CONTEMPORARY PAINTING IN SCOTLAND

BILL HARE

Best wishes
Bill Hare

CRAFTSMAN HOUSE

First published in 1992 by Craftsman House BVI Ltd., Tortola, BVI
Distributed in Australia by Craftsman House,
20 Barcoo Street,
East Roseville, NSW 2069, Australia

Distributed internationally through the following offices:

USA	**UK**	**ASIA**
STBS Ltd.	STBS Ltd.	STBS (Singapore) Pte Ltd.
PO Box 786	5th Floor, Reading Bridge House	No. 25 Tannery Road
Cooper Station	Reading Bridge Approach	Singapore1334
New York	Reading RGI 8PP	Republic of Singapore
NY 10276	England	

ISBN 976 8097 27 2

Design   *Craftsman House, Sydney*
Typesetter   *Craftsman House, Sydney*
Printer   *Kyodo, Singapore*

CONTENTS

Acknowledgments vii
Preface viii
Introduction 1

The Artists

Reinhard BEHRENS 22
John BELLANY 26
Elizabeth BLACKADDER 30
Dennis BUCHAN 34
Joyce CAIRNS 38
Steven CAMPBELL 42
Russell COLOMBO 46
Calum COLVIN 50
Stephen CONROY 54
Fred CRAYK 58
Ken CURRIE 62
Alan DAVIE 66
David DONALDSON 70
Kate DOWNIE 74
David EVANS 78
Alexander FRASER 82
Lys HANSEN 86
Gwen HARDIE 90
John HOUSTON 94
Ian HOWARD 98
Peter HOWSON 102
Margaret HUNTER 106
Matthew INGLIS 110

Callum INNES 114
Alan JOHNSTON 118
John KIRKWOOD 122
Jack KNOX 126
Henry KONDRACKI 130
Eileen LAWRENCE 134
Tom LAWSON 138
Keith McINTYRE 142
Bruce McLEAN 146
John McLEAN 150
Alexander MOFFAT 154
John MOONEY 158
Elizabeth OGILVIE 162
Glen ONWIN 166
James PATTISON 170
Fred POLLOCK 174
Barbara RAE 178
June REDFERN 182
Iain ROBERTSON 186
Duncan SHANKS 190
Peter THOMSON 194
Frances WALKER 198
Alison WATT 202
Kate WHITEFORD 206
Adrian WISZNIEWSKI 210

One-Person Exhibitions 214
Bibliography 224

For my wife, Liz

ACKNOWLEDGMENTS

would like to thank the following people for the support and help which they have given me in writing this book: Duncan Macmillan, Andrew Patrizio, Marjorie Cuthill, Valerie Fiddes, my wife Liz, and most of all, the artists and their Galleries. I would also like to thank my editor, Nevill Drury, who commissioned this book from Craftsman House in Sydney, and Caroline de Fries for assistance in design and production of the book.

PREFACE

In my introductory essay to this book I write that, 'Both within and outside
Scotland, the 1980s have been hailed as a remarkable success story for Scottish
Art'. In that essay I have tried to give some of the main reasons for this 'success
story' by looking at contemporary Scottish painting in relationship to its historical
development. There is, however, another important factor to consider when
discussing the condition of contemporary art in Scotland. I would like to raise
this briefly now.

I refer to the political situation in Scotland through the 1980s.

It should immediately be pointed out that the majority of artists selected for this
survey of contemporary Scottish painting are in no way politically motivated in their
art. Yet, as with everyone else, these artists are affected by the political climate of
the country they live in. Furthermore, this is certainly the case with the public and
private institutions which support the arts in Scotland and have a vested interest in
their success.

For most politically aware people in Scotland the 1980s has been, to say the
least, a frustrating period. This stems from what is now referred to in Scotland as
the 'Referendum Fiasco' of 1979. In that year the nearly defunct Labour Government
introduced a referendum on devolved political/economic power to the Scottish
people in an attempt to stave off the Scottish Nationalist threat to their electoral
power in Scotland. However, although the majority of Scots who voted plumped for
devolution, a group of frightened Labour members of Parliament managed to deny
the will of the Scottish people through introducing the requirement of a 40 per cent
minimum vote on the *total* electorate — in other words an unused vote was counted
as a no vote! Since then the Labour party, whom the Scottish electorate continues to
support, has been defeated at four consecutive general elections by a Conservative
Government strenuously committed to the union of Scotland and England ruled
from Westminster. Thus, to all intents and purposes, the Scottish people have been
politically disenfranchised.

This situation has created a political vacuum in Scotland which has been most spectacularly filled by the creative achievements of Scottish artists and writers. They, unlike the politicians, have addressed the cultural and social issues which are directly relevant to most people in Scotland. It is those artists and writers who have been the true heroes and heroines of the 1980s. However, they work within a Scottish art scene which is a complicated one. For example, both right and left wing cultural institutions have been keen to claim the success story of Scottish art for themselves; there is also the never-ending rivalry between Glasgow and Edinburgh and between national and local arts organisations — and from certain quarters the predictable accusation of a 'sell-out' when critical and commercial success is recognised, especially if that recognition comes from south of the border. Success, as with failure, is a complex business in Scotland.

I draw the reader's attention to these political and cultural issues because I feel they are relevant to the story of Scottish art over the last decade. They should not alter our appreciation of the aesthetic quality of Scottish painting represented in this book, but I hope an awareness of such issues will add a little more to our understanding.

PAST AND PRESENT: AN HISTORICAL VIEW OF SCOTTISH ART IN THE 1980s

To the outside world Scotland no doubt appears to be a small and remote place. Thus, it must come as a surprise that such a country should have contributed so much to human thought and endeavour. This is especially true in the area of science and engineering. In the arts, however, the international respect for the great triumphs of Scottish literature has not unfortunately been equally enjoyed by Scottish painting. While the rest of the world reads and admires the writings of Scott, Burns, Carlyle, Stevenson and MacDiarmid, the history and achievement of Scottish painting is only now beginning to be appreciated by the wider public, both in Britain and abroad. This growing acknowledgment of the importance and distinctive character of Scottish painting has been recognised mainly because of the tremendous energy and serious commitment that has marked the art scene in Scotland in the 1980s. The aim of this book, therefore, is to survey the breadth and vitality of recent Scottish painting, and present the individual contributions that the selected artists have made.

Both within and outside Scotland, the 1980s have been hailed as a remarkable success story for Scottish art in general and painting in particular. The international reputation of the Scots — both those of the older generation such as Alan Davie, John Bellany, Bruce McLean and Elizabeth Blackadder and also the new emerging painters such as Steven Campbell, Ken Currie, Peter Howson, Adrian Wiszniewski, Gwen Hardie and Kate Whiteford — speaks for itself. While there have been the usual accusations in some quarters of over-hype (what the Scots term 'here's tae us, wha's like us'), the last decade has undoubtedly been the most exciting and rewarding for Scottish art this century.

As we move into the 1990s, however, and begin to experience the harsh effects of the international economic recession, the art scene in Scotland, as is the case worldwide, is beginning to contract and exude much less confidence than before.

Yet it should be said that this loss of nerve is more an attitude to be found in the art market and institutions than amongst the artists themselves. Still it does allow some sceptical commentators to dismiss the 1980s as a freak, 'flash in the pan' phenomenon. I take a different view, and will attempt to show that the achievements of the artists included in this book have not appeared 'out of the blue', but are built on a long tradition within the history of the visual arts in Scotland. To gain a fuller understanding of contemporary Scottish painting it is necessary to be aware of the historical and social forces which Scottish artists have inherited and experienced. This introductory essay will, therefore, present recent Scottish painting within a much wider historical perspective than the last decade.

My reference, a moment ago, to the present restrictions brings me to the first and possibly the most important factor in any discussion of Scottish art — the question of patronage. The fact that over the centuries many of Scotland's most successful artists have found it necessary to leave their country to develop their careers is indicative of the financial and cultural difficulties a small country like Scotland faces. This is especially so when it has such close economic links with its larger next-door neighbour, England. This continuing problem of sustaining a vibrant, indigenous visual arts community against an unsympathetic economic background goes back at least to the early 17th century. With the Union of the Crowns in 1603 and the departure of the Scottish court to London, state patronage of the arts also moved south. Along with the loss of royal and aristocratic support there was the additional burden of a national church, whose extreme Protestant attitudes were hardly conducive to large ecclesiastical commissions. Therefore it is little wonder that until the Enlightenment era of the 18th century, there was only limited and local activity in the visual arts in Scotland. However, from the mid-18th century, progressive Scottish society turned its back on the religious conflicts of the previous era, and set to transform itself into a dynamic modern community. In all areas of social, economic and cultural endeavour, the Scots of the Enlightenment strove after fuller intellectual understanding and material progress. This progressive outlook was also reflected in the spectacular developments in painting and some of the major names of Scottish art: Allan Ramsay (1713–1784), Henry Raeburn (1756–1823) and David Wilkie (1785–1841) are the products of this period, sometimes known as 'The Golden Age of Scottish Painting'.

It may seem that there can be little connection between the painting of the Scottish Enlightenment and the work of the artists included in this book. However, behind the superficial appearances of differing period fashions and styles there are fundamental connections and shared concerns between Scottish painting, past and present.

Firstly, although the Scottish Enlightenment was on the whole a secular phenomenon, it shared with Scottish Protestant theology a strong commitment to the profound importance of individual personal experience. The moral philosophers of the period sought for a deeper understanding of the inner life of the human mind and senses, but within a social, rather than a spiritual, framework. Turning now to contemporary Scottish painting with its strong emphasis on the figure, for instance, one can also see a broadly similar involvement with particular human and social experiences rather than universal abstract speculations. The second important ideal which contemporary painting has inherited from the Scottish Enlightenment is the conviction that art, like all important human activities, is ultimately an intellectual discipline. This, I believe, can be discerned both in the paintings and the statements of the artists in this book. The work of these painters can be seen as an on-going dialogue between the workings of the human eye/mind and the natural and social order of the world around them. For these artists the basis of this empirical confrontation with reality is the intellectual development of trained perception through close observation and long practised skills of drawing and painting. This then brings us to the position of the Academy and the central importance of the four art schools in Scotland.

The concept of the Academy came into being during the 16th century in Italy. The learned and rational aspects of art were emphasised along with design and drawing as the basis of academic training. However, it was the French, in the 17th century under Louis XIV and his first minister Colbert, who devised the definitive model for the modern art academy. Over the next two centuries art academies were established in every country which had aspirations to be part of the international civilised community. The influence of such institutions reached its zenith during the 19th century with, for example, the virtual cultural dictatorship of the French Salon in Paris, and to a slightly lesser degree, the Royal Academy in London. Since the rise of modernism in this century, the academies have lost their former authority and become, in most cases, merely another relic of a past era.

In Scotland, however, they do things differently, and the Royal Scottish Academy has remained powerful enough even today to engender both respect and resentment in the native artistic community. To understand this is to be aware of the strong sense of tradition that characterises the outlook of most Scottish artists. Although many of the painters included in this book would regard themselves as radical, in that they wish to change people's attitudes to a wide range of different concerns, they are not iconoclastic avant-gardeists who desire to obliterate the past and solely concentrate on being fashionably new for novelty's sake. This frantic pursuit of trendy novelty, which has dominated the cosmopolitan art centres throughout the 1980s, and which many, like the leading critic Robert Hughes, vehemently denounce, has fortunately found little encouragement in Scotland.

Why Scottish artists, right up to the present, should have such a strong sense of tradition, probably goes back to the establishment of the Royal Scottish Academy in Edinburgh at the beginning of the 19th century. Firstly, the RSA was a fairly late arrival, compared to its French and English counterparts, and, as such, because of its long and difficult birth, was even more highly valued in Scotland. Secondly, because the country had lost its political sovereignty with the Union of the Parliaments in 1707, any institution which gave focus to national identity was, and in many cases still is, greatly honoured. Thirdly, the Academy gave its members, as a body of professional citizens, not only a sense of social status, but also a voice in the nation's cultural affairs — whether it has exercised that voice enough and in the right manner depends for each artist on which side of the social and artistic barricade they choose to belong. Fourthly, another vitally important function of the Academy was as an educational institution for the training of students. In the Academy studios the handing on and exchanging of ideas about the execution and purpose of art could be facilitated from one generation to the next. Since the late 19th century the RSA has shed this educational responsibility to the four regional art schools in Edinburgh, Glasgow, Dundee and Aberdeen. Yet such is the moderate size of the artistic community in Scotland that there are still close links between the Academy and the art schools, as many of the teaching staff there are also leading members of the RSA. Therefore it comes as no surprise that there is a decidedly academic character to much Scottish painting, particularly with its emphasis on draughtsmanship and painterly technique. The influence of an academic outlook in Scottish painting is further reflected in the conventional subject matter which most artists tend to choose for their work. I will return to this a little later.

Again to take up this question of patronage in Scotland, an important function of the RSA has been to exhibit annually the work of its members and selected practising artists from all over the country. In many cases, this was the only opportunity that some painters had to present their wares to the general public, and, as such, was an important event in the Scottish art calendar. However, throughout the 19th century resentment towards the RSA began to grow, as it was felt by many that it merely catered for the art establishment in Edinburgh. Other towns and cities, especially Glasgow, therefore, began to set up their own independent exhibition societies. This burgeoning sense of local identity and civic pride was a sign that the wealth generated by commerce and industry was spread throughout Scotland during the Victorian era. The trend towards greater decentralisation encouraged patronage on a local scale, as well as establishing numerous civic art galleries which are still important exhibition venues and public purchasers of Scottish art. The location of artistic centres throughout Scotland, with local art galleries, art schools, workshops and studio spaces, gives Scottish art a wide spread of regional variety, which hopefully is reflected in the selection of painters included in this book.

Fortunately public patronage still continues to be an important source of support for Scottish artists. This can be seen in the list of works in public collections that many painters in this book present. Not only does the work purchased by a local authority, a university, the Scottish Arts Council or the Scottish National Gallery of Modern Art, give artists some well-earned financial reward, and impetus to their career, but further encourages them to risk producing more challenging and experimental work which would be unlikely to find a buyer in the private market. In Scotland quite a high proportion of art produced in the 1980s was geared to address, both through scale and subject, a public audience rather than a private patron.

On the other hand, it has to be admitted that Scottish art in this century has not been loyally supported by the private collector, who has preferred to buy historical rather than contemporary work. This lack of support has contributed, until recently at least, to the steady exodus of many of Scotland's best artists. However, on the positive side, it has meant that the art of those exile Scots has been enriched by contact with the leading international art movements. This of course is not a recent experience for Scottish painters. The importance of direct contact with the work of other artists outside Scotland has always been seen as a vital requirement for widening a young painter's horizons. In the 18th century most serious-minded Scottish painters made their pilgrimage to Rome, while Paris became the artistic mecca for the Scots during the modern period up to the immediate post-war years. Now, with the aid of postgraduate travelling scholarships, many of the younger artists in this book have made prolonged study visits to the more recent art capitals, such as New York and Berlin. Therefore, artists in Scotland do not rely solely on their experience of international art by passively browsing through art magazines and looking at slides. They try to make direct contact with the historical and contemporary art of other countries which they feel can help them to enrich their

own work. One of the most gratifying aspects of recent Scottish painting is the way
it reflects an equally balanced dialogue between the international art scene and its
own indigenous native culture. Unlike earlier periods in the 20th century when most
Scottish art was a mere pastiche of imported styles, the best painting being produced
now has its own distinctive individual character. To realise how this has been achieved
it is necessary to have a brief look at Scottish painting in the modern period.

Apart from the heroic efforts of isolated figures such as James Cowie (1886–1956)
and William Johnstone (1897–1981), who remained outside the mainstream of the
art establishment, the painting produced in Scotland until the last war was fairly
undistinguished. To be fair, in some ways this was not solely the fault of the artists
themselves — many of whom had immense pictorial facility. Rather they were the
inheritors of an accumulating problem that had bedevilled Scottish art since the early
19th century. This perennial dilemma involved the crucial issue concerning the
choice and treatment of subjects which were appropriate to the authentic Scottish
experience.

The debate on the whole question of Scottish identity goes right back to the
Union of 1707. Then Scotland gave up its political independence to become a junior
partner in the rapidly expanding firm of Great Britain and the British Empire. This left
Scotland financially better off, but a nation without a civic government — so creating
a schizophrenic situation for the Scots whose hearts might be in the Highlands,
while the rest of their bodies were controlled from London. Initially, however, the
intellectual excitement and optimistic outlook of the 18th century Enlightenment,
with its committed belief in universal order both in the human and natural world,
seemed to transcend and so largely deflect attention from Scotland's own particular
identity problems. One only has to look at the great portraits of Allan Ramsay or
Henry Raeburn to sense that the artists also shared the confidence of their patrons.
And although an air of uncertainty began to appear in the later work of Raeburn and
David Wilkie, it was not really until the Victorian era that the belief in painting as a
vital part of the intellectual climate of Scottish society began to be lost in a cloud of

Highland mist.

For most of the later 19th century much of Scottish art, as with Scottish industry, moved into the export business. Thus, instead of working for the direct demands of a Scottish public, painters now supplied manufactured images of Scotland for an outside market. Furthermore, this fed back into the home demand for painting, where private patronage was mainly taken over by industrialists who, wishing to forget the polluted source and human cost of their wealth, preferred an image of Scotland which was steeped in rural nostalgia. Such was the whole-scale involvement of Scottish Victorian art, in presenting a one-sided, distorted view of life in Scotland — with endless pictures of desolate cottages and ruined castles swathed in swirling mists or sanitised farm labourers and their families praying round the family bible — that one would hardly know from the painting produced in the 19th century that Scotland was one of the most advanced industrial countries in the world. The received image of Victorian Scotland has been a toss-up between soaring mountain tartanry or humble cottage kailyard.

It was little wonder then, that by the beginning of this century many of the young progressive Scottish artists were reacting strongly against the dark brown Victorian paintings of sentimental narratives and romanticised Highland landscapes. These 'modern' artists, such as The Scottish Colourists like F.C.B. Cadell (1883–1937), Leslie Hunter (1871–1931), and S.J. Peploe (1871–1935), eagerly made contact with the most avant-garde ideas in painting, especially those being developed in Paris in the first decade of this century. They were determined to eschew all the anecdotal subject matter and slick illustrative style which had dogged 19th century Scottish painting. Following the example of the Fauves (the Cubists were too radical and far too dark), these early 20th century Scottish modernists began to move the focus of subject matter in Scottish painting away from the human figure within a particular identifiable social context, to concentrate on 'pure', non-literary motifs such as the humble still lifes and incidental glimpses of the natural world. Thus they could fix all their creative energies solely on the pictorial problems of compositional arrangements and colour harmonies. Unfortunately, the content of such paintings was so nondescript that stylistic quotation became its main *raison d'étre*, resulting in mere pastiches of modern art: with a tint of French Fauvism, a stroke of German Expressionism and a later dash of Abstract Expressionism, most 20th century Scottish painting was all style and no substance.

This *belle peinture* school of modern Scottish painting, as it became known, has dominated the art scene in this country for most of the century, and against which many of the later artists in this book have strongly reacted. Yet these *belle peinture* artists were merely the latest victims of the continuing crisis of identity within Scottish society and culture. In their determination to avoid the accusation of being parochial and reactionary, they rushed to embrace the cosmopolitan values of modernism and shed most of the distinctive characteristics of Scottish art. Unlike their French, German, or Spanish counterparts, who could adopt the language of modern painting to reflect their own indigenous cultural and social experiences, most earlier 20th century Scottish painters turned their eyes away from the past, or from what was going on in the streets and work places throughout Scotland. Thus the bland, modernistic pictures they produced were not only 'politically correct', but also completely safe to be placed on the walls of any middle-class drawing-room. Even if such paintings were a little over-sensuous for the Scottish puritan temperament, these expressions of decorative delights were produced with so much refined taste that they would never offend anyone with any degree of genteel sensibility. In contrast to much Scottish painting today, little of the work of The Scottish Colourists or the later Edinburgh School of W.G. Gillies (1898–1973), William MacTaggart (1903–1981) and John Maxwell (1905–1962), took up the challenge of modern art as a dynamic vehicle for critical engagement with contemporary Scottish experience.

Isolated outraged voices, such as that of Hugh MacDiarmid, hammered against such vacuous, unrepresentative examples of modern art — but to little avail. The *belle peinture* school of Scottish painting, with its stranglehold on the RSA, the Scottish art schools and the very limited commercial gallery system, continued to dominate and stultify the art scene in Scotland for most of this century until the 1960s. Before then, Scottish painters who had serious ambitions to further their art within a wider international context — William Johnstone, Robert Colquhoun (1914–62), Robert MacBryde (1916–72) or Alan Davie, for example — felt it incumbent on themselves to move elsewhere. Yet few of these émigré artists lost their deep sense of their native roots. They may have left their country but, as the exiled Czech musician Rafael Kubelik described his own feelings, they kept their nation in their hearts. These artists continued to draw creative strength from their Scottish origins, while acting as an inspirational example to younger artists. This was certainly the case with both Johnstone and Davie, and later, John Bellany.

By the 1960s, however, the liberating euphoria that was generated by that decade began to take effect on the creative arts in Scotland. On the visual arts scene the situation began to change immeasurably for the better. And it can now be seen that much of the ground work which led to the success story of Scottish painting in the 1980s was laid two decades earlier.

Firstly, some of what happened in the 1960s had beneficial effects which were more psychological than practical. For instance, the opening in Edinburgh of the Scottish National Gallery of Modern Art in 1960, unfortunately did not create a great new source of state patronage for Scottish artists, but it did, however, grant a degree of status to modern art which the general public had previously refused to recognise. Another event in the mid-1960s was staged to alter people's attitude towards contemporary art. Following the example of the great French Realist painter, Gustave Courbet, and also inspired by the critical views of Hugh MacDiarmid, the young art students, John Bellany and Sandy Moffat, defiantly hung their uncompromisingly realist paintings on the railings outside the sanctified portals of the RSA during the Edinburgh International Festival. Such a gesture sought to emphasise that art, if it has any real justification for serious critical attention, should be both relevant to a whole range of human experiences and accessible to all who wish to widen their social, intellectual and emotional awareness. These pictures hanging out on the street demanded attention and consideration at a time when there was a growing feeling that painting was a dying art form. Furthermore, following in the great tradition of Northern European art, these two young artists returned the figure and pictorial narrative to a position of central importance in their work — not in any anecdotal sense, but with monumental significance. As can be seen from much of the work by the younger figurative painters in this book, Bellany's and Moffat's example and teaching have been extremely influential on the art of the 1980s.

On a more directly practical level, the most important development on the Scottish art scene in the 1960s was the creation of The Scottish Arts Council in 1967. Unlike other public art institutions, its brief was to support directly artists in advancing their careers, and widening the availability of contemporary art to the general public. The manner in which this has been achieved was through giving financial help to individual artists in the form of awards and bursaries, and at the same time by funding semi- and non-commercial galleries to exhibit a wide range of different types of contemporary art from Scotland and abroad. Thus, not only were opportunities increased for artists to present their work through one-person and group exhibitions, but also a new seriously interested public was created for the visual arts. Such was the case, for example, when Richard Demarco invited, the then little known Joseph Beuys to show and perform in Edinburgh in the early 1970s. The great German artist's ideal of art and life being an integral part of each other, and his strong metaphysical emphasis on the living force of the spirit in the material world, struck a deep sympathic chord with many people in Scotland. Beuys' artistic philosophy has proved a lasting inspiration to a number of Scottish artists, especially those whose art deals with social and environmental issues. Through his art and example, Beuys invited artists to broaden the whole basis and approach of their work, and look for new ways to address crucial questions, both in human society and the natural world. And with the spread of non-commercial galleries, Scottish artists could now be much more ambitious and challenging in their art.

Over the last two decades, not only has the network of galleries expanded, but

the sheer number of artists practising throughout Scotland has increased dramatically.
The whole atmosphere of change and expansion has been most noticeable in
the Scottish art schools, where the majority of the students now train to become
professional artists, rather than art teachers, which tended to be the case in the past.
Furthermore, there is a much stronger sense of solidarity and supportive community
amongst artists working in Scotland, especially with the younger generation, who
look to each other for mutual support. This is reflected in the establishment of the
many artist-run workshops and galleries throughout the country. For example, there
are at present five Scottish print-makers workshops throughout the country, and
many of the painters in this book are also extremely fine print-makers in their
own right.

Yet for all the creativity which has been engendered in the Scottish art scene
since the 1960s, there are still certain deficiencies, apart from the continual
government under-funding which is the perennial curse of the arts in this country.
For instance, there is little serious art criticism in Scotland, and this deficiency has
at least two detrimental effects. Firstly, without the critical support, it is difficult
to create a more informed public who are seriously interested in the visual arts.
Secondly, the wider international status of Scottish art in general and individual
artists in particular, is dependent on the attention that is given by non-Scottish
critics. Not surprisingly, such outside occasional visitors cannot be expected to have
the same degree of understanding and sympathy as that of home-based writers.
Therefore, without solid critical back-up, artists are even more vulnerable to the
shifting moods of taste and fashion on the international art scene.

In addition to this lack of sustained critical support, there is no consistent private
buying and collecting of contemporary art in Scotland. As a result, although many of
the more successful Scottish artists now choose to stay and work in Scotland, they all
have dealers from outside. While it should be stressed that most painters feel their
galleries are understanding and supportive of their art, in a commercial world certain
pressures can be exerted on individual artists to meet outsiders' views of what is the

appropriate image for Scottish art, as happened in the 19th century. Yet all that being said, it is exhilarating and gratifying that Scottish painting should be creating such critical and commercial impact abroad. I would now like to look at some of the reasons for this upsurge in interest that has been generated by contemporary Scottish painting.

It was pointed out at the opening of this introduction, that, on the international scale of recognition, the visual arts, until recently, have been much less conspicuous than other areas of Scottish achievement such as science or literature. That is not to say that Scotland has not produced major figures in painting, such as Allan Ramsay and Henry Raeburn in the 18th century, David Wilkie and William McTaggart (1835–1910) in the next, and during this century, William Johnstone, J.D. Ferguson (1874–1961), Joan Eardley (1921–63), Alan Davie, and John Bellany. However, it has to be conceded that in most general books on the history of art, Scotland's contribution tends to be overlooked. I would suggest that this lack of recognition has little to do with the quality of serious work produced by Scottish artists over the last three centuries, but more to do with the fact that historians and critics tend to be of the shared opinion that art can only be created in the great cosmopolitan centres of the art world such as Rome, Paris or New York. Scottish art, as with that of many other neglected countries, has suffered greatly from this blinkered outlook. However, one of the most important changes that took place during the 1980s, was the undermining of the modernist ideal of universal conformity to general principles of aesthetic credibility. As the monopolistic authority of institutionalised modernism finally began to disintegrate from the 1960s onwards, alternative interpretations of the development of modern art began to emerge. Therefore, with the influence of centres of cultural authority starting to be challenged from all points of the compass, Scotland, as with other previously marginalised countries, was well placed to flourish in the new critical democratic climate. Now, many people were beginning to realise that there were possible alternative readings of the history of 20th century art to the officially sanctioned canon of French Impressionism — American Abstract

Expressionism. For example, critics began to recognise that just as important was the great Northern European tradition of modern art from Van Gogh, Munch, the German Expressionists and Realists, through to the COBRA group and up to Beuys, Baselitz and Kiefer. Within that history of realist/expressionist painting, Scottish art clearly had a secure place and distinctive tradition. This has given contemporary Scottish painting much more confidence and a keener sense of its own identity in its relationship to the outside art world. At last that long native tradition of Scottish art with its emphasis on direct observation, psychological analysis, metaphysical speculation and moral and social criticism can be clearly placed within the much wider context of international 20th century art.

Furthermore, when we turn to the current art scene, many of the common stylistic characteristics which critics have discerned in the 'New Painting' of the 1980s — bold figuration, evocative narrative, emphatic technique and poetic atmosphere, for instance — have always been distinguishing qualities in much of the best of Scottish painting. Unlike previous periods when Scottish artists felt it beholden on themselves to disguise the authentic character of their natural artistic inclinations with modernistic fancy dress, contemporary painters can express themselves in their inherited pictorial tradition and be appreciated by the rest of the world. In the 1980s Scottish painting at last rediscovered its own voice!

In the 1980s 'subject' as opposed to 'motif' returned to centre stage in contemporary Scottish art. None of the artists in this book, however, can be seen as merely illustrators. All are concerned to allow their medium of expression to formulate the appearance and character of their imagery. As such, the personal vision of these artists is not only expressed through their choice of subject, but also by their stylistic method of interpretation and presentation. This concern with developing a personal style is vitally important. For style is the distinctive — some may even say the uniquely individual — voice of the artist; the means by which the artist gives a recognisable presence to a painting and so allows the spectator to engage in a dialogue of ideas and feelings with the work itself.

Looking through this book one is struck by the sheer range and variety of work being produced in the area of contemporary Scottish painting. Therefore, I feel, unlike previous eras in Scottish art, it would be a very difficult, if not impossible task to formulate any unifying characteristics based on stylistic similarities. So is there any other approach that might present the artists in this book as a more coherent school of painting? I think that might be possible, if we move our attention away from the question of stylistic expression and concentrate on choice and interpretation of content. Then internal connections between various artists begin to emerge.

The most immediately recognisable group within these Scottish artists is the abstract painters. Although Scottish figurative painting received much of the critical attention during the 1980s, high quality abstract painting continued to be produced throughout the decade. The Scots, in fact, were pioneers in the development of 20th century British abstraction, especially through the painting of William Johnstone, William Gear (1915–) and the early work of Alan Davie. Not surprisingly, because of the Scots' long established concern with the metaphysical dimension of experience, the work of these earlier Scottish abstract painters was closely connected with surrealism. Thus, in their paintings they used the power of intuitive gesture, the force of expressive colour, and the associative meaning of shapes and symbols, to release primordial aspects of the human psyche and make links with the primitive and natural world. This surrealist dimension to early abstraction, however, is not so noticeable in contemporary Scottish painting. On the whole, the current abstract painters seem to have less concern for the psychological release of spontaneous expression than for the more formal demands of pictorial composition and colour relationships. Gesture and application of paint is still of crucial importance, but now more for its own sake, and less for any symbolic or metaphysical expression. The sources of inspiration for the abstract painters in this book seem to vary from initial connections with specific aspects of the outside world, as, for example, in the work of Denis Buchan, Alexander Fraser (when he was an abstract painter), Jim Pattison and Russell Colombo, to those other abstractionists such as John McLean, Fred

Pollock, Iain Robertson, Callum Innes and Alan Johnston, whose pictures are much more independent and rigorously 'pared down' to the essential language of drawing and painting.

While it is clearly easier to recognise and group the abstract artists, I think it is also possible to make meaningful connections between other painters in this book. Thus, by doing so, the variety of work can be viewed within a more structured framework which makes connections and interrelationships more likely to be perceived.

The common factor which links most of these Scottish painters is their art education. Most of them studied at one of the four art schools, and a good number teach or have taught there. These institutions pride themselves on their long-standing commitment to traditional academic values based on drawing, respect for materials and a knowledge of the great art of the past. Looking through their work this becomes very evident: quality draughtsmanship, technical facility and intelligent, witty reinterpretation of artistic conventions and genres are the hallmarks of much contemporary Scottish painting. And it is with the broad concept of the different genres, that is, the academic classification of painting into different types of subject matter, that it is possible to group the non-abstract painters in this book.

Briefly, a short explanation of the genre system might be required here. Originally this method of classification was formulated in the academies to help to differentiate between a great painting and a merely good one. At the top were the great history paintings as they concerned themselves with universal, high moral themes taken from the Bible and the Classics. Then came portrait painting, because, as was usually the case in the past, it dealt with the most important people in society. Next were the pictures that presented the everyday life of ordinary people. This type of painting was known — and thus can cause a little confusion — as 'genre'. Finally, at the bottom end of the academic league table of excellence, was landscape and lowly still life — where human subject-matter was less likely to be included or was excluded altogether. This hierarchy of artistic judgment based on the humanist notion of man being the measure of all things, was overturned in the modern, urban era, with the collapse in the belief that the academies were the sole arbitrators of aesthetic standards. For example, most of the innovative art of the 19th and 20th centuries was in the area of landscape and still life. However, although the value judgments connected with the genre system have been abandoned, the broad division of painting into these different types of subjects still exists, both for the artists and their public. Furthermore, the choice and treatment of subject is in many ways still the most important basis of understanding between the work of art and the spectator.

Firstly, which group of artists in this book could be regarded as history painters? It may seem contradictory, but the artists whom I would classify as history painters have little interest in resurrecting visions of the past. Scottish art, particularly in the 19th century, has had more than its share of that. Today the painters working within this particular genre are drawn towards history painting for its moral and intellectual authority, not for its retrospective tradition. The best history painting in Scotland concerns itself with modern, not past times, engaging in a critical dialogue with its public on such crucial issues facing human society as the nuclear threat, chronic environmental pollution, social and economic injustice. The history painters in contemporary Scottish art are those who most overtly use the rhetorical power of painting to make critical observations about social and political issues. This would cover the work, for example, of Ken Currie, John Kirkwood, Glen Onwin, Fred Crayk and Tom Lawson. I would also classify Kate Whiteford as a history painters, as her work, through its use of ancient signs and symbols, deals with the origins of social and cultural identity.

The recurring question of identity brings us to the second genre, portraiture. Here the individual's sense of his or her own personal and social identity becomes the focal point. Portraiture was the dominant subject in 18th century Scottish Enlightenment painting, when the study of human nature and society was the main concern in philosophical thinking. However, during the 19th century, portraiture was superseded by the rise of landscape painting and there are few conventional portrait painters in contemporary Scottish art — although David Donaldson, Sandy Moffat, John Bellany, Fred Crayk and Alison Watt have produced some excellent work in this area. Yet, if we widen our view of the aims of portrait painting to encompass the broad notion of it as a close analysis of experience and identity, expressed by the powerful presence of the human figure, then a whole group of artists comes together. I refer to those painters such as Gwen Hardie, June Redfern, Lys Hansen and Margaret Hunter. These artists present for our scrutiny the figure, usually nude and female, in order to raise disturbing questions concerning gender and sexuality, liberty and conformity, and the shifting relationship between inner and outer reality in the psychology of human experience. It is also possible to see similar concerns in the work of Adrian Wiszniewski.

When art moves from examining the individual human experience to the wider social one, we are usually dealing with genre painting. Within the Northern European tradition, Scottish art has a long association with this kind of painting going back to David Allan (1744–1796) and the great David Wilkie, who established genre painting as a serious subject in art history. This type of subject matter, the everyday life of ordinary people, became debased and discredited when Victorian artists and their public used it as a vehicle for sentimental elegies to a mythical lost world of rustic arcadia. Not surprisingly, there has been little genre painting of significance in Scotland during this century. However, since John Bellany expanded the potential for this type of subject matter onto a heroic scale with his monumental pictures of the Scottish fishing community, there has been a great revival in genre painting. Joyce Cairns and Keith McIntyre are artists who have most readily responded to Bellany's example. Others, such as Peter Howson, Stephen Conroy, Henry Kondracki and Peter Thomson, have dealt with the alienation and the ritualistic harshness and humour that characterises much of everyday modern life, this time within an urban context.

Since the 19th century, Scottish landscape painting has become by far the most popular subject in art, both with artists and their public. This is hardly surprising since Scotland, although a small geographical entity, is blessed with a vast range of different types of scenery. Yet it was not only its scenic qualities which made the landscape so alluring to the Scots. With the lack of nationhood, the people of Scotland desperately needed a symbolic substitute for such a loss, and the landscape, with all its historical and tragic associations, fitted the role perfectly. Contemporary Scottish landscape painters do not necessarily avoid the historical associative dimension of the subject, but they are also closely attentive to the specific qualities of the natural world as something to be respected in their own right. The approach to landscape painting as represented in this book can be broadly divided into two. On the one hand, there is the expressive gestural response which links with such figures from the past as William McTaggart and Joan Eardley, and here includes John Houston, Barbara Rae, Duncan Shanks and Kate Downie, who treats the urban scene very much as a landscape. On the other side, in the tradition of William Dyce and James Cowie, there is the meditative, analytical method, with its emphatic graphic character which is practised by Frances Walker, Liz Ogilvie and Reinhard Behrens.

Finally, we come to the last group of artists in this book, the still life painters. From what would appear to be the least inspiring type of subject, these artists produce a wide range of high quality painting, which can hold its own against any of the other genres. Again, the explanation for this phenomenon may go back to the influence of art school training in Scotland and its emphasis on close and prolonged study from the model/object. Yet what transforms the work of these artists from what could be a fairly dry academic exercise are the different techniques employed, and the concentrated intensity of their vision. To appreciate the wide range of technical approaches, one only has to compare the meticulous analytical work of David Evans, Eileen Lawrence or John Mooney, with the robust painterliness of Jack Knox, or the elusive visual poetry of Elizabeth Blackadder and Ian Howard.

The ultimate strength of still life painting lies in the fact that, essentially, it is the most characteristic of Scottish art. By this, I mean it involves the very foundation of the practice of the visual arts in Scotland: that is, the direct confrontation between the artist and his subject, where study can be at its most analytically concentrated. The best of all Scottish art, both past and present, has had this empirical basis — where close observation and hard-won technical facility have allowed the artist to examine and translate into marks, signs and images the world of appearances.

Furthermore, through the intensity of the artist's interrogation, this world of appearances begins to open up to all kinds of social and metaphysical speculations on the nature of things and their relationship to each other.

I am conscious that the 'genre' groupings that I have just applied to the artists in this book could be accused of being arbitrary. There are some artists who cannot be pinned down to one type of subject, and move freely, for example, between landscape and still life. I have only placed such artists within a certain grouping because I feel that they produce their best work when painting that particular type of subject. But I realise that is only a personal view. What is more important is how each artist uses, in a positive or critical manner, the conventions associated with each of the genres. For instance, the history painters exploit the traditional scale and moral authority associated with that type of painting to question and attack a whole range of political and social attitudes. While, on the other hand, the still life painters take a genre which is usually not regarded as having a serious intellectual status, and, through their sustained observations, raise all kinds of thoughtful questions about the connections between ourselves and the world of objects with which we surround ourselves.

Lastly, there are artists whose work cannot be readily placed within the broad spectrum of the academic genres at all; for example, Matthew Inglis, Alexander Fraser, Calum Colvin, Steven Campbell, Bruce McLean, or Alan Davie. That is as it should be. All art which wishes to remain vital needs to question and extend existing conventions, as well as having a healthy respect for the great traditions of the past. In addition, artists must also have a keen sense of their own personal, social and cultural identity, while at the same time being receptive to ideas and influences from outside. After a lengthy and generally disappointing period in 20th century Scottish art, the contemporary painters seem to have got the balance right again. Hence their remarkable successes over the last decade, both in Britain and abroad. Furthermore, Scottish art in the 1990s, despite the unfavourable economic conditions and the great uncertainty about Scotland's political future within the United Kingdom, can continue from strength to strength.

REINHARD BEHRENS

Reinhard Behrens was born in West Germany in 1951. He trained at Hamburg College of Art (1971–78), then undertook a postgraduate course at Edinburgh College of Art (1979–80). Since then he has settled in Scotland, teaching at Edinburgh College of Art (1982–84) and Gray's School of Art, Aberdeen (1986). In 1987 he moved to Fife where he is now working as a full-time artist.

There is a late 18th century portrait by Henry Raeburn of Sir John Clerk of Penicuik and his wife, grandly surveying their estate. The hillside behind them is bare, but Sir John, through his pointing gesture, which quotes Michelangelo's *God the Creator* of the Sistine Chapel, indicates that he will soon turn this part of the Scottish countryside into a cultivated garden. In many ways Reinhard Behrens has sought through the imaginative power of his art to create the opposite — a vast wilderness of terrible austere beauty, which he has given the mythical identity of Naboland. Although this arctic wasteland is an invention of the artist's acquisitive imagination and exists only through the associative power of images and objects to evolve their own history, the popular success of the Naboland pieces must lie in the familiarity and accessibility of the materials that Behrens uses. These tie in closely with his experiences of Scotland: the epic landscape backdrops and many of the found objects, which act as pseudo-archaeological evidence of the vanished human presence, are directly taken from his findings when travelling around the mountains and seashores of this country.

The work of Behrens clearly places him within the Northern European tradition and more specifically relates his art to Romanticism. Many of the themes in the ongoing saga of Naboland; man's doomed struggle with the overwhelming forces of untamed Nature; the vanished travellers lost in their search for some elusive goal; the few scattered traces of a past visit to this inhospitable land by explorers from our civilisation — all link his work to the northern Romantic temperament.

Yet, there is also a clear 20th century dimension to his art. Following the Dadaists and Surrealists he demonstrates the ability of the artist to alter the significance of images and objects by taking them out of their found context and literally placing

Ring of Brodgar, Orkney, 1980,
Pastel and pencil on board, 70 x 50 cm

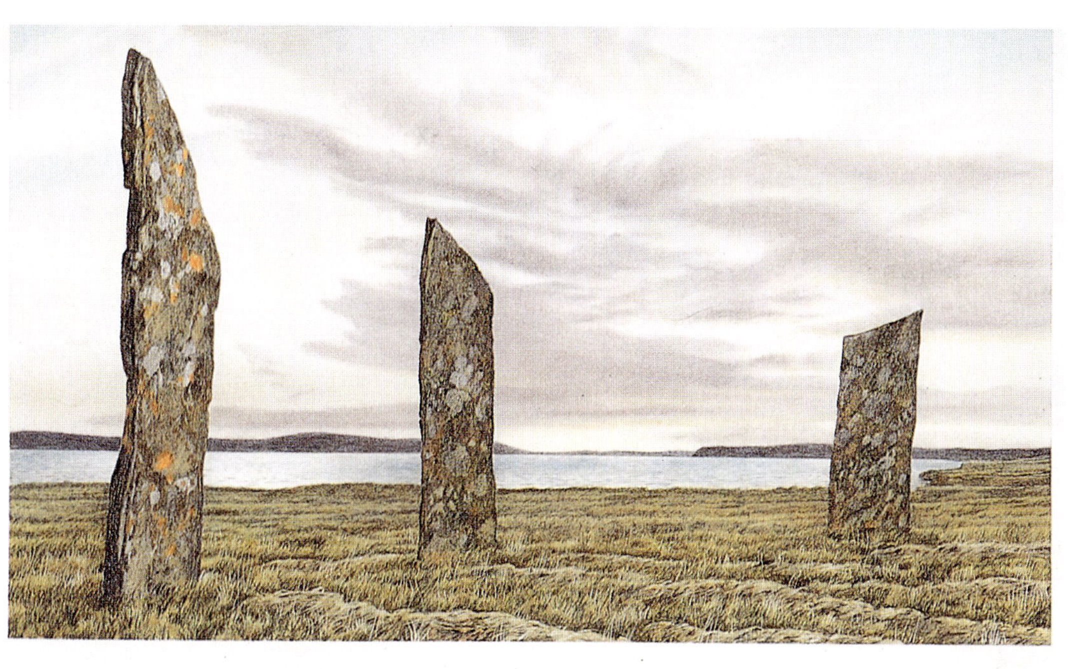

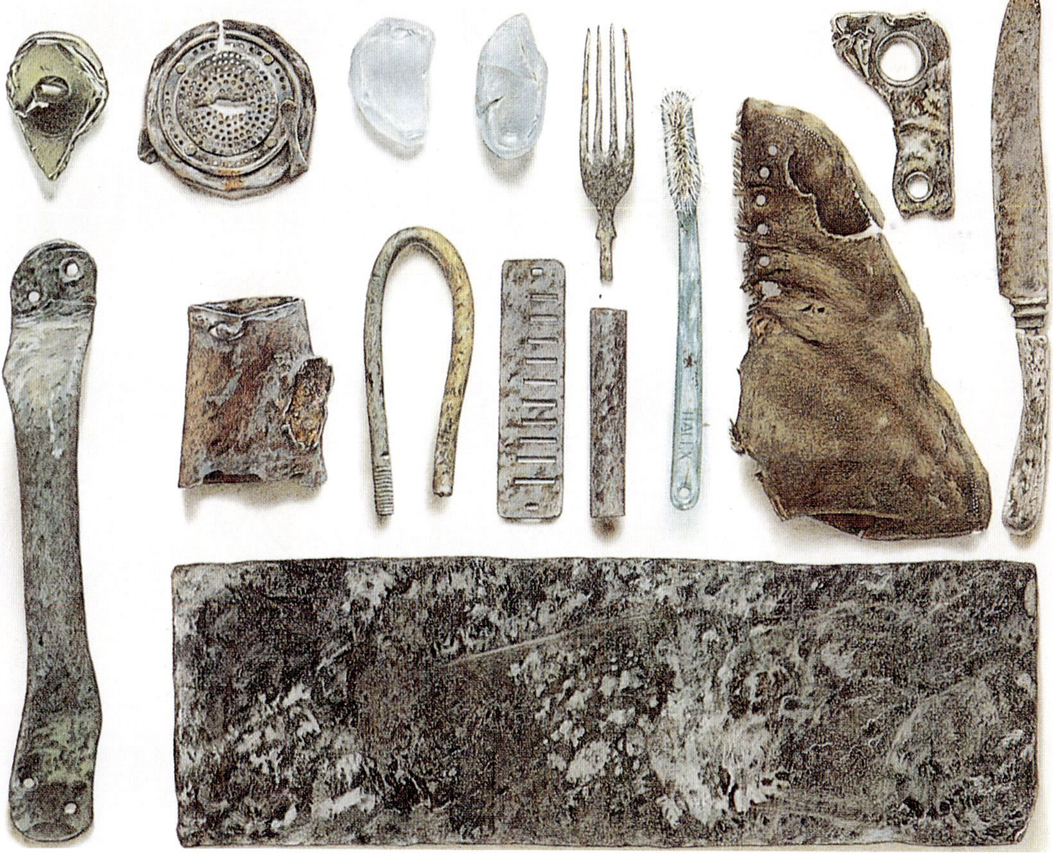

them in another world. This he does so convincingly by the meticulous attention to detail he shows in the way he paints and arranges the various Naboland settings. Finally the seemingly total authenticity of his installations is achieved by his witty use of museum-style presentation; calling into question how much we consume as history is in fact pure fantasy — like Naboland.

The numerous exhibitions on the Naboland theme which Behrens has created have been seen to popular and critical acclaim throughout Scotland since the early 1980s. He has won various awards, including one from IBM (1985) and a Scottish Arts Council major bursary (1987).

Artist's Comment

Naboland to me is not so much a dream country of my own, but rather the shared sum of associations that are stirred up in everyone who looks at my drawings, paintings, prints and objects.

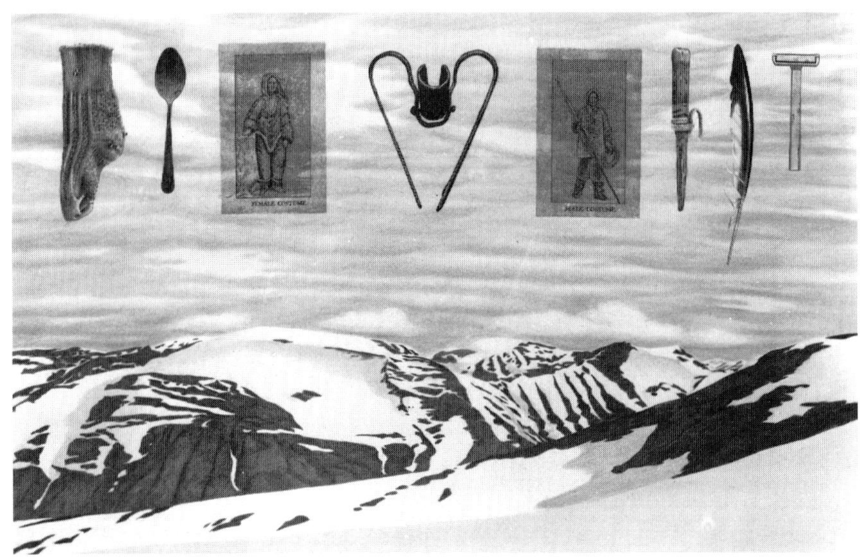

Inuit Valentine, 1989,
Pastel, pencil on board, 50 x 70 cm,
Collection of the artist

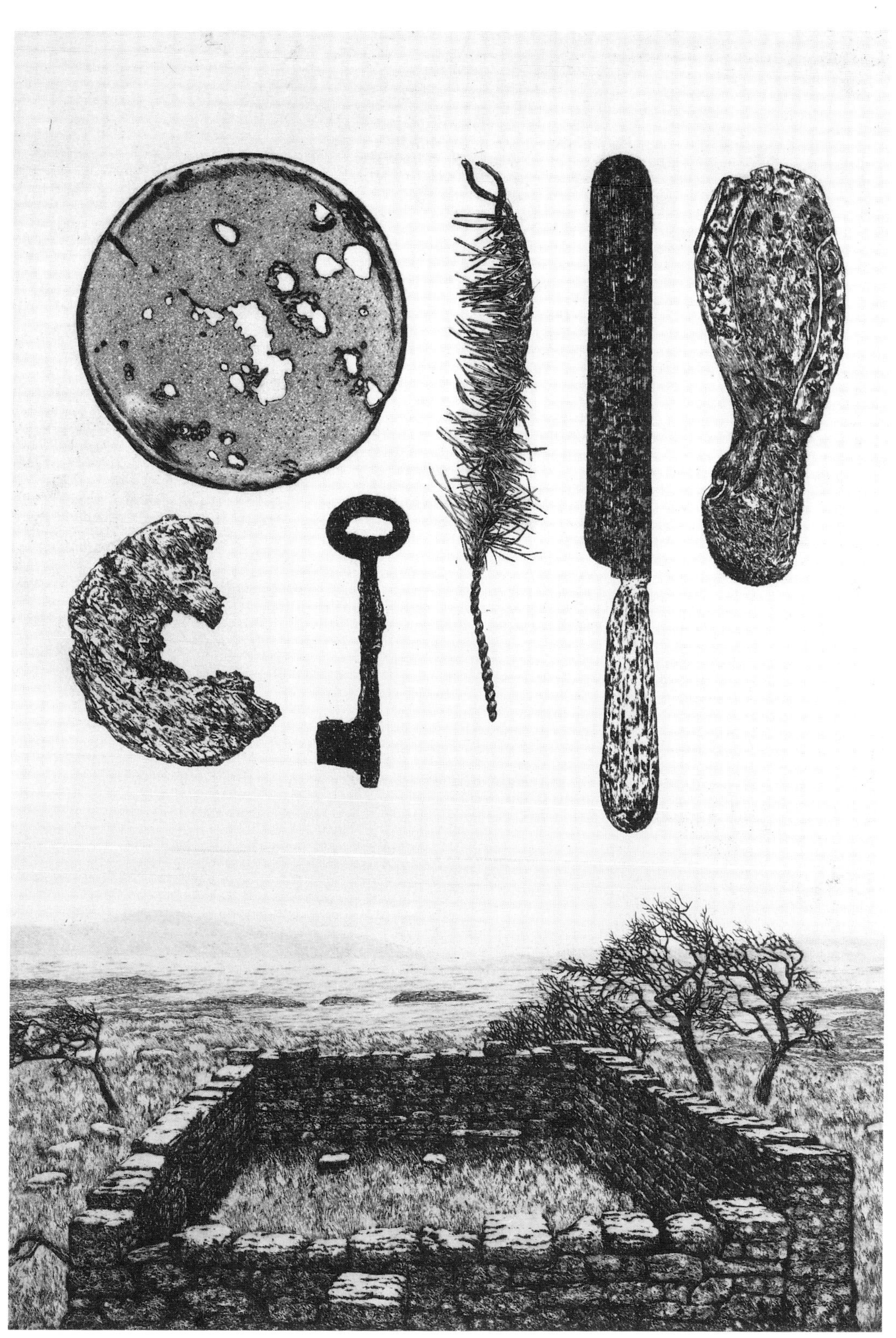

Boreraig, Skye, 1986,
Etching, 50 x 33 cm,
Courtesy of the Fine Art Society

JOHN BELLANY

John Bellany was born in 1942 in Port Seton, a small fishing town at the mouth of the Firth of Forth. He trained at Edinburgh College of Art (1960–65) and went on to the Royal College of Art, London (1965–68) where he studied under Peter de Francia. During the 1960s and 1970s he held various lecturing posts in a number of English art colleges. After a serious illness in 1984 he has devoted all his working time to painting. His career is now one of the most successful of any British artist, as witnessed by his major retrospective in 1986–87 at the Scottish National Gallery of Modern Art, Edinburgh and Serpentine Gallery, London.

Within contemporary Scottish painting, John Bellany is undoubtedly the most influential figure of his generation. His work, with its distinctive personality, has made a strong impact on the course of painting in this country. It would not be an exaggeration to say that nearly all the younger artists working in a figurative manner today have responded in some degree to the example of his achievement.

When Bellany began to train as a painter in the early 1960s, Scottish art was in a sorry state. The dominant mode of painting as practised by the art establishment of the art colleges and RSA was still a decorative form of Fauvism going back to The Colourists. Any artist wishing to develop a serious alternative to the complacent art scene in Scotland went elsewhere. Bellany, with a few others, was the first to offer a serious challenge within Scotland to the ubiquitous *belle peinture* manner of Scottish painting. Following the example of the leader of modern Scottish literature, Hugh MacDiarmid, Bellany attached his painting to the great realist/metaphysical tradition of Northern European Art. While still at art college he began to produce work that dealt with the harsh physical and social realities of the fishing community with which he had deep personal attachments. These pictures were painted in an uncompromising fashion, both in the dark, brooding manner of expression and the monumental dimension of scale — they were the first serious figurative pictures painted in Scotland for more than a generation.

Bellany moved and settled in London in the mid-1960s. There he continued to feel an outsider, being a committed figurative painter when the cosmopolitan art

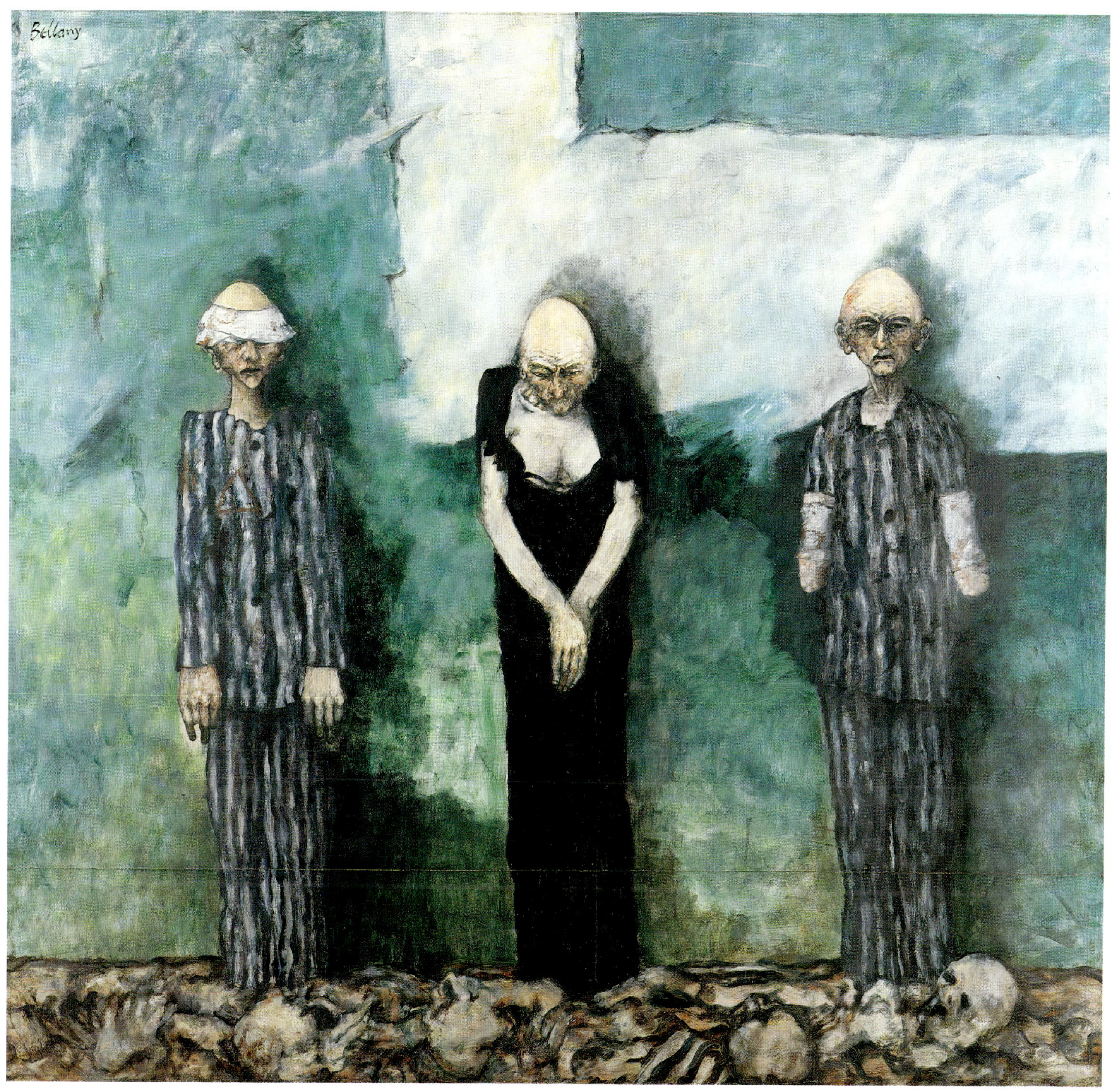

Pourquoi?, 1967,
Oil on board, 200.5 x 213 cm,
Courtesy Fischer Fine Art Limited, London

scene was still taken up with vapid late modernism. Yet he had supporters such as Peter de Francia and John Berger as well as the continuing friendship of Sandy Moffat and Alan Bold. Artistically the major boost to his development after moving south was his first-hand acquaintance with modern German painting, especially the work of Beckmann. From the German artist's example, he began to evolve a repertoire of personal iconography, mostly connected with the sea, which gave his paintings a profoundly tragic mood. His mysterious figures and strange creatures were firstly presented in a strong hard-edged style, but by the later 1970s his technique had become so violently expressive that by the time of his breakdown some of his work was almost gesturally abstract. Since his recovery, he has reverted to a more controlled handling. He continues to use the same subjects and imagery, but now in a more ironic manner. Despite all these sea-changes in Bellany's career he remains the great humanist painter of contemporary Scottish art.

John Bellany has had exhibitions all over the world. His work is represented in numerous private and public collections, including the Museum of Modern Art, New York, and the Tate Gallery, London.

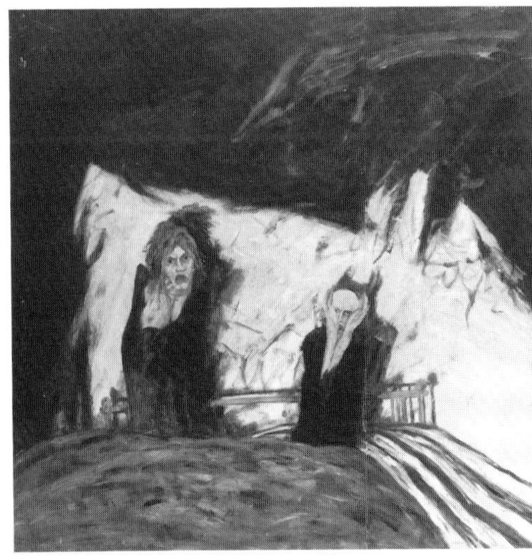

The Fright, 1968,
Oil on canvas, 182.9 x 182.9 cm

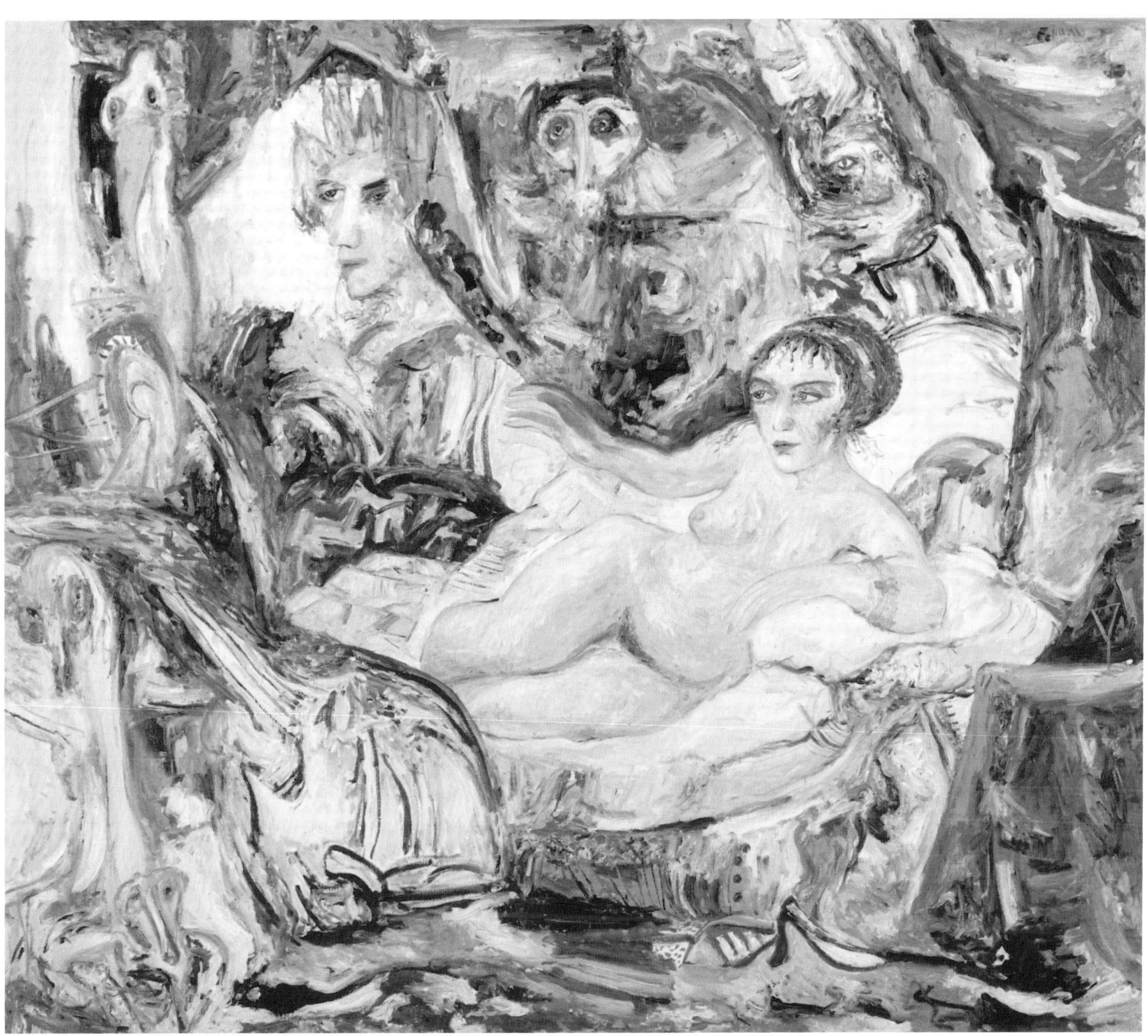

Danäe: Homage to R. II, 1991
Oil on canvas, 182.9 x 213 cm

ELIZABETH BLACKADDER

Elizabeth Blackadder was born in Falkirk in 1931 and studied Fine Art at Edinburgh University and College of Art from 1949–55. From 1962 to 1986 she lectured in the Fine Art Department of Edinburgh College of Art. She currently lives and works in Edinburgh.

Blackadder's development, from her early student days to her current practice, has been typified by an ever-increasing confidence and delicacy in the technique of still-life painting. Her training at Edinburgh College of Art, under the then Head of Painting, William Gillies, built a foundation in sensitive brushwork and the power of colour. Over the years, the artist has perfected a distinctive way of painting in watercolour which has won her acclaim in Scotland and beyond.

Blackadder focuses on the intimate and controlled environment of the studio, arranging diverse memorabilia across her table which are then transposed into paint. Flowers, vases, cats, paper, textiles and leaves float on pale grounds, in part representing themselves but also forming abstract, loosely woven shapes across the paper. Like the memories associated with the objects themselves, they seem to float randomly, soon to be dispersed. The translucent quality of watercolour helps add to this feeling of transitory reality, of the insubstantiality of the material world. In effect the background acts as the table on which the objects sit, tilted up towards the spectator, reducing perspective and three-dimensional space as well as inviting absorption into the artist's diverse textures.

Her technique is a dialogue between the paint and the paper; over the years, Blackadder has worked with the lucid, irreversible effects of watercolour, where major changes cannot be made and a confidence of touch is necessary to secure the right weight and balance. This evokes very strongly the manner of Japanese artists whose sense of touch and the eloquence of the calligraphic mark has clearly been an inspiration to the artist, as the many Japanese objects and references in her work illustrate. Both Blackadder's technique and subjects seem far removed from the world beyond the studio, yet, as personal memorabilia, they hint at travel and a lifetime of collecting.

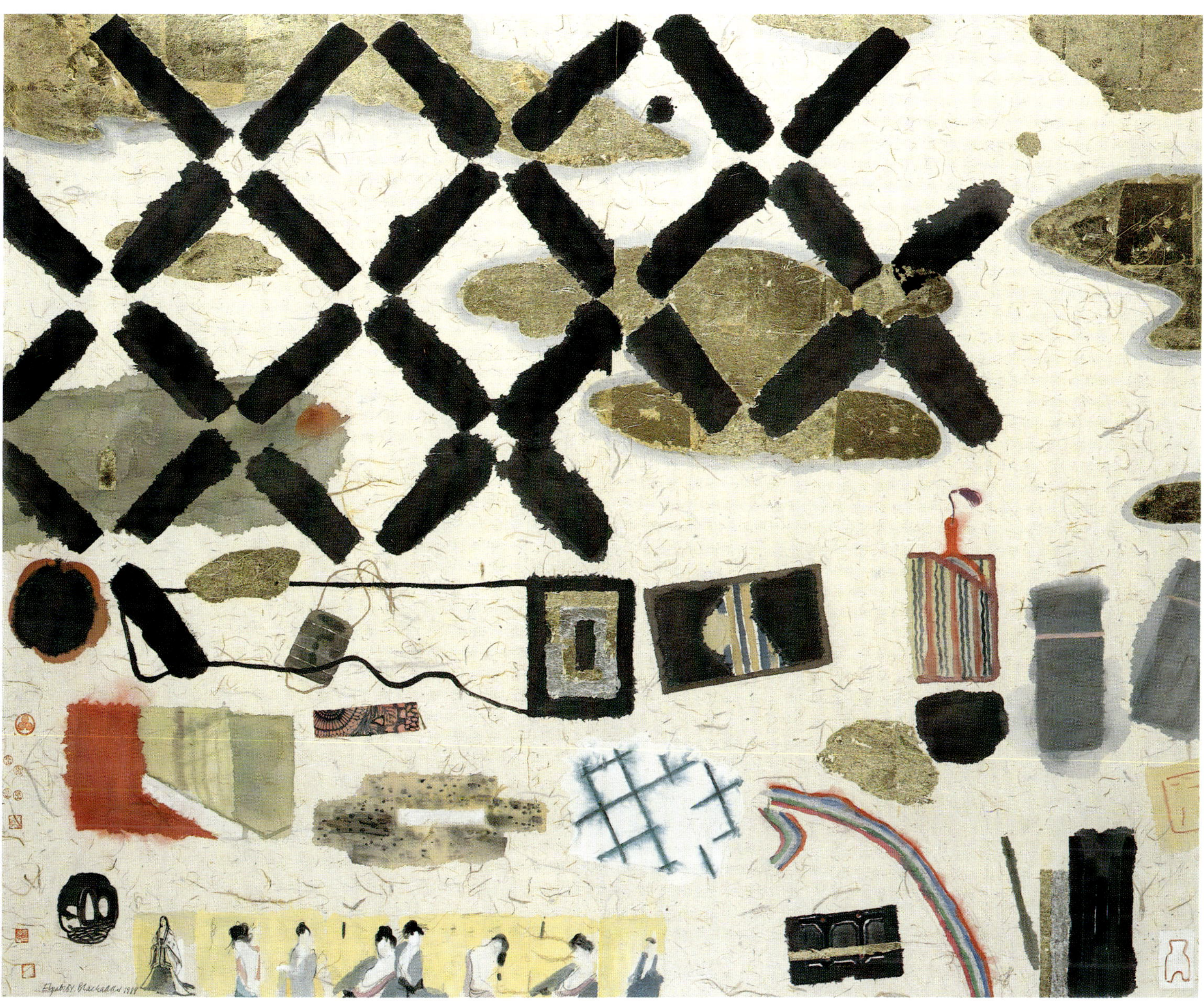

Figures and Still Life, Kyoto, 1988,
Watercolour/gold leaf, 99 x 126 cm,
Private collection
Courtesy Mercury Gallery, London

The artist is represented in many private and public collections worldwide, including the Tate Gallery, the National Galleries of Scotland and the National Museum of Women in the Arts, Washington DC.

Artist's Comment

There is the danger, perhaps, of being put down as only a watercolourist — the feeling that it is not so serious a medium and that it is somehow feminine. I have always worked from the thing seen, no matter how much I move away from the source.

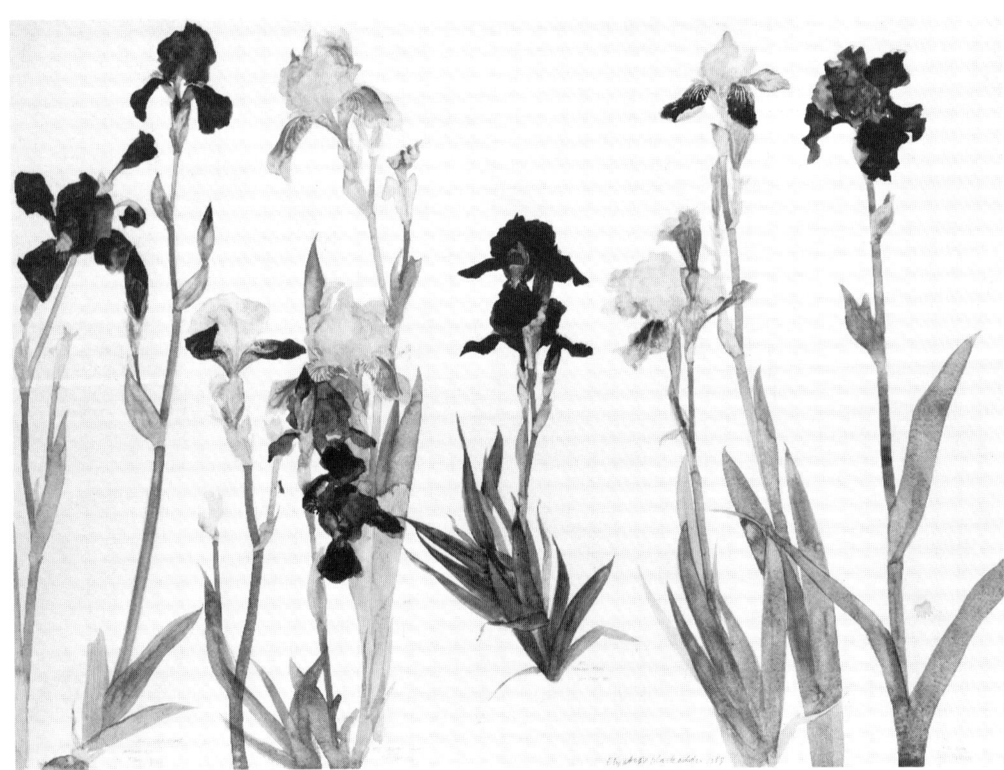

Studies of Irises, 1983,
Watercolour, 69 x 104 cm,
Private collection

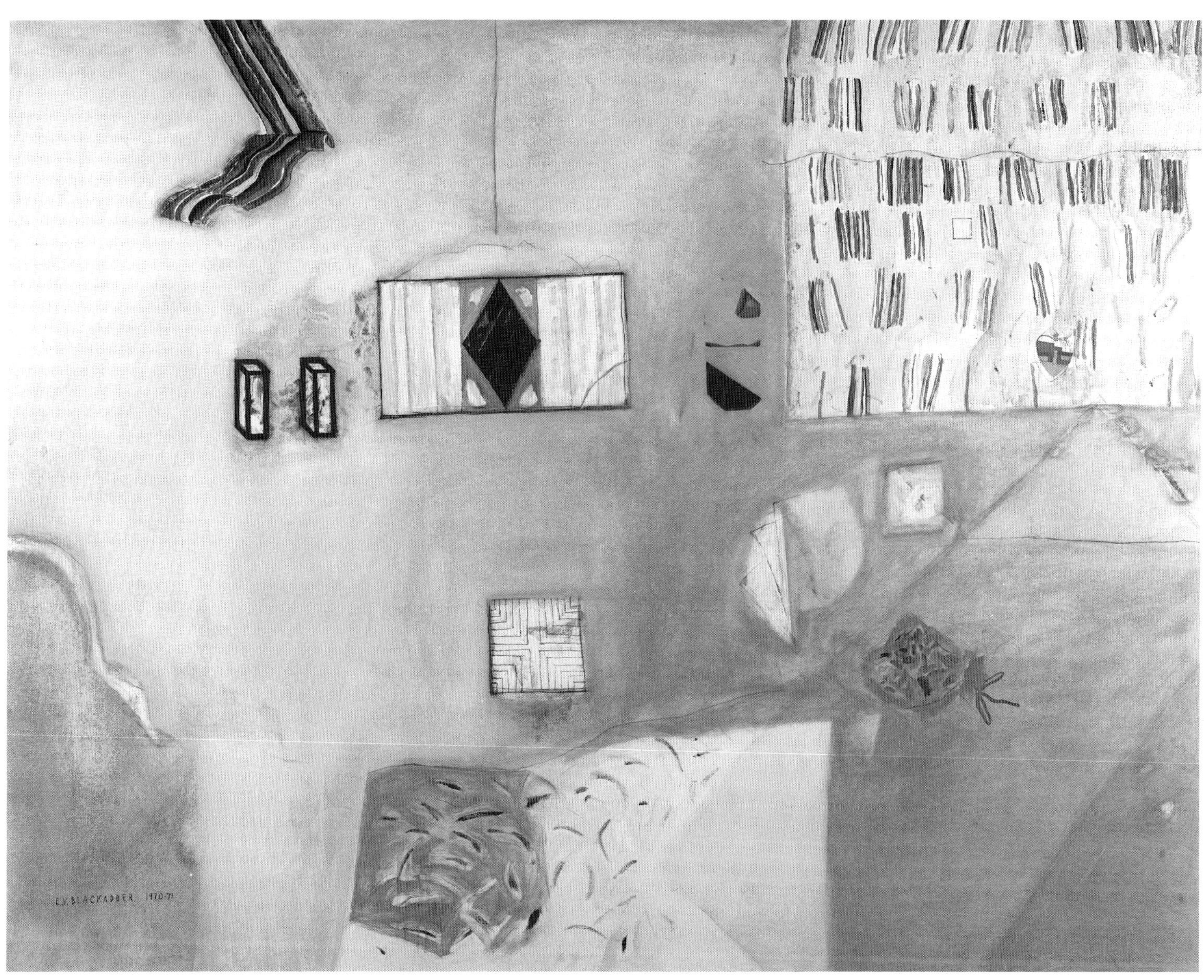

Grey Table, 1970–71,
Oil on canvas, 112 x 142 cm,
Private collection

Dennis Buchan was born in Arbroath in 1937. He studied at Dundee College of Art (1954–58) and then did various part-time teaching jobs until he was appointed lecturer in painting at his old college in Dundee where he continues to teach. He has won a number of awards over the years, both from the Royal Scottish Academy (of which he is a full member) and the Scottish Arts Council.

Dennis Buchan's work represents a type of painting which is greatly admired in certain quarters of the Scottish art scene. His paintings are widely viewed as fine examples of the 'painterly' qualities of Scottish art. More specifically his work can be seen to demonstrate that the rich colourist tradition of Scottish painting can be fused with more recent international developments such as Abstract Expressionism and painterly Pop Art without the complete loss of that necessary distinctive sense of indigenous character. This achievement may result from his disinclination to more total abstraction. For, although Buchan's finished paintings might appear on first acquaintance to be purely arrangements of colours and shapes without reference to anything outside themselves, they have in fact evolved through an abstracting process from the artist's response to natural phenomena. Yet the 'natural phenomena' which inspires his paintings need not always be taken from the observed world, although many are, even to the point of the retention of a recognisable image such as a figure or a still life object. However, other sensuous experience such as 'the rich textures and rhythms of music' can act equally as a stimulus. Whether the initial inspiration for his paintings be a distant seascape, a view of a garden, the lively atmosphere of a cafe interior or a moving passage by Mahler or Sibelius, his paintings, with their highly accomplished interplay of strong contrasting colours and patterns, present a complex experience of heightened intensity.

Dennis Buchan has had exhibitions throughout the United Kingdom. In Scotland he tends to show at the Royal Scottish Academy, although he has exhibited in commercial galleries like the Compass in Glasgow (1975). His work is represented in private and public collections, such as the Scottish Arts Council and Leicester University.

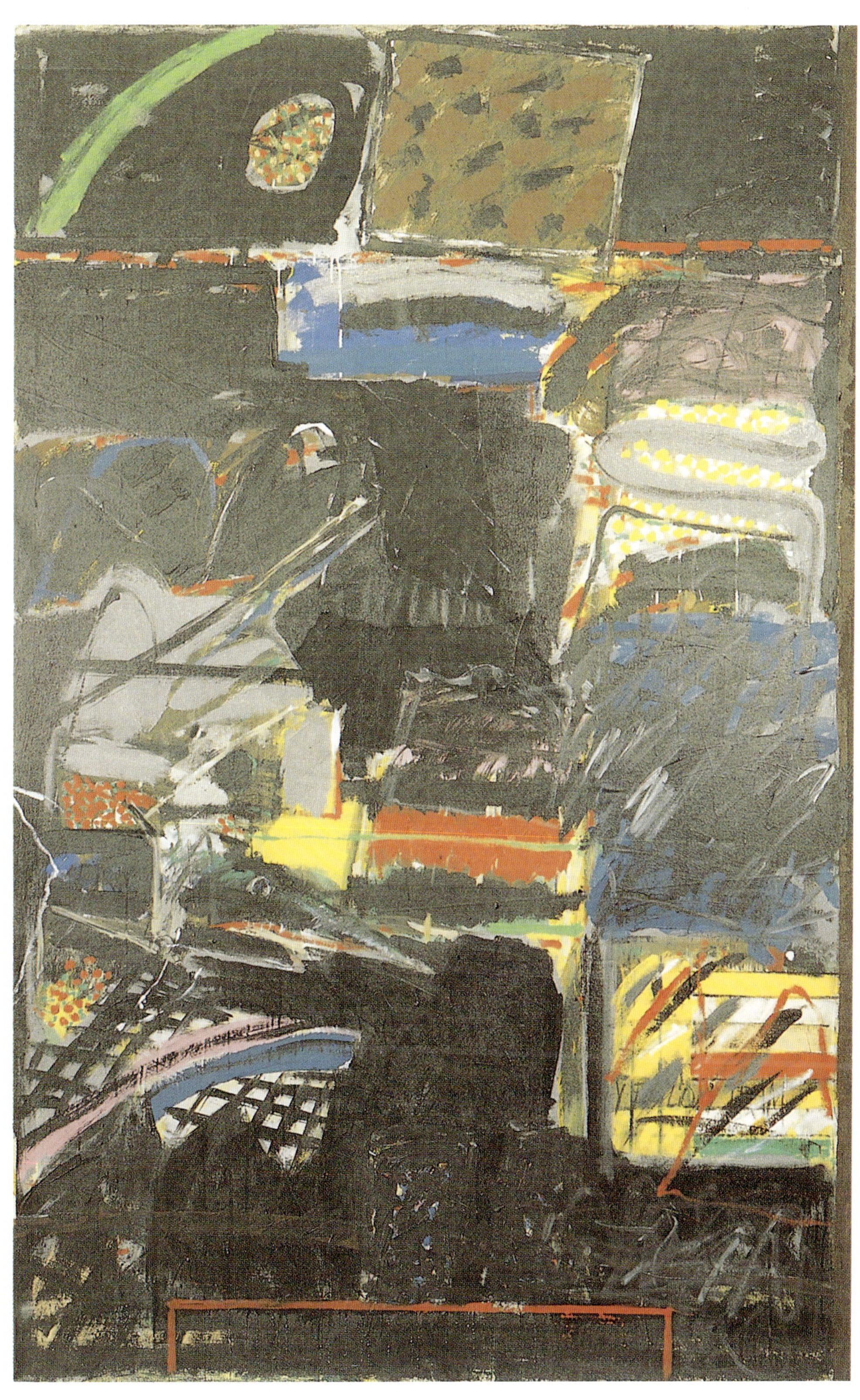

Night Quay, 1991,
Acrylic on canvas, 200x 130 cm,
Photograph: Malcolm J. Thompson
Collection of the artist

I have always felt I had affinities with artists concerned with the environment in perhaps an oblique and atmospherically expressive way and I myself try to absorb the excitement of ambiguous interior/exterior relationships which at the moment can be summed up as being — A Cafe, A Beach, A Harbour, An Environment experienced, measured, felt and interpreted.

Shore Series, 1987,
Acrylic on canvas, 125 x 115 cm,
Photograph: Malcolm J. Thomson

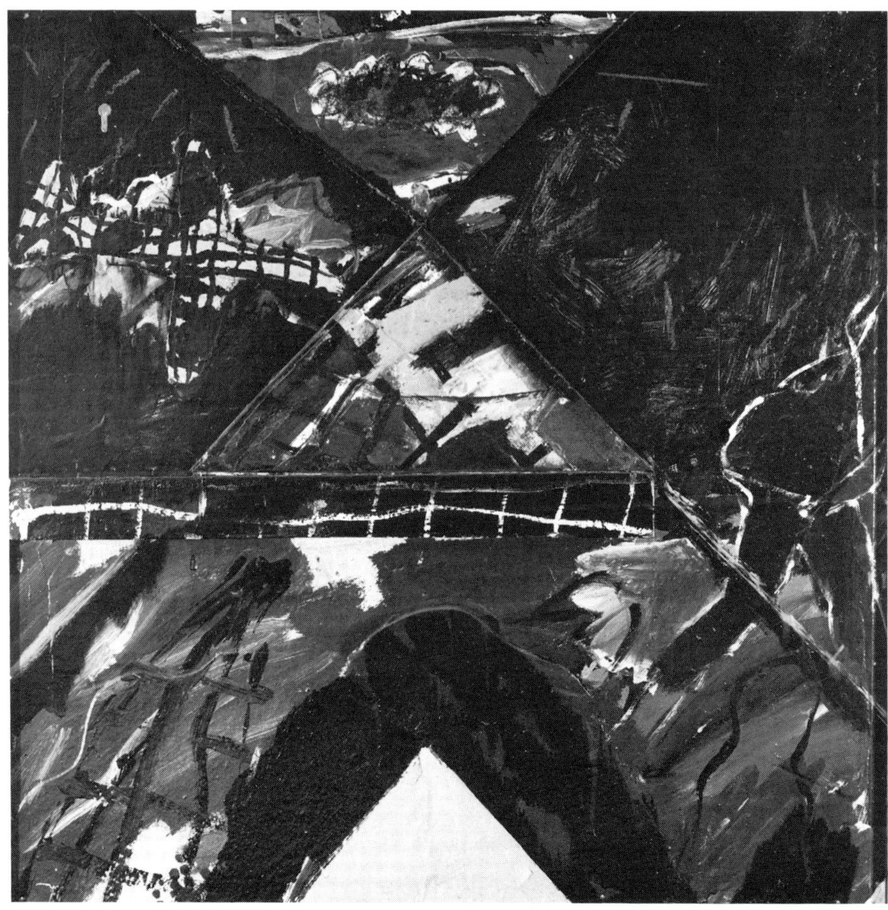

Garden Series, 1975,
Acrylic and collage on hard board, 125 x 115 cm,
Photograph: Malcolm J. Thomson

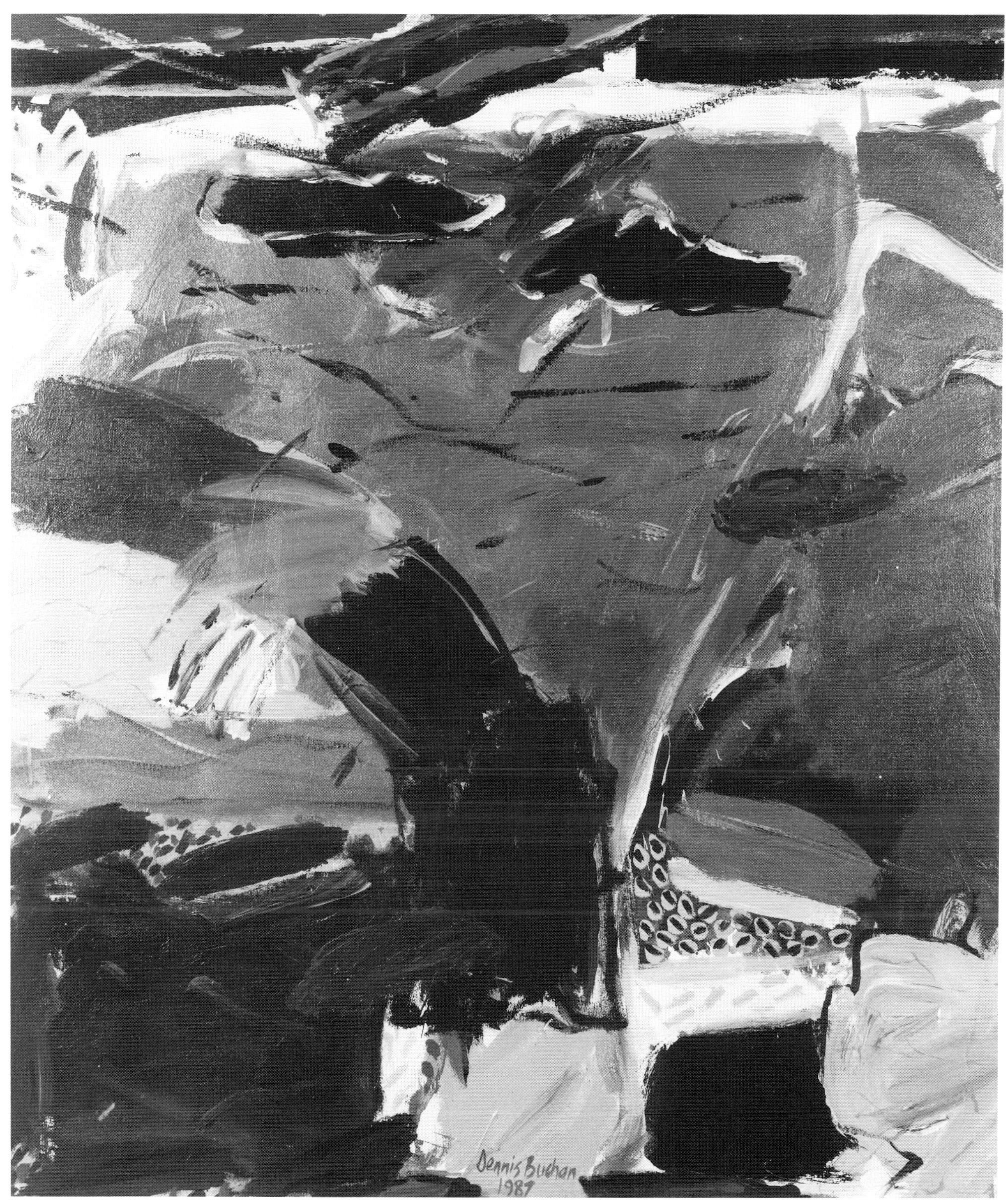

Dennis Buchan
1987

JOYCE CAIRNS

Joyce Cairns was born in Edinburgh in 1947. She studied at Gray's School of Art, Aberdeen (1966–70), then gained her Master of Art at the Royal College of Art, London (1971–74) and obtained her art teaching qualification from Goldsmiths College, University of London in 1976. She then returned to Gray's in Aberdeen where she is a lecturer in the Drawing and Painting Department.

Over the last ten years, Joyce Cairns has emerged as a figurative painter of great expressive power. The central concern in her work has always been autobiographical and psychological investigation through personal and imaginative experience. In her earlier paintings of the 1970s mythological themes dominated and were treated in a pseudo-religious fashion, with pictures sometimes taking the form of altarpieces for example. Stylistically these earlier works were strongly influenced by 19th and 20th century Symbolists, such as the Pre-Raphaelites, Chagall and Kokoschka.

In 1976 she came back to Scotland, after a period in London. With her return to her social and artistic roots and finding a studio at the mouth of Aberdeen harbour, she began to shed the earlier self-enclosing mysticism. Her work, as with the best of North European art, became grounded in actual experience; avoiding the picturesque, her pictures are now usually set against the background of the community life and maritime activity next to hand around the harbour. Yet the subjects are still treated in a highly personal and imaginative manner. By using expressive perspective and distortion in her complex compositions, Joyce Cairns fuses elements of her own life history with dramatic and comic scenes of high passions in which emotional, sexual and political forces interact in grand scenes of human experience.

Joyce Cairns has won many awards for her painting and has exhibited in Scotland and England. Since 1980 she has had solo exhibitions in Glasgow, Aberdeen and Edinburgh. In 1991 she signed with the Odette Gilbert Gallery, London. Her work is represented in many private and public collections throughout Great Britain and abroad, including the Scottish Arts Council and the Contemporary Arts Society, London.

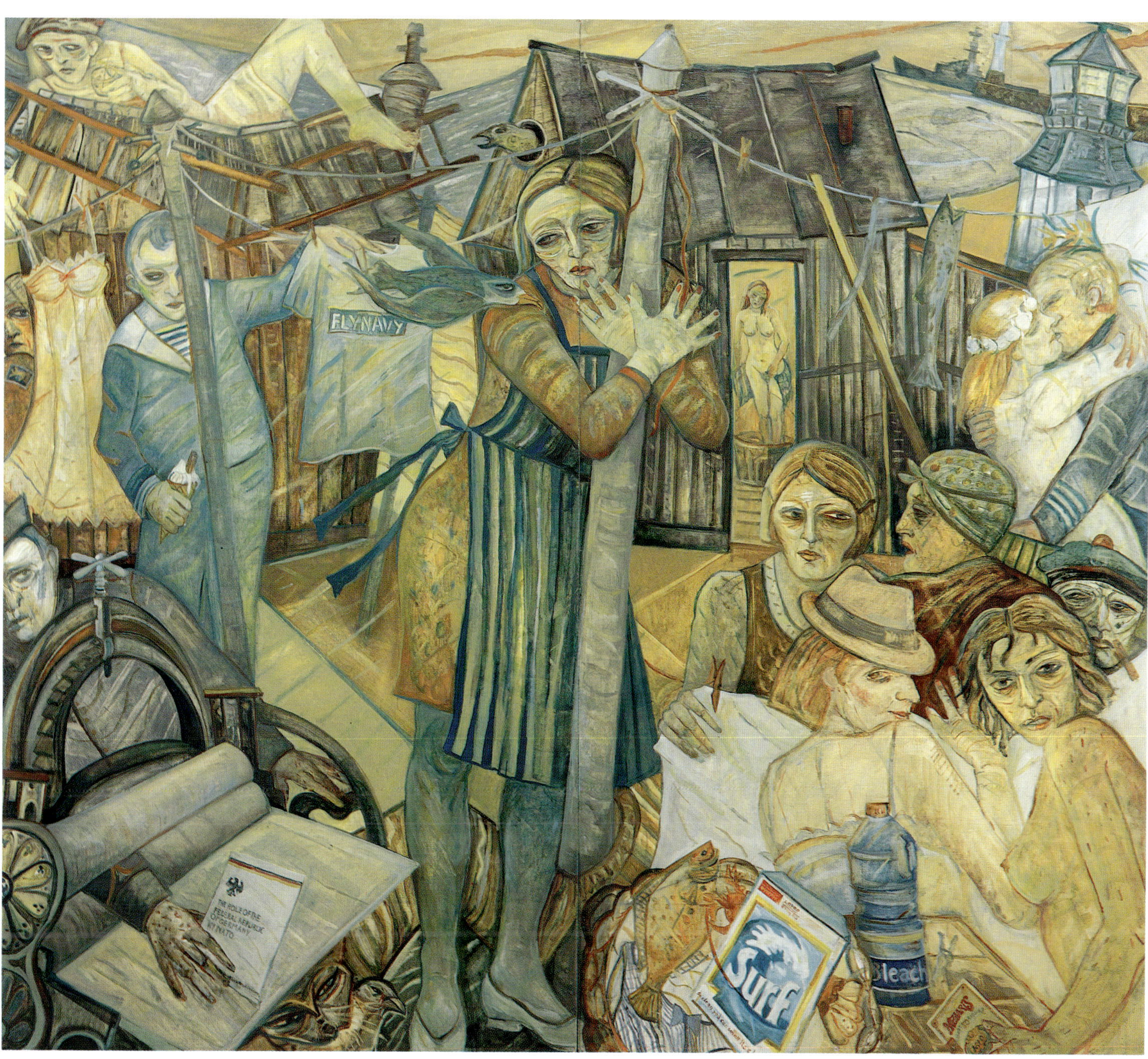

The Drying Green, 1990,
Oil on board, 213 x 244 cm,
Photograph: Robin Wilson
Collection of the artist

Artist's Comment

*I see life as a comedy. It's about living and experience, a burlesque with evil
undertones.*

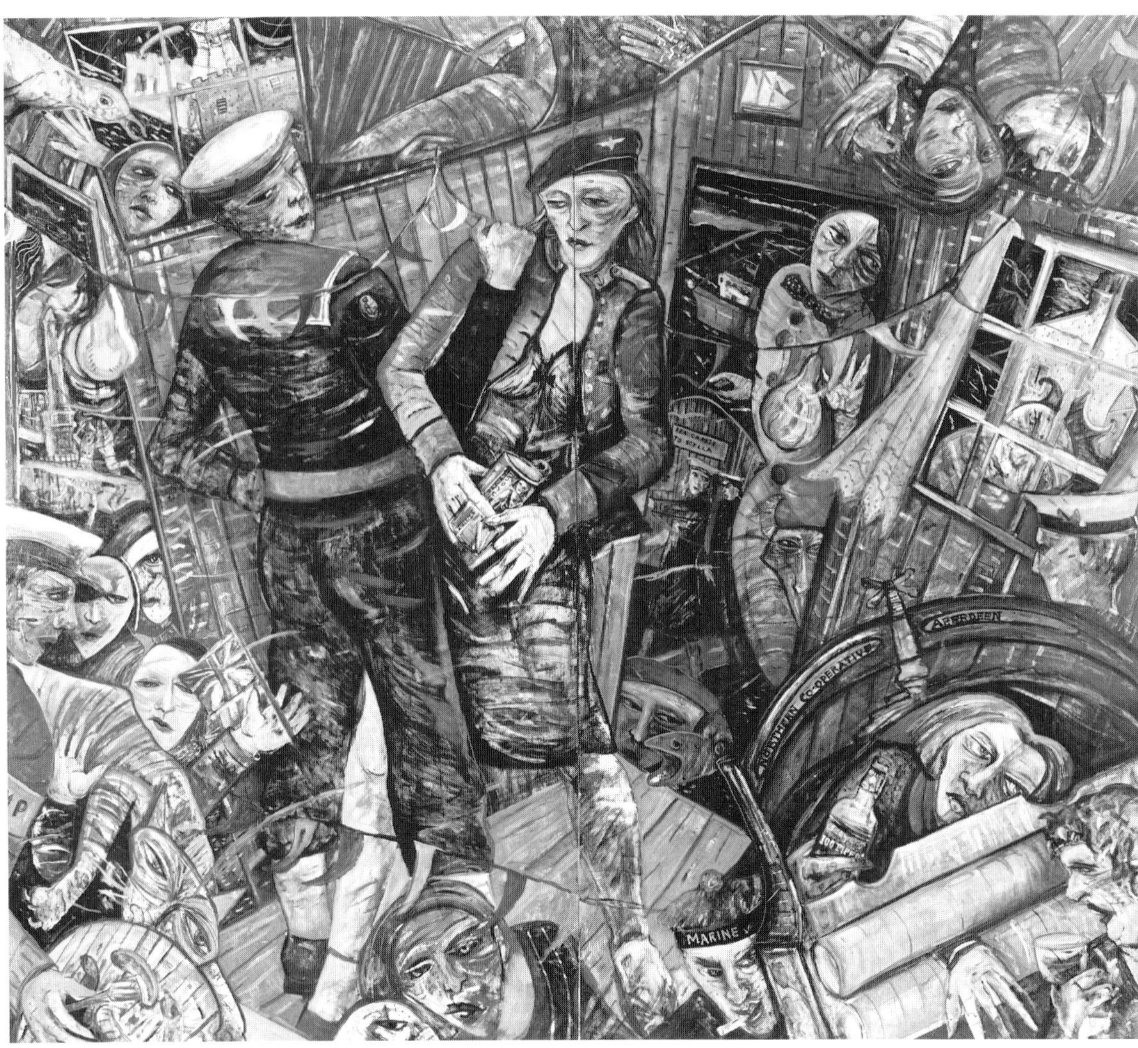

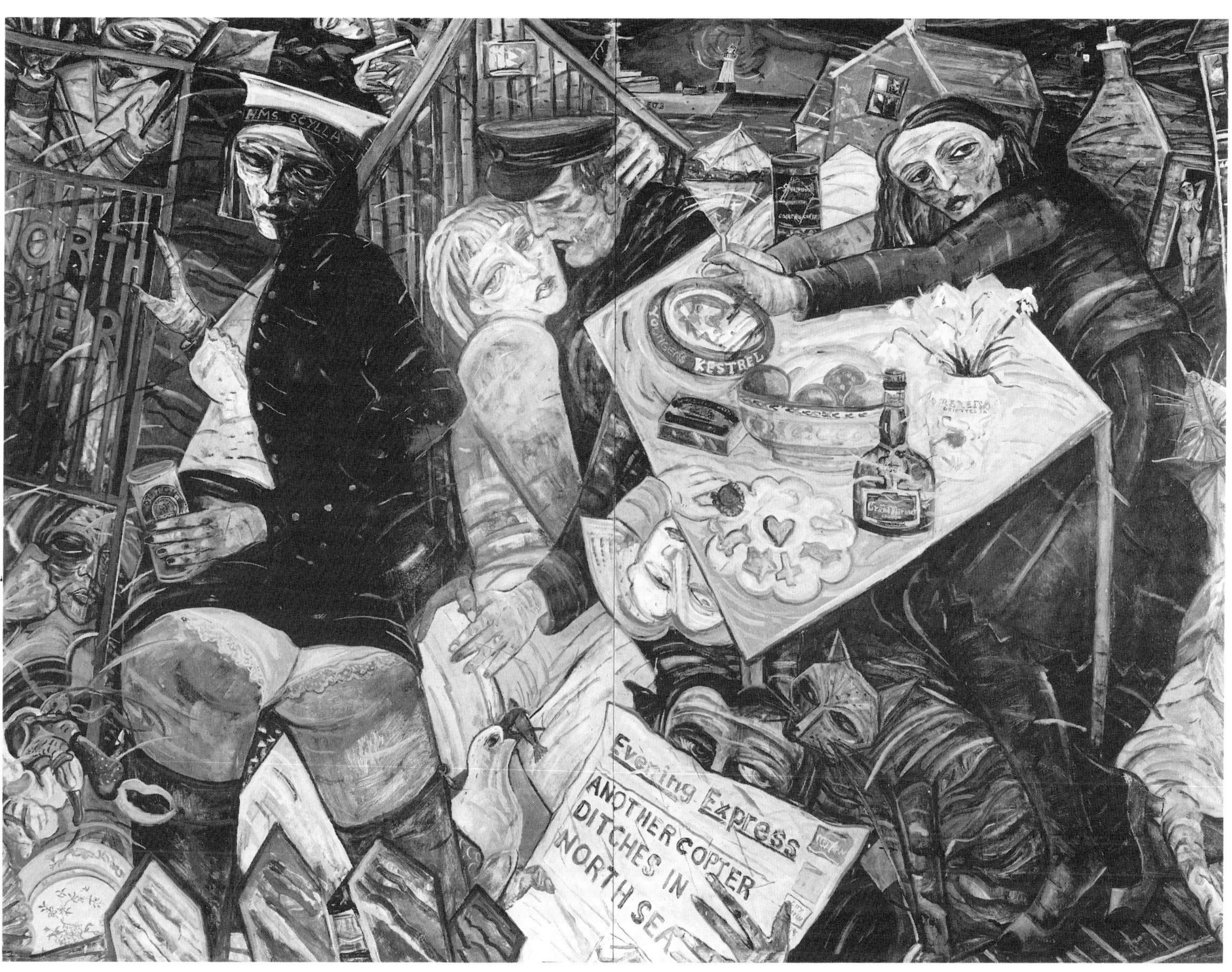

A Cold Wind Blows Over the North Sea, 1989,
Oil on board, 183 x 244 cm,
Photograph: Mike Davidson

Scenes in the Sheddie, Footdee Street Party, 1986,
Oil on board, 213 x 244 cm,
Photograph: Mike Davidson

Steven Campbell was born in Glasgow, Scotland in 1954. He worked for seven years as a steel works maintenance engineer before attending Glasgow School of Art between 1978 and 1982, after which he won a Fulbright Scholarship to New York. After internationally acclaimed successes in painting in New York he has returned to Scotland where he currently lives and works.

Of all the Scottish artists who rose to prominence in the 1980s, Campbell perhaps made the biggest international impact with his large, enigmatic canvases, with titles and subjects which sought to confuse rather than enlighten: *Two Humeians Preaching Causality to Nature* (1984) or *Building Accusing the Architect of Bad Design* (1984).

Campbell embraces a wealth of ideas and a huge cast of characters taken from all aspects of life and fiction. His early work at Glasgow School of Art consisted of performance art, and an intense theatricality and feeling of farce is carried over into many of his paintings. Characters enter and exit the stage which Campbell creates, with a demonstrative bravura designed to challenge the viewer, rather than soothe and comfort. Whilst Campbell's way of painting is expressive and assertive, his subjects are rarely directly emotional, preferring to play with ideas from a mainstream European tradition: philosophy, science, Cubism, Surrealism, collage and modern film are all alluded to in his work.

Campbell's paintings are littered with traditionally dressed figures and are set amongst claustrophobic surroundings, such as forests and derelict buildings. There exists in each work a complex layering of meanings which counterpoints the density of the detail that the artist crams in.

Even if we are familiar with all the ideas Campbell raises, he deliberately disrupts us if we try to piece together any definite story or specific event. This playfulness, under which lies a more serious questioning of how we piece together everyday experience, is very much part of a wider strain in contemporary figurative art; Campbell's place in the top bracket of European painting in the 1980s and beyond seems secure.

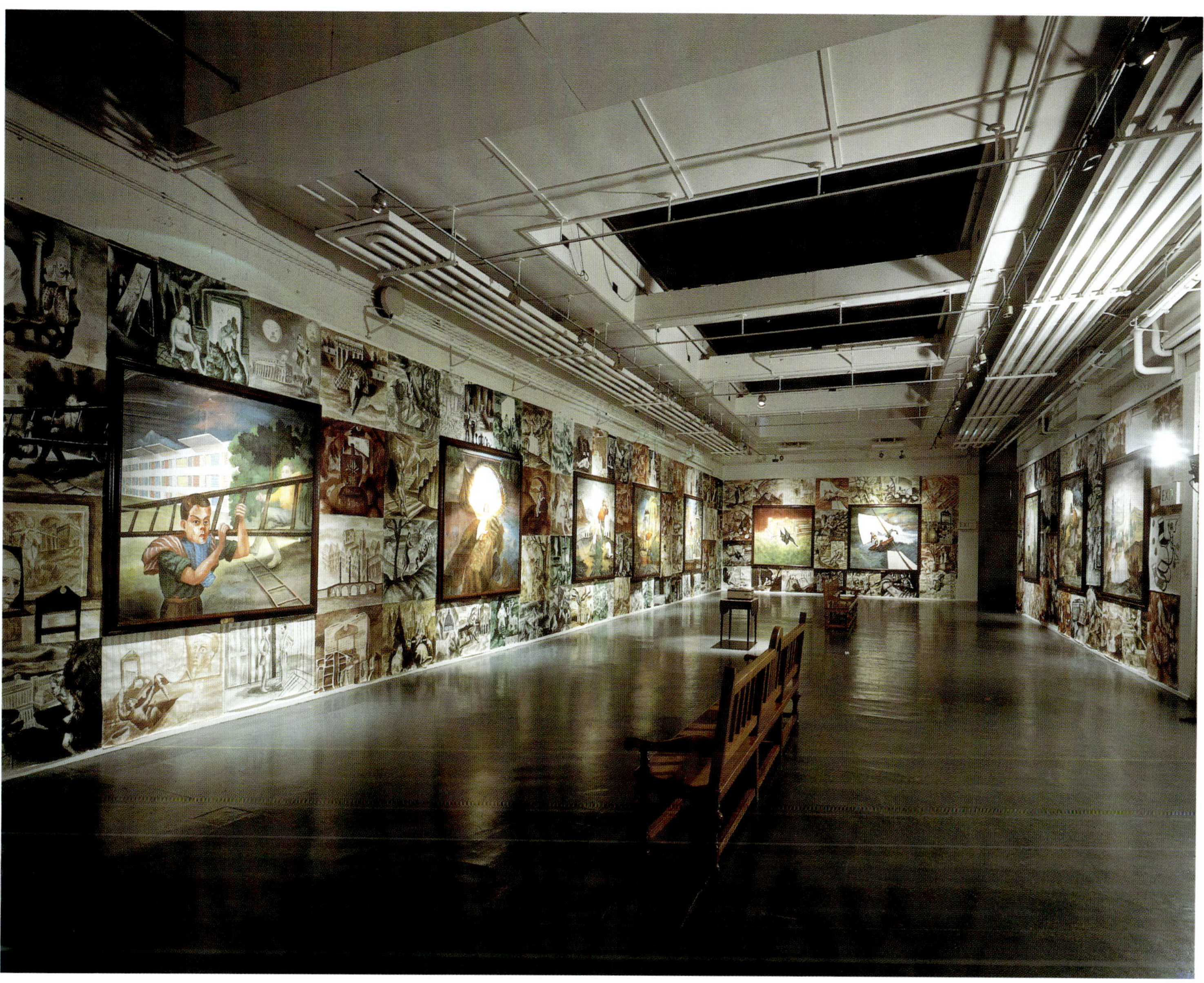

Installation: 'On Form and Fiction',
Third Eye Centre, Glasgow, March 1990

Campbell's first solo exhibition was at the Barbara Toll Fine Arts, New York, in
1983 and he has subsequently shown extensively around the world in major shows
in Europe, Japan, the United States and Australia.

Artist's Comment

*The painting starts off as one thing and if that doesn't work I try something else until
a memory of all these things is in it but none of them is particularly true except the
one I've picked to title the work. The picture is a summing-up of all the mistakes; it is
what's left.*

*The Man who Gave his Legs to God
and God did not Want Them*, 1987,
Oil on canvas, 239 x 209.5 cm,
Photograph: Prudence Cuming
Associates Ltd

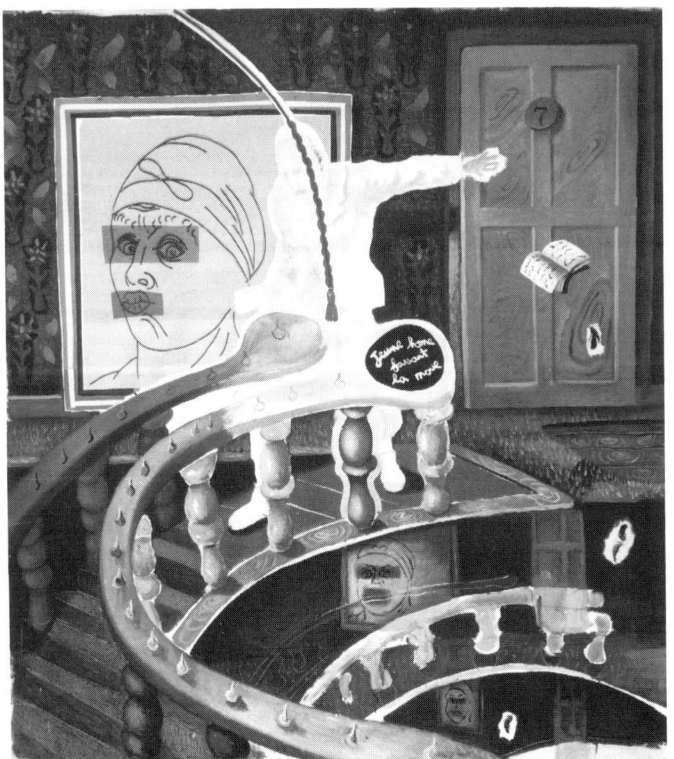

The Drunken Poet/Red Stripe, 1989,
Oil paint and collage, 188 x 170.2 cm,
Photograph: Prudence Cuming Associates Ltd

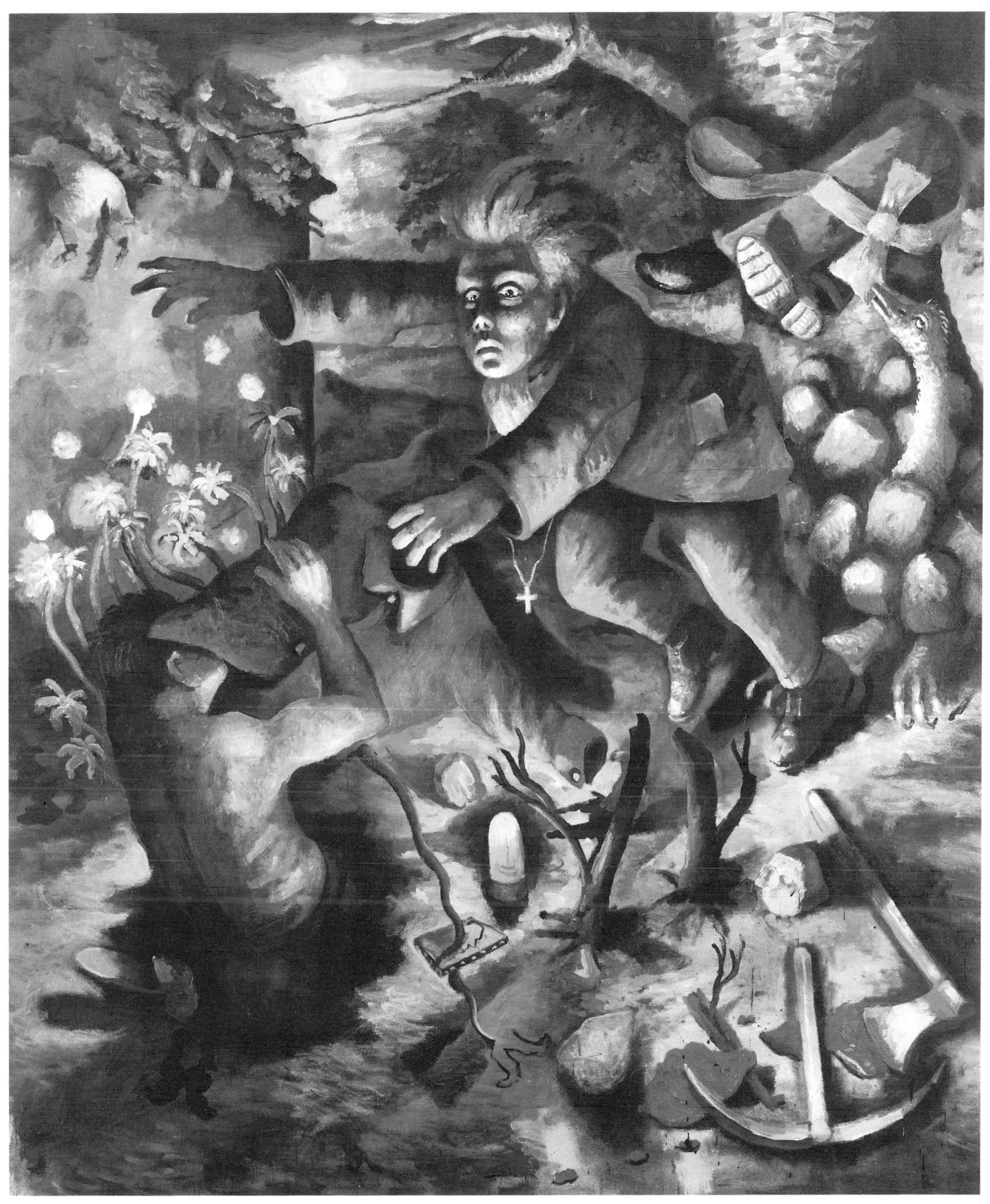

Russell Colombo was born in London in 1947. He moved north in the 1960s and graduated from Edinburgh College of Art in 1973. In 1980–81 he studied for a Diploma in Art Therapy at St Albans College of Art and now works part-time as an art therapist near Edinburgh.

Although English/Italian by birth, Russell Colombo's work can be accommodated within the Scottish painting tradition. He trained in Edinburgh and his instinctive feeling for expressive gesture and colour harmonies relates his work to the broad development of 19th and 20th century art in Scotland. That said, however, the main influence on his manner of painting has been the Abstract Expressionists, particularly lyrical painters like Sam Francis. Following the example of these trans-Atlantic artists, Colombo has sought to present his paintings as fields of broken colours which inter-link to create an all-over surface of vibrant pattern. Yet, despite the American influences, Colombo's work has also distinctive Scottish features. Firstly, his initial sources of inspiration tend to come from landscape, whether Scottish or from his travels abroad. Secondly, his paintings, as with many of the other artists in this book, are concerned to penetrate below surface appearances and investigate the geological and biological structures of the natural world.

Although Colombo has always been a committed abstract painter with no discernible figuration, his paintings are still deeply concerned with human experience. The ultimate theme in his work is the expression of the human need for a sense of underlying order and the integration between the perceptive powers of our senses and the macro- and microscopic forces of the physical world. As such, his best paintings are an open-ended dialogue between the creative powers of art and Nature.

Since the late 1970s, Russell Colombo has exhibited regularly in group and solo shows. Amongst other galleries, he has exhibited in The Fruitmarket and Talbot Rice Gallery in Edinburgh. His work is represented in a number of private and public collections in Scotland, including the Scottish Arts Council and Edinburgh Art Galleries.

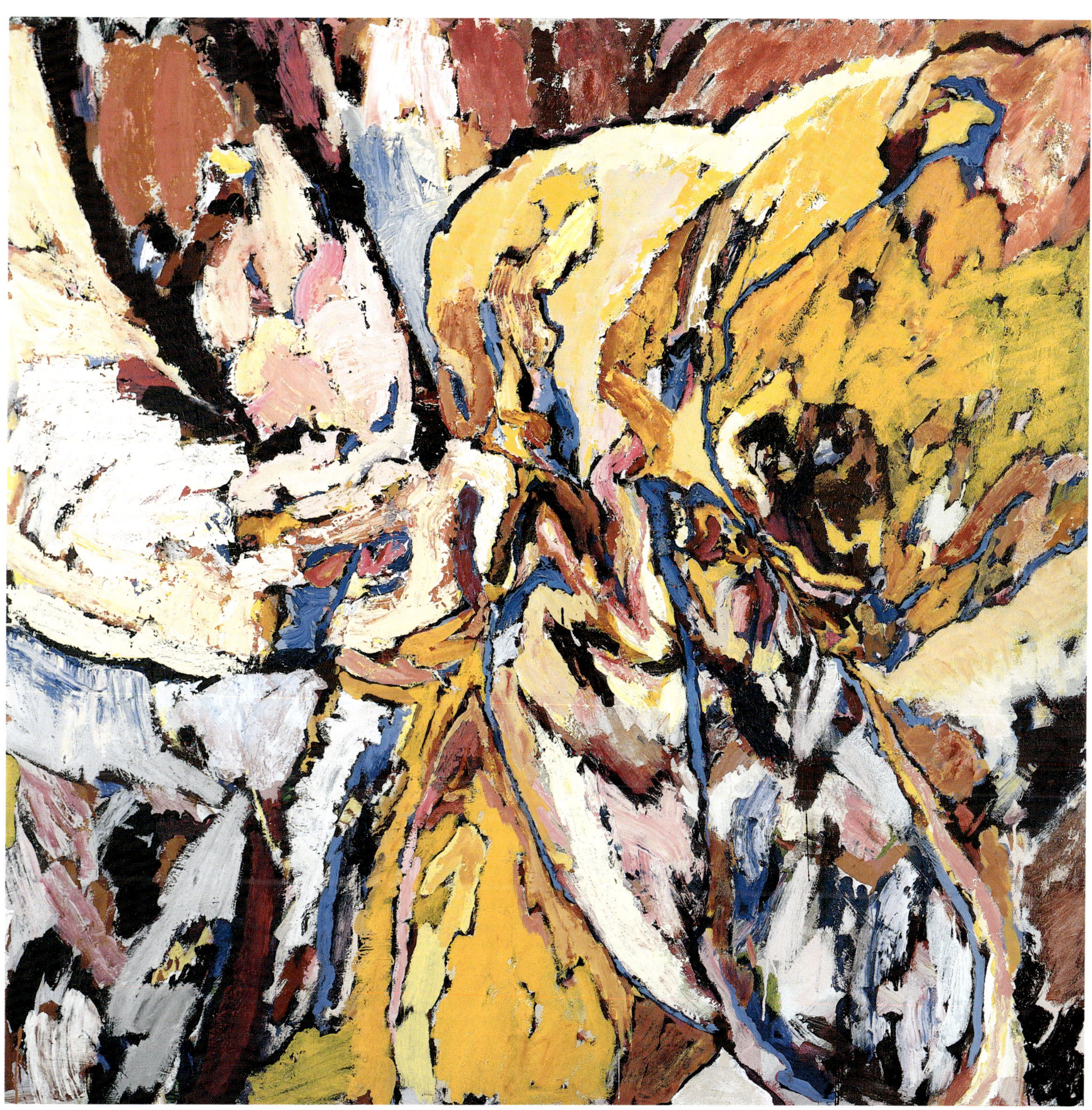

C.M.V. Special, 1990,
Acrylic on canvas, 183 x 183 cm,
Photograph: Joe Rock
Collection of the artist

Artist's Comment

I agree with the Taoist notion that the universe is a dynamic state of flowing energy, the essence of which cannot be named.

My painting is an attempt to find a visual metaphor for the unnamable.

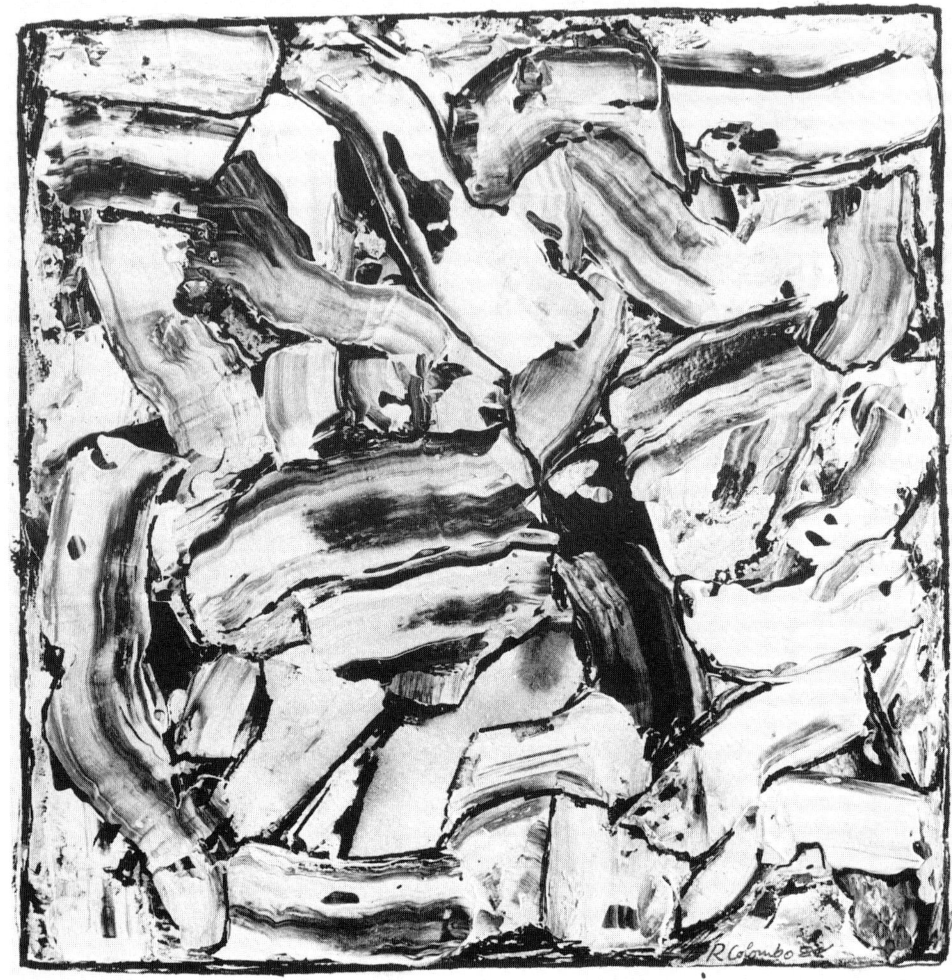

Untitled, 1988,
Acrylic on board, 61 x 61 cm,
Private collection,
Photograph: Joe Rock

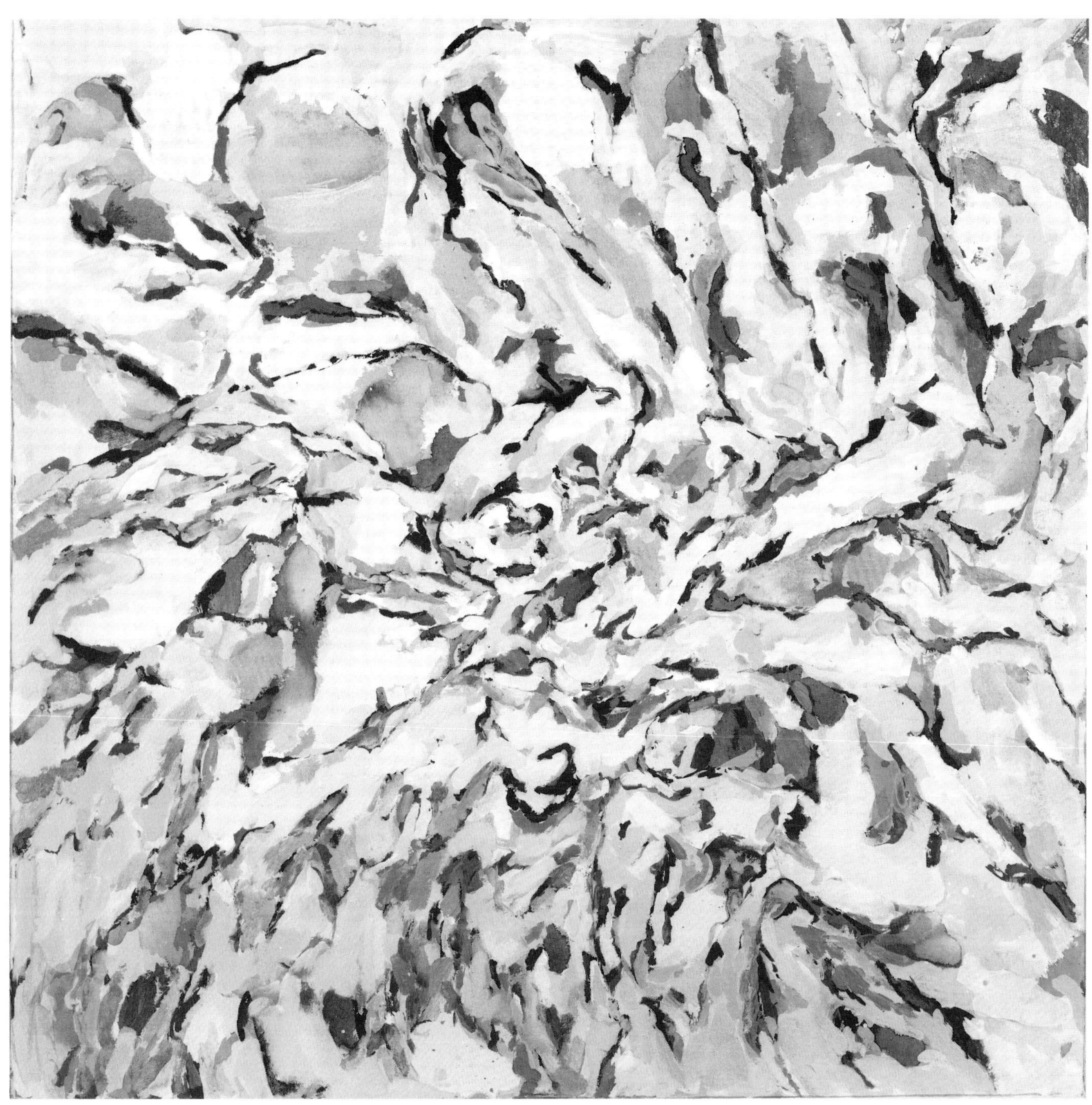

Tiperweir, 1986,
Acrylic on canvas, 122 x 122 cm,
Private collection,
Photograph: Joe Rock

Calum Colvin was born in Glasgow in 1961. He studied at Duncan of Jordanstone College of Art, Dundee from 1979–83, progressing through the Painting and Sculpture Departments, before finally concentrating on photography, which he studied at the Royal College of Art, London from 1983–85.

Colvin has been one of the most prominent young artists in Scottish photography in the 1980s — a period when that art-form has been particularly lively in this country. His method is to construct, then paint over, three-dimensional environments in his studio. He then photographs the finished piece, discarding it in preference to the two-dimensional cibachromes, which become the final art work.

The assemblages are made out of a variety of objects, including domestic ephemera and furniture, kitsch ornaments, books and magazines, musical instruments and Scottish memorabilia. Through a variety of visual and literary references, we are given clues to the meaning of each work. Across this dense still life, which can be decoded like a Victorian Pre-Raphaelite painting, Colvin paints a second layer of images, creating another set of meanings which interweave across the first. The blue, trumpeting boy in *Deaf Man's Villa* (1989), although a complete painted image in itself, actually spreads across a real record player and a dissembled mannequin. This is a typical juxtaposition where the subject of the male nude and music are doubled in two very different types of representation; one cheap and household, the other steeped in the Classical tradition.

Colvin enjoys resurrecting traditional images in art, favourites being Botticelli, Bosch and Ingres as representatives of both the perfect and bizarre in the history of art. Highly charged images of male and female forms point to a concern with sexuality, where the image and the reality are often unconnected. The sexually restrained Northern tradition, which has become a part of Scottish art and literature, is confronted in Colvin's uninhibited celebrations.

The artist creates a studio fantasy, mocking the narcissistic obsessions of much art of the past, but also paying homage to the complex systems we have developed in Western art, from Renaissance perspective to the fractured world of Cubism, the

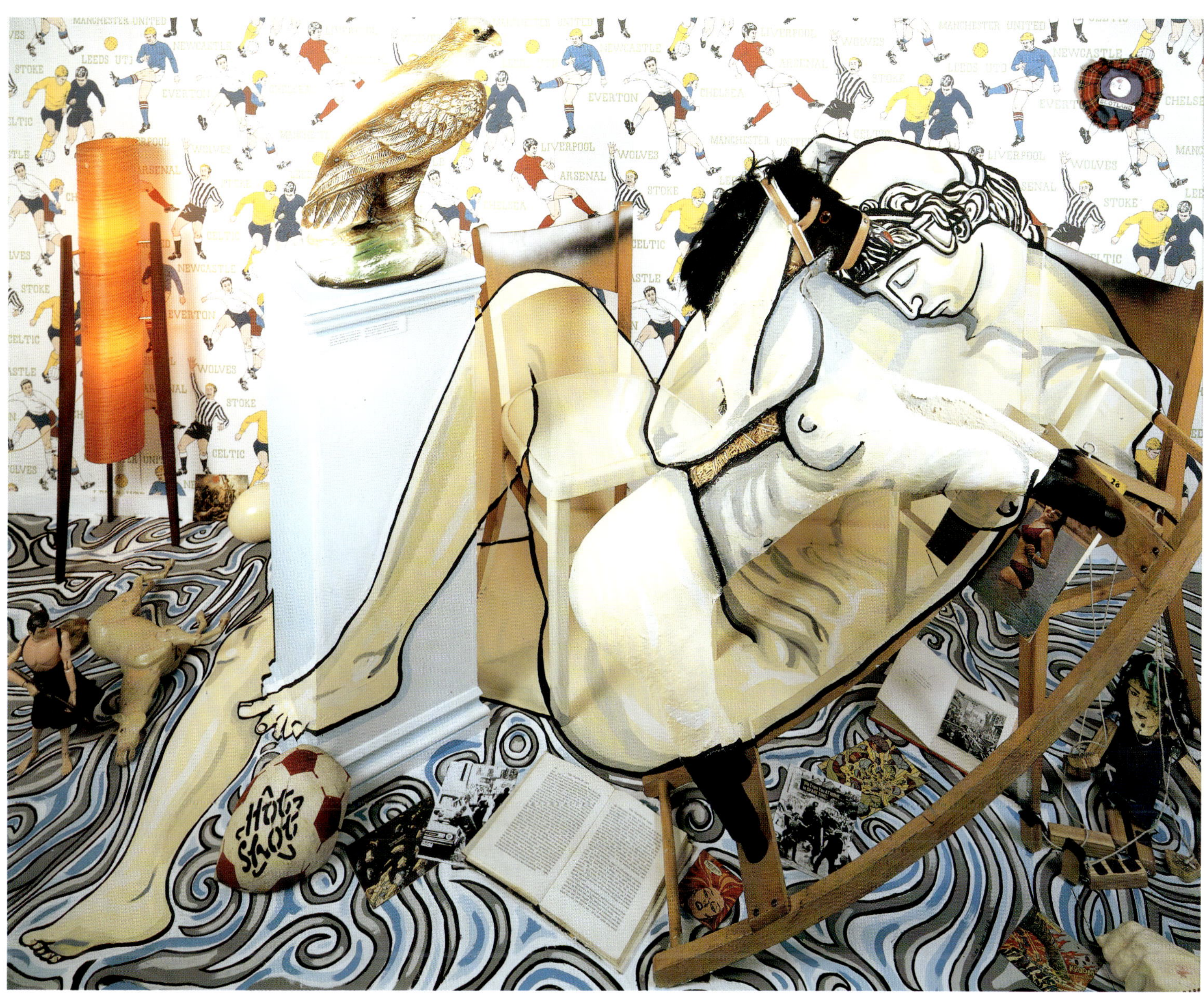

Incubus, 1988,
Photograph, 122 x 155 cm,
Courtesy Salama-Caro Gallery

visual jokes of Surrealism and the supposed 'reality' of photography. Colvin gives us very real proof that the camera can lie just as well as the painted canvas. High art, high gloss finish and high irony are the staple ingredients of Colvin's vision.

The artist has exhibited worldwide and is represented in major international private and public collections including the Metropolitan Museum of Art, New York, and the British Council, London.

Artist's Comment

I want to keep people guessing. A double take at two or three removes. Some artists seem so sure, so dogmatic. I'm not like that.

Brief Encounter (centre panel), 1990, Cibachrome of mixed media construction, 155 x 122 cm

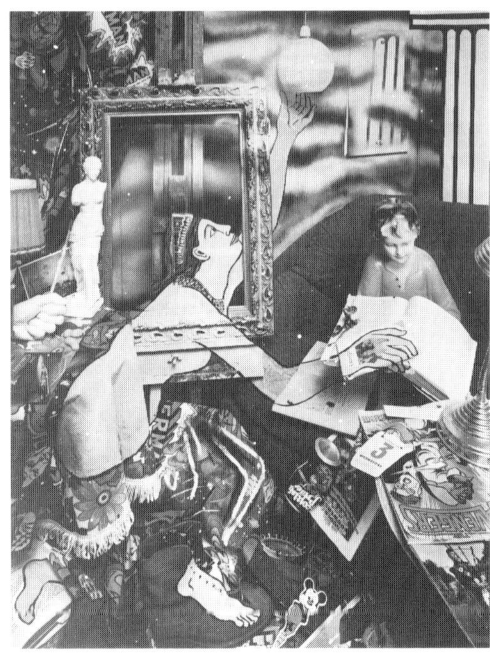
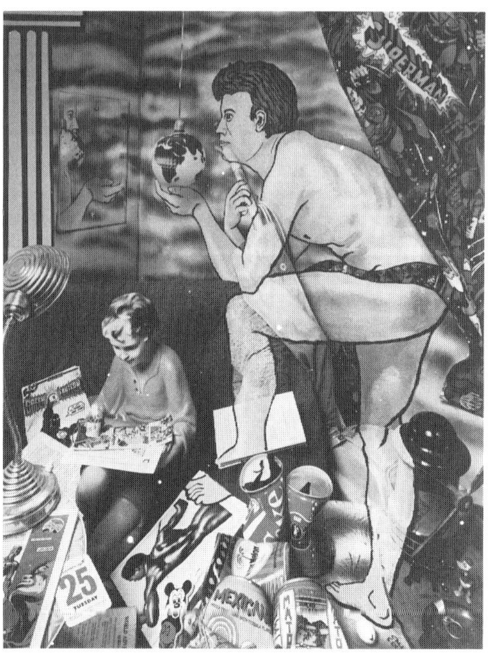

Heroes I and II, 1986, Cibachrome of mixed media construction, 155 x 122 cm (each)

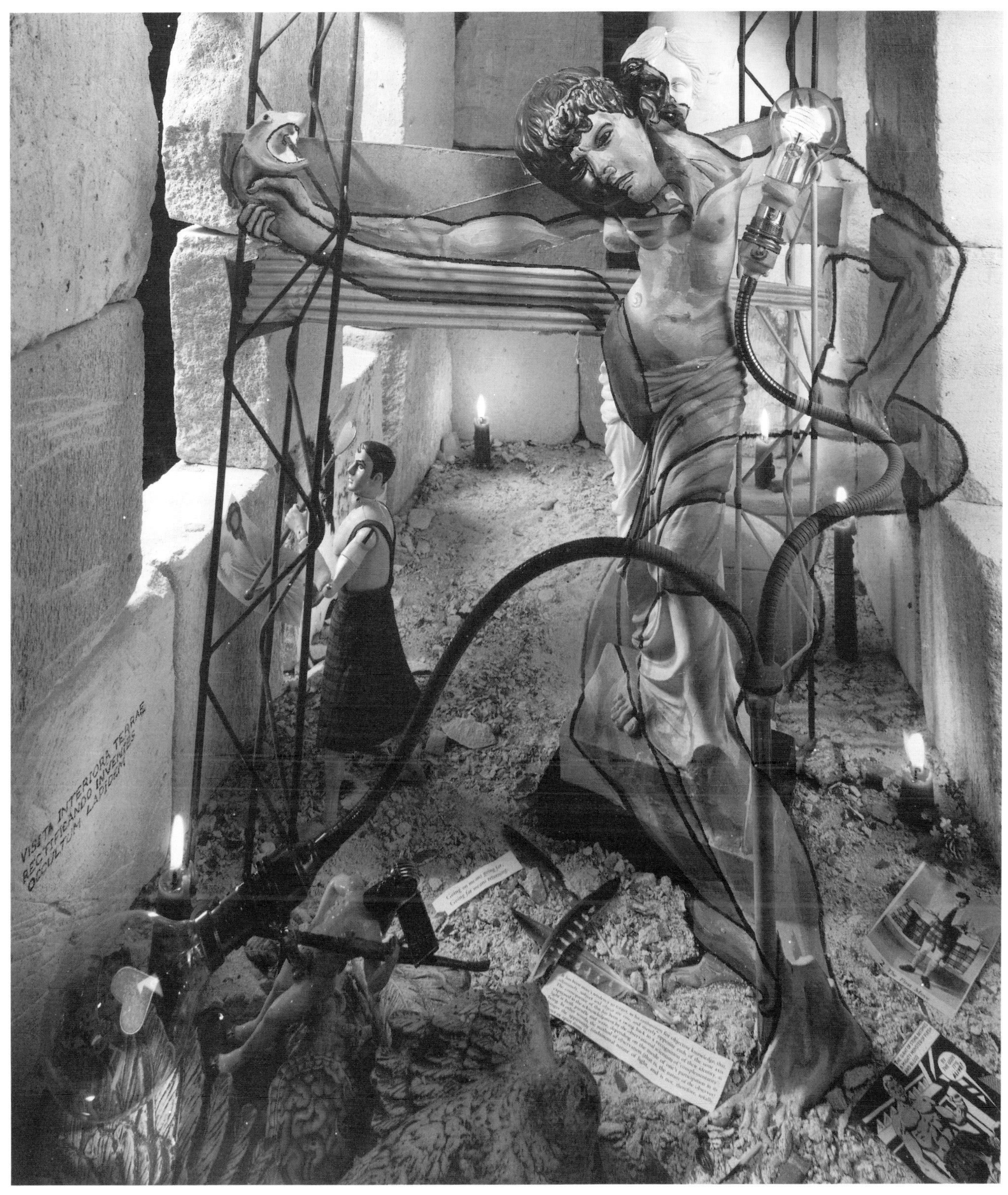

VISITA INTERIORA TERRAE
RECTIFICANDO INVENIES
OCCULTUM LAPIDEM

Stephen Conroy was born in Helensburgh, Scotland in 1964. He enrolled at the Glasgow School of Art in 1982, completing his postgraduate studies there in 1987.

Conroy is one of the most prominent new names to emerge after the ascendancy of contemporary Scottish figurative painting in the mid-1980s. Conroy's example is unusual given the tendency of his peers at Glasgow School of Art to either react against the figuration of Steven Campbell and Ken Currie into conceptual art or to attempt to emulate unsuccessfully the style of these artists. Conroy's favoured subjects have often been of populated interiors, which exploit references to earlier art, most especially that of Degas, whose austerity and formal innovation is clearly inspirational for Conroy. Often his subjects inhabit an airless environment, where the artist manipulates a variety of light sources — consequently, a sense of theatre is deliberately evoked in many 'set-piece' paintings, depicting figures placed in cafes, artists' studios, opera halls and laboratories.

The claustrophobic atmosphere which he encourages also contains obscure narrative clues rarely enough for the viewer to work out exactly the story. Figures seem to pause, uncommunicatively, between action, their faces betraying no emotion. To bring out their poetic quality, Conroy chooses oblique titles, such as *One Idea Too Many* or *Further and Better Particulars* — a technique of secrecy reminiscent of Steven Campbell.

Whilst Degas and the Impressionists have exerted a strong stylistic influence, the inclusion of bizarre imagery and enigmatic references looks much more to Surrealist art, especially that of de Chirico. Even closer to home is the relationship between Conroy and an important Scottish artist of the 20th century, James Cowie, who also worked in a highly self-conscious Surrealist style. Conroy's manner, like Cowie's, clearly represents a reaction to the overly expressionist, colourist tradition in Scottish art.

In a relatively short career to date, Conroy has exhibited in solo exhibitions in London, Glasgow and Manchester, as well as group shows including *The Vigorous*

Living the Life, 1988,
Oil on canvas, 152.8 x 122.3 cm

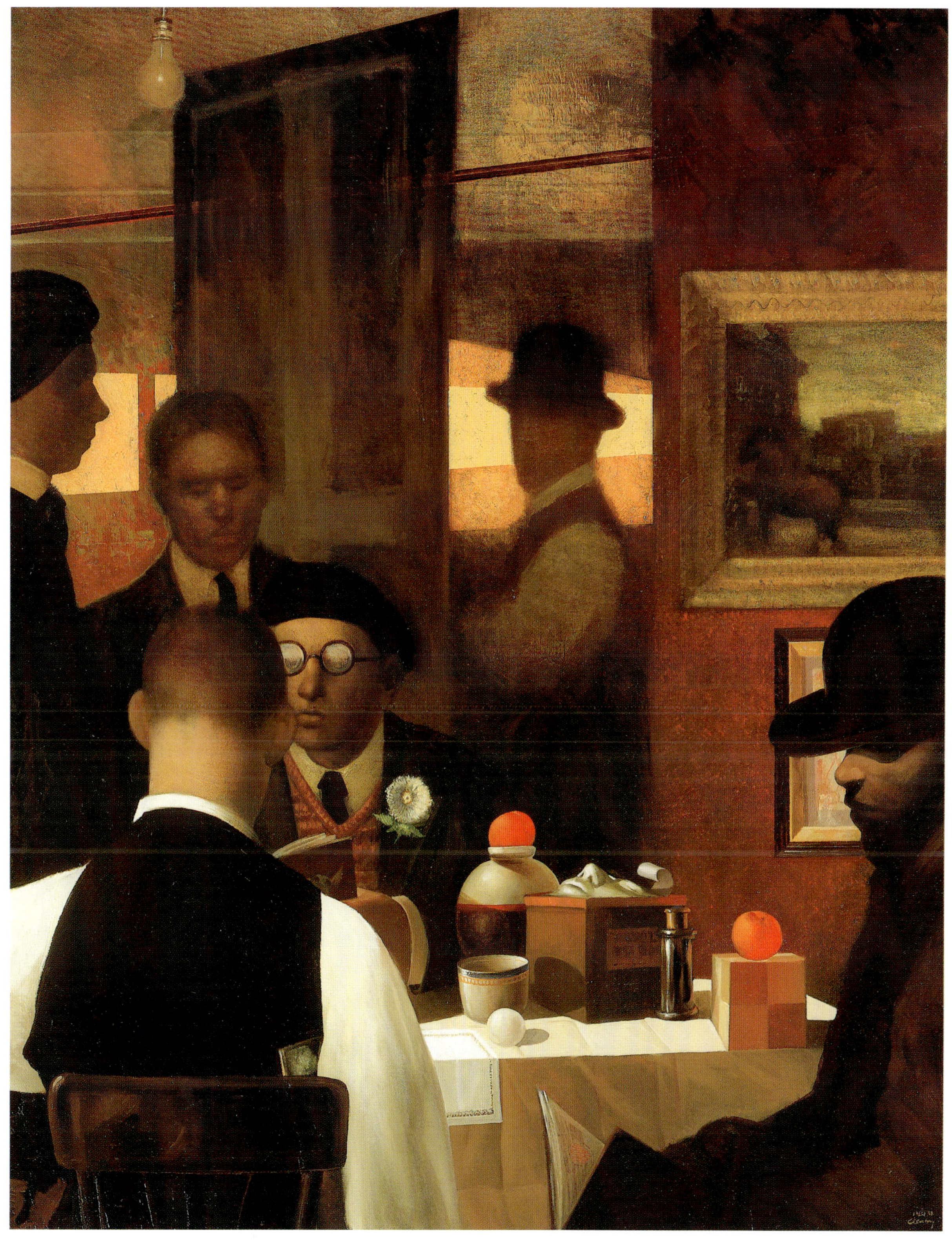

Imagination (1987), Scottish National Gallery of Modern Art. He is represented in public collections throughout the United Kingdom, including the Scottish National Gallery of Modern Art, Glasgow Museums and the Scottish Arts Council.

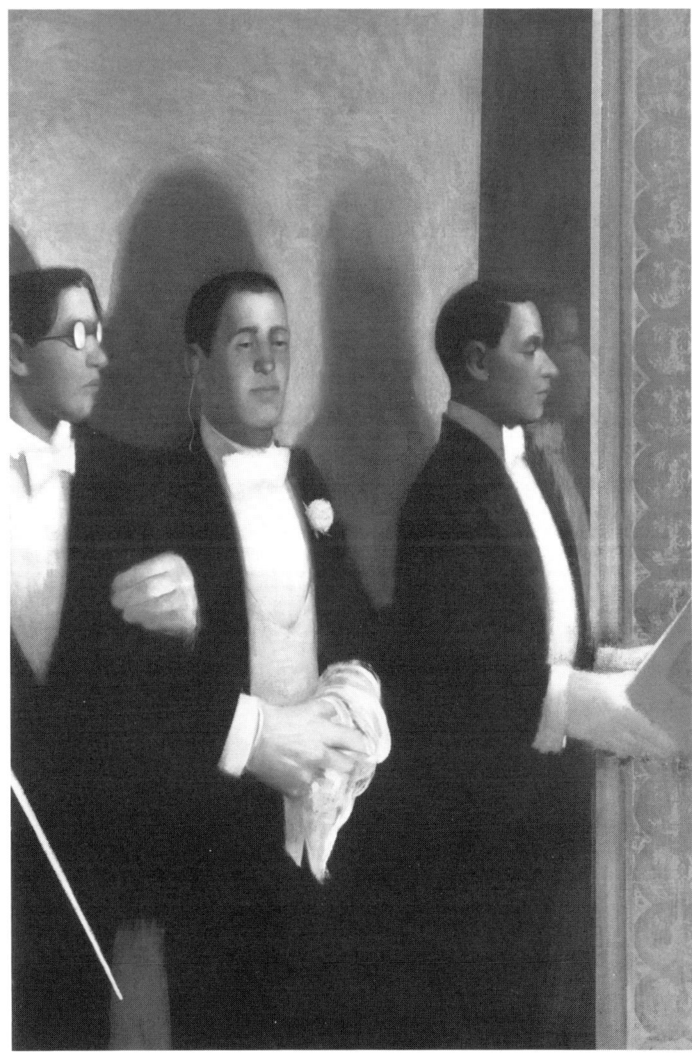

E Muoio Disperato (I Die Despairing), 1989,
Oil on canvas, 152.4 x 101.6 cm,
Photograph: Prudence Cuming
Associates Limited

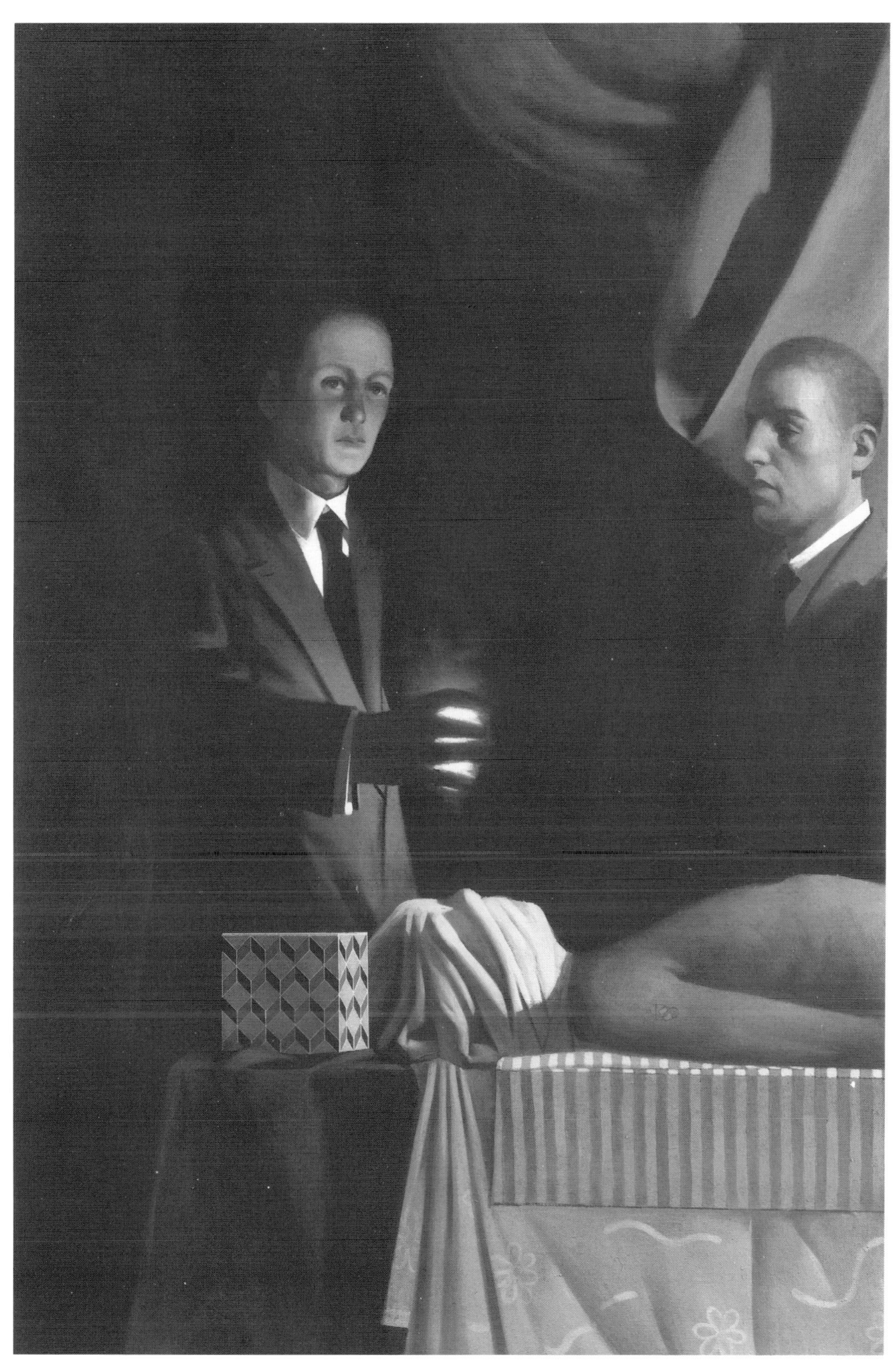

Alchemy (left panel), 1990,
Oil on canvas, 183.5 x 121.9 cm,
Photograph: Prudence Cuming
Associates Limited

FRED CRAYK

Fred Crayk was born in Portsmouth in 1952, but grew up in Inverness. Before becoming a student at Duncan of Jordanstone College of Art, Dundee (1972–76) he studied for a year in Paris. His postgraduate year was at Edinburgh College of Art and until recently he was an art teacher at a secondary school in industrial West Lothian between Glasgow and Edinburgh.

From his training at art college in Dundee, with its academic emphasis on the disciplines of drawing and painting from life, Fred Crayk has developed into a powerful figurative painter. However, being a political and artistic radical, he has sought in his art to subvert the traditional view of Scottish painting. He rejects the typical subjects associated with Scotland, such as the idyllic rural landscape or the quaint fishing village bobbing by the sea, for the harsh realities of late industrial and contemporary urban life. The major intent behind his work is to disturb complacent bourgeois attitudes and stimulate argument as to the purpose of art. Crayk feels that middle class sensibilities are basically romantic and nostalgic and so his art seeks to confront the conventional idealisation of Nature and History with the material reality of political upheaval and social experience. As such, the power in Crayk's work has the tension of opposites — the romantic artist as hero, but social outcast; Nature as creative and moral inspiration, but victim of blind greed; each of us as members of human society, but willing or unwilling competitors in the dog-eat-dog world of modern consumerism.

Crayk eschews his natural ability to paint in a sensually attractive way. He mixes his paints with various materials to build up layers of rough impasto. With pictorial composition, he likewise rejects ideas of balance and harmony in favour of awkwardness and disjunction. His paintings exploit the tension between abstraction and representation, causing a Brechtian sense of alienation, which, nevertheless, offers tremendous stimulus for the eye as well as the mind.

Fred Crayk has exhibited in group and solo exhibitions since the mid-1970s inside and outside Scotland. He has had important shows in Glasgow and in Edinburgh. He has won a number of prizes and scholarships, including the Scottish Art Council's

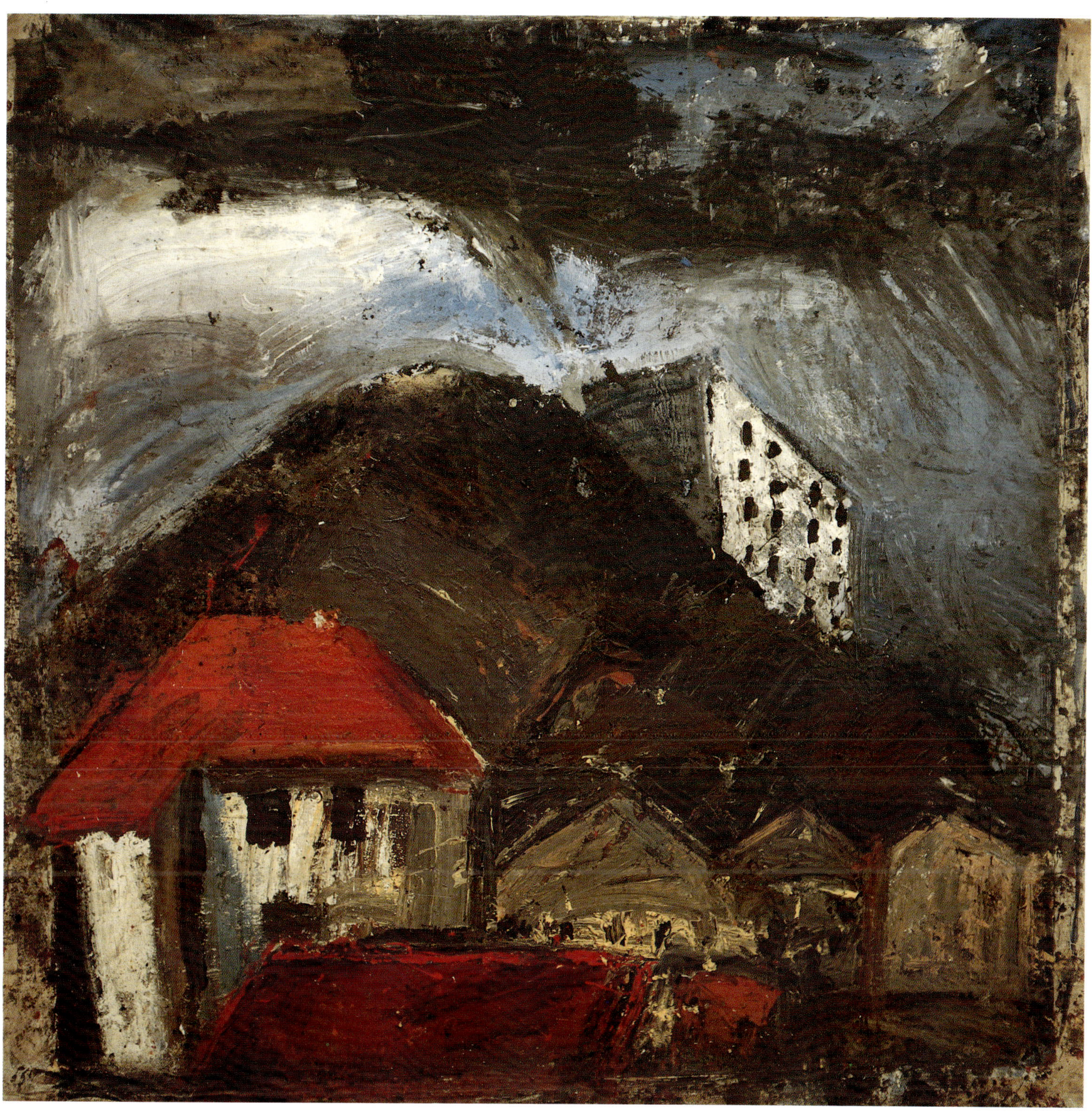

Parnassus: Heap and Dwelling, 1991,
Acrylic on canvas, 216 x 224 cm,
Photograph: Ralph Hughes
Collection of the artist

prestigious Amsterdam Bursary (1980). His work is represented in private and public collections, such as the Scottish Arts Council and the IBM collection.

Artist's Comment

I have developed my painting as a response to different aspects of modern industrial society and the distorting effects it has on what is known as 'Nature'. At the core of my thinking is the tenuous relationship between man and Nature in an increasingly artificial environment.

The Dark Passion of the Soul, 1991,
Acrylic on canvas, 142 x 135 cm,
Photograph: Ralph Hughes
Collection of the artist

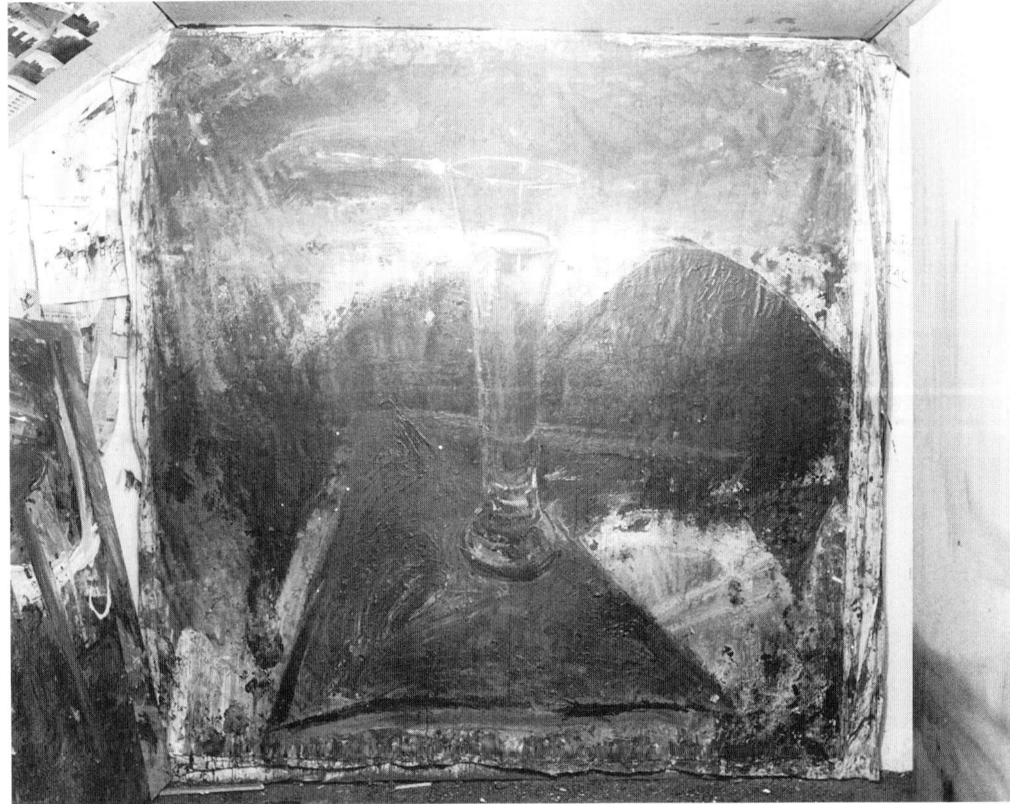

Alba, Oh Alba, 1991,
Acrylic on canvas, 218 x 224 cm,
Photograph: Ralph Hughes
Collection of the artist

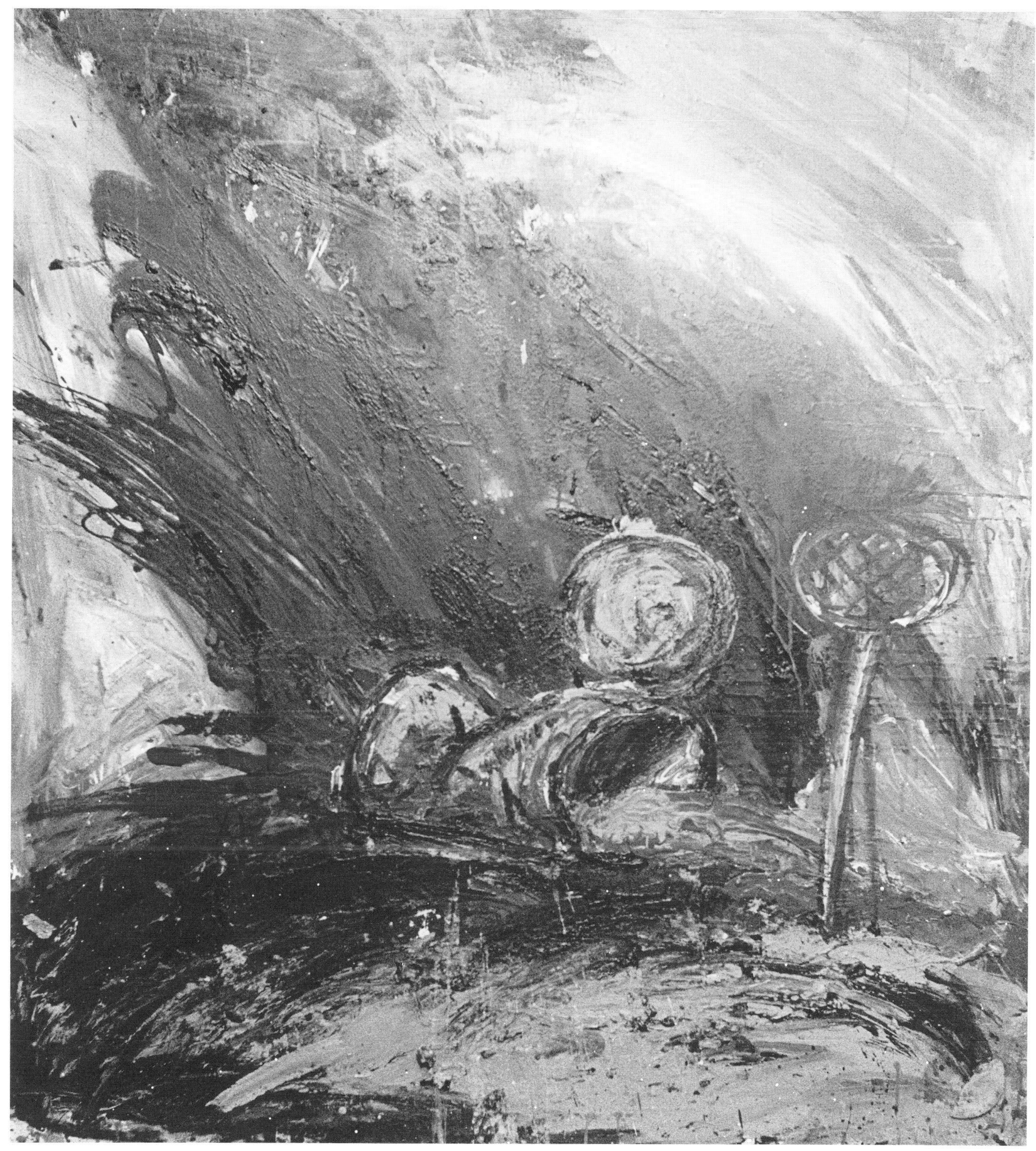

KEN CURRIE

Ken Currie was born in North Shields, Northumberland in 1960 to Scottish parents. After studying social sciences in Scotland, he trained as a painter at the Glasgow School of Art from 1978–83. He still lives and works in Glasgow.

Currie soon rose to prominence for his assertive and graphic images of working-class life. A thoughtful political artist, Currie in his early work sought to highlight the plight of whole communities, especially those who were seen as the victims of industry and urban decay. The Glasgow shipyards, the protest march, the slums and the bars have been his subjects — representing a sustained attempt to get beneath the veneer of life as so many people in the Western World have experienced it. His latest work has shown more attention to the plight of the individual, rather than the group, within that society. Certainly, the kind of subjects Currie deals with have often only occupied the fringes of Scottish art, yet their topic, the lives of the mass working population of Scotland, have held the political centre stage for many years — the prominence and popularity of Currie's work has helped to bring this paradox into focus.

In 1987 Currie completed a panoramic commission for Glasgow's People's Palace Museum, which depicts two centuries of the city's history, starting with the Calton Weaver's Massacre of 1787 and leading up to life on the front line of recent industrial unrest. To emphasise the continuation of struggle and the involvement of art in this struggle he has used as inspiration a number of past artists who likewise did not divide their artistic and social beliefs, such as Fernand Léger, Diego Rivera and Kathe Kollwitz. In his latest work, a slightly more generalised and gothic mood pervades his paintings, still steeped in the history of art, yet more directly emotional and painterly. It marks a widening of the expressive power of his work.

Although Currie's work can often seem pessimistic, it is the complex mixture of past injustices and future possibilities which remains the essential theme.

Currie's first exhibition was at the Glasgow Arts Centre in 1982, called 'Art and Social Commitment' whilst his first international show was at the RAAB Galerie in Berlin in 1988. He has been in numerous group exhibitions, most particularly 'New

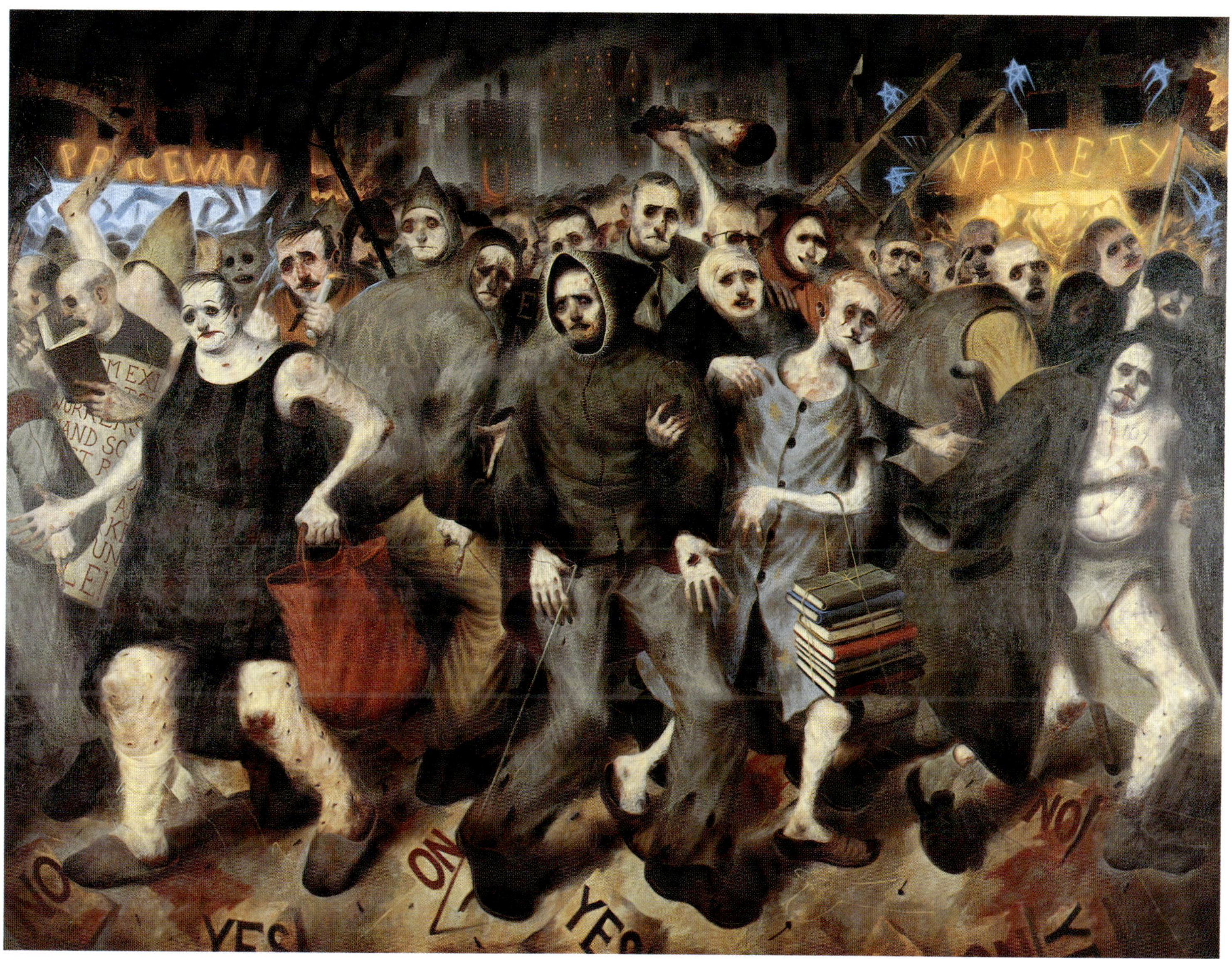

The Street, 1990,
Oil on canvas, 274 x 365 cm,
Courtesy RAAB Gallery, London

Image Glasgow' (1985). 'The Vigorous Imagination' (1987) and 'Scottish Art Since
1900' (1989).

Artist's Comment

*I don't want to just look back nostalgically to the past. It can't be fossilised — it has
to be living.*

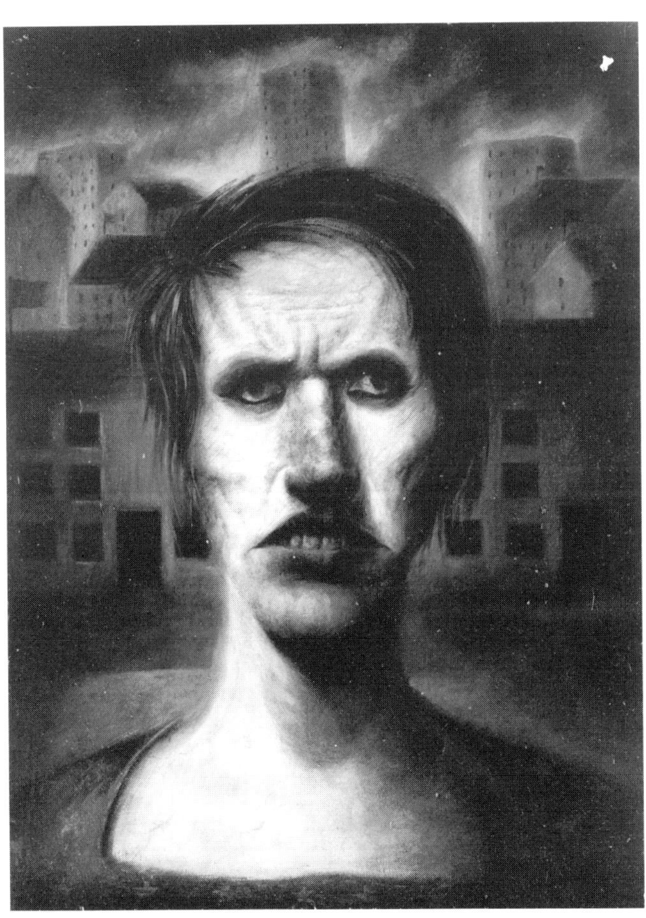

Head of a Realist, 1989,
Oil on wood, 46 x 33 cm,
Photograph: Antonia Reeve,
Courtesy RAAB Gallery, London

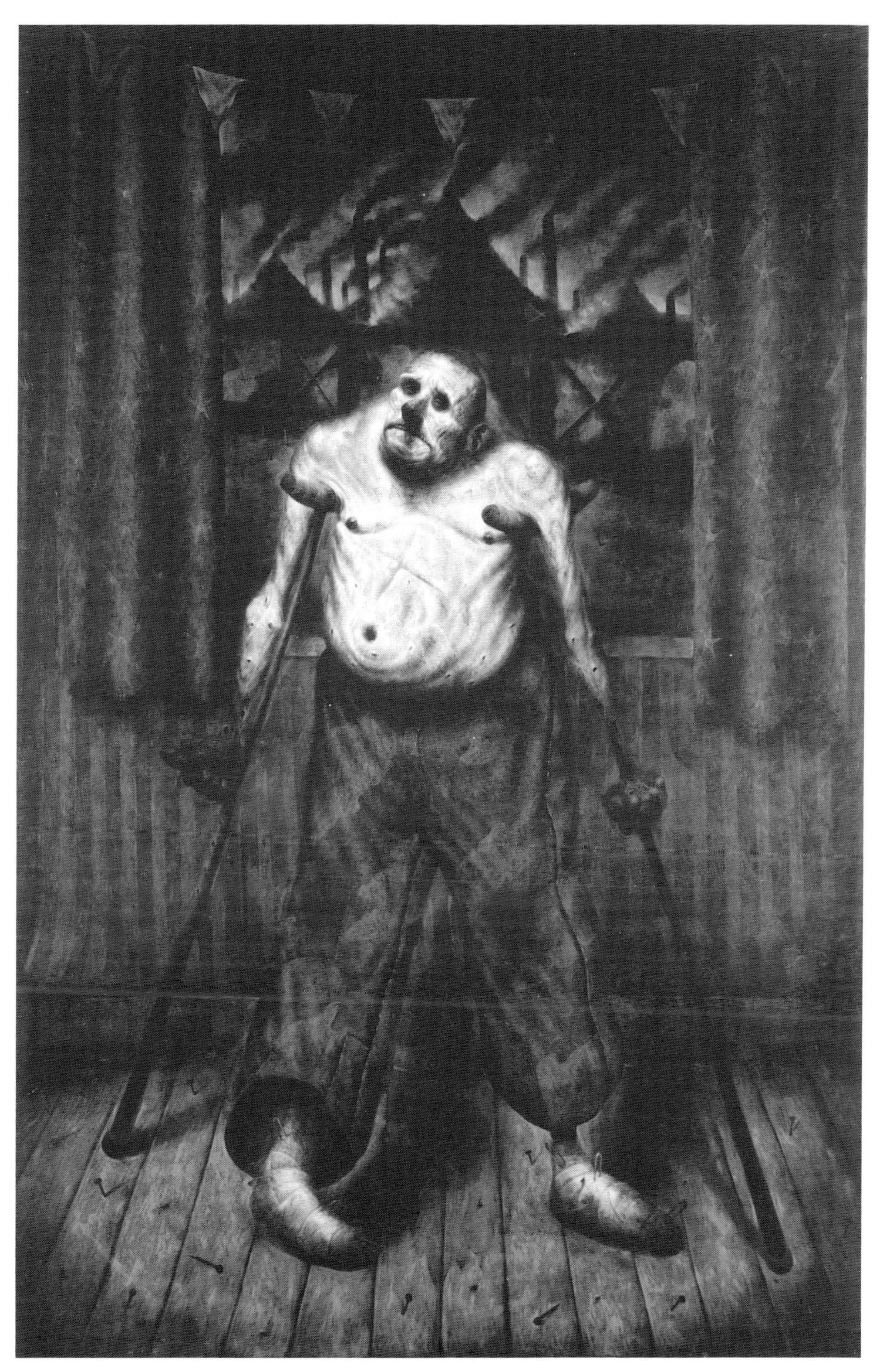

Scottish Stoics (triptych, central panel), 1989,
Oil on canvas, 274 x 183 cm,
Photograph: Antonia Reeve,
Courtesy RAAB Gallery, London

Alan Davie was born in 1920 in Grangemouth, Scotland, the son of a painter and etcher. Between 1937 and 1940 he studied at Edinburgh College of Art and began his life-long interest in music. In 1947 he briefly became a professional jazz musician but left on a scholarship around Europe in 1948 to study a wide variety of art and develop his own painting, which, after a long career, has established Davie as Scotland's most prestigious painter since the Second World War.

Such is the complexity of Davie's interests, working methods, influences and ideas, he is a difficult artist to categorise. He was the first British artist to be introduced first-hand to early American Abstract Expressionism, in Venice in 1948 by a supportive and influential Peggy Guggenheim. Thus, Davie's early roots lie in European Surrealism and its adaptation by American artists into aggressive and personal expressions of intense emotion.

A dark and mystical atmosphere hangs over Davie's work of the late 1940s and 1950s, exploring primitive subjects in rich colours. The exuberance of the 1960s with its rebelliousness and free spirit is reflected in a lighter, more colourful and open direction in Davie's paintings, which were strongly linked to the intuitive improvisations of jazz — a continuing interest for the artist. Themes of liberation and playful sexuality are counterpointed by a more esoteric attitude involving Eastern religion and a belief in the non-rational forces of human nature. Painting for the artist is not about the creation of individual objects but a continuing process which involves other activities — all of which result in an intense and direct experience of Nature — such as underwater swimming, sailing and gliding.

Davie's more recent painting has employed a more studied method, working from ink drawings and gouaches and gathering in a rich diversity of sources, including Indian, South American and African art. All are mixed intuitively with other abiding symbols, characteristically made Davie's own. Now in his 70s, Davie's output is undiminished and continues to command international respect for its integrity and complexity.

Davie has enjoyed a lifelong professional relationship with his gallery Gimpel Fils,

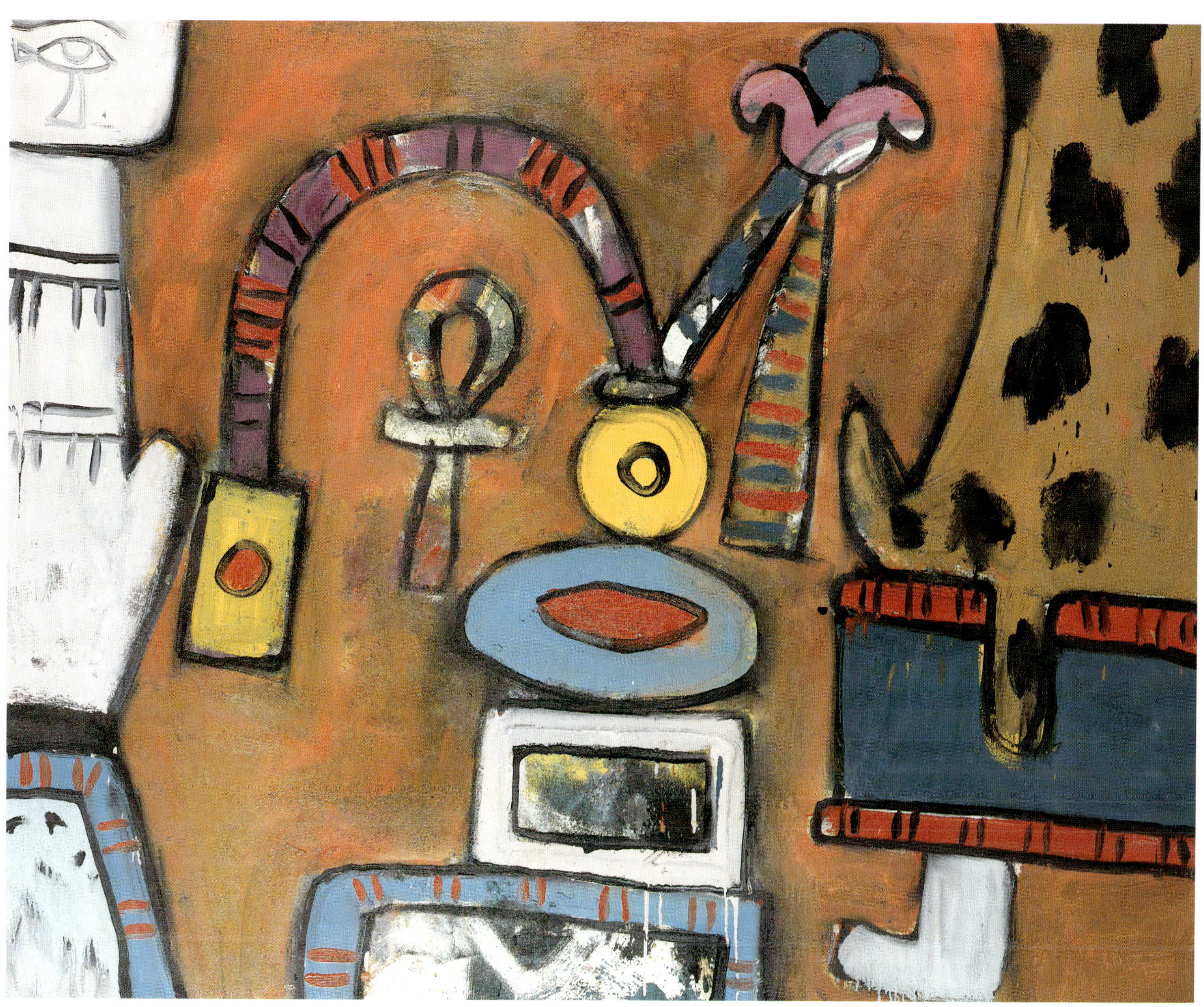

Portrait of a Scribe No 2, 1965,
Oil on canvas, 122 x 152.5 cm,
Private collection, USA

and has had many major exhibitions worldwide including the Whitechapel Art
Gallery, London (1958), the Stedelijk, The Netherlands (1962) and his largest
retrospective, at the McLellan Galleries, Glasgow (1991). He is also represented in
some of the biggest international collections in the world, including the Tate Gallery,
London, and the Museum of Modern Art, New York.

Artist's Comment

*I feel very close to the alchemists of old and, like them, I have in the end reached
some enlightenment in the realisation that my work entails a kind of symbolic self-
involvement in the very processes of life itself.*

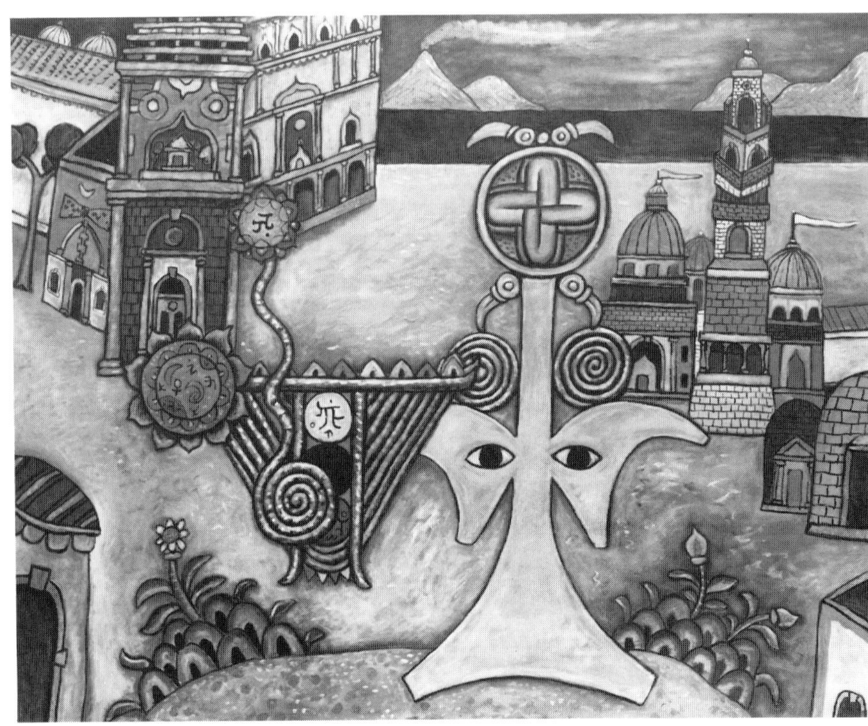

Hallucination with Gold Pectoral, 1984,
Gouache, 59.5 x 73 cm,
Collection of the artist

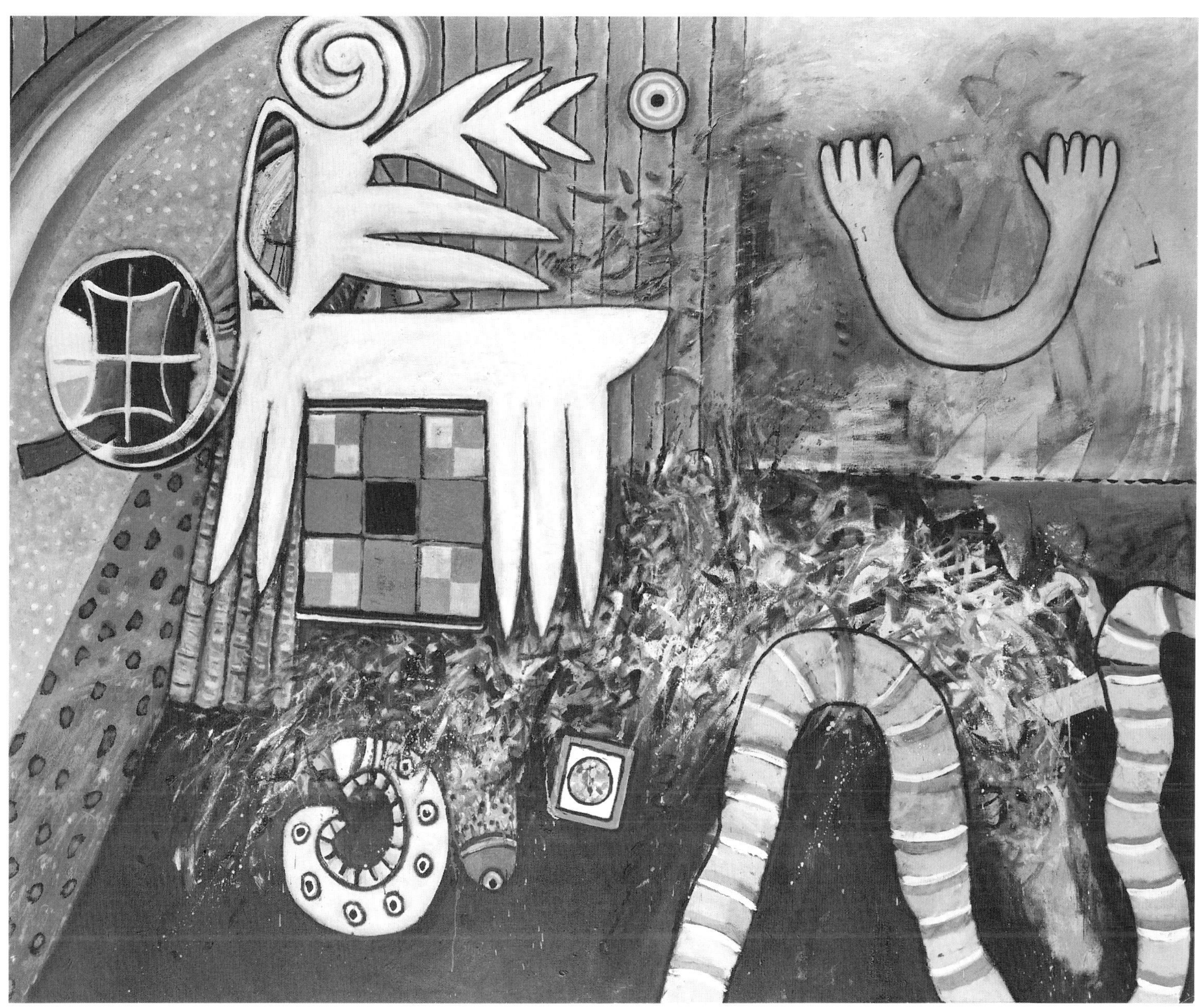

Haussa Spirit No. 2, 1974,
Oil on canvas, 173 x 213 cm,
Collection of Gimpel Fils

David Donaldson was born in Chryston, Lanarkshire in 1916. He studied at Glasgow School of Art (1932–37) and went on to teach there from 1938, becoming the Head of Drawing and Painting (1967) until he retired in 1981. He has had a very distinguished career, including honorary degrees from both Strathclyde and Glasgow Universities. He was appointed as Painter to Her Majesty the Queen in Scotland (1977).

It is frequently claimed, sometimes to the point of ad nauseam, that the true mark of Scottish painting is its 'painterliness'. What this is usually taken to mean is the artist's hedonistic celebration of the sensual qualities of paint, through rich colour, succulent impasto and bold intuitive brushstrokes, which almost model in relief the objects and shapes in the picture. Many would feel that David Donaldson is a master of that school of Scottish painting. He is, but he's more.

The *belle peinture* style, as practised by the majority of 20th century Scottish painters, has proved to be extremely limited. This is demonstrated by the vacuous repetitiveness both in subject and treatment, of the work of the minor Scottish Colourists and their followers. By contrast, Donaldson, over a long and prolific career, has continuously managed to triumph over this.

He has achieved this for two or three important reasons. Firstly, as a college teacher for most of his working life, he has a deep knowledge and respect for the academic tradition of his profession. As such he does not choose his subjects simply for their picturesque qualities, but also for the potential challenge to solve the pictorial problems that the subject will present in relationship to the history of that particular genre. Over the years he has worked in all the academic genres from biblical figure composition to humble still life. Furthermore, because he has such a wide knowledge of painting and is gifted with such virtuosity of technique, he has the ability to adopt his stylistic approach by incorporating and referring to all manner of different types of painting. Donaldson may not claim to be a cerebral artist, but he is a very knowledgeable one. Secondly, he is also an extremely perceptive and humorous artist and this too places him firmly within the history of Scottish painting.

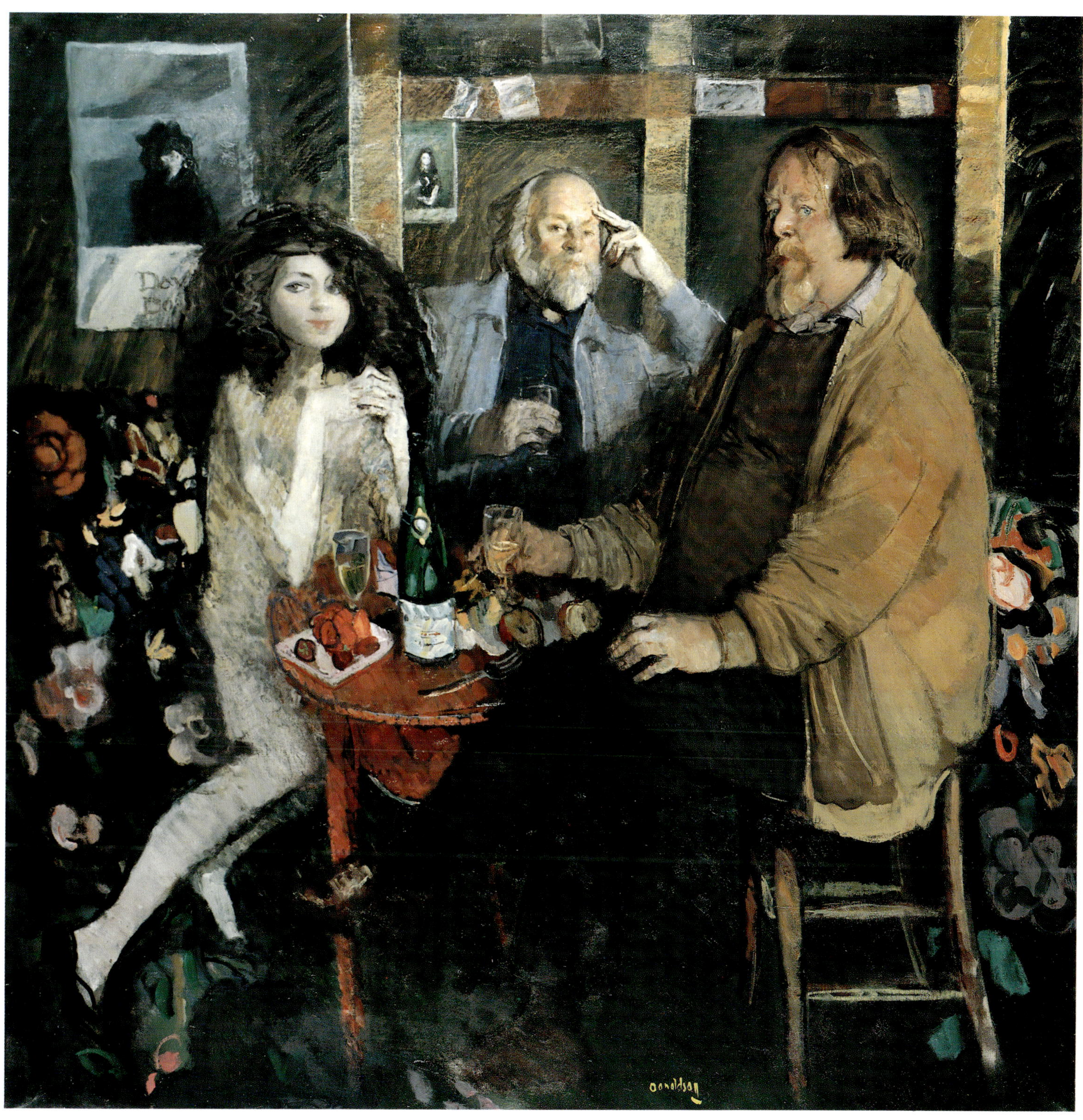

Annette and the Elders, 1980–81,
Oil on canvas, 152.4 x 152.4 cm,
Private collection

For if his chosen method of painting, with its insistence on direct observation and
working straight onto the canvas without preparatory drawings, makes him an heir
to the methods of Raeburn, his sharp-eyed observation of the comic dimension of
human character and its failings links him with David Wilkie. Finally a third reason
why his paintings are more than mere *belle peinture* is that, for all their sensual
delights, there is a strong decadent undercurrent to them. Donaldson, like Burns,
demonstrates in his art a keen Calvinistic awareness of the transience of physical
beauty and pleasure — but that does not stop him enjoying and sharing it while
he can.

It was not until he retired in 1981 that Donaldson began to exhibit extensively,
both in Great Britain and abroad. He was honoured with a major retrospective by
Glasgow Art Gallery in 1982. He has works in many private and public collections,
including those of Her Majesty the Queen and the Scottish Arts Council.

Artist's Comment

*If you keep the original inspiration — that which fascinates you at the beginning —
for a year, or a month or half an hour or for however long it takes — you might
arrive at a conclusion.*

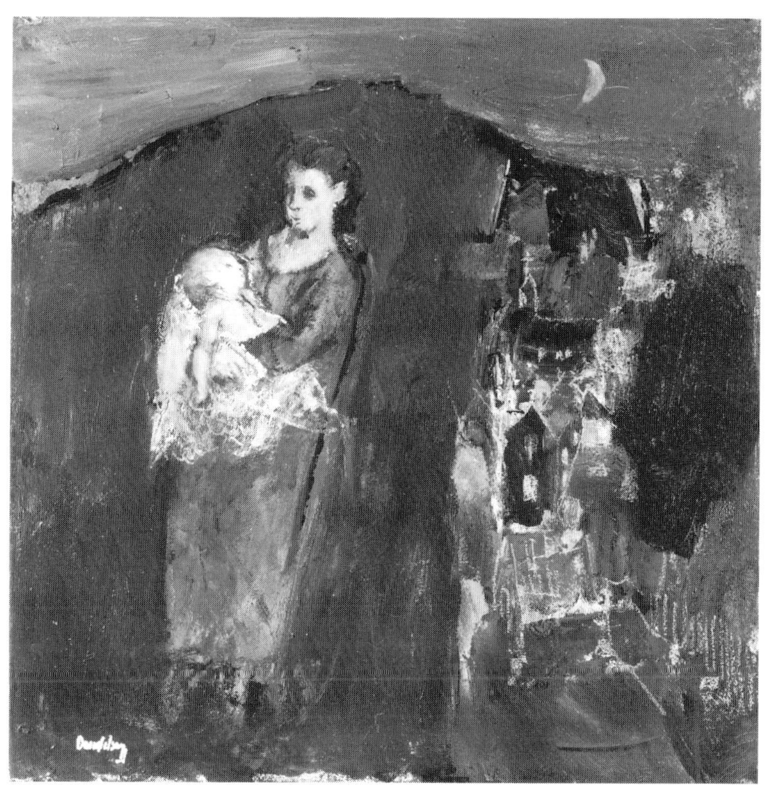

Exodus II, c. 1971,
Oil on canvas, 45.7 x 45.7 cm,
Private collection

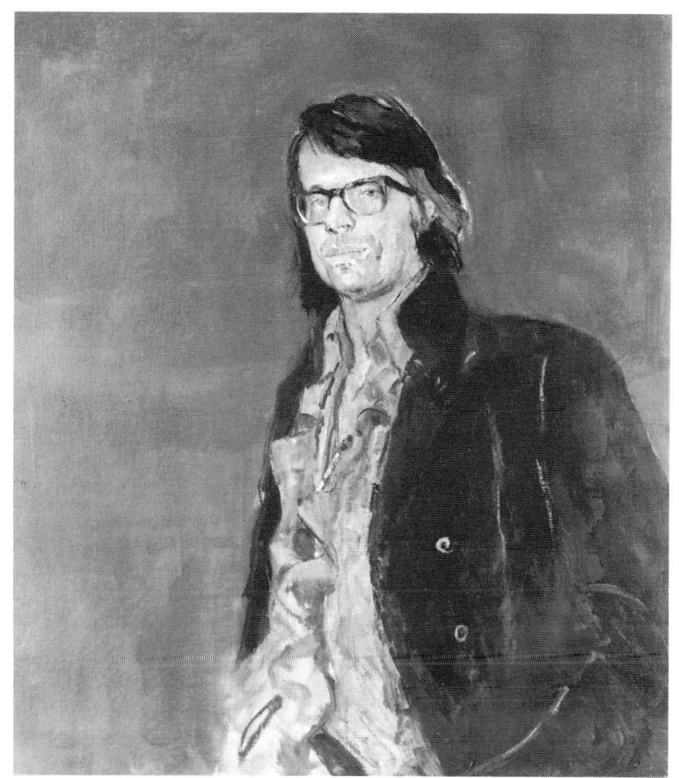

Bobbie McIntyre of Sorn, 1974–75,
Oil on canvas, 101.6 x 91.4 cm,
Private collection

Kate Downie was born in North Carolina and in 1958 trained in Drawing, Painting and Postgraduate Studies at Gray's School of Art, Aberdeen. She has travelled extensively abroad and taught in Aberdeen and Newcastle. In 1983–84 she won the Scottish Arts Council Residency to Amsterdam. Downie currently lives and works in Edinburgh.

Downie is very much an artist of the city. Over the last 200 years or so, the urban landscape and mass population has pervaded the natural landscape and artists have struggled to visualise the impact of our towns and cities — the problem being how to form a language sensitive to the vibrancy and severity of our modern world. The French poet Baudelaire has been most associated with the appeal to artists to tackle city subjects head on: for him, modern life was 'rich in poetic and marvellous subjects. The marvellous envelops and soaks as like an atmosphere, but we don't see it'. Downie, too, invites us to see and appreciate the ferocious activity of the city through her highly expressive paintings — there is a clear connection between the teeming energy of Baudelaire's Paris (where Downie worked for a year from 1988–89) and the speed of her brush as she seeks to capture fleeting incidents before they vanish. In the panoramic sweep, the zooming perspective and the detail the artist picks out, she echoes the dynamism of film and photography.

In 1990 she exhibited a series of works, *Urban Circus*, which focused on famous Parisian landmarks and numerous road intersections where traffic and people converge. She describes herself as having 'a love/hate relationship with the city. Some of the Paris myths are very powerful and I wanted to break some of them down. There is a huge trade in romanticism yet they have a massive traffic problem and incredible pollution'. Few Scottish artists can be said to be treating the urban world with as much insight and vigour.

Downie has held many artist-in-residence posts, most particularly ones allied to industrial companies, and has had one-person exhibitions in Britain and Europe. Her work is in many private and public collections in the United Kingdom and worldwide.

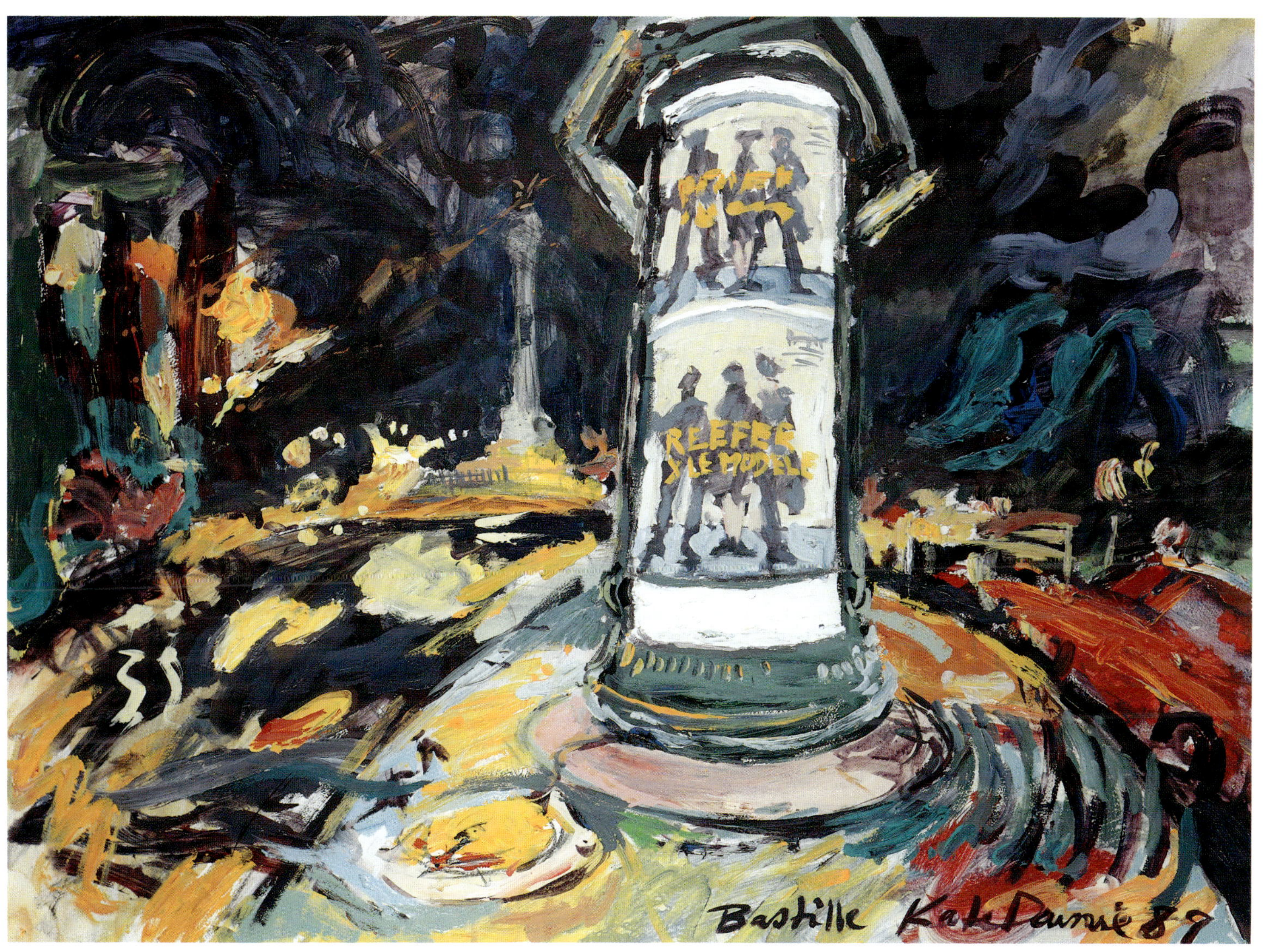

Bastille Night Painting I, 1989,
Acrylic on paper, 75 x 105 cm,
Photograph: Antonia Reeves
Collection of the artist

Artist's Comment

The extraordinary and the magnificent are, for me, bound up with what is mundane and sometimes awful. Most of the places in a city where I base my work are very particular to me, yet almost 'non-places' to the people who pass through them. The streets are neither private nor communal, though they are a large part of people's lives. I am a fixed point in the flux; I focus and directly observe where others glance.

The experience of 'being there' confronts the grand concepts of city planners and transport systems. In both a positive and a negative sense I carry these concepts and use them to set up an edgy counterbalance between function and emotion.

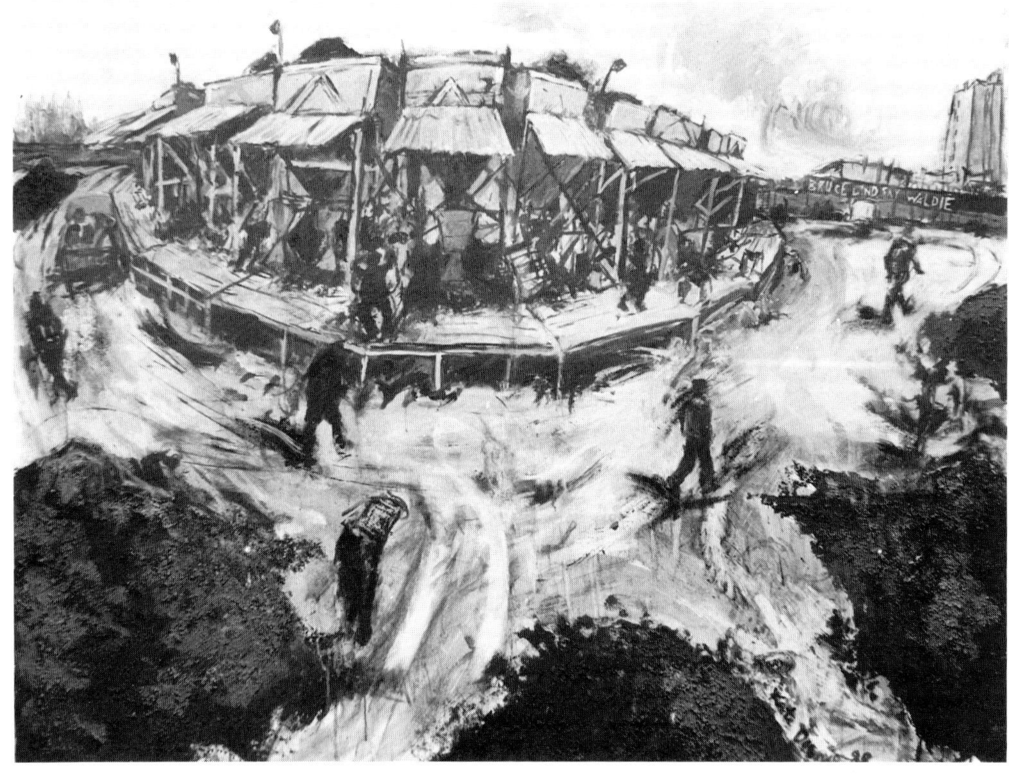

The Coal Men, 1988,
Acrylic and coal on canvas, 153 x 200 cm,
Photograph: Kate Downie

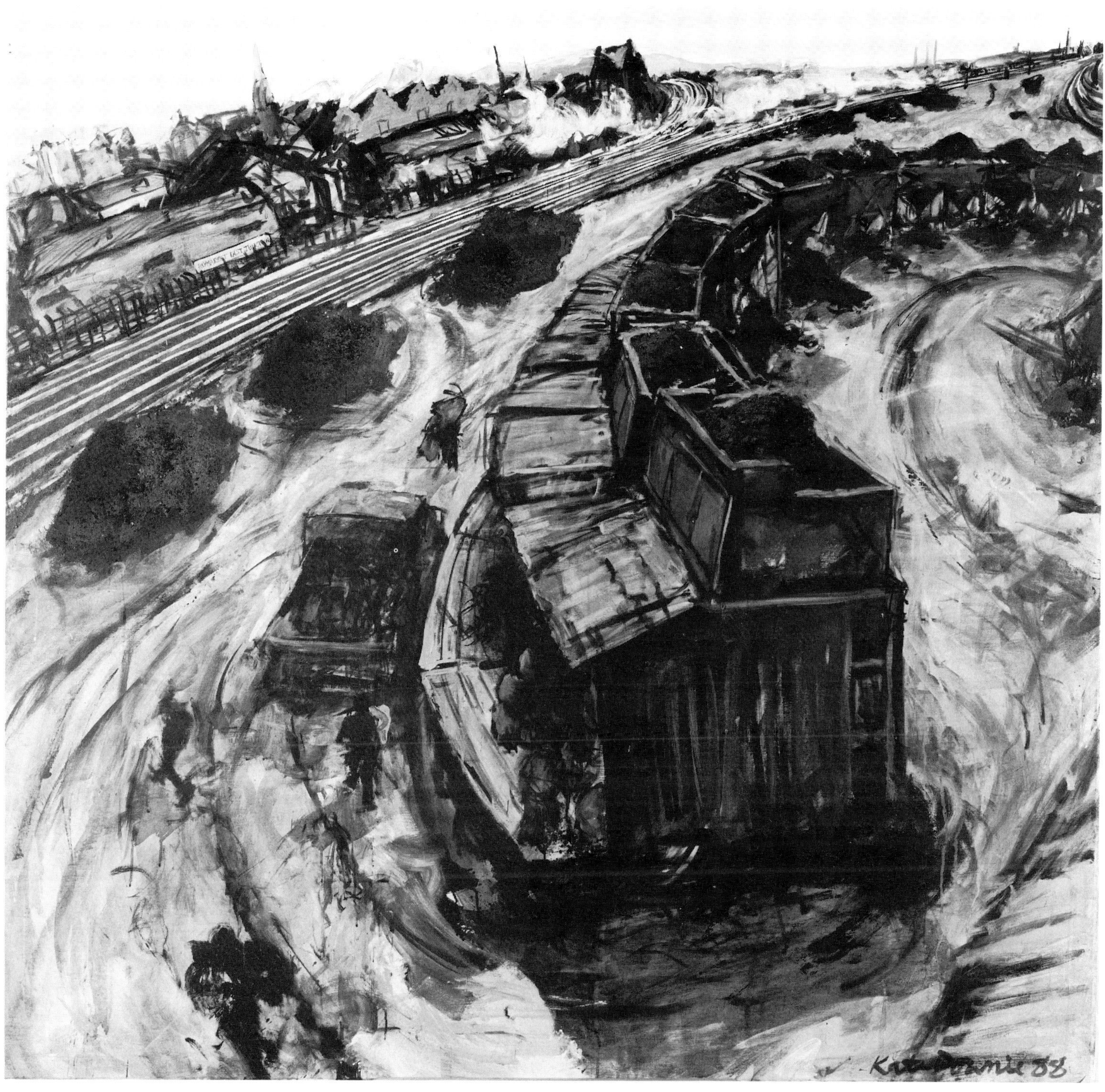

The Coal Yard, 1988,
Acrylic and coal dust on canvas, 170 x 177.5 cm,
Photograph: Antonia Reeve

David Evans was born in Abercarn, Gwent, Wales in 1942. He studied at Newport College of Art (1959–62) and then at the Royal College of Art, London (1962–65). Since then he has taught at Edinburgh College of Art. He was awarded the Granada Arts Fellowship at the University of York (1968–69) and took a year out to research for his paintings by travelling throughout the USA (1975–76). He lives and works in Edinburgh.

It is generally agreed that modern art begins around the middle of the 19th century. If that is the case then the notion that its development is one of clear progression is hard to accept; there seems to have been a break along the line between the early and later stages. For example, all the great pioneers of modern art, from the Impressionists to the Cubists, agreed with Courbet that painting was a 'concrete' art dealing exclusively with the relationship between human perception and the material world. However, a radical shift in emphasis took place with the development of painting towards abstraction. Modern art lost its materialistic aims and began to take on an overtly mystical character. Furthermore, so successful were advocates of abstraction with their appeals to the pursuit of higher spiritual values of universal significance that most figurative art, unless it was academic classicism, was deemed to be of a very limited and mundane nature.

When David Evans began his career in the 1960s the last great triumph of abstraction, post-war American Expressionism, was sweeping all before it in England, but made little impact with the conservative Scottish art scene. Maybe the artistic climate in Edinburgh was more conducive to a natural figurative painter of Evan's detached analytical temperament and this allowed him to develop his painting in the methodical and intensely committed fashion which is a distinctive quality of his work. He is a highly skilled delineator of what he observes, whether is he is working directly in front of the subject (in the form of a tableau set up in the studio for example) or from a photograph. Much of the immediate attraction of his paintings must lie in their carefully considered compositions and painstaking method of execution. Yet the more lasting appeal of his best work may operate at a deeper level, in that it seems

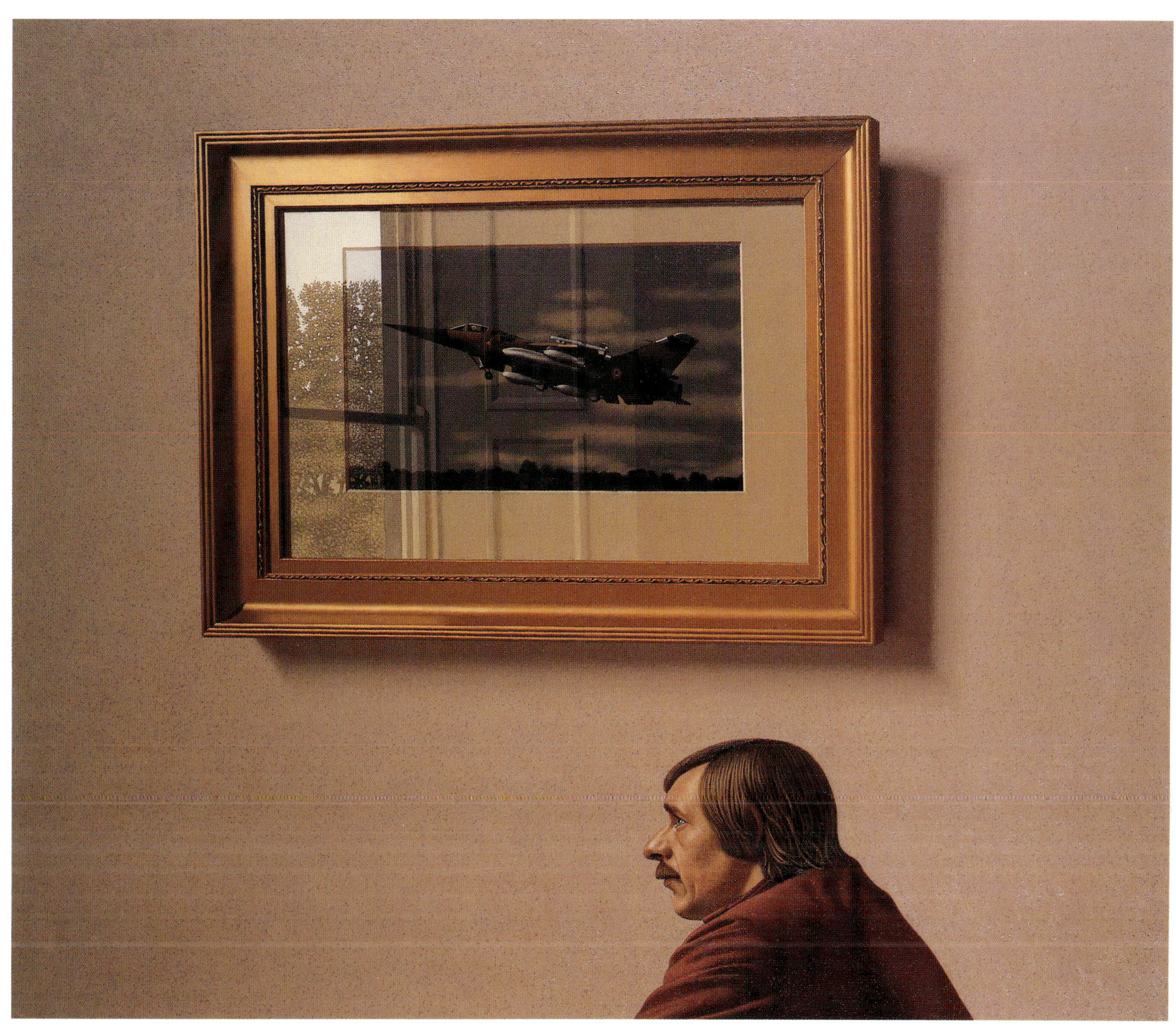

Summer Mirage, 1985,
Oil on canvas, 107 x 132 cm,
Collection of the Royal Scottish Academy

to reconsider the special relationship between the material world of light and substance and the act of painting, which has been so crucial to the art of the past. Taking ordinary and everyday subjects such as motorways, neon signs and figures in empty hotel rooms, he arranges and presents these scenes in such a particular light that they take on an intriguing presence which suggests all kinds of deeper psychological realities. Evans' paintings can sometimes be slightly contrived, however. At their best, like Vermeer's, they infuse the 'ordinary and everyday' with such intense mystery that they refute the notion that figurative art is incapable of presenting universal insights on the human condition.

David Evans has shown mostly in Edinburgh and London and had a major retrospective exhibition at the Fruitmarket Gallery, Edinburgh in 1982. His work is represented in a number of private and public collections throughout Britain, including the University of York and the Scottish Arts Council.

Artist's Comment

My interest in something might be triggered off by an object seen in a particular context or the way an object looks in a particular light, light playing a dominant role in my pictures, finding it a convenient way to present an object, or a particular mood and perhaps the whole reason for doing the picture.

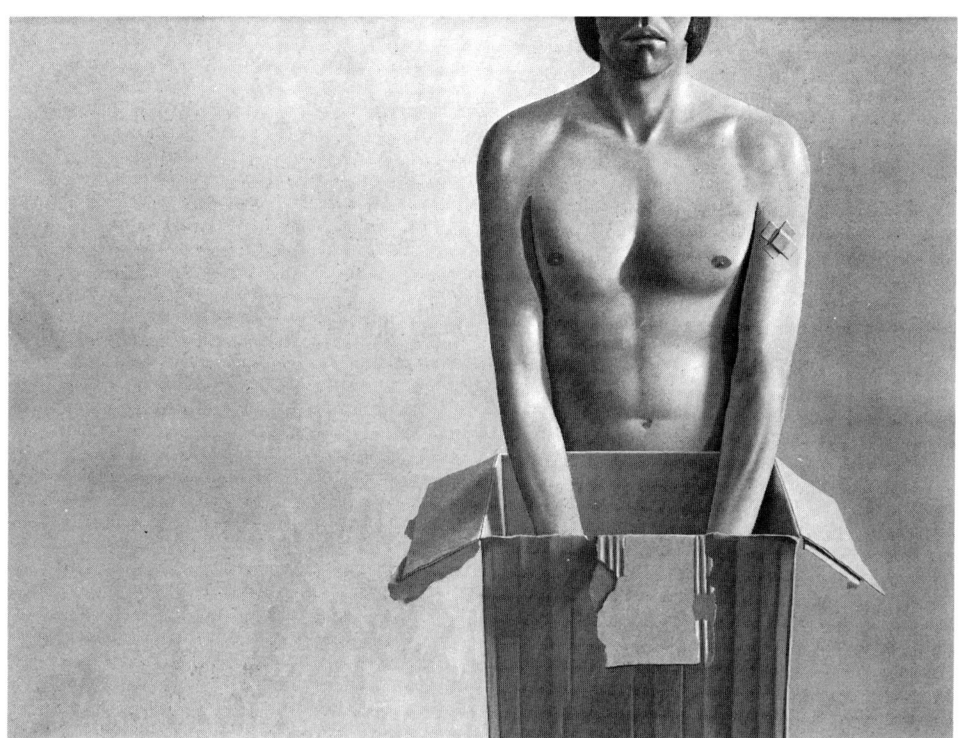

The Birdcatcher, c. 1980,
Oil on canvas, 102 x 127 cm,
Photograph: A.G. Ingram Ltd

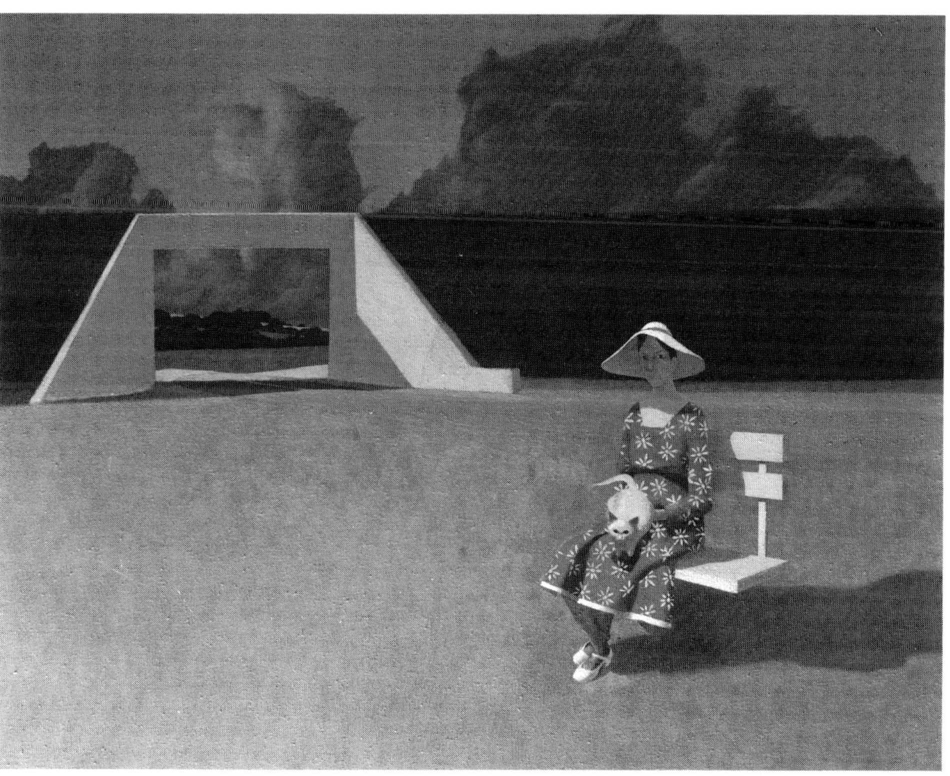

Portrait of an Afternoon, 1972,
Oil on canvas, 101.6 x 127 cm,
Private collection

ALEXANDER FRASER

Alexander Fraser was born in Aberdeen in 1940. He studied at Gray's School of Art, Aberdeen (1958–62) and is now a senior lecturer in charge of Painting there. He has won many awards for his painting and is an active figure on the Scottish art scene, through his work on the Scottish Arts Council and the Royal Scottish Academy committees.

The most exciting thing about the development of Alexander Fraser's paintings over the last ten years or so, is the many issues they raise about the nature of painting itself. In the 1970s his work moved out of the figurative mode into abstraction but has returned to being strongly representational again. This is in no way a reflection of the artist's attempt to follow fashion, but rather a demonstration of the seriousness of the commitment he has towards the art of painting. Being of a generation who had been led to believe that painting was the vanguard of modern art and abstraction its greatest triumph, the essential nature and function of painting in the postmodern era of the 1980s was much more problematic for him than for the young vigorous neo-expressionists just out of art school. No one was more aware of the bilingual nature of painting: how it could speak for itself and of its own reality, or be made a translator of some other outside reality which the artist wishes to express through the language of pictorial imagery.

In the early 1980s Fraser seemed committed to the modernist position, celebrating the autonomy of painting. Then he produced very large paintings of all-over swirling pigment which explored the possibility of pure painting. In these monumental works saturated colour and gestural marks created their own sense of order and meaning and communicated through their own evocative language of sensory stimulation and poetical allusion. However, fairly soon after he had mastered this heroic all-over style of painting, he became dissatisfied with these abstract compositions of 'interlocking loops of space'. He wanted to 'sober up' his paintings and evolve a more systematic method, where he could introduce a straight line and a flat area, which could be reworked if necessary. Using Velazquez's *Las Meninas* as a starting point, he gradually began to work into the picture surface of his paintings

The Gray Mare, 1990,
Acrylic on canvas, 137 x 102 cm,
Collection of the artist

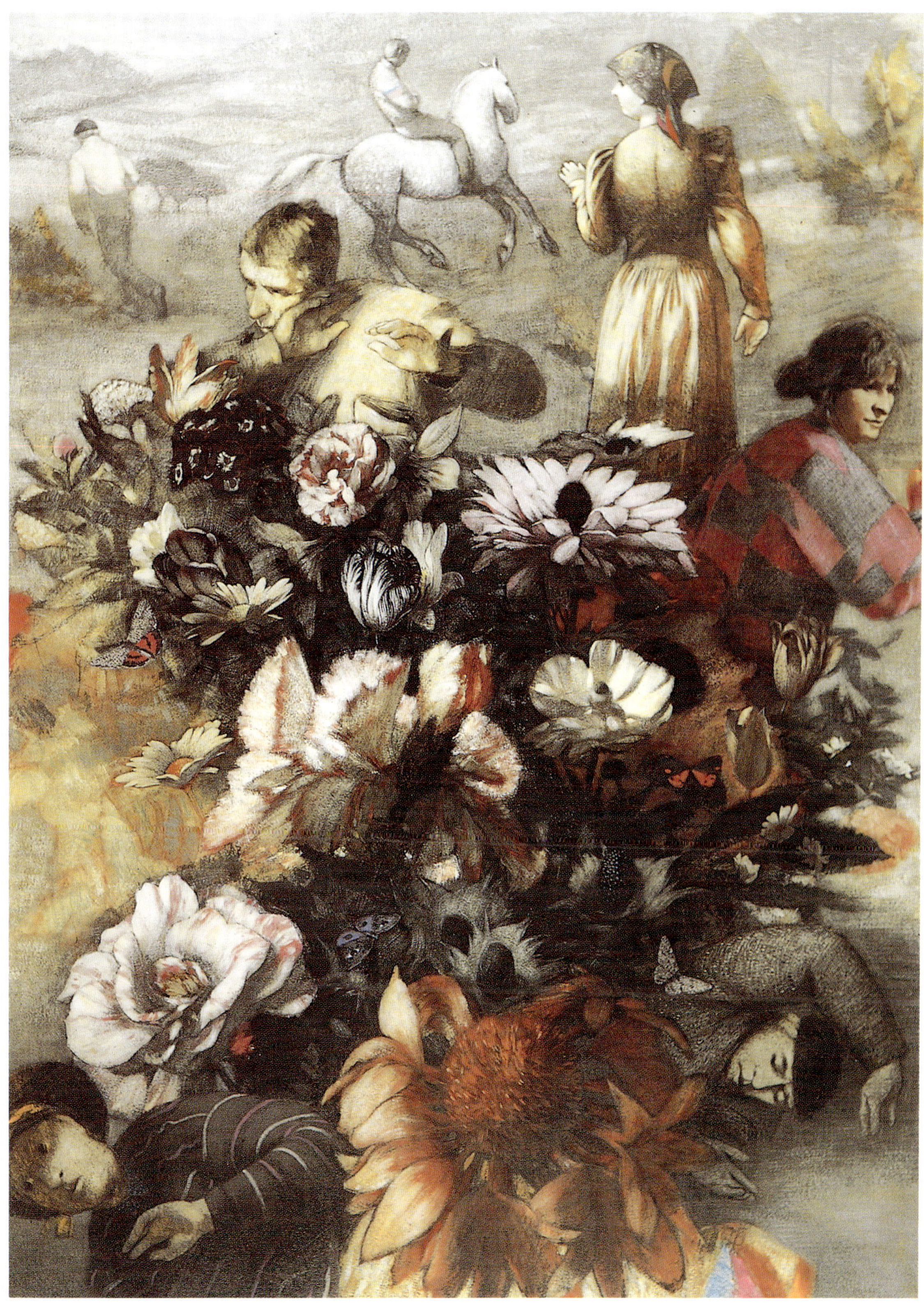

and thus introduced pictorial space and volumetric form back into his painting.
Since then, because he is such a consummate draughtsman, it is not surprising that
figures have reappeared in his pictures. Coinciding with this return to figurative
representation has been a radical shift in technique towards a highly analytical
method of painting, which presents finely detailed images of great clarity, but not
at the expense of atmosphere and mystery.

Alexander Fraser has exhibited widely and his work is represented in many private
and major public collections in Scotland, as well as the Contemporary Arts Society,
London.

Artist's Comment

*I think that I have been too interested in form and easily distracted by ART. Recently,
I acknowledged how much I had been suppressing and I gave up ART — I now paint
pictures. I paint my family and my environment transformed by myth.*

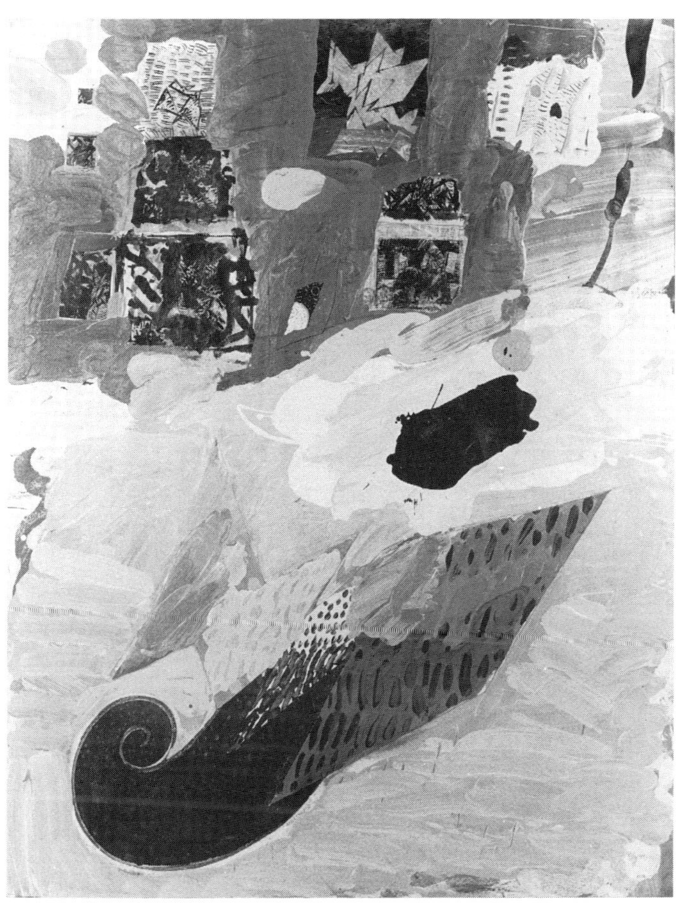

Study for 'Helen visiting Ranakpur', 1987,
Acrylic on paper, 137 x 102 cm,
Private collection

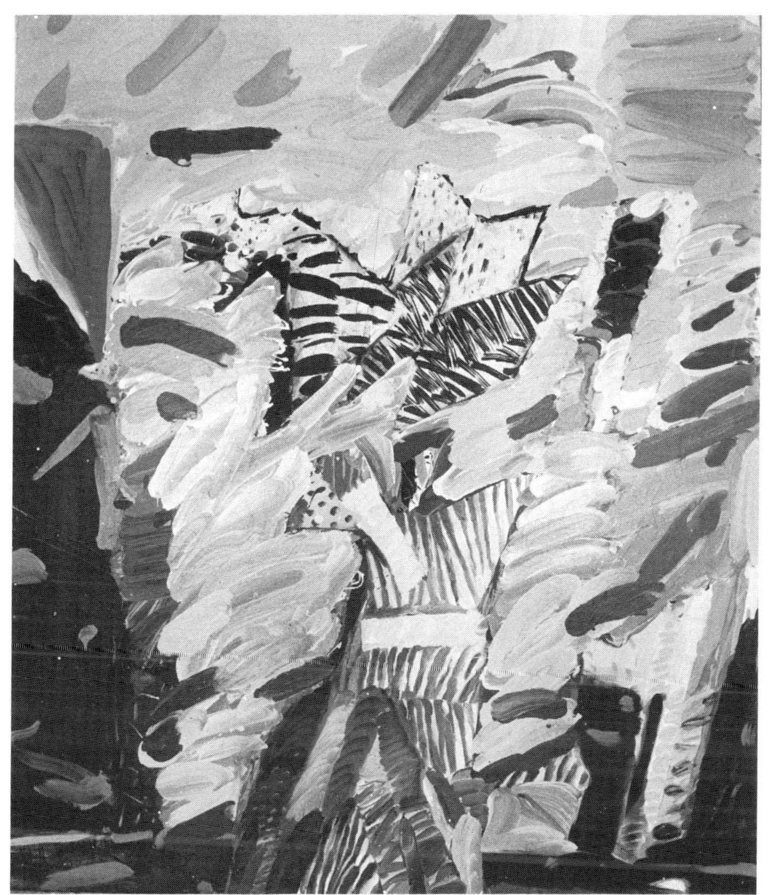

Woman in Striped Dress, 1986,
Acrylic on canvas, 274 x 244 cm,
Collection of the artist

LYS HANSEN

Lys Hansen was born in Falkirk. She studied at Edinburgh College of Art (1955–59) and Edinburgh College of Speech and Drama (1955–58), then went on to a course in Fine Art Studies at Edinburgh University (1961). She began her career as school art teacher then had to devote most of her time to bringing up her young family. It was not until the later 1970s that she had the opportunity to return fully to her painting, now fuelled with new found sources of creative energy. Since then she has emerged as one of the most powerful expressionist artists working in Scotland. Throughout the 1980s she has won many prizes and awards, one of which allowed her to work in West Berlin (1985), which was an important stage in her recent development.

Throughout the 1980s the human figure has become very much the central subject in painting again. Yet, few contemporary artists are as obsessed by the subject as Lys Hansen. Most painters will present their figures within some wider context and setting, whether domestic, historical or poetical. In Hansen's case, however, nothing is allowed to detract from the obsessive concentration on the human presence. Backgrounds, if there is any space left, are vigorously painted out. Thus, the arena of action in each painting is reduced to a shallow box, forcing the figures into all kinds of painful and disturbing contortions as they desperately seek enough room to 'breathe and have their being'. Furthermore, as she is primarily concerned with the female form, the struggling torsos and distorted features of her figures affect us in a different manner than, for example, Michelangelo's *Slave* sculptures. Her figures generate a powerful psychic resonance which challenges the viewer's attitude to the position and treatment of women within a wide range of artistic, sexual and social contexts.

Hansen's large scale paintings, with their expressive use of anatomical distortion, vivid non-naturalistic colour, claustrophobic composition and overwhelming immediacy, work on many levels. For example, one of the things they do is attack the conventional idea of the female nude as a reclining figure laid out for the voyeur's gaze. Hansen's women dare to have a life of their own, even if they seem to be

Grip, 1985,
Oil on canvas, 183 x 152 cm

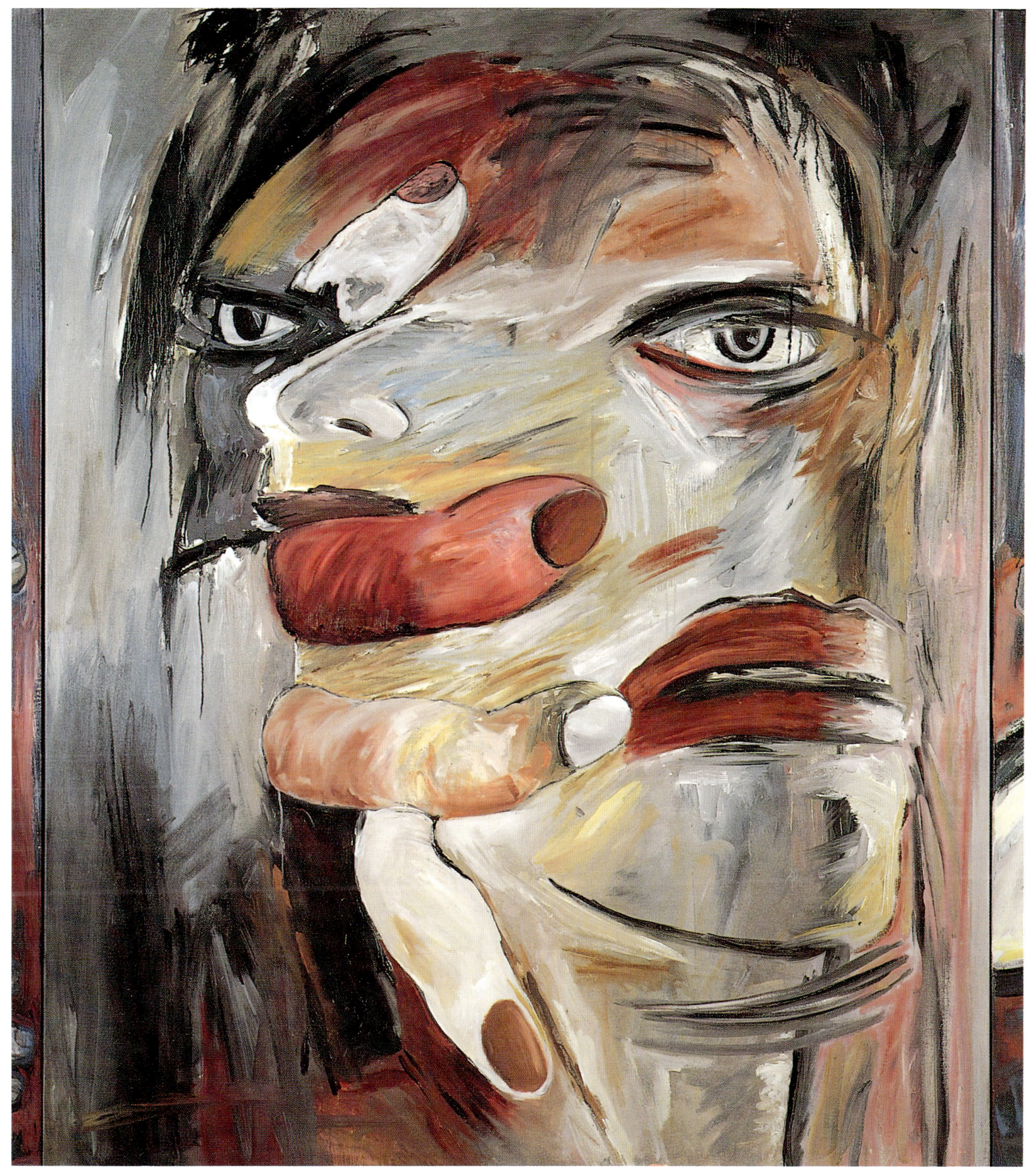

involved in heightened moments of frantic moral and psychological crisis. Yet, taking her work as a whole, Hansen's paintings are open-ended dramatic narratives and can be seen as various stages in an on-going flowing of self-discovery and reintegration.

Since renewing her career in the 1970s, Lys Hansen has had major solo exhibitions in Glasgow, Edinburgh and London. She has works in a number of private and public collections in Scotland, including the University of Stirling and the Scottish Arts Council.

Artist's Comment

The women in my paintings are volatile inhabitants of my canvases and full of primal energy; they are seen as active subjects, not as passive objects.

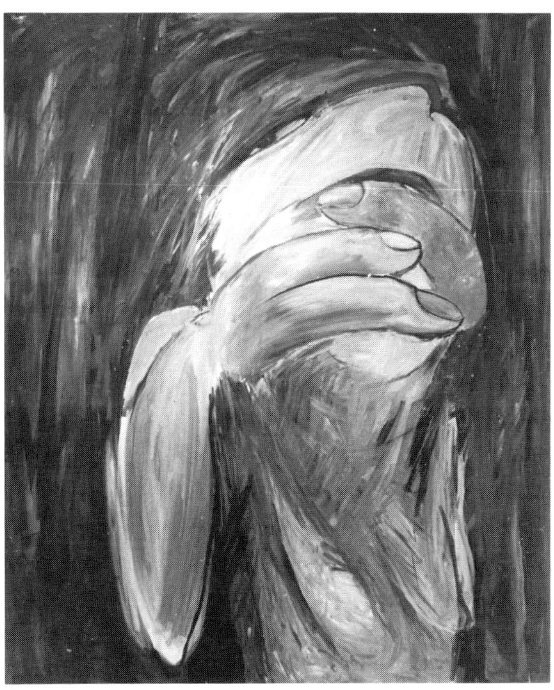

Say Nothing, 'Berlin Trilogy' (left panel), 1985,
Oil on canvas, 183 x 152 cm

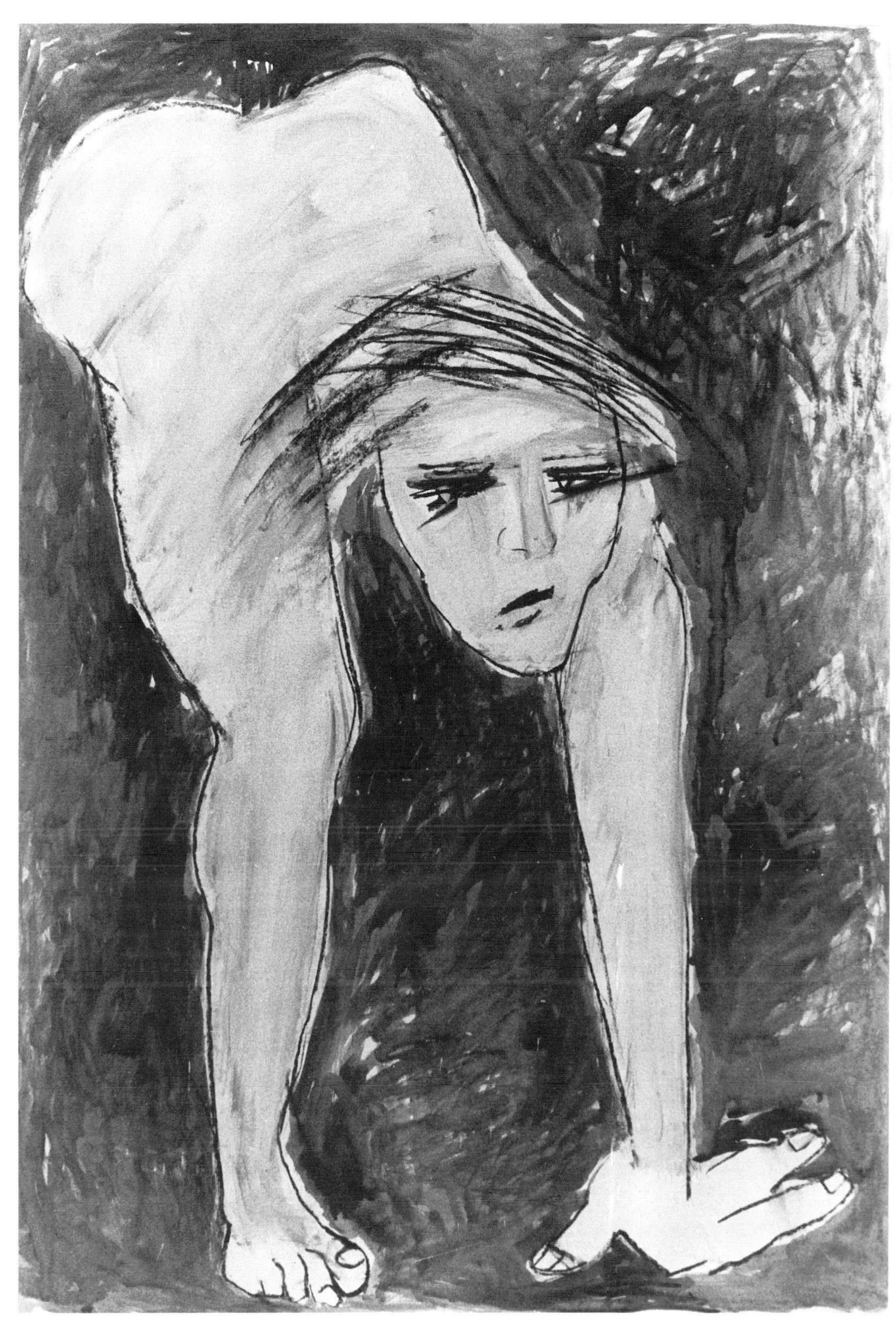

Allein, 1985,
Pastel, charcoal and gouache,
122 x 84 cm

Gwen Hardie was born in Newport, Fife in 1962. She trained at Edinburgh College of Art (1979–84), then went to Berlin under a DAAD Scholarship and studied under Georg Baselitz (1984–85). Since then she has been a full-time painter in Berlin (1984–90) and London (1990–).

There are two main concerns in Gwen Hardie's work. The first concern is how to represent the female figure in a manner that is not merely subservient to the traditional iconography of that universal subject, but is truthful to the body's feminine physicality and sexual identity. Her second concern — and this deals with the way the artist presents her subject — is how to control the presence of her figures in relationship to the size and shape of the enclosing picture frame. These two crucial aspects of her work were already being addressed in her first exhibited paintings which she produced in her final year at art college. Mainly using herself as model, which she still does, she focused on specific areas of the figure, by placing her subject close to the frame and so excluding any external distraction. Thus, she created in her paintings of the mid-1980s a powerful introspective mood, which gave the treatment of her enlarged heads and torsos a feeling of genuine monumentality rather than being merely overblown in a Michelinesque manner.

Although these early works challenged the usual domestic scale and vision of most female painting in Scotland, her painterly technique still remained within the Scottish academic tradition. In Germany, under Baselitz's direction she was encouraged to experiment and began to move to a much more tactile method of expression. This was achieved by discarding the use of brushes in favour of applying the paint by sponges and then even more directly using her hands and fingers. The parts of the body depicted in these new paintings (1985–86) became so enlarged that the viewer was invited to rediscover the landscape of the human body from a newly born baby's viewpoint. This desire to return to the origin of awareness and perception also led to a series of simple linear figure paintings which were clearly inspired by primitive and prehistoric pictographic methods. In these works the whole figure for once is on display, set or floating against a neutral background. Here the

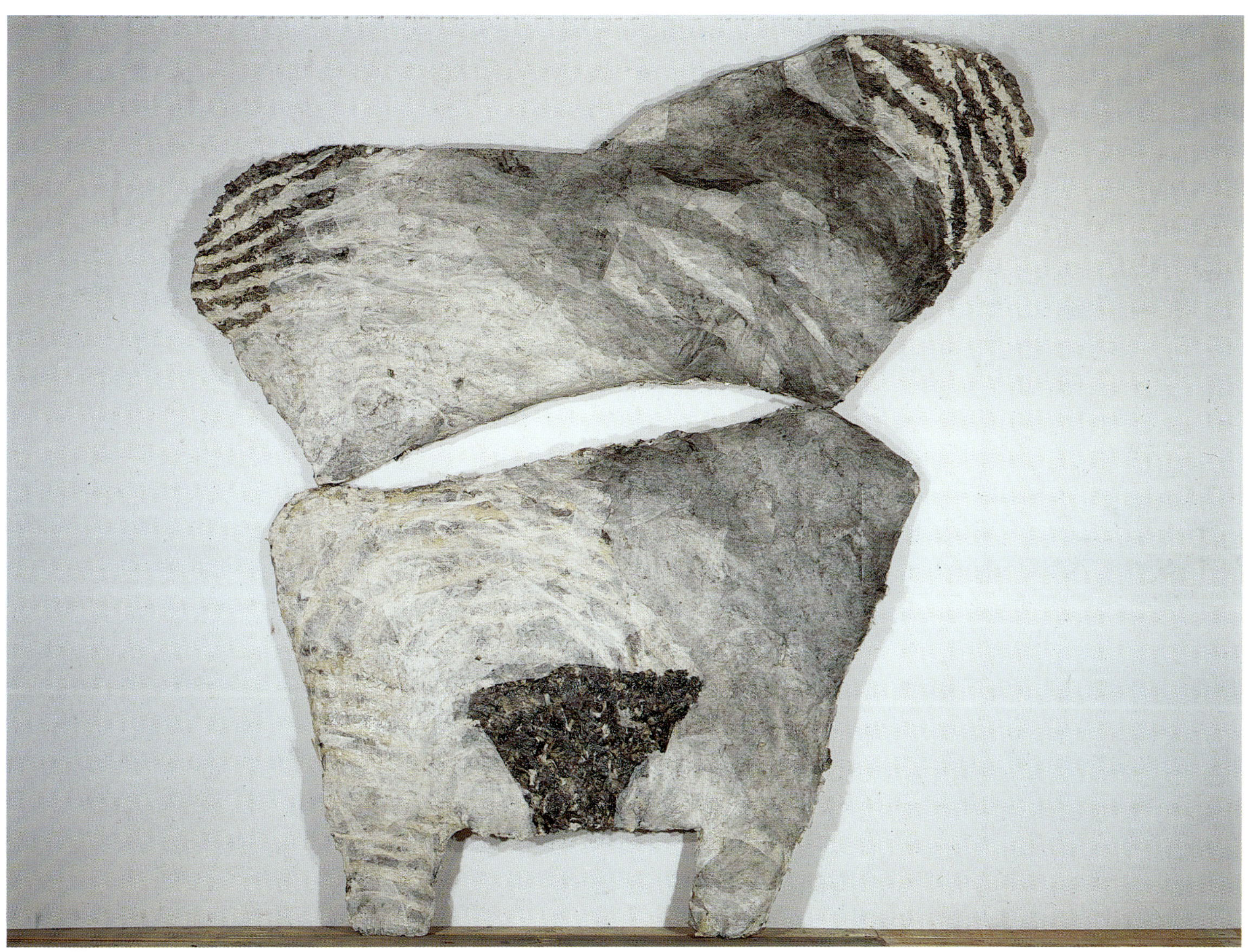

Perch, 1988,
Paper, glue, acrylic, wire and iron rods, 274 x 274 x 15 cm,
Courtesy Fischer Fine Art Limited, London

outline drawing depicts the female form and emphasises those anatomical areas of greater importance such as the vulva and womb. Yet there is no division, but a free flow between the internal and external being of the figure.

In her recent work, although the subject remains constant, the interest has shifted back to the outer forms. Taking the device of enlarging sections of the body to their ultimate conclusion, her latest paintings are like enlarged microscopic views of skin and tissue. Also, with her acute tactile sense she has moved into creating sculptured figure forms of layered paper, where the emphasis is on the elasticity of the outer skin. Her new works are much lighter in mood — sexy rather than sexual.

Gwen Hardie has had major exhibitions in Britain and abroad and has rapidly built up an international reputation. She is connected with Annely Juda Fine Art, London. Her work is represented in many private and major public collections, such as the Metropolitan Museum, New York, and the Scottish National Gallery of Modern Art, Edinburgh.

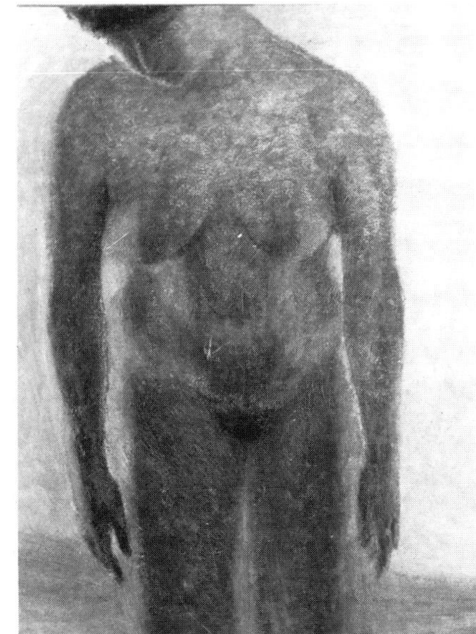

Me and Sea, 1984,
Oil on canvas, 152 x 122 cm

Coupling, 1988,
Acrylic on canvas, 200 x 200 cm,
Courtesy Fischer Fine Art Limited, London

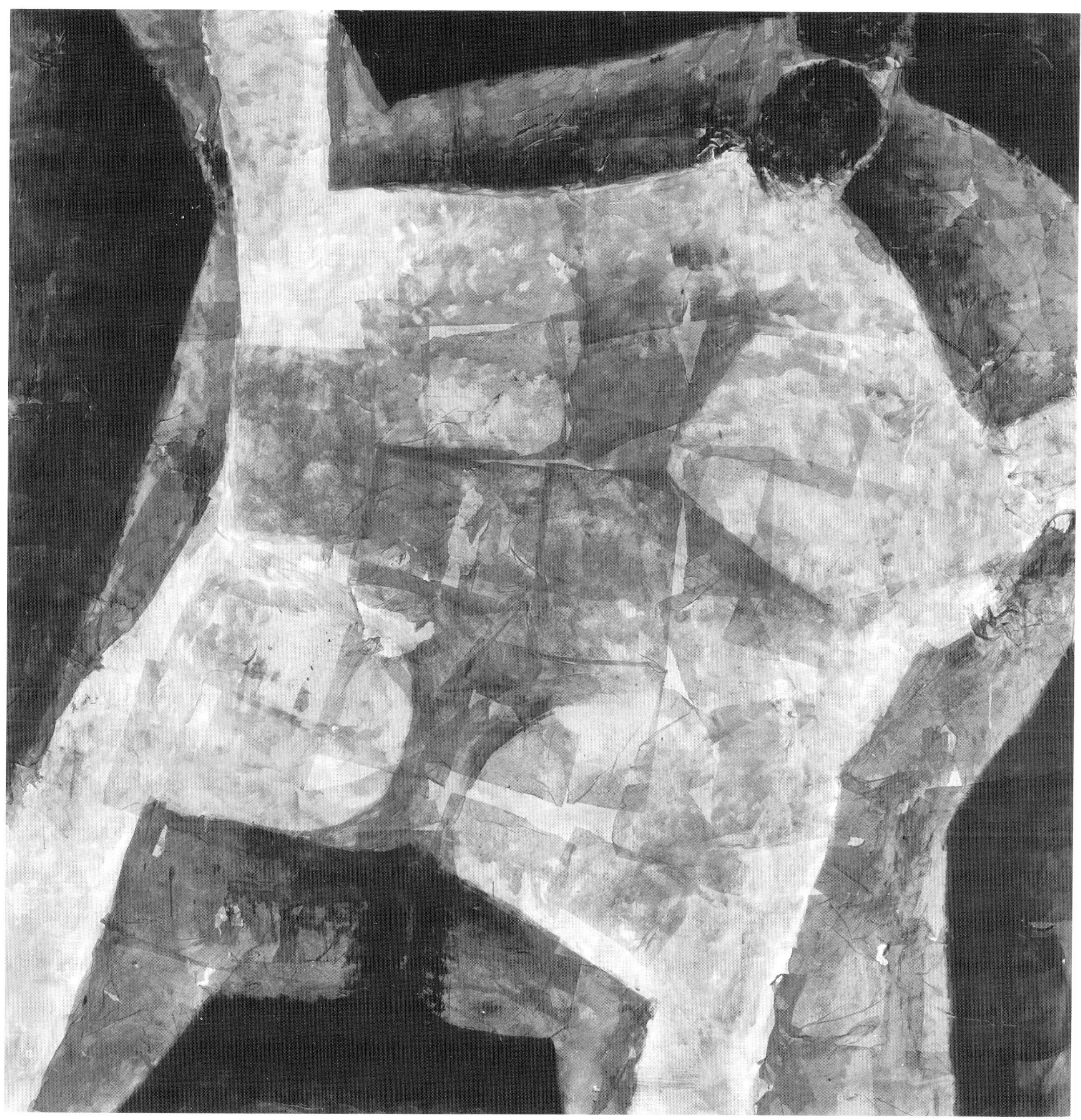

JOHN HOUSTON

John Houston was born in Buckhaven, Fife in 1930. He studied at Edinburgh College of Art (1948–54), where he went on to teach in the School of Drawing and Painting from 1955–89, becoming deputy head from 1982 until he retired. He has won many awards and became an elected member of all the important Scottish art institutions. For his services to art in Scotland he was awarded an OBE in 1990. He is married to the painter, Elizabeth Blackadder.

Stand anywhere in Scotland and the sea is not far away. The same might be said when looking at a John Houston painting. As with his two illustrious predecessors, William McTaggart and Joan Eardley, Houston is not exclusively a maritime painter, but even when he is tackling other subjects and themes, the sea's imminent presence can be felt. If he paints a still life the subject more than likely will be oysters or a lobster; recently he has turned his attention to figure painting and his favourite theme in this area of his work is, not surprisingly, the beach party. Of course, he does produce works with no overt maritime content.

Yet taking his prolific output as a whole, there is a strong impression that he is truly at his best, working on full cylinders, when he is directly painting his favourite seascapes, such as Firth of Forth with the Bass Rock on the far horizon.

As with the sea there is a restless energy in all of Houston's paintings, which is reflective of his romantic temperament. Like his 'constant companion and hero' Turner, he is an inveterate traveller. His wanderings, which have taken him all over Europe, North America and the Far East, have developed in him an acutely sensitive eye to the constant shifts and changes in atmospheric mood and climatic conditions. The weather in all its varying moods is a constantly recurring theme in his work; even the treatment of his figures is as much a reflection of the natural environment around them as an expression of their psychological states of mind.

His travels have also brought him into contact with a wide range of artistic movements such as German Expressionism, American Abstraction and Japanese Zen painting. Ever responsive to new ideas and experiences, he has gained something from all the different cultures and landscapes he has visited in the development of his

A Day by the Sea, Summer, 1990,
Oil on canvas, 203 x 203 cm,
Collection of the artist

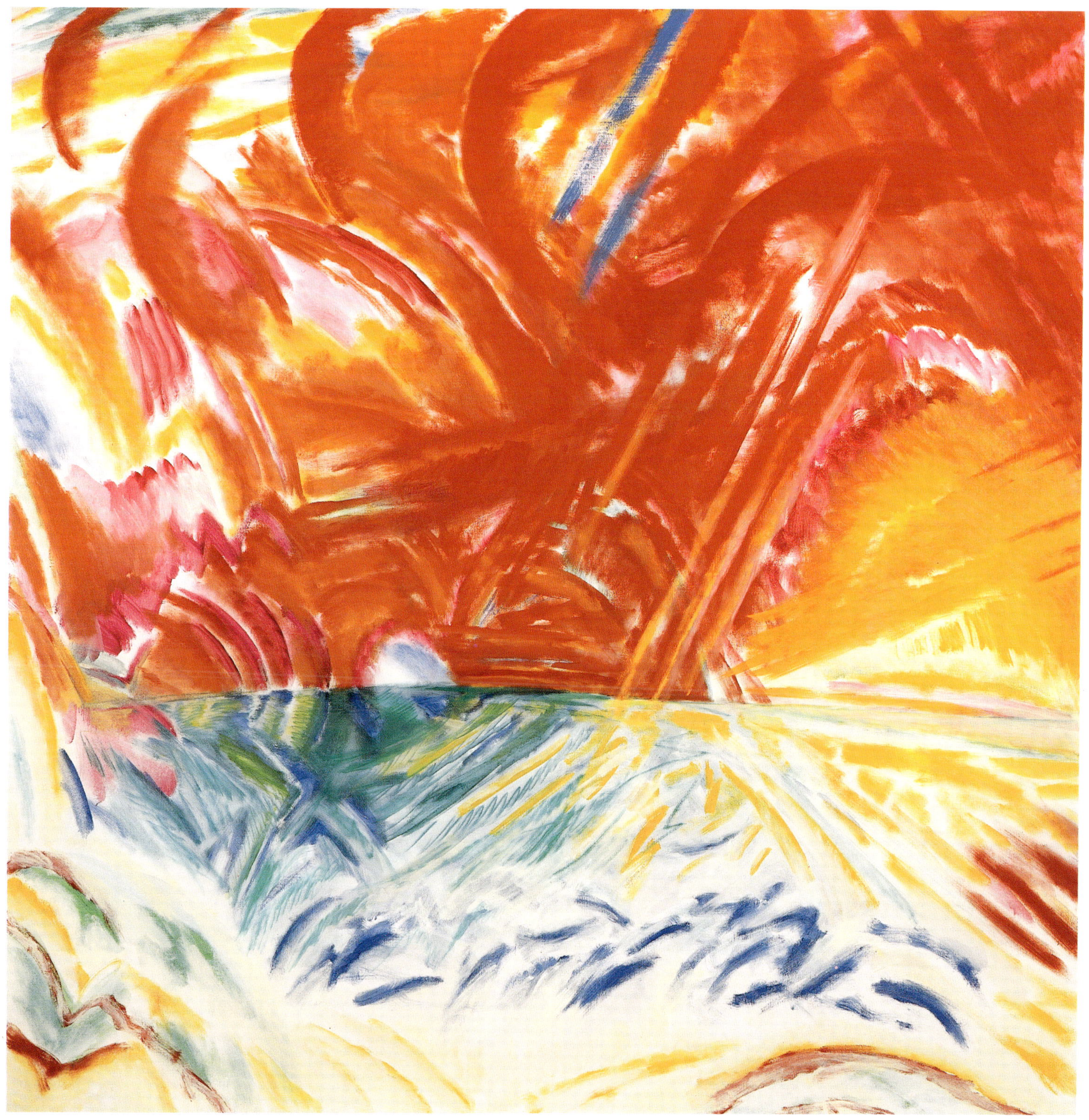

free colourist painting techniques. Equally at home working on canvas or paper he now has such control over his medium that he is equally a master of the intimate interior world of the still life or the apocalyptic universe of the sublime seascape.

John Houston is one of the most successful Scottish painters and regularly exhibits his work in Scotland and London. He has had a long association with both the Scottish Gallery and the Mercury Gallery. His work is represented in innumerable private and public collections both in Britain and abroad, including the Walker Art Gallery, Liverpool, the Vincent Price Collection, USA, and Scottish National Gallery of Modern Art.

Artist's Comment

The paintings grow as you paint them; in a way they are painting you.

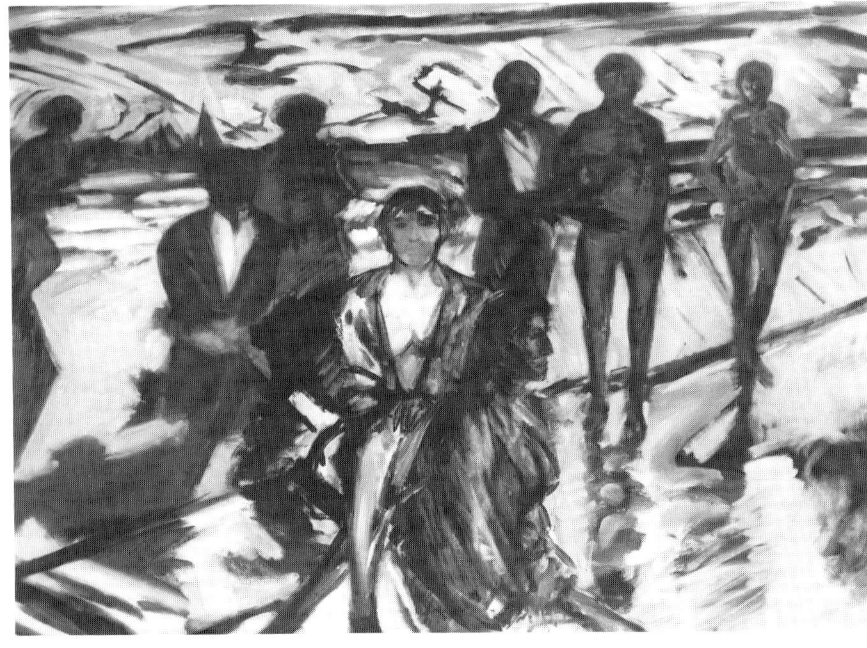

Beach Party, 1986–90,
Oil on canvas, 173 x 244 cm,
Collection of the artist

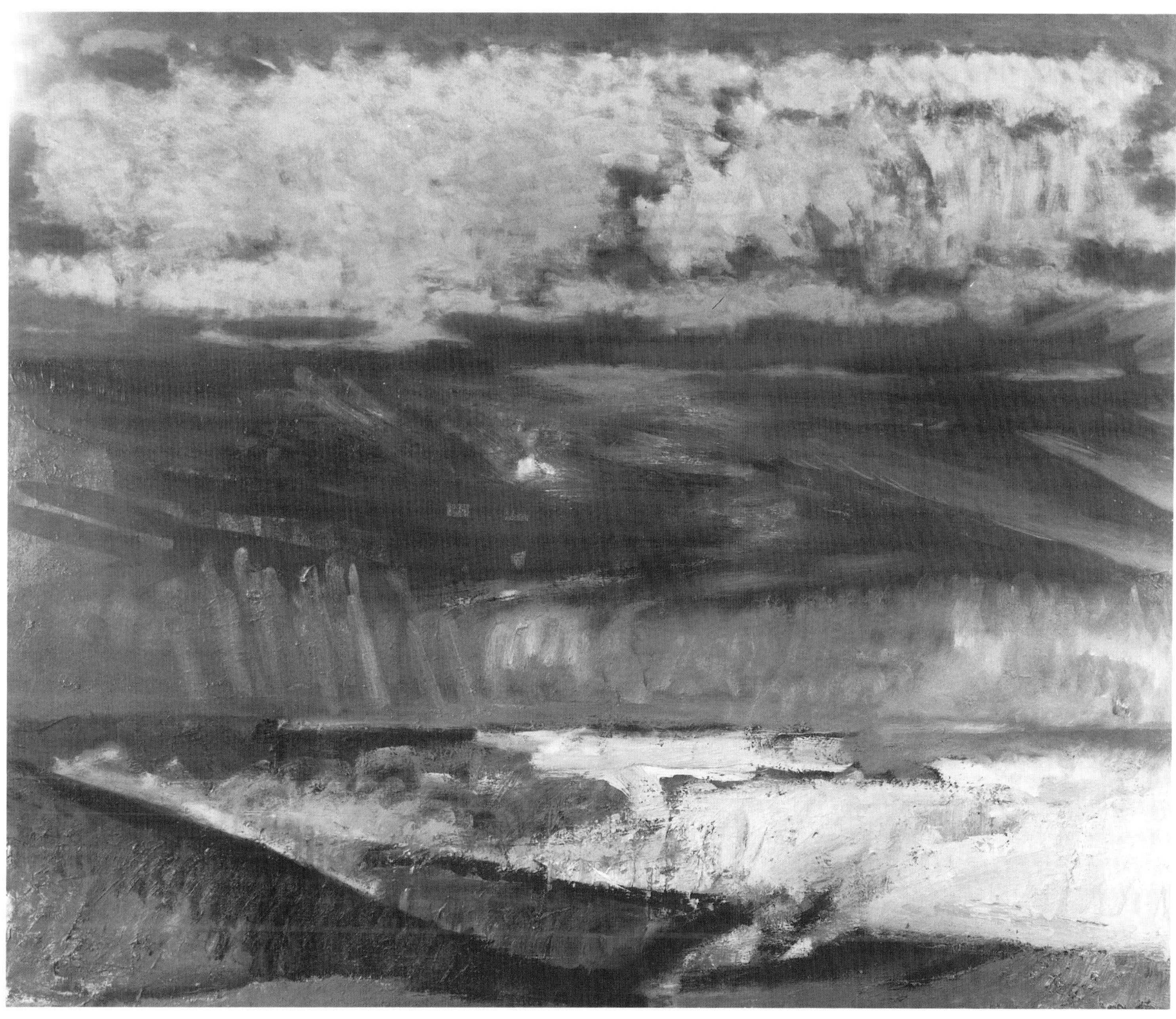

Gullane Bay, 1984–85,
Oil on canvas, 152 x 183 cm,
Private collection

IAN HOWARD

an Howard was born in Aberdeen in 1952 and studied at Edinburgh University and Edinburgh College of Art for his Fine Art degree (1970–75). He gained a postgraduate scholarship to Italy (1976) and was appointed a lecturer at Gray's School of Art, Aberdeen (1977–85). Since 1986 he has been Head of Painting at Duncan of Jordanstone College of Art, Dundee. Over his career he has won many awards and prizes for his paintings.

Ian Howard is an intellectual artist. In Scottish terms he could be seen within that analytical approach to painting which produced from North East Scotland such earlier artists as William Dyce and James Cowie. Like Cowie there is a strong metaphysical dimension to his work, deriving in his early paintings from a similar interest in the art of the Italian Renaissance, where scientific perspective could ironically also create mysterious relationships. This fascination with such artists as Piero della Francesca developed from his academic study of art history and archaeology at University. In the work of the late 1970s and early 1980s he adapted the altarpiece format to play intriguing visual games with spatial composition and pictorial narrative. The technique he employed tended to be of a graphic linear nature, simulating a fresco style appearance. This created a clarity of presentation which emphasised, by contrast, the ambiguity of meaning attached to the complex structure of buildings and machines which dominated the scenes depicted.

While still retaining, if not intensifying, his deep interest in the metaphysical power of objects on the human perception and imagination, Howard's paintings have radically developed throughout the 1980s. Since the early part of the decade his work has shifted in treatment from what might be called the Albertian concept of painting as a window onto a silent, static world to a fully blown baroque one, where rumbustious movement and sensual delight in the plastic tactile qualities of painting are the order of the day. If the earlier works were mockingly serious, the later paintings are the reverse —witty comic dramas within the Surrealist tradition of visual pun and games. Possibly taking his lead from 20th century art's obsession with the object, the subject matter of his later 1980s paintings has moved from exterior,

Triad, 1989/90,
Mixed media on wood, 183 x 183 cm,
Photograph: Malcolm Thompson
Collection of the artist

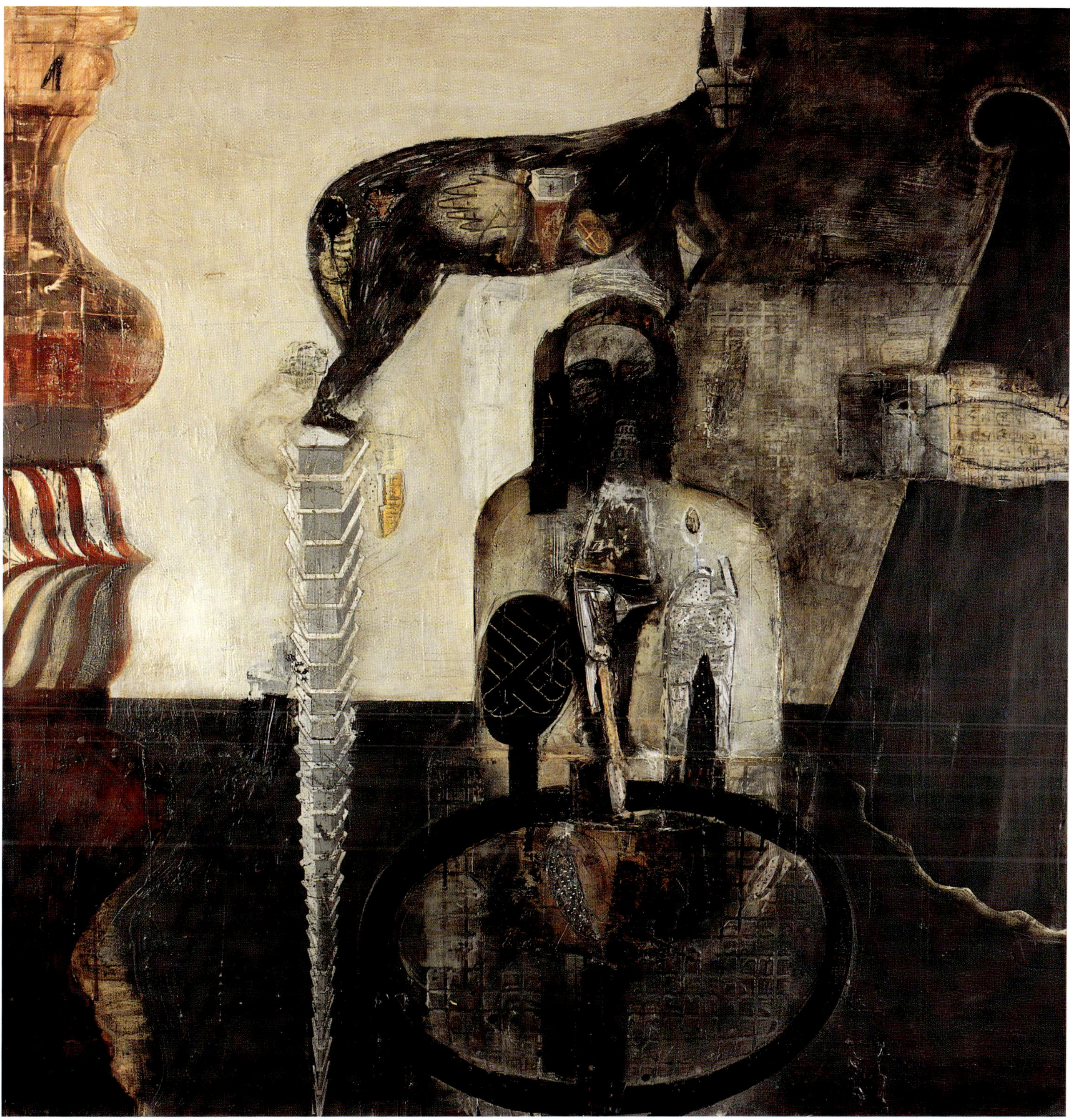

architectural and sculptural concerns to the interior world of domestic still life. A new
iconography has also evolved which is less elitist and esoteric and more connected
with local experience and popular culture. One of the major successes of these works
is Howard's ability to merge stylistically, by adopting postmodern eclecticism: a range
of influences from Picasso, de Chirico, Walt Disney through to Scotland's own comic
strip heroes like *Oor Willie*. Howard's works have always been great fun, intriguing
both visually and intellectually. His latest work, however, seems to be taking on a
more sombre reflective mood and it will be fascinating to see how this develops.

Ian Howard is one of the most successful middle generation painters working in
Scotland. Apart from his meteoric rise in the academic world, he has had a number
of very successful exhibitions, most notably his one-man Third Eye exhibition which
was shown in Glasgow, Edinburgh, Dundee and Aberdeen in 1987–88. His work is
represented in many private and public collections, including the Arts Council of
Great Britain and the Contemporary Arts Society, London.

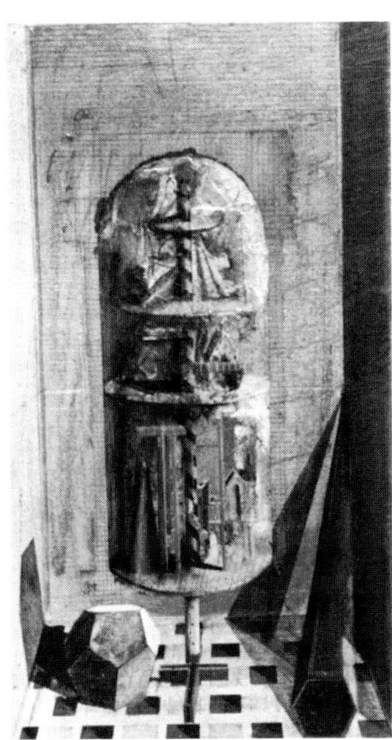

Still Life # 1, 1990,
Mixed media on paper, 102 x 76 cm,
Private collection

Capsula Ex Rabbit, 1987,
Acrylic on canvas, 244 x 244 cm,
Private collection

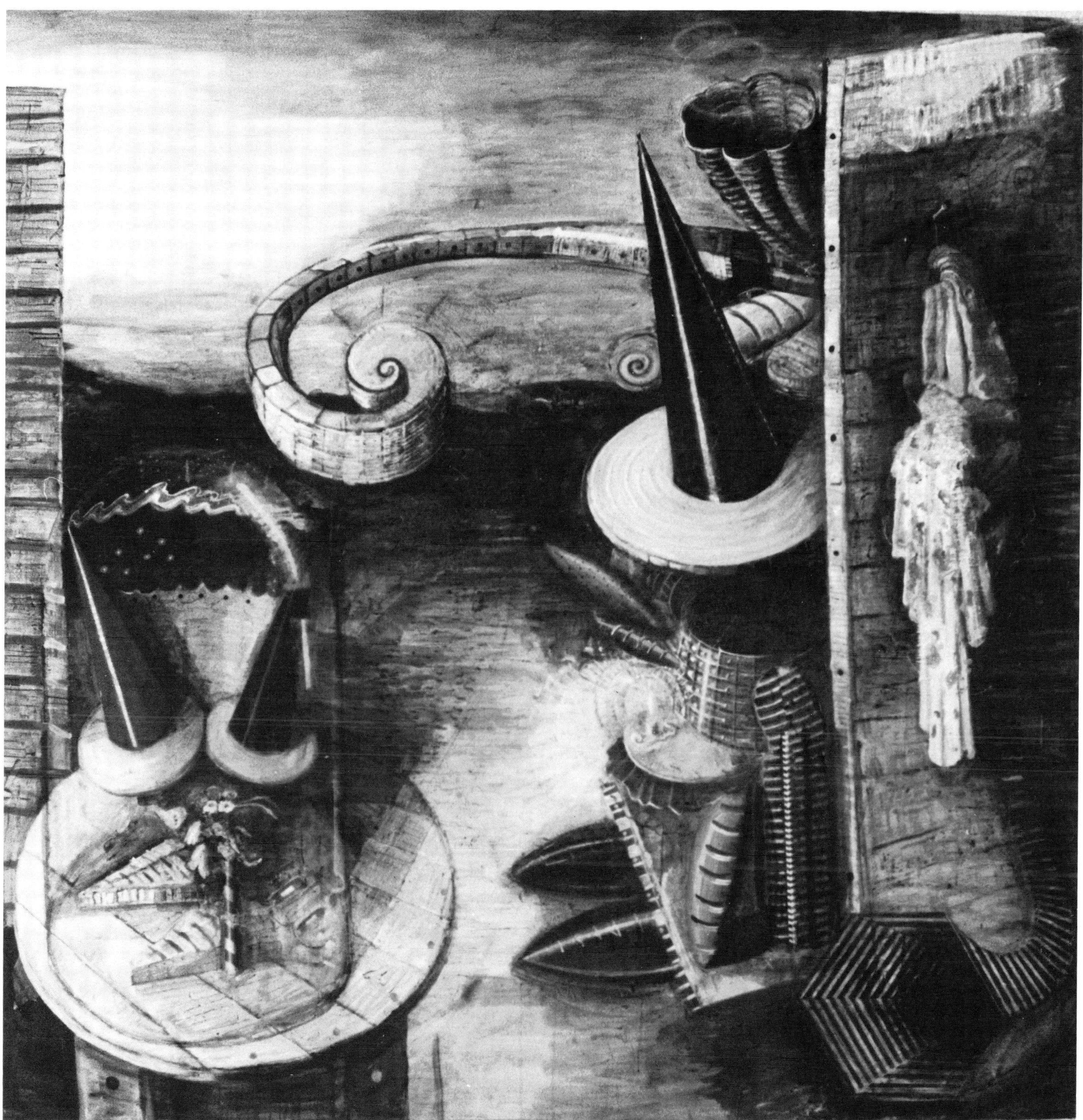

P eter Howson was born in London in 1958, moving to Scotland in 1962. He trained at Glasgow School of Art from 1975–77, returning two years later to complete his studies in 1981. After teaching briefly at Glasgow School of Art in 1985, he now lives and paints full time in Glasgow.

Howson achieved international recognition in the 1980s, alongside other Glasgow painters such as Currie, Campbell and Wiszniewski, for his aggressive and direct images of working class life. There is a long and distinguished history of committed social painting which goes back in Britain to Hogarth, in France to Daumier and in the United States to artists like Thomas Hart Benton and George Bellows. The figurative exuberance of these artists, as they expanded and deepened their own genres of portraiture and history painting, has become a key influence for artists in Glasgow, most particularly Peter Howson. Whilst maintaining a strongly theatrical and graphic style, he has avoided the blind pursuit of effect for its own sake and succeeded in introducing a highly engaging narrative and symbolic complexity into his work.

His dramatic paintings often explore as their subject the male environment, from mercenaries and the urban homeless ('dossers') to shipbuilders and musclemen. The format varies from single portrait heads to large scale modern-day allegories. The handling of paint is part gritty and earthy, yet also employs graphic techniques of caricature, popular art and styles of past art which add further layers of meaning. Howson's figures burst with athleticism, caught in a theatrical posture, whether as group compositions, such as *Death of the Innocent* (1988) or in single figure subjects, such as *The Heroic Dosser* (1987). But more than this, Howson often hints at some kind of moral dilemma, both for the subject and for us as spectators. His characters appear physically strong yet, as exploited victims within society, are weak in comparison to the superior forces which control their lives. We too are challenged in the way we respond to Howson's depictions of the casualties of modern life. Many artists, in Scotland and elsewhere, have chosen simply to ignore these difficult issues, yet in a powerful and gripping manner, Howson has brought these questions

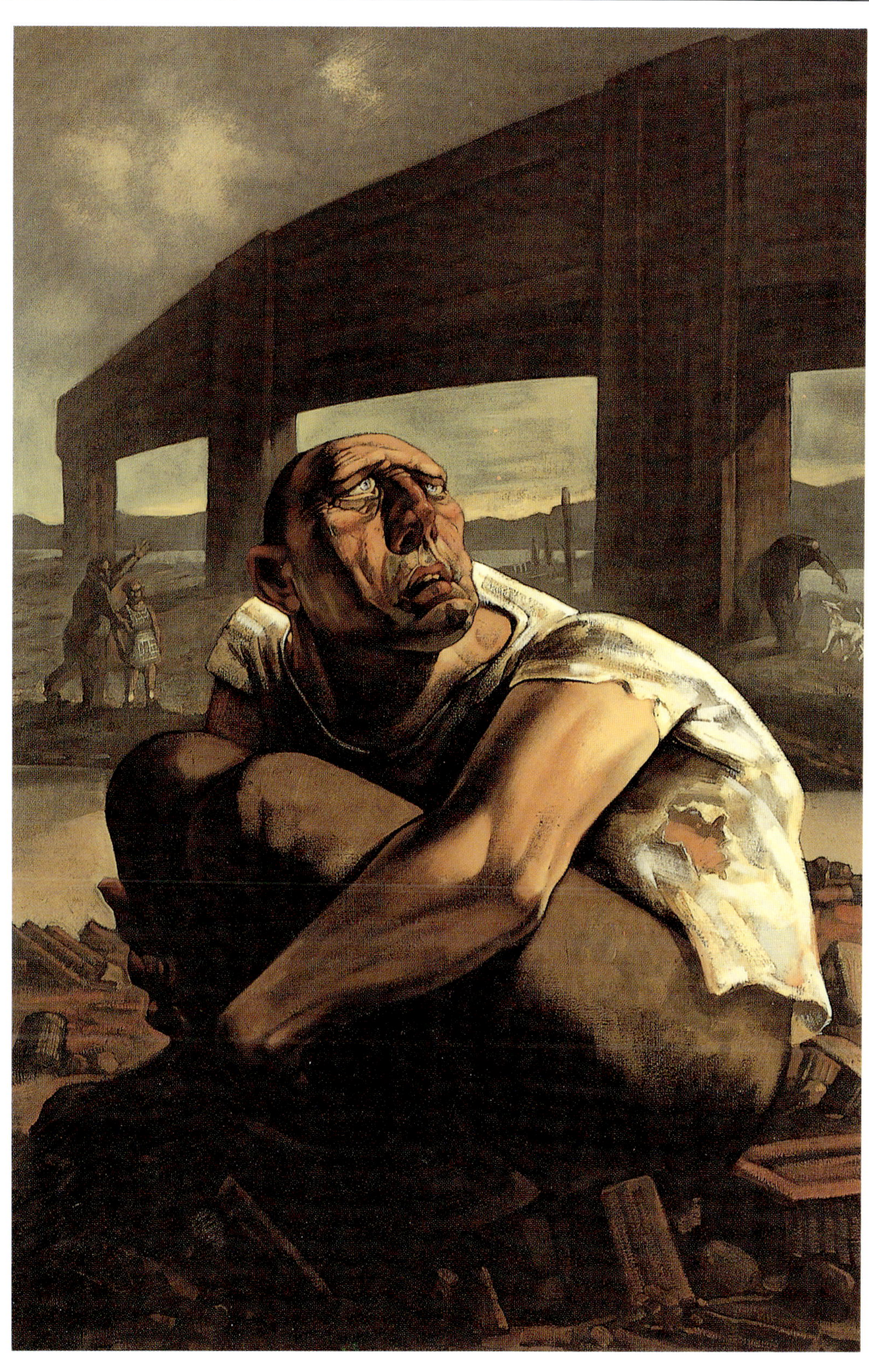

The Bridge to Nowhere, 1991,
Oil on canvas, 189 x 128 cm,
Courtesy Angela Flowers Gallery, London

to the fore.

The artist's work is represented in many major public and private collections throughout the world, including the Museum of Modern Art and the Metropolitan Museum of Art, New York, and the Tate Gallery, London.

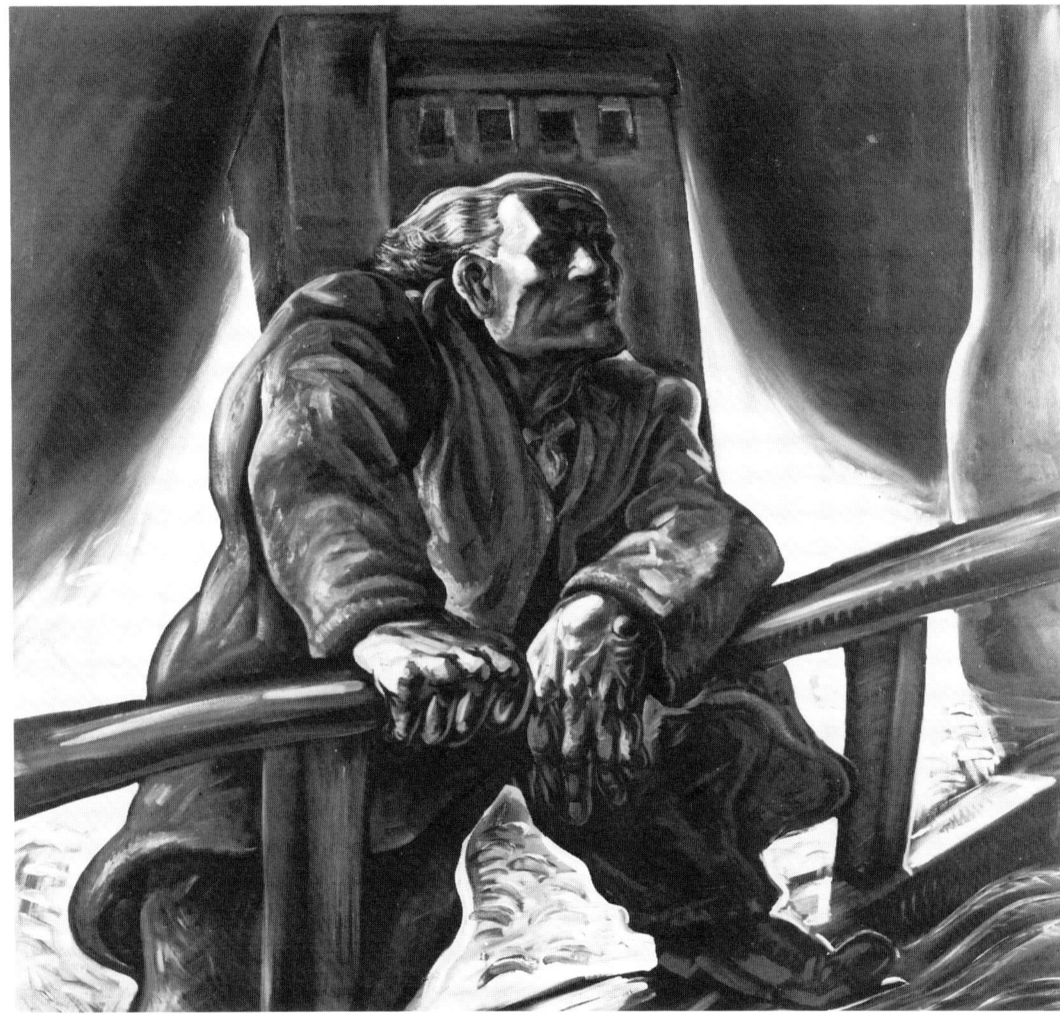

The Heroic Dosser, 1987,
Oil on canvas, 213.5 x 213.5 cm,
Courtesy Angela Flowers Gallery,
London

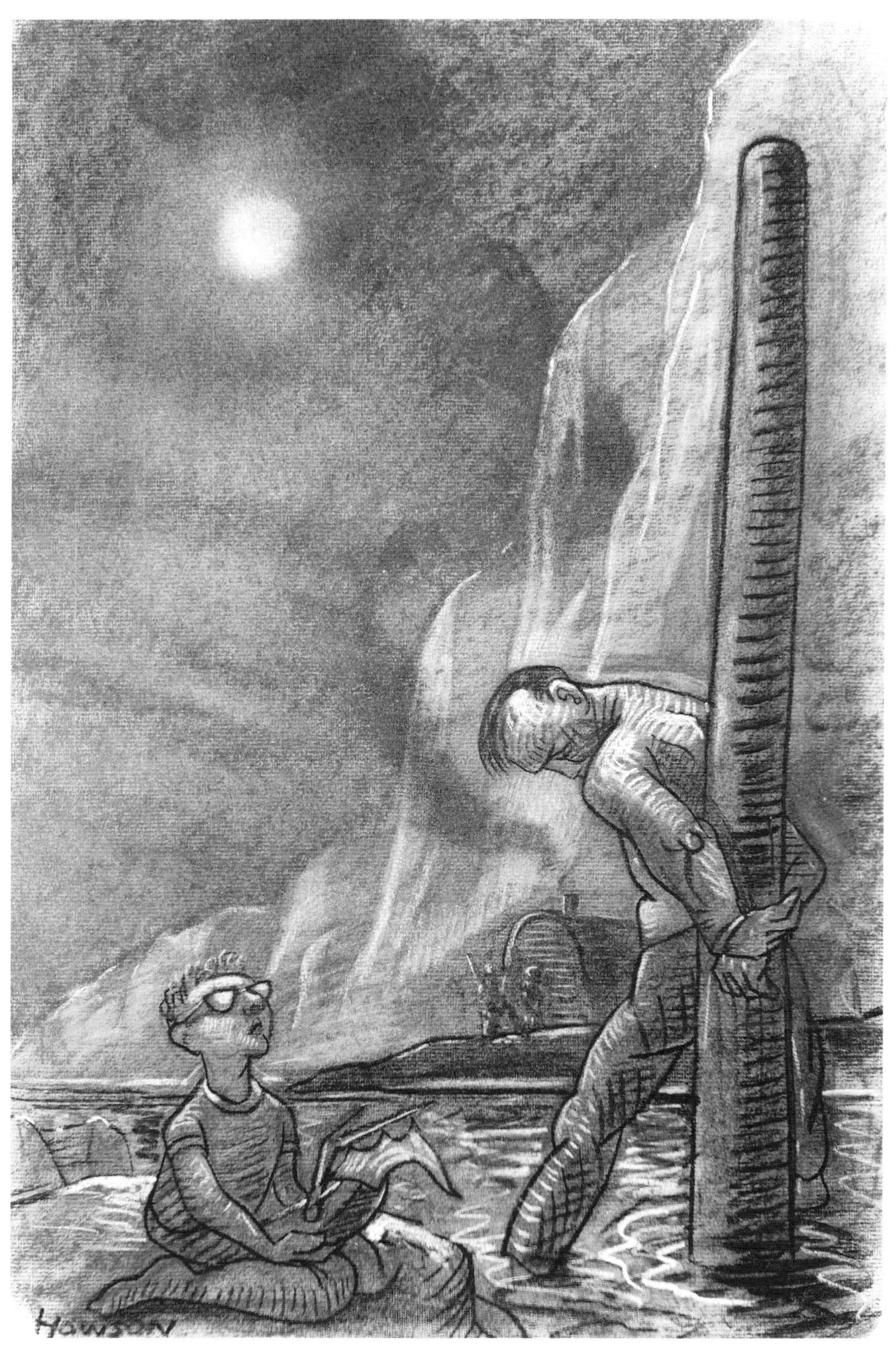

Broken Boat, 1990,
Pastel on paper, 65 x 50.8 cm,
Courtesy Angela Flowers Gallery,
London

Margaret Hunter was born in Irvine, Ayrshire in 1948. She was a single parent of two children when she determined to go to Glasgow School of Art (1981–85). Demonstrating a strong individuality in her art and no little self will she gained postgraduate entrance to study under the guidance of Georg Baselitz at Hochschule der Kunste, Berlin. A full-time artist, she now splits her working year between her studios in Berlin and Scotland.

Margaret Hunter makes no bones about the influence Georg Baselitz has had on her work. His teaching and example, along with her studious visits to the Museum of Ethnography in Berlin, have all played a significant part in the development of her powerful style of representation which captures the directness and vitality of primitive art. This certainly places her work firmly within the Expressionist tradition of modern art and particularly connects it with much 20th century German painting. However, it should be pointed out that the radical wing of Scottish Art also contributed to the emergence of European Expressionism as far back as the 18th century. For example, David Allen described his illustrations for that eulogy to the simple life, Allan Ramsay's *The Gentle Shepherd*, as not offering expensive smooth engravings, but expressive and characteristic designs.

Margaret Hunter's paintings could also be seen as expressive and characteristic designs, particularly as there is a strong graphic dimension to her work, along with the emotive use of raw colour. Furthermore, as with David Allen, her primitivism is not a self-conscious exercise or some futile attempt to recapture a dimly remembered past state of innocence. On the contrary her art is motivated by her committed belief in the continuous psychological bond, as expressed by human creativity, between our pre-civilised pantheistic origins and the postmodern pluralistic world we have made for ourselves. Delving below surface appearances, her paintings seek through expressive line, colour, texture and archetypal forms, to celebrate our common humanity.

Margaret Hunter shows regularly in Scotland and London, as well as in other European countries on the Continent. She is exhibits with the Vanessa Devereux Gallery, London.

Carrying the Egg, 1990,
Oil on canvas, 145 x 104 cm,
Courtesy Vanessa Devereux Gallery, London

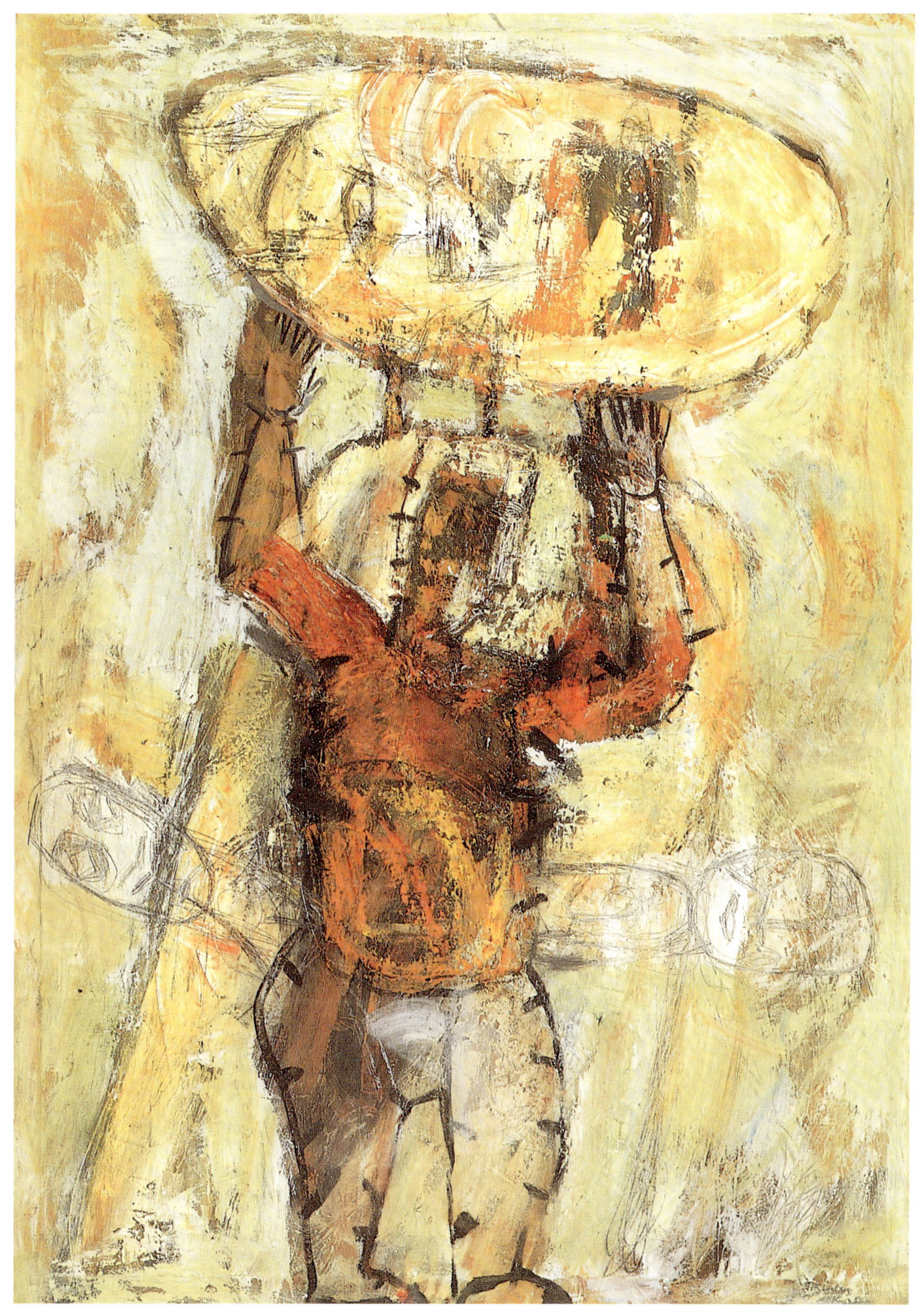

Artist's Comment

I am always astounded by the inventiveness of tribal art, abstraction and stylisation, and this has inspired my recent work.

It seems to me that the unsophistication and honesty of primitive art can be used to address and reveal the 'inner' person of today. The idea of peeling away the layers of consciousness is reflected in my method of painting. By overlaying paint, faint marks and images can be seen below the surface and the tension between line and colour is used to communicate feeling and emotional intensity.

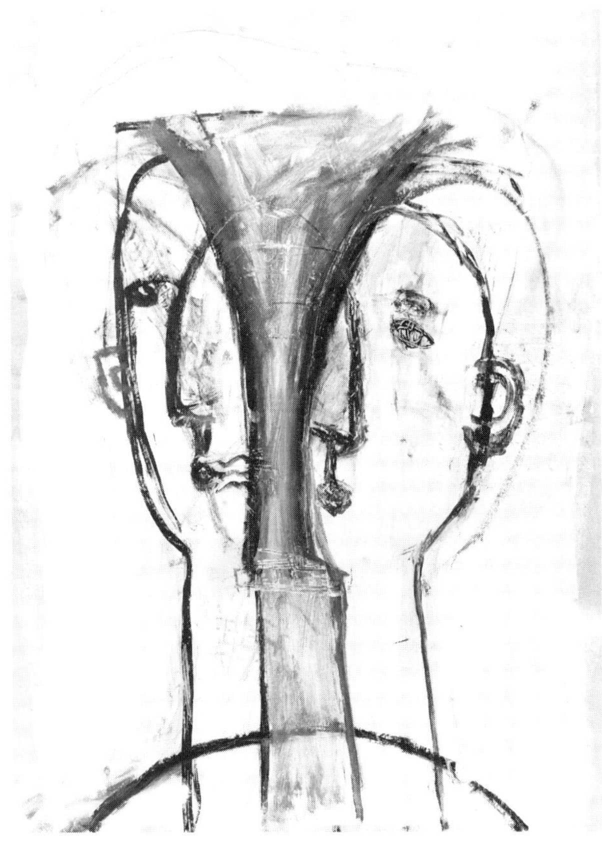

Whisper, 1988,
Mixed media on paper, 157 x 99 cm,
Collection of the Scottish National Gallery of Modern Art

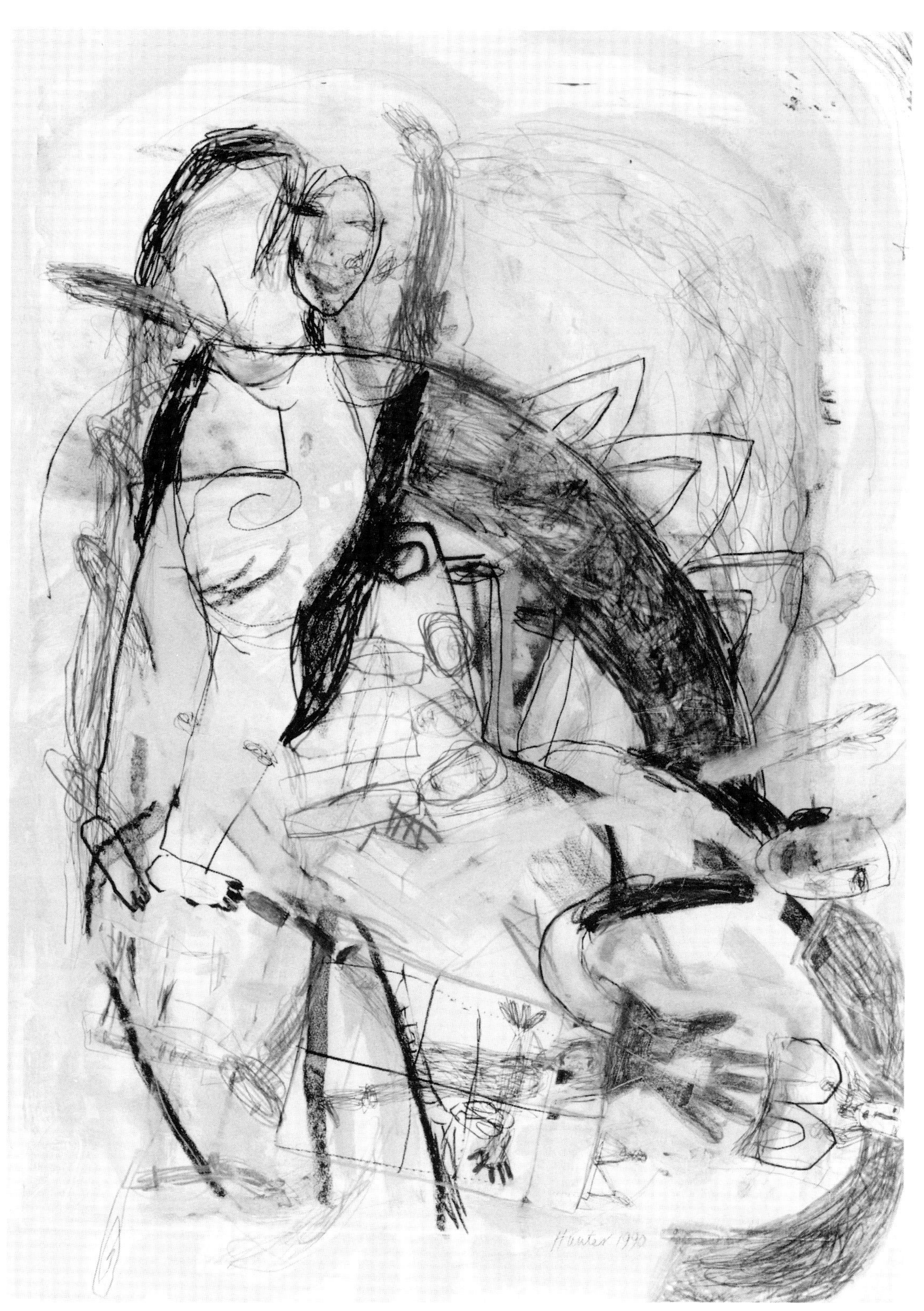

Upside Frau, 1990,
Mixed media on paper,
116 x 85 cm,
Photograph: Antonia Reeve,
Courtesy of Vanessa
Devereux Gallery, London

Matthew Inglis was born in Stirling in 1958 and trained at Edinburgh College of Art (1976–81), where he was a student in the Tapestry Department. Since then he has been working, with the help of various odd jobs and a Scottish Art Council award for young artists (1984), to develop a career as a full-time artist. He was artist-in-residence at the Crawford Arts Centre, University of St Andrews, in 1988. At present he lives and works in Edinburgh.

Matthew Inglis' training in the tapestry department at Edinburgh College of Art prepared him to maintain a fairly flexible attitude to his means of artistic expression. What kind of artist he is, is difficult to define and he has no desire to be pigeon-holed as a painter or sculptor. This open approach is also reflected in the way he handles his materials, for although he frequently uses three-dimensional objects in his work, they are treated in a pictorial rather than a formalistic manner. He is a superb image maker of witty and provocative ideas.

Broadly speaking there are three main aspects to his work: his free standing sculpture which is not relevant here, his 'boxes', or 'Incident series', which present incongruous scenes in the form of miniature tableaux, and lastly his wall panels which in contrast to the enclosed world of the boxes are open-ended in their presentation and thematic concerns.

As with the earlier Dadaists and Surrealists, Inglis believes that art need not be a conscript, but a challenge to the authority of logic and materialism. His aim as an artist is to free the power of the imagination both in himself and his audience, to stimulate our capacity to wonder and delight in the irrational. This he achieves with the found objects he arranges in his boxes, by presenting the viewer with an alternative, *Alice Through The Looking Glass* world. Here the normal laws of perspective, scale and narrative are overturned — for example, a giant's boot comes crashing through the clouds onto the roofs of a quiet suburban street in *Revenge* or monstrous ears literally grow out of the wallpaper in an ominous piece entitled *Walls Have Ears*. Yet behind all their anarchic humour there is a serious debate concerning our complex relationship with the material world of objects we have created for

Water (detail), 1989,
Mixed media,
Photograph: Heidi Kosaniuk
Collection of the artist

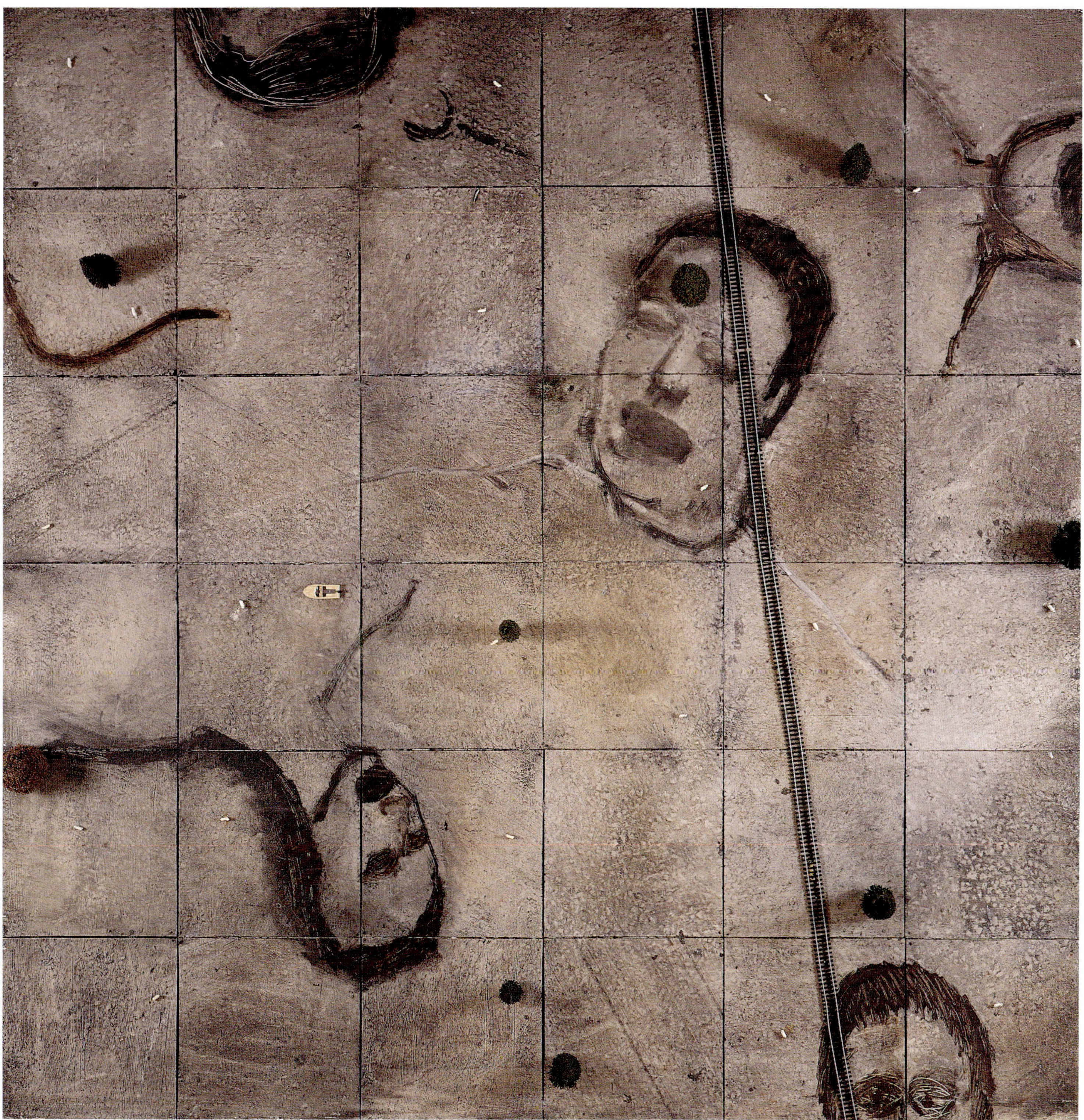

ourselves, particularly in our contemporary consumerist society.

If the box series in Inglis' work are pictorial and narrative in format, his panels are painterly and poetic; they concern themselves more with personal issues, dealing with the psychology of private experience rather than public ritual. The panels tend towards the contemplative, using the evocative qualities of colour, texture and scale to stimulate feelings and associations about the individual self and the relationship with our social and natural environment.

Robert Rauschenberg said that his work was where art and life met, and the same could be said of Matthew Inglis. Inglis exhibits frequently throughout Scotland and abroad. His work is represented in a number of private and public collections, such as the Scottish Arts Council and the BBC.

Artist's Comment

One of the fundamentals of my work is the friction caused by the clash between social/political objectives, personal objectives and aesthetic objectives.

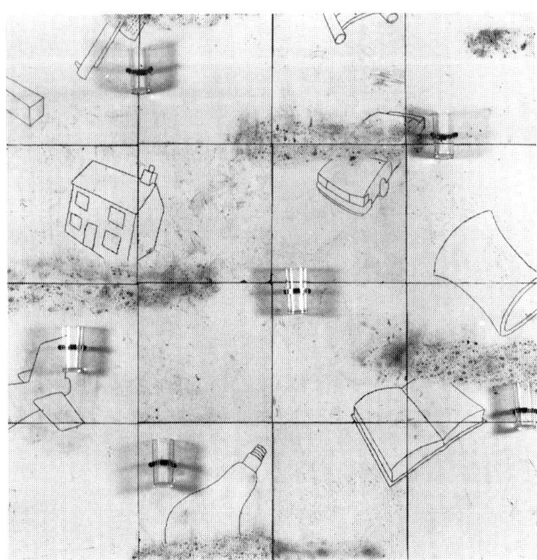

Water (detail of trilogy), 1991,
Fire on gloss paint on hardboard, glasses, 152 x 152 x 20 cm,
Photograph: Heidi Kosaniuk
Collection of the artist

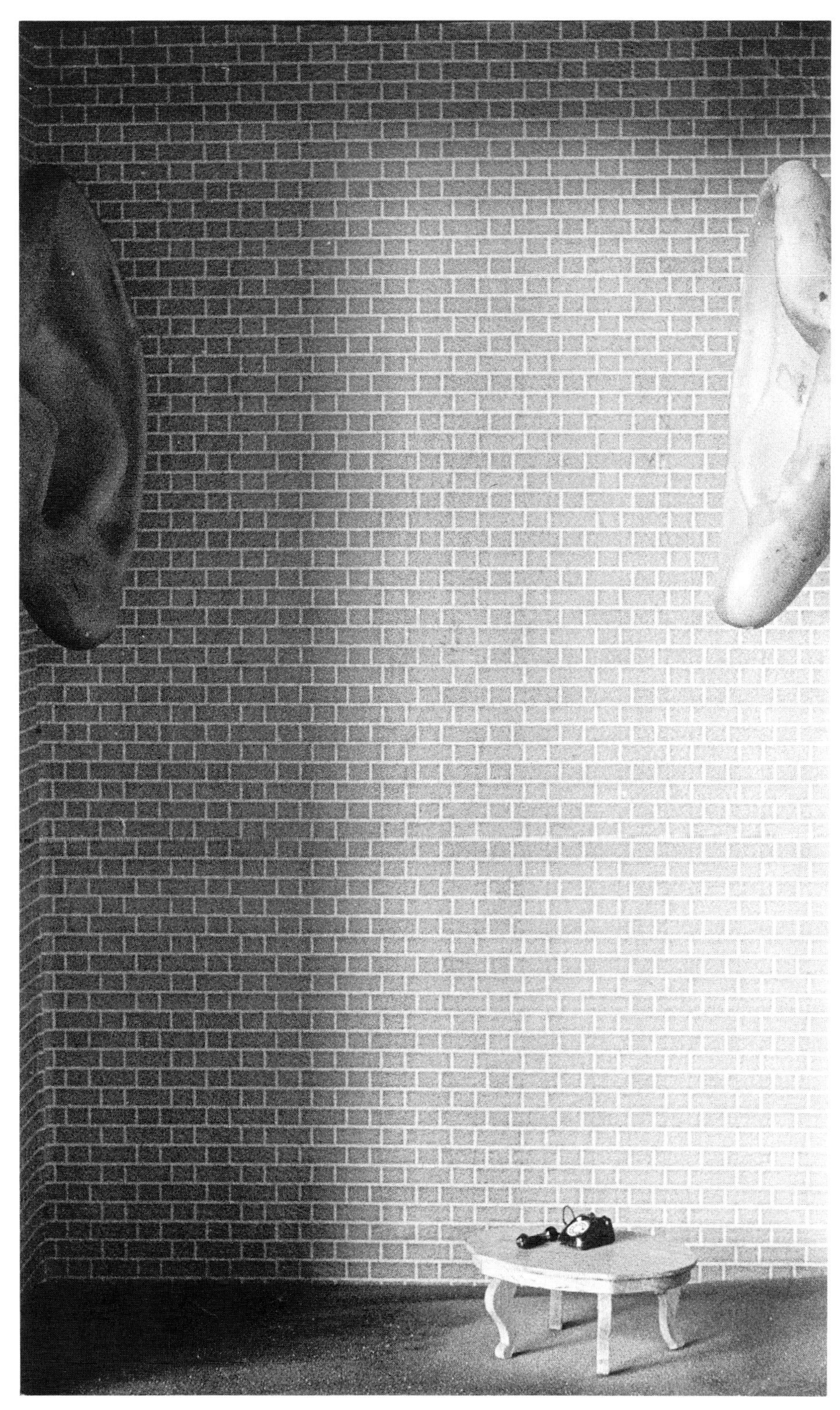

Walls Have Ears, 1990,
Oil on wood, paper, ears, toys, 45 x 30 x 15 cm,
Photograph: Ralph Hughes,
Private collection

CALLUM INNES

Callum Innes was born in Scotland in 1962 and took his postgraduate degree in Painting at Edinburgh College of Art (1984–85) after completing a Bachelor of Arts degree at Grays School of Art, Aberdeen. In 1987 he was awarded the Amsterdam Residency by the Scottish Arts Council. He currently lives and works in Edinburgh.

Innes' painting illustrates the variety of contemporary art in Scotland which, in the public eye at least, is so dominated by large-scale figurative work centred around Glasgow. Innes has turned away from any trace of the human presence in his work, developing instead a far more restrained and abstract means of expression. His paintings consist of tightly controlled skeins of paint, applied evenly across a wax paper surface, then overlaid with drops and dribbles of turpentine — creating glowing layers of translucency. As the turpentine dries, the paintings can change quite noticeably, which has become an intrinsic part of the artist's working method.

On an intellectual level, Innes parallels in paint the qualities of decay and organic growth associated with natural substances, whilst on an emotional level, deep mysterious feelings of memory and introspection are evoked in the gentle surfaces thus created. In his paintings' very self-effacing qualities we are paradoxically drawn in to explore them further, more so than in more demonstrative works by other artists which may offer quicker although less enduring returns. In some respects, Innes' work reflects an almost scientific interest in the microscopic fabric of the natural world — a topic which has been the focus of Scottish arts and sciences for many years and which provides an illustration of the interweaving connections between the organic, the controlled, the accidental and the poetic sides to Nature. Although still at an early stage in his career, the thoroughness and sensitivity of his current work — and its appreciation in Europe and the United States — bodes well for the future.

Innes has had solo exhibitions in Aberdeen, London, Los Angeles and Edinburgh. Important group shows include 'The British Art Show III' and the 'Kunst Europa'.

Repetition Two, 1991,
Oil on canvas, 75 x 62 cm

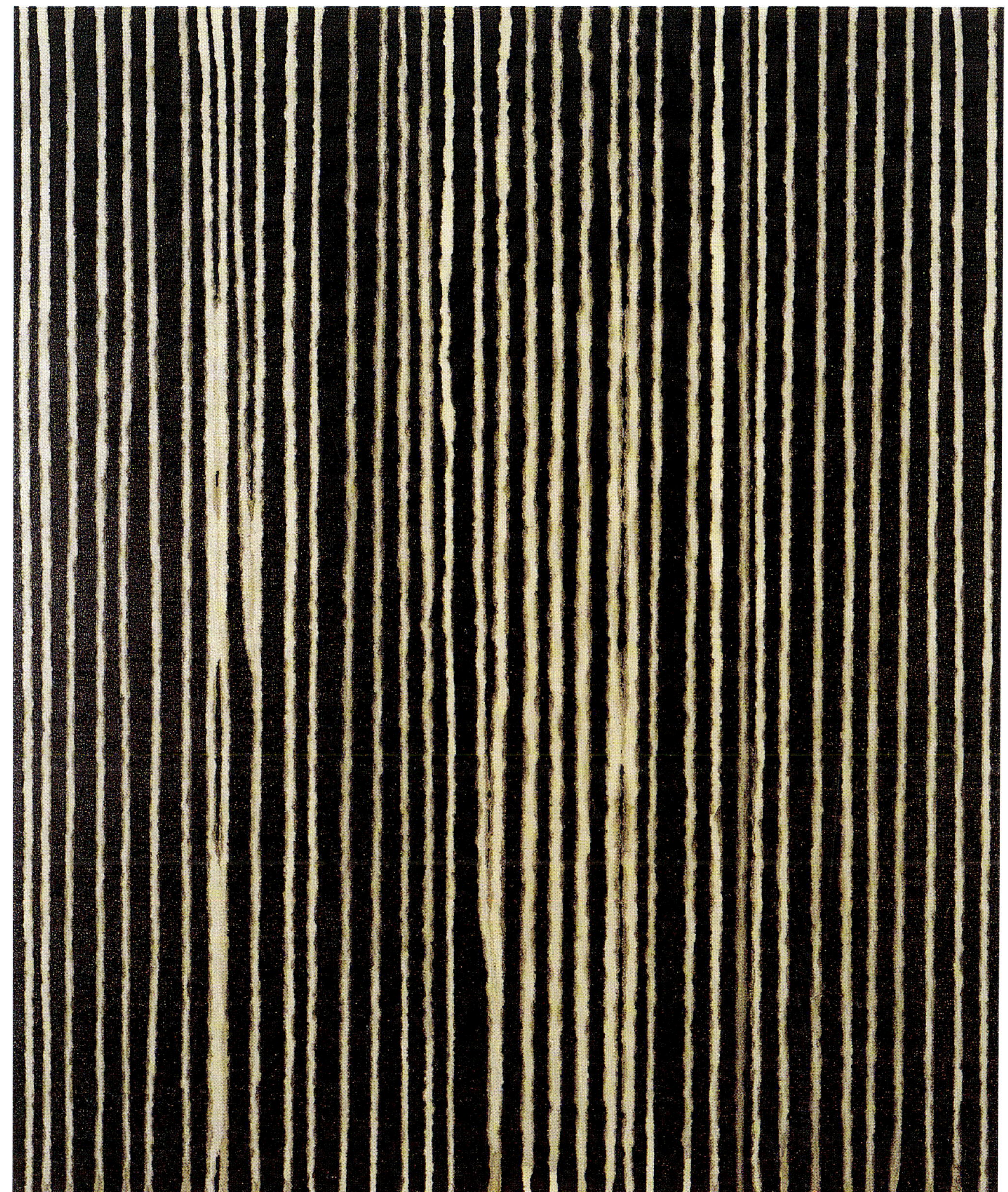

Artist's Comment

Painting is usually additive: my paintings are built up and erased. They often appear to have an essential frailty. When a painting is done, I don't feel that my personality is hanging on the wall, for all to see. It is a piece of work that I have organised and then presented.

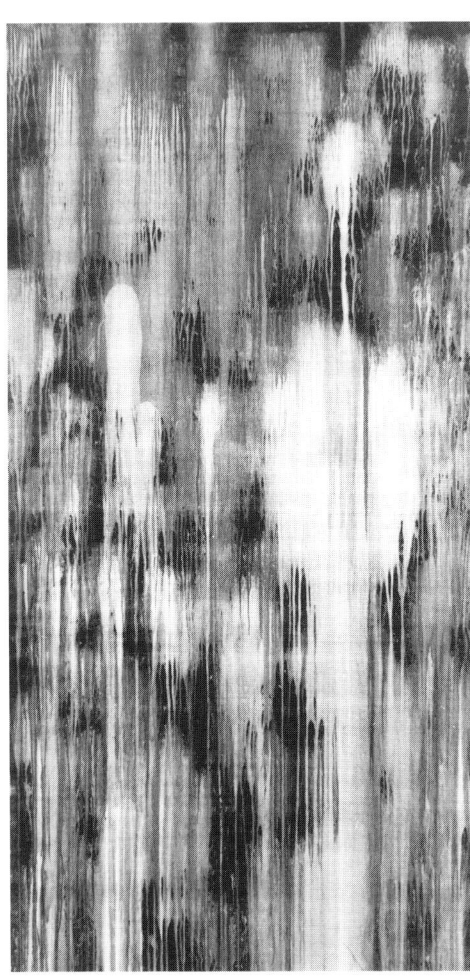

Untitled, 1990/91,
Oil on oil paper, 210 x 100 cm,
Photograph: H. Kosaniuk,
Courtesy Frith Street Gallery, London

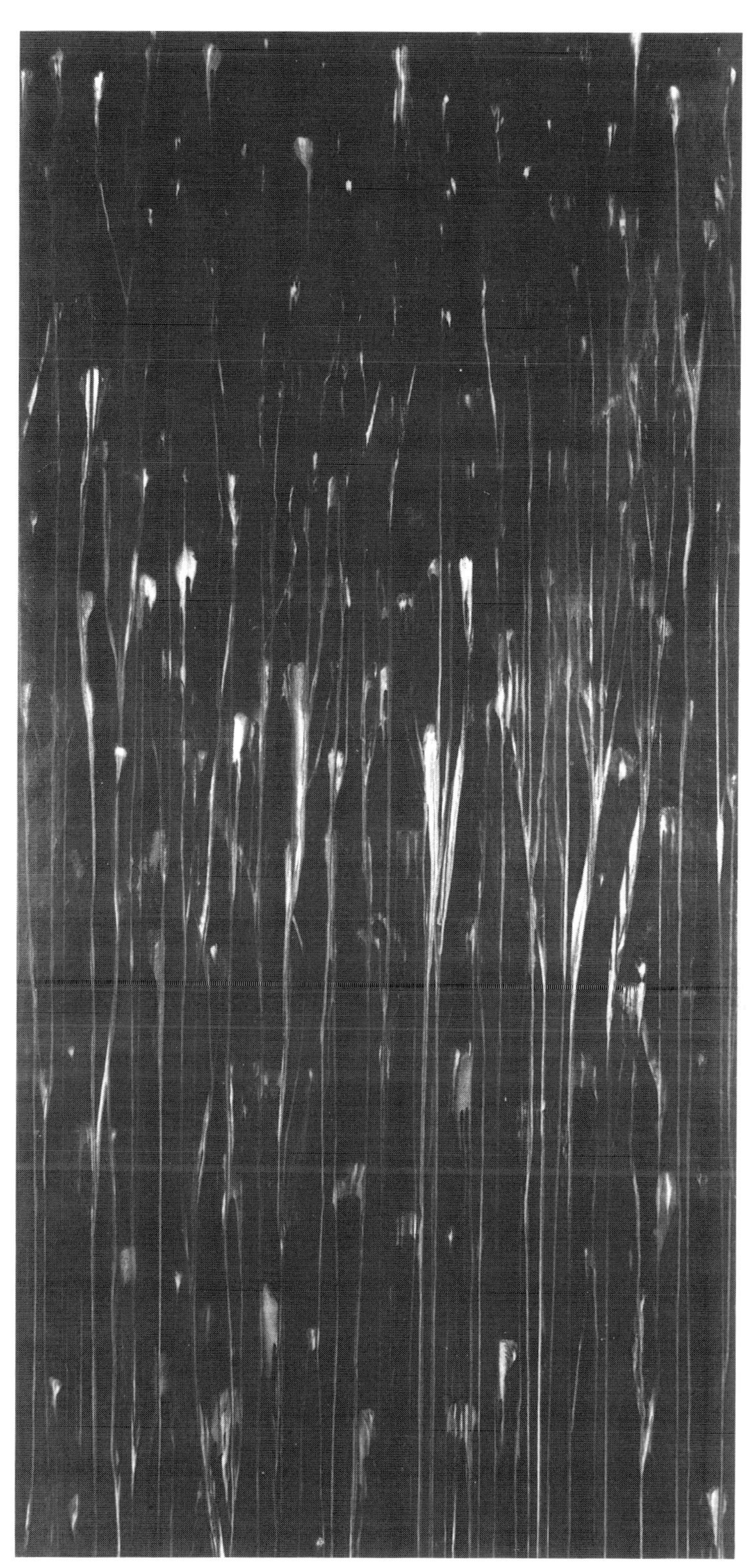

Untitled, 1990/91,
Oil on oil paper, 210 x 100 cm,
Photograph: H. Kosaniuk,
Courtesy Frith Street Gallery, London

Alan Johnston was born in Edinburgh in 1945 and trained at the Royal College of Art, London, and the Kunstakademie, Dusseldorf. He currently teaches in the Fine Art Department of Edinburgh College of Art.

Johnston's severe and philosophical art has found more ready appreciation in Europe, New York and Japan than in the more figurative and colourist traditions dominant in Scotland. His work demands a good degree of concentration from the spectator, who is invited to have a familiarity with major European and Eastern artists and thinkers, as well as the confidence to bring their own emotional responses too.

Johnston's drawings suit both the neutral and sympathetic space of modern architectural sites as well as the art gallery. In discrete wall drawings the artist has installed internationally from Wuppertal and Dusseldorf, Germany, to Edinburgh, Rome and Yamaguchi, Johnston imposes himself quietly on a variety of city environments.

'Nature develops the spirit of place' is a sentiment coined by James Joyce and one keenly appreciated by Johnston whose contemplative art rests on a response to Nature — not a sun-drenched Mediterranean paradise, but a harsher, more muted Northern landscape. Johnston's inspiration is rooted in the artists and writers of the Northern Europe such as Joyce, Casper David Friedrich and Edvard Munch, and their concern with a lucid flowing evocation of time and space. Johnston's art, too, is one of involvement; the belief that humans are part of Nature, not as outside observers. A rounded view of art and Nature such as this is close to Eastern philosophy and art, which, too, has been a great inspiration to Johnston, backed up by many trips to Japan made by the artist.

In both Japanese and Celtic art the dominance of the vertical format resonates with independence and solitude as well as embodying the relationship to sound and music intervals. All these ideas are of great importance and interest to the artist, whose attitude to Nature in many ways goes appreciably beyond the art genre of 'landscape'.

The artist is represented in private and public collections around the world and

Untitled, 1986,
Gesso, acrylic and charcoal on linen,
244 x 183 cm,
Photograph: Jacobson Studio
Courtesy Jack Tilton Gallery

has had major one-person exhibitions in Oxford, Yamaguchi, New York and
Edinburgh.

Artist's Comment

*One was dealing with a true sense of space in the drawn form. What I was looking
for is this: a total visuality of experience: a total sensibility in seeing which governed
all ideas of place, interval and time.*

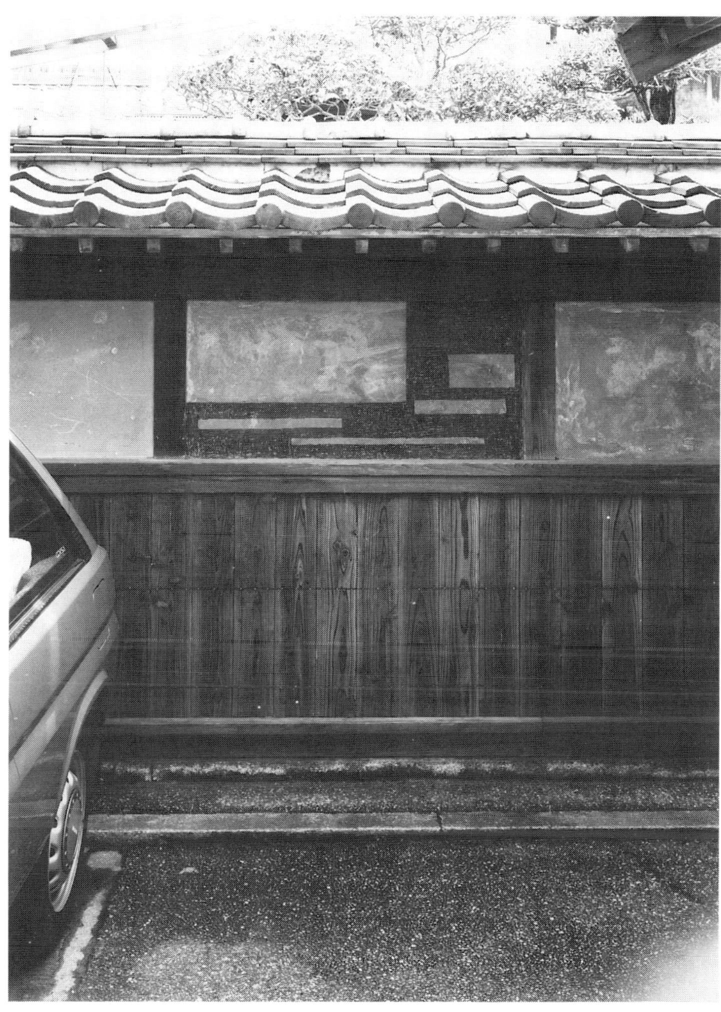

Wall Drawing, Japan, 1989,
Photograph: Alan Johnston

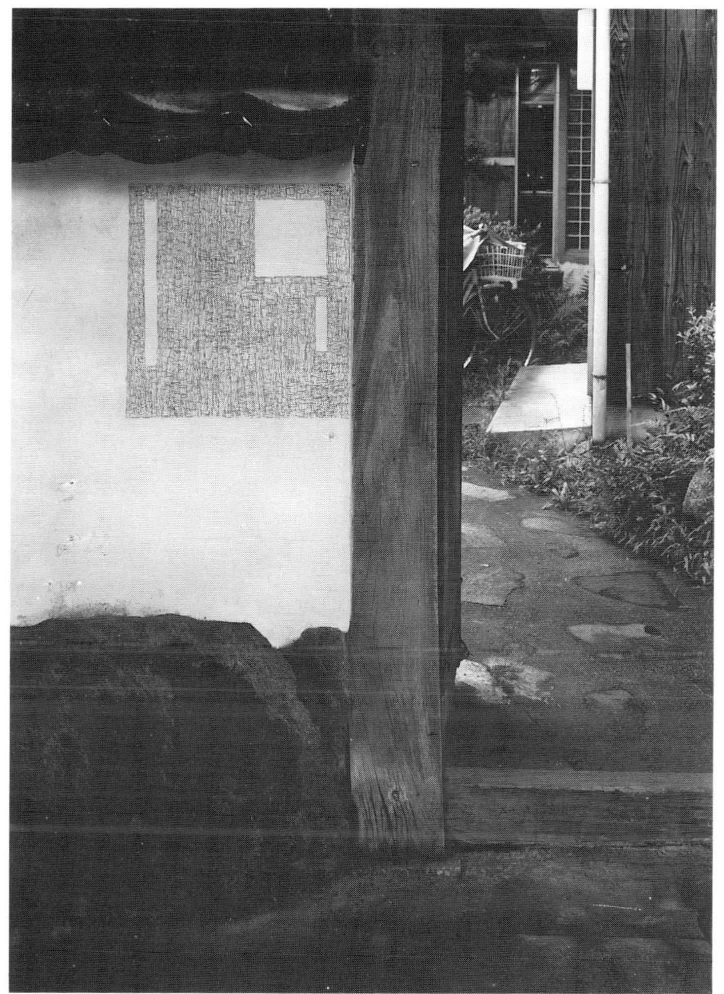

Wall Drawing, Japan, 1989,
Photograph: Alan Johnston

John Kirkwood was born in Edinburgh in 1947 and trained at Duncan of Jordanstone College of Art, Dundee (1965–70). He teaches children with special educational needs in an Edinburgh school.

Strictly speaking, John Kirkwood should not be termed a painter. Being a radical artist who expresses strong social and political criticisms, it is not surprising that he avoids his work being too closely associated with such a culturally 'respectable' medium as painting. If he can be categorised, Kirkwood might be described as a multi-medium practitioner, which reflects his belief that the most characteristic aspect of our technological world is its multi-various means of continuous communication. Thus, he feels that modern art should not remain dominated by a linear narrative attitude, but should partake of the simultaneous multilateral experience of contemporary reality — 'Visual art can reveal many aspects at the same time very effectively, because it can be illogical and it can show oscillation'.

Broadly speaking there are three main mediums of expression in Kirkwood's work which, although varying in physical size and technical execution, interrelate and complement each other to create a unified vision of human, social and environmental concerns. The most conspicuous aspects of his art are the large sculptural relief panels which he has continued to produce since art college. These panels — some abstract, others with specific pictorial images, such as landscape — are collectively called *Bulkheads*. Epic in scale, sombre in mood and tragic in vision, the *Bulkheads* express a deeply pessimistic view of recent human history. The earlier panels, with their use of mass-produced components, dealt with the irresponsible dissolution of heavy industry and as such had a more specific Scottish relevance, but in recent years the artist has focused his attention in his panels on the awesome threat to worldwide political and ecological stability that increases with every major military conflict. The *Bulkheads* are truly History Paintings. They operate on a factual as well as metaphorical realm of reality, giving them a Goyaesque nightmare quality of profound psychological intensity.

If Kirkwood's relief panels tend to be formal in composition and funereal in

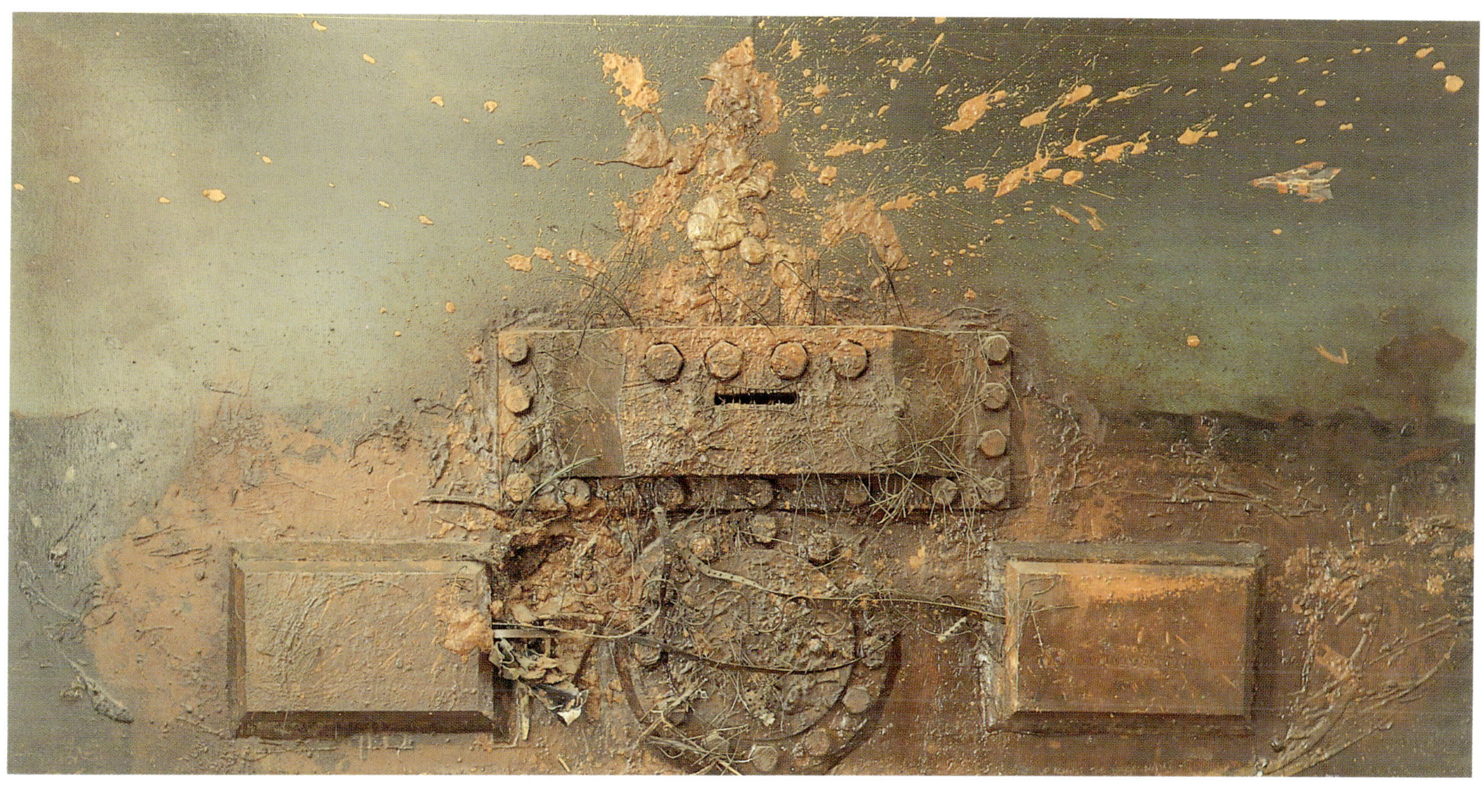

Up Against the Juggernaut, 1987,
Mixed media, 122 x 244 cm,
Photograph: Ralph Hughes

mood, his other two chosen means of expression — photomontage and hand-coloured etchings — are by contrast fluid and dynamic. They more obviously reflect his fascination with the 'flux of things' between order and chaos in forces operating at all levels of experience from nuclear warfare to electromagnetic energy. His photomontages, employing a whole range of different types of images — for example, grainy documentary to high gloss photography — present scenes of chaotic destruction where the ruthless pursuit of economic and military superiority reach their apocalyptic climax. In a very different mood his etchings, executed in a non-artistic engineering drawing style, celebrate the dynamic power of matter to create and recreate at the sub-atomic level of universal existence. Here Kirkwood seems to be echoing William Blake's belief that 'energy is eternal delight'.

John Kirkwood has had a number of solo exhibitions. Until now he has mainly shown his work in Edinburgh. He has also had a number of Scottish Arts Council awards and his work is represented in their collection as well as other institutions, such as the Contemporary Arts Society, London.

Artist's Comment

In my etchings I want to show order and chaos, the flux between the two, while the Bulkheads are an attempt to return social and ethical values to the art of modernity.

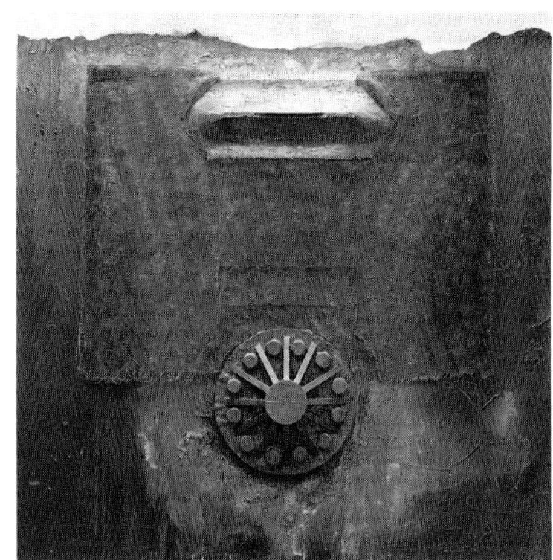

Bulkhead with Beak and F15 Overhead,
1980,
Mixed media, 183 x 183 cm,
Collection of the artist

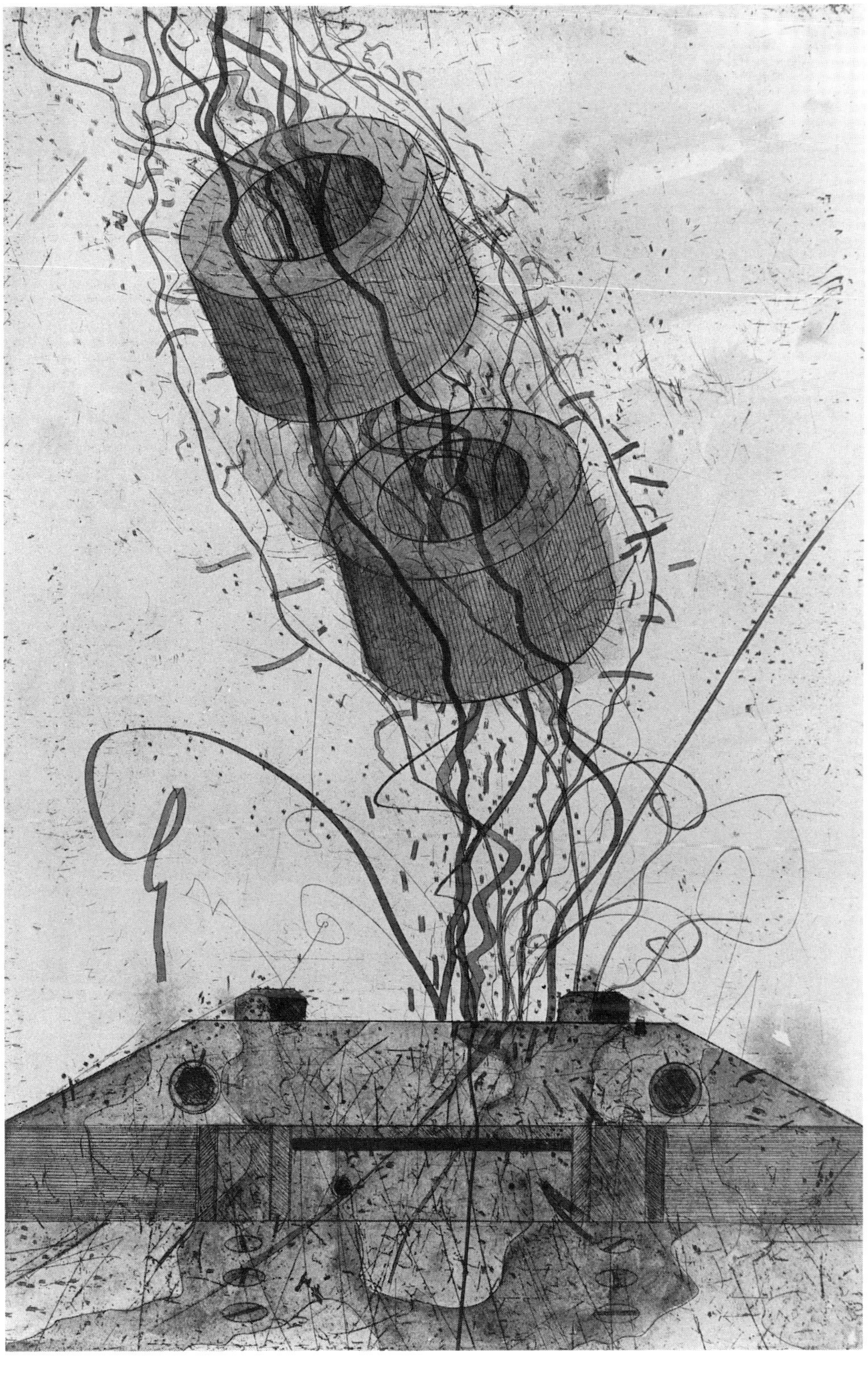

Discharge Crack II, 1977,
Hand tinted etching, 89 x 51 cm

Jack Knox was born in Kirkintilloch in 1936 and studied at Glasgow School of Art from 1953–57. He attended the André Lhote Atelier, Paris, in 1958. After teaching for a time at the Duncan of Jordanstone College of Art he was appointed as Head of Drawing and Painting at Glasgow in 1981.

Knox has held a prominent position in Scottish and British painting in general as early as 1971, when he had a highly successful one-person show at the Serpentine Gallery, London. He was fortunate enough to see the major exhibition of American Abstract Expressionism in Brussels in 1959 — the experience influenced him deeply and Knox's confident handling of paint and dramatic technique are indebted to some of the great American artists such as Gottlieb and Motherwell.

His favourite subjects are luscious still lifes and domestic scenes, strongly theatrical and physical in character. The various accoutrements which the artist assembles hold their own space with an assertiveness reminiscent of the best of Dutch 17th century still life painting, where the material existence of the objects is emphasised. Clearly, all the articles Knox paints — such as bicycles, coffee pots, plants and bread — are meant to be picked up, handled, used as part of everyday life. Yet, an actual human presence is absent in Knox's paintings — so, as if to compensate, his still life subjects seem to have an animated and anamorphic quality, which make them spring from the canvas. The artist's expressive and emphatic handling of paint, developed over his long career, adds to the life of each work. The repeated still life motifs have become familiar stock images for the artist, yet, despite their availability, they are never drawn directly from life and hence have a mysterious presence. As he says —'I remember the essence. What isn't remembered isn't worth remembering!' Underlying the assertive depiction of everyday objects, then, there is a personal and subjective imagery not far below the surface.

The artist has had important one-person exhibitions in Edinburgh, London and Glasgow, as well as group exhibitions across the United Kingdom and Europe. He is represented in many public and private collections throughout the world, including the Scottish National Gallery of Modern Art and the Scottish Arts Council.

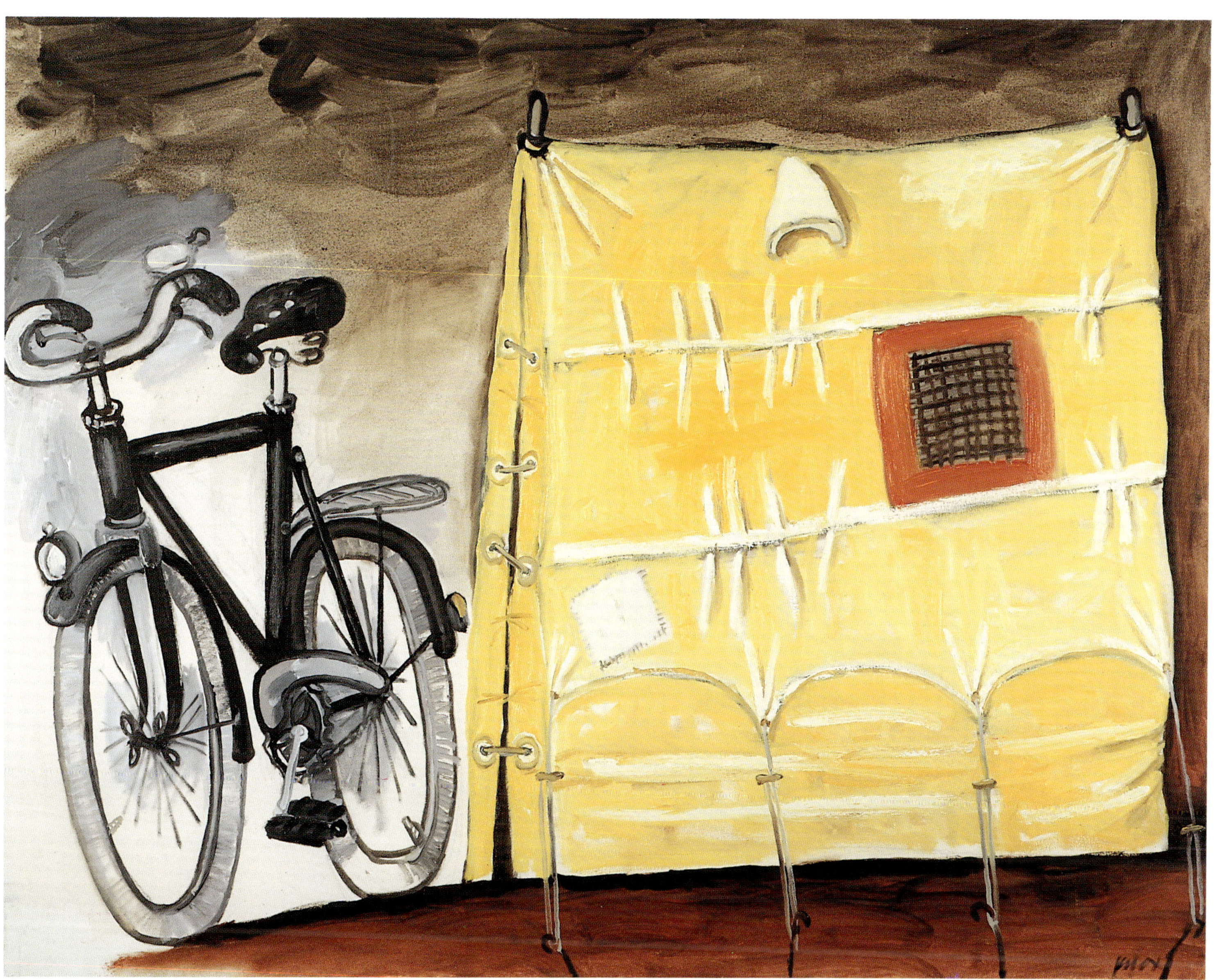

Bike and Tent, 1989,
Oil on canvas, 114 x 147 cm,
Photograph: Antonia Reeve

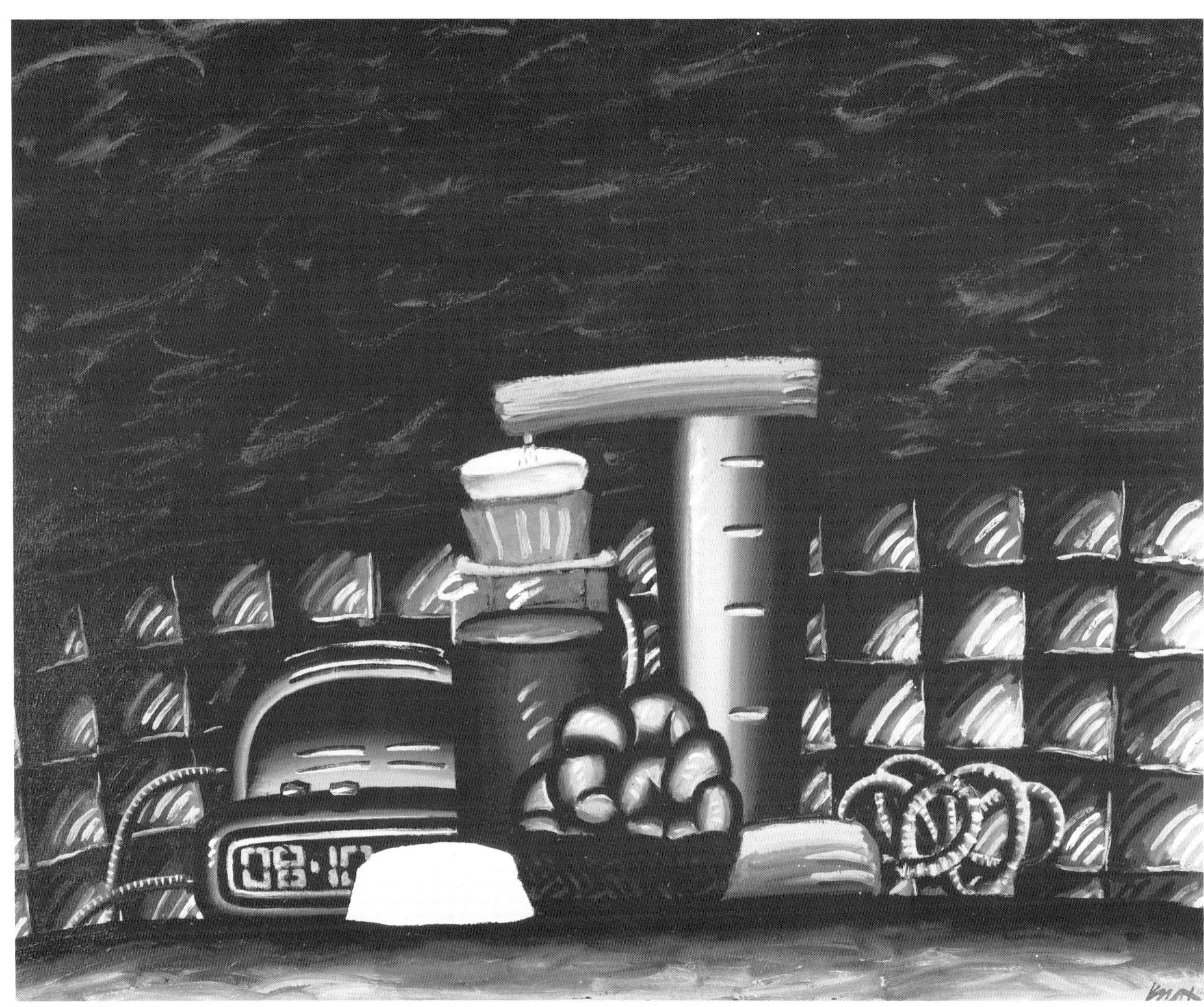

Breakfast, 1982,
Oil on canvas, 122 x 152 cm,
Photograph: Sean Hudson,
Collection of the artist

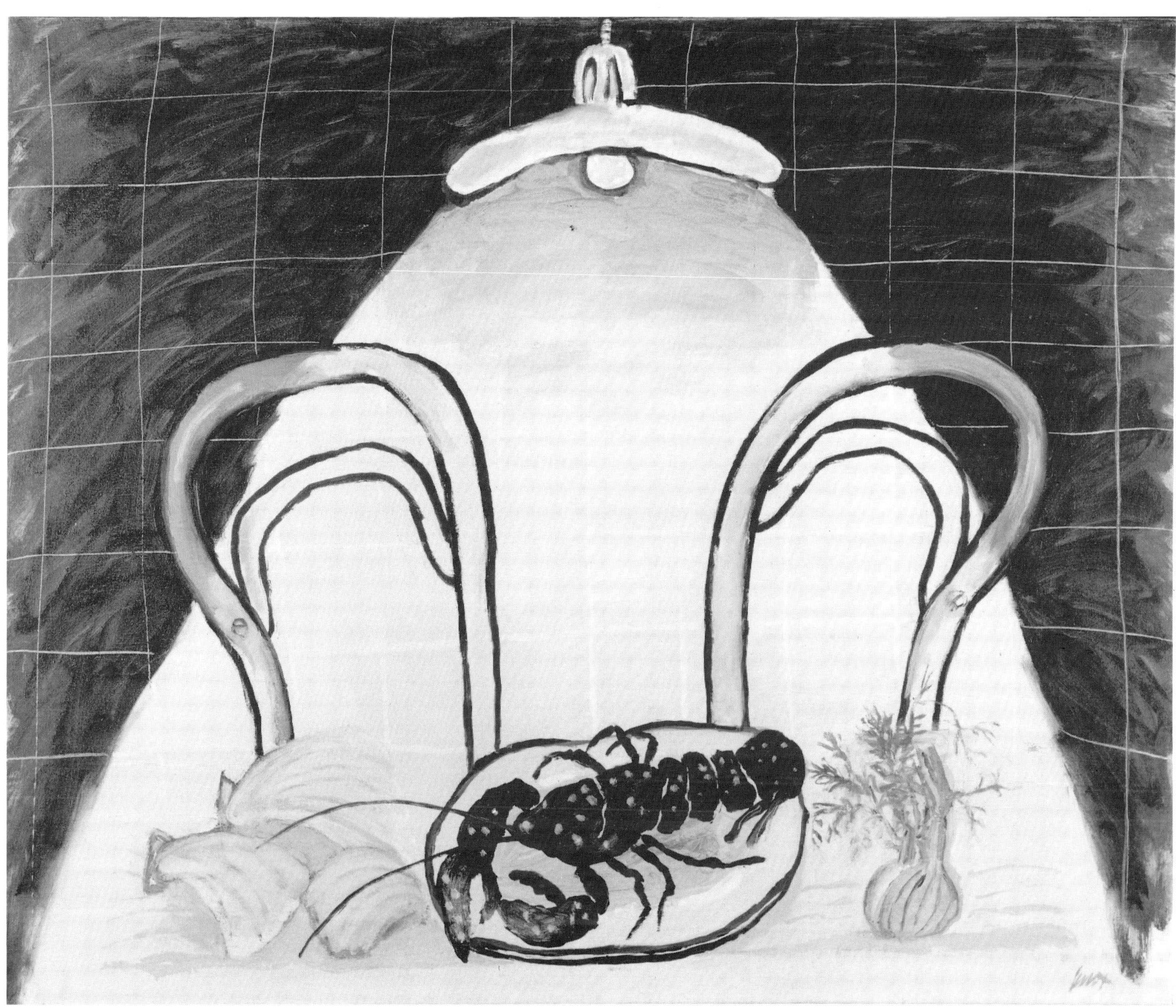

Kitchen, 1989,
Oil on canvas, 112 x 137 cm,
Photograph: Antonia Reeve,
Collection of the artist

Henry Kondracki was born in Edinburgh in 1953. He went to Byam Shaw School of Art (1981–82) and graduated with First Class Honours from the Slade School of Art, London (1982–86). Since then he has concentrated on his career as a painter, attaching himself to the Vanessa Devereux Gallery and, more recently, to the William Jackson Gallery, London.

In a recent interview in *Scam* magazine (August/September 1990), Henry Kondracki discussed his art in this way — 'It's a feeling that you're trying to get over and you're using these images to try to transmit that feeling, just as Giotto did when he put those angels in the sky when Christ was lying dead. The angels look as if they've been knocked back, in a state of grief, and it's as if something physical is hitting them. Giotto's trying to transmit the idea of grief knocking you over.'

Despite the way it is sometimes taught, the history of art is not a straightforward progression with all artists working towards some common goal of agreed excellence. The course of art throughout the centuries is full of twists and turns, deviations to the right and left and out and out 'U' turns. It is necessary at times for certain artists to take a reverse view of the history of painting and seek to go right back to the primeval, primitive and psychological origins of creativity. This has been one of the great revitalising forces of modern art from Gauguin to Miro. As the above quotation shows, Henry Kondracki, likewise responds to the directness of original sincere art as a stimulating demonstration of the continuing expressive power of narrative image-making to move people as profoundly now as it did in the past. His own painting clearly reveals his faith that such an intuitive form of pictorial language is still eminently valid. As such it can just as well deal with the psychological reality of his own personal history along with the everyday experiences of modern life, as it did with the Passion of Christ in Giotto's day. Yet, as with the early Renaissance master, Kondracki's paintings are the product of a highly skilled and clear-sighted artist. The crude, seemingly slap-dash appearance that his work can initially suggest is partly a result of his strong reaction to the 'tasteful and gentle rendition' of much of Scottish academic painting. By contrast, his own paintings are

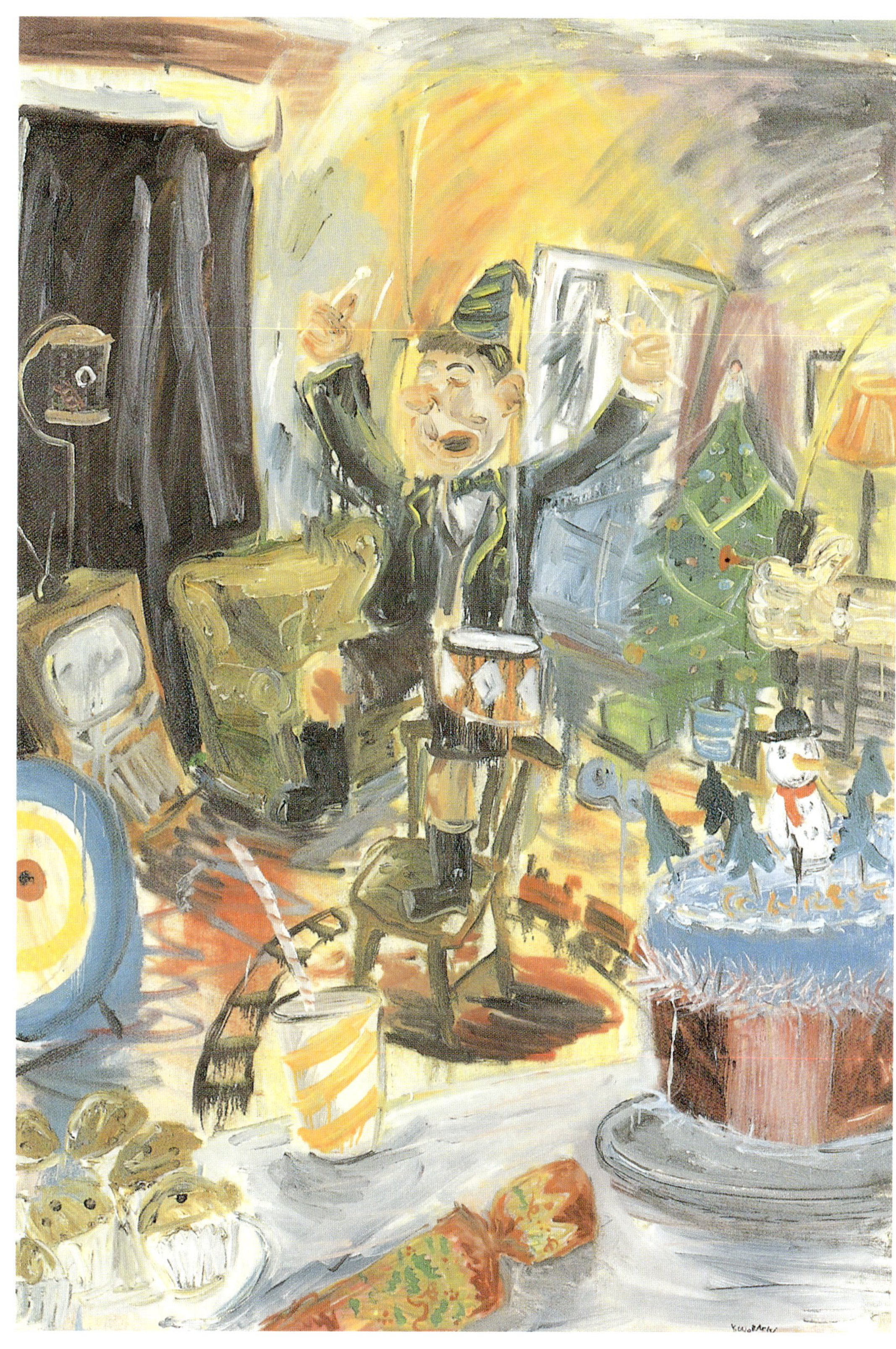

Party Piece, 1990,
Oil on canvas, 152 x 107 cm

raw and exuberant. Yet they are also highly controlled exercises in picture making.
This is demonstrated by the scale on which he can paint, the complexity of some of
his compositions, the evocative power of his tragi-comic narratives and, most of all,
the sheer manipulative power he has over the medium of paint. Kondracki's pictures
have a fresh immediacy which delights, but also a mysterious aura which fascinates.

Henry Kondracki has had considerable success with one-man shows in Edinburgh
and London as well as Melbourne (13 Verity Street Gallery, 1988). He has won a
number of awards and his work is represented in private and public collections, such
as the British Arts Council.

Artist's Comment

I attempt to portray the beauty, ugliness and extraordinariness of everyday living.
I build images that are a synthesis of thought, memory, emotion, fact and fiction.

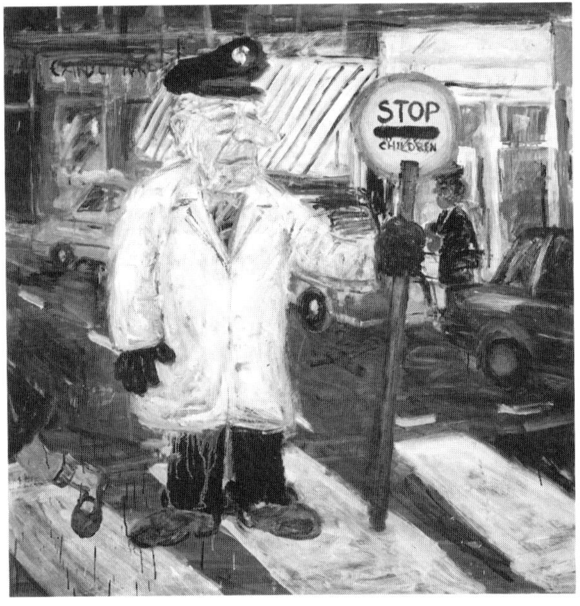

Lollipop Man, 1991,
Oil on board, 122 x 122 cm

Mersey Beaucoup, 1986,
Oil on canvas, 183 x 183 cm

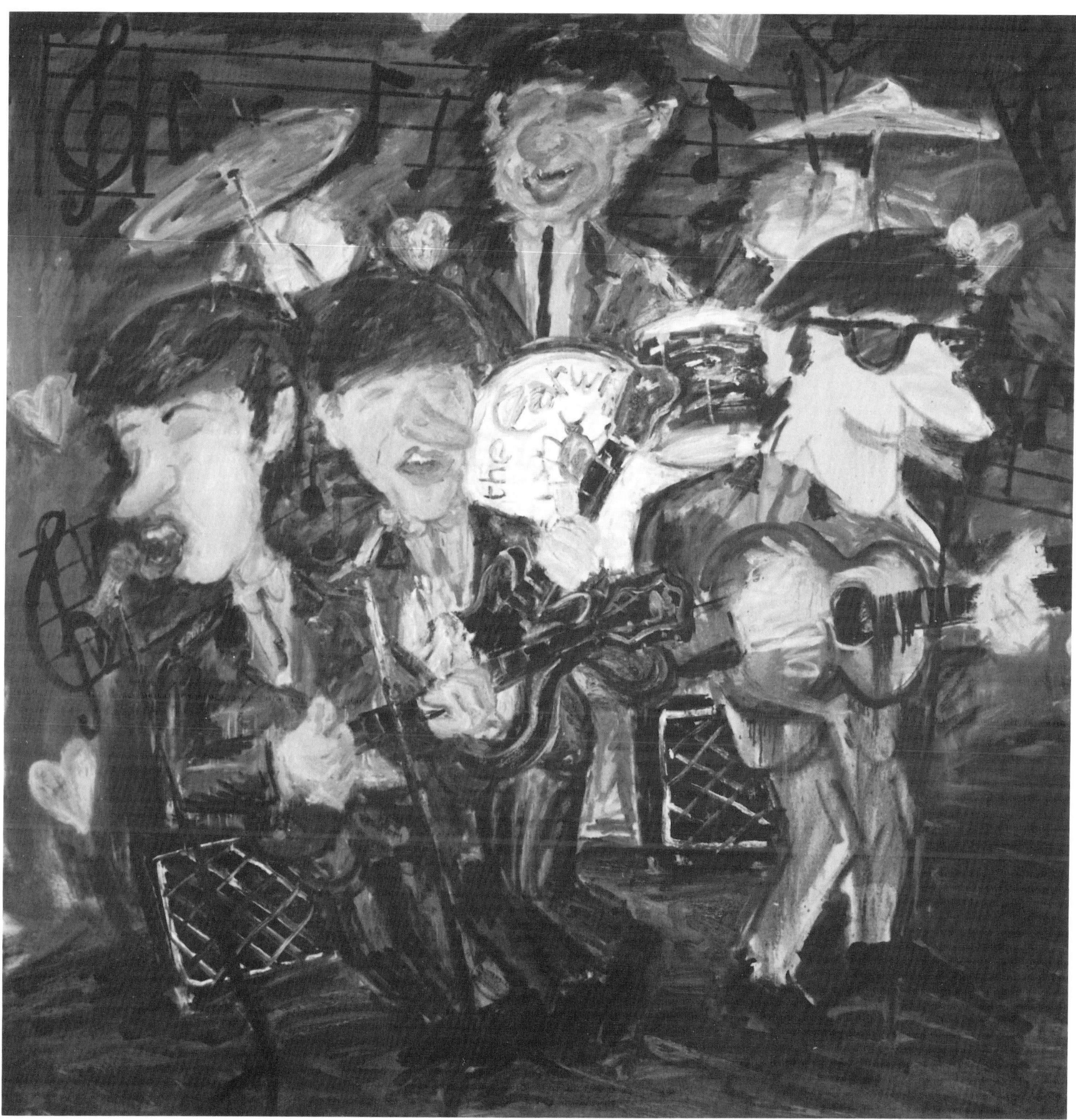
the Garwi

EILEEN LAWRENCE

Eileen Lawrence was born in Leith, Scotland in 1946. Between 1963 and 1967 she took her Diploma at Edinburgh College of Art, graduating with postgraduate qualifications in 1968. She currently lives and works in Leith, near Edinburgh.

Lawrence's paintings are highly symbolic and evocative. Her preferred medium is watercolour, which she uses on an unusually large scale and in an innovative way. Across the picture plane are scattered images often relate to flight and birds — feathers and eggs predominated in her early work. This imagery is directed to seemingly contradictory ends, at one time both highly realistic, even to the extent of using real objects embedded into the surface, whilst at the same time being mystical and meditative. She explores, instinctively, the relationship between the real and the spiritual worlds —after all, this has been a serious concern in British art going back at least as far as William Blake, who aspired to 'see the world in a grain of sand'. Lawrence follows Blake in the belief that an intensely detailed and searching analysis of the real world can lead us directly to wider questions of religion and human existence.

Prior to 1985, the predominance of black and white, as well as an imaginary script which appeared in many works, all evoked the power of religious texts — particularly the Taoist *Book of Changes* and *The Egyptian Book of the Dead*. These and other scripts operate in a similar way to Lawrence's method, exploiting the non-specific power of sequential images —objects are made to float across a pale ground, rising to the surface as if rooted in a deep, subconscious dream-world.

A visit to Turkey in 1985 brought with it an interest in the heightening powers of colour, earth-reds, golds and blues turning into even stronger hues as her work developed. At one and the same time, Lawrence shows great intellectual, almost scientific, discipline in the way diagrammatic depictions are laid before us in her paintings, whilst never allowing the treatment to become merely descriptive. They always allude to a world as spiritual and mysterious as it is real.

Lawrence has participated in one-person and group exhibitions throughout the United Kingdom and Europe. She is represented in major public and private collections in the United Kingdom, Europe and the United States.

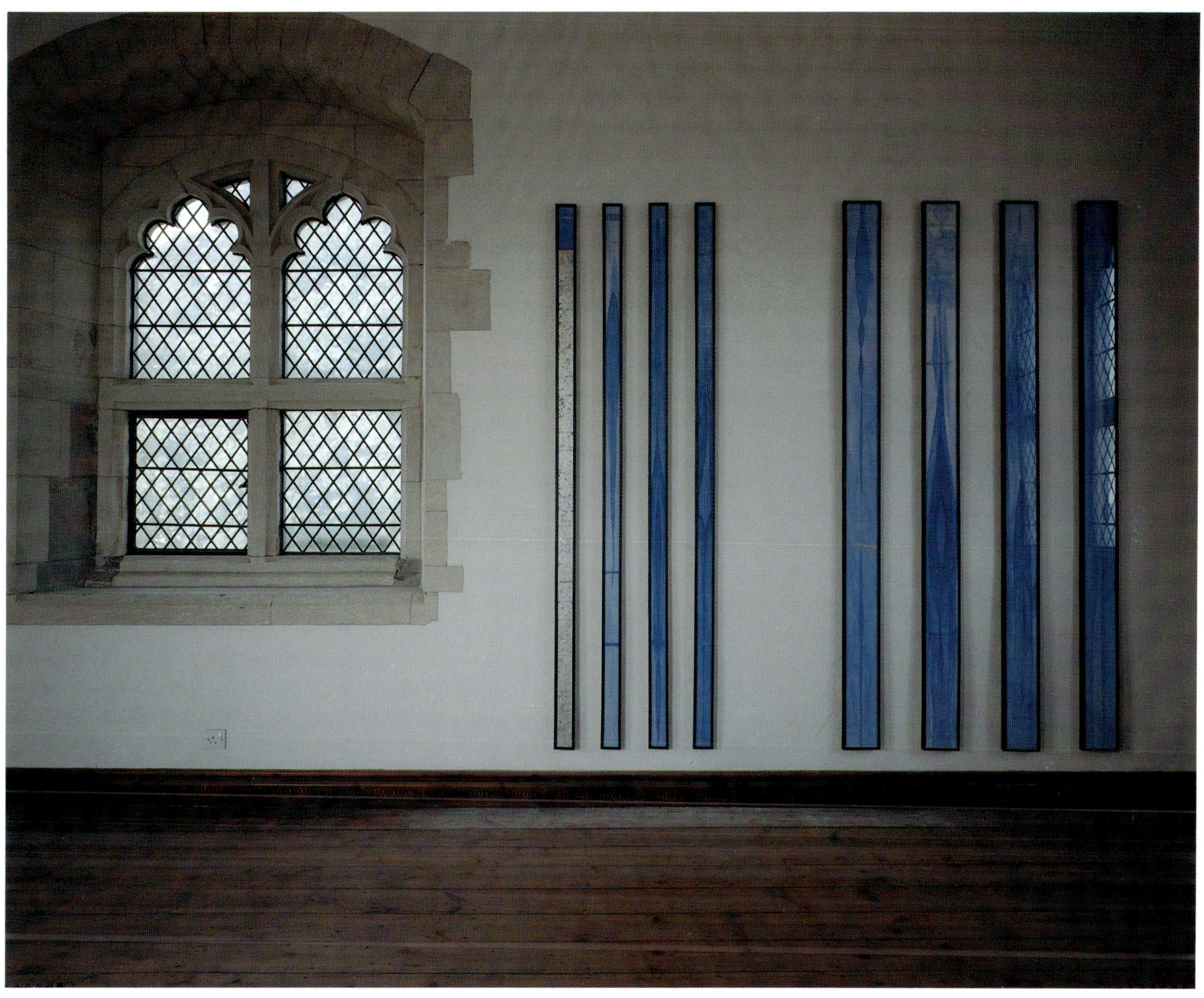

Lincoln Prayer Sticks, 1990,
Watercolour on paper, 240 x 8 cm and 240 x 15 cm,
Photograph: Rod Shone

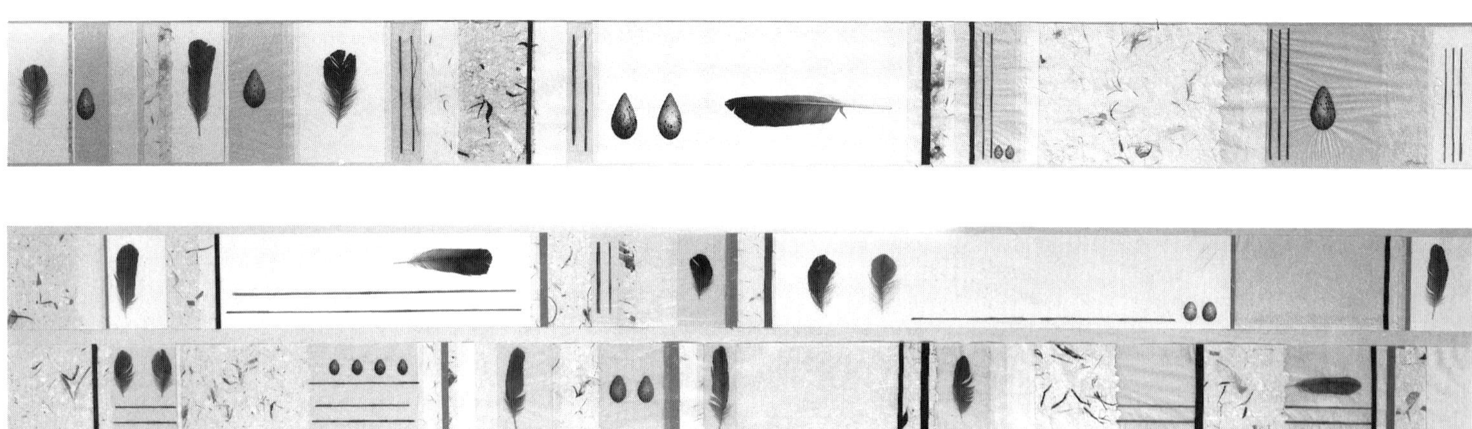

Scroll I, 1977,
Watercolour on paper, 25 x 240 cm

Scroll III, 1977,
Watercolour on paper, 38 x 244 cm

Heron Cone, 1986,
Watercolour and gold leaf on paper, 62 x 50 cm

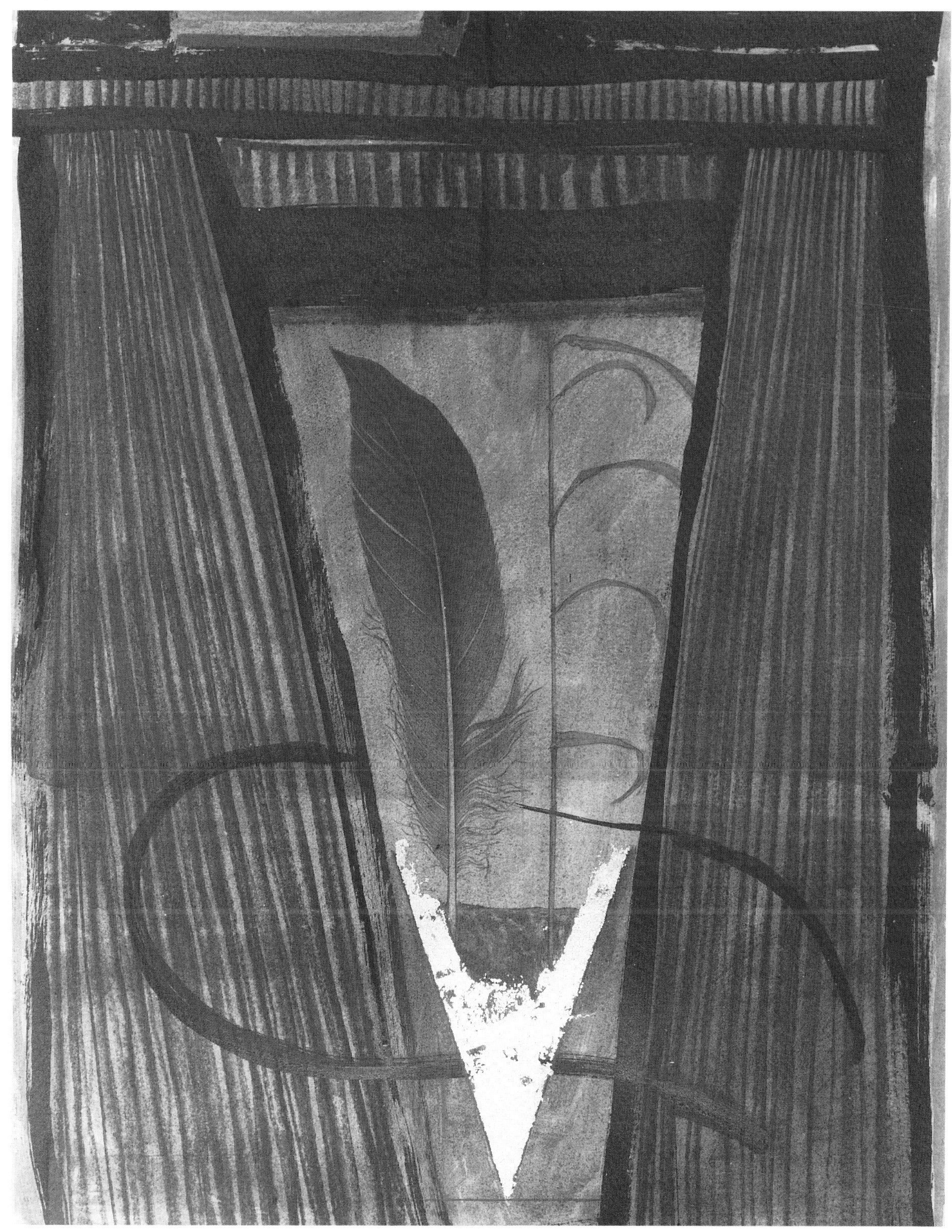

Thomas Lawson was born in Glasgow in 1951. From 1969 to 1973 he studied at the University of St Andrews, before completing two years postgraduate study at the University of Edinburgh. He subsequently left for New York in 1975. He currently lives and teaches in Los Angeles, USA.

Lawson is very much an outsider in terms of indigenous Scottish painting, having moved to New York early in his career and having his first one-person exhibition in Scotland as recently as 1990. Although Lawson often uses oil paint, he seldom leaves the surface of the canvas unified in the traditional sense, choosing to disrupt the image by overlaying dots, lettering and other marks. This serves to remind us that we are looking at an artificial creation produced by the artist and that the once coherent vision of our world no longer holds true today. Whilst this attitude to oil painting is not unique among Scottish artists, its stylistic progressiveness has meant that Lawson's work has found more ready acceptance in the art worlds of the United States and Europe.

From 1977 Lawson has used a variety of sources for his paintings, from children's comic books to newspaper photographs, which were begun in 1979. The importance of these sources was that they were originally intended to be seen once, then thrown away. The artist transferred the crude lines and colouring of newspaper reproductions into paint, resisting any temptation to allow the sensual textures of oil to come to the fore. Two worlds, one of everyday pulp, the other of 'high' art, were made to collide — a technique Lawson picks up and develops from the artists of the Pop generation in the 1960s. Two series in particular, one of murdered corpses (1981), the other of injured children's faces (1982), are highly charged, despite the dead-pan handling. In the latter we are shown the reality of some young people's lives, who have been long since separated from the supposed innocence of childhood. That this theme has been an enduring one in art enables Lawson quite deliberately to open up the whole question of aesthetic emotion as it is channelled towards art works and the very serious, yet often distanced, feelings we experience when hearing of public tragedies on the news.

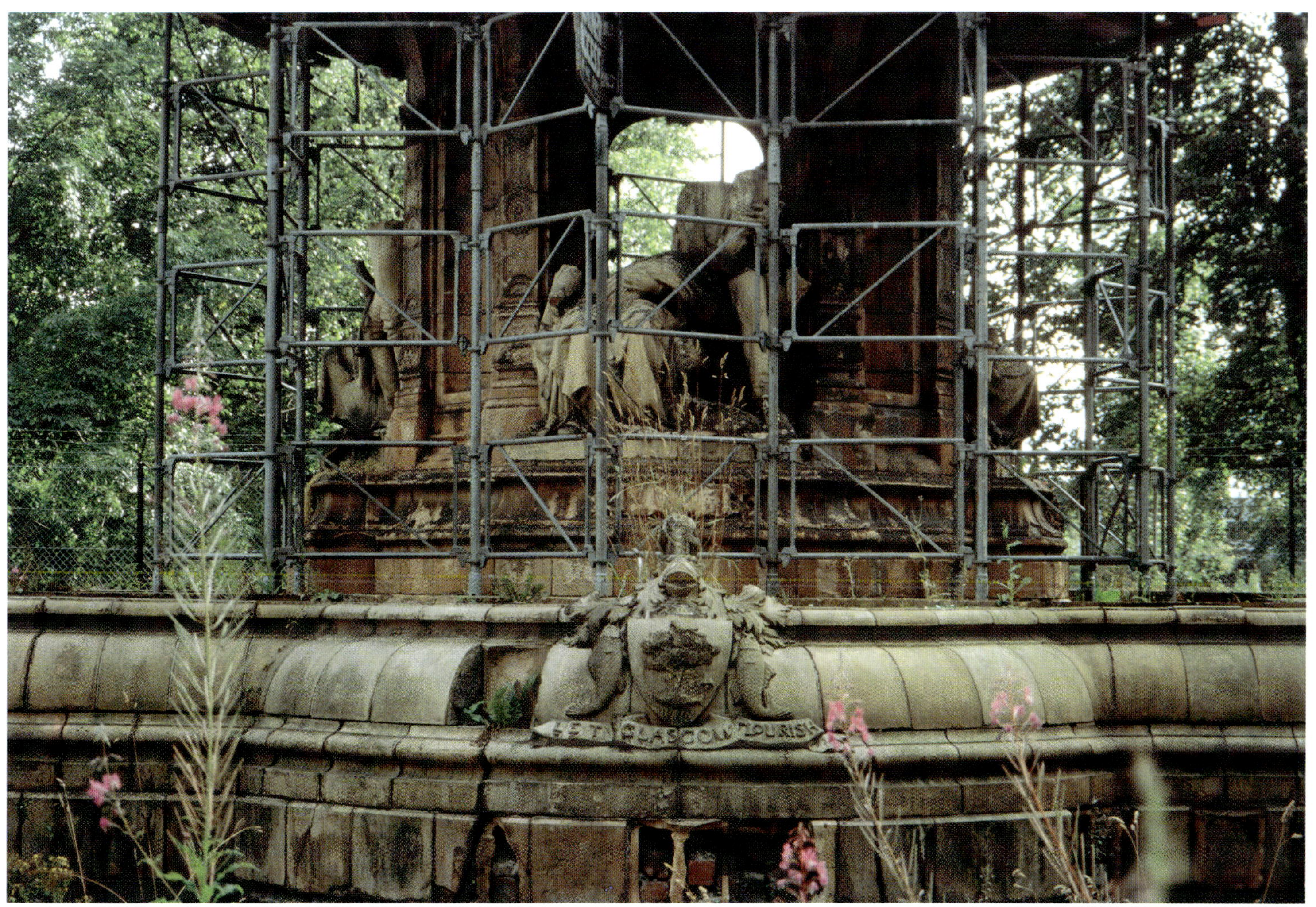

Glasgow Green and Flourishing, 1990,
Scanachrome on canvas, 400 x 600 cm
Photograph: Thomas Lawson

In a different direction taken more recently, Lawson has expressed his interest in
the social power of public sculptures and all they embody in terms of civic ambition
and symbolism —they hover like anonymous spectres over many of our most
important cities and are evoked in a variety of the artist's pieces such as *Glasgow
Green and Flourishing* (1990, Glasgow) and *Angel Caido* (1991, Madrid). Lawson
relies on his own ambivalence between the false values they impose on a city's
populace and the nostalgic affection for absolute verities which these sculptures seek
to personify and encourage.

As well as his work as an artist, Lawson has received international recognition
for his critical writing and has been invited to curate numerous exhibitions of
contemporary art. His work is represented in many public and private collections of
contemporary art worldwide.

Artist's Comment

*What I'm interested in as an artist is participating in culture. I work with the materials
of culture, that is, the pre-existing framework and that is what intrigues me. The
evidence of culture is what I look at and think about and mess with in some way, so
it is inevitable that I have to use images that exist already. The idea of searching for
some kind of original image through material is an absurdity to me. The images are
there and I translate them in various media, alter their context, make them
something else. This translation certainly flirts with the possibility of meaning, but
ultimately sets out to deny the simple-minded readings normally associated with
figurative art. Stories are better told in the pub than on the walls of a gallery.*

Wild Horses, 1989,
Acrylic on masonite, neon lights,
wood, 231 x 351 x 14 cm,
Courtesy Metro Pictures, New York

He Shot His Best Buddy, 1981,
Oil on canvas, 122 x 249 cm,
Courtesy Metro Pictures, New York

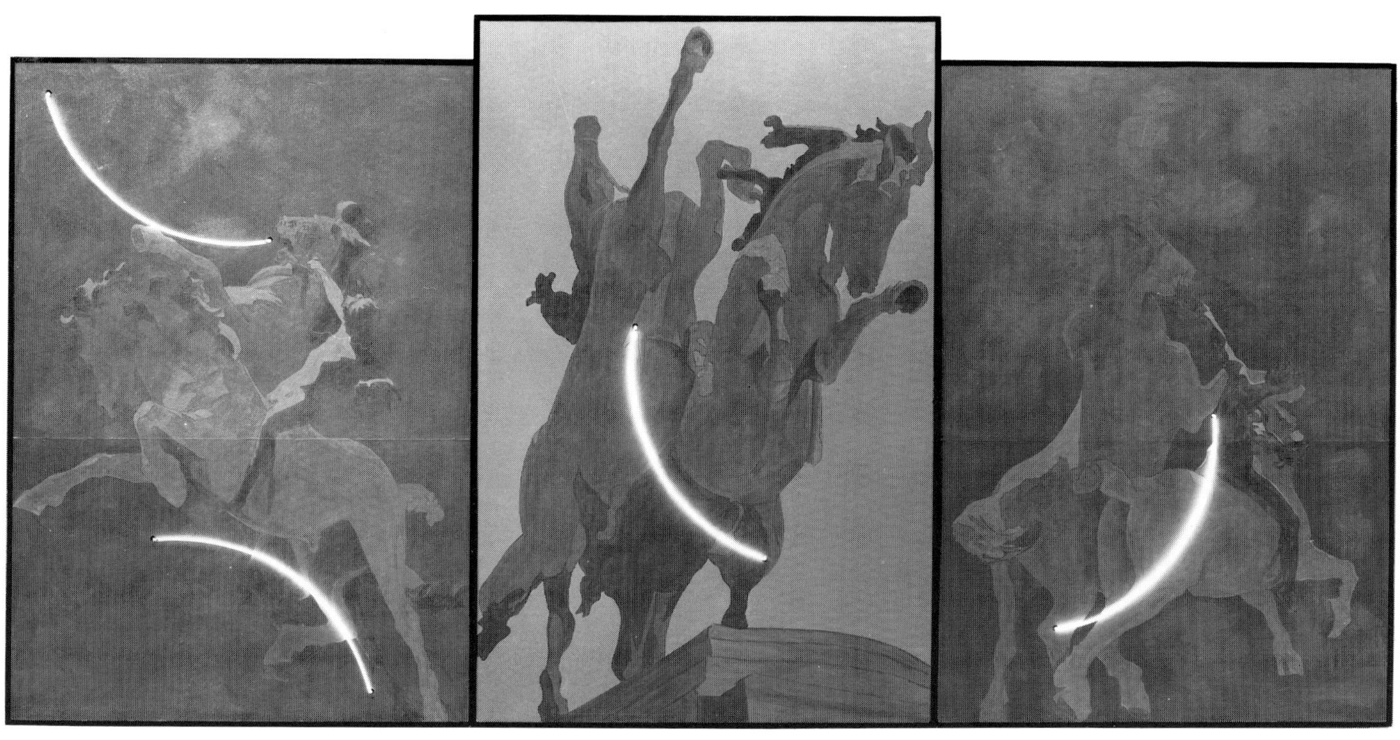

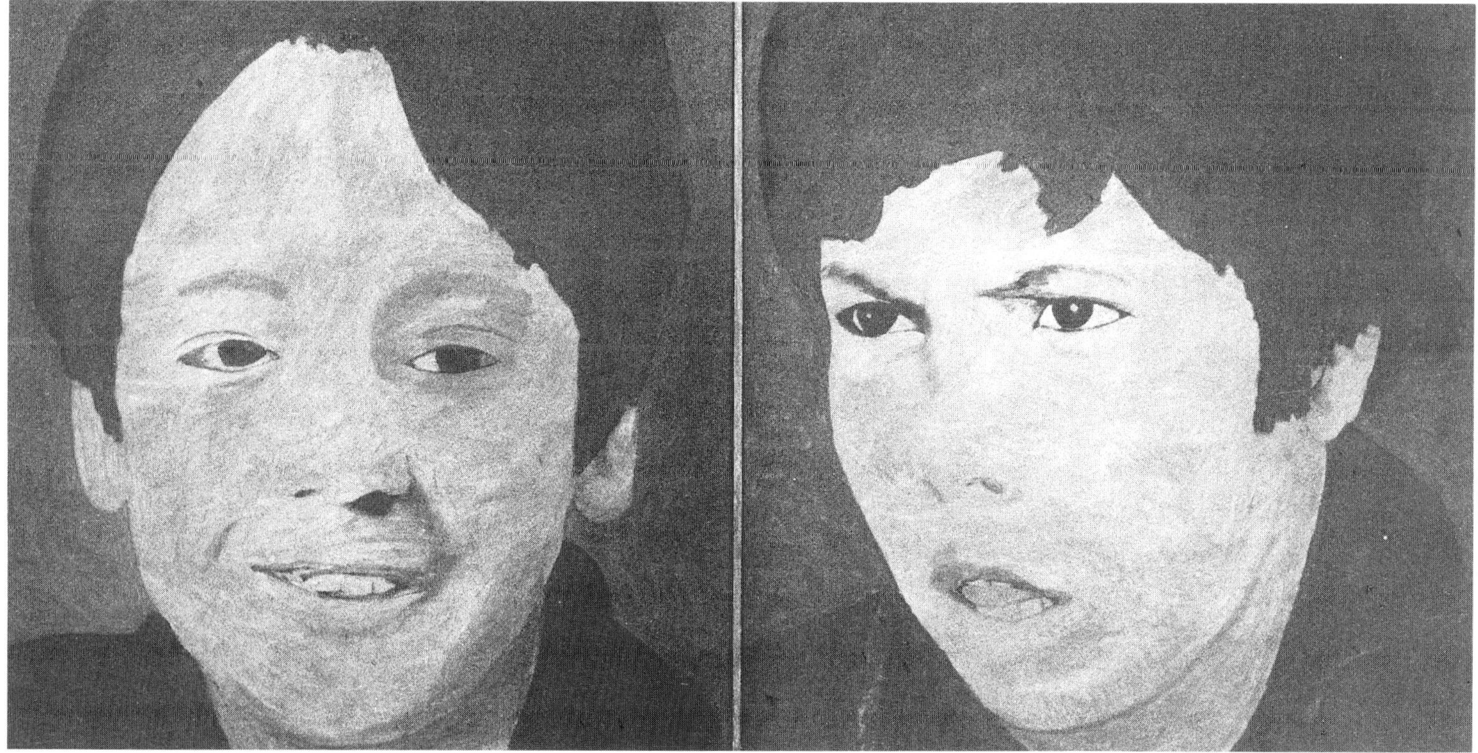

KEITH McINTYRE

Keith McIntyre was born in Edinburgh in 1959 and studied Drawing and Painting at Duncan of Jordanstone College of Art, Dundee from 1978–83. Since 1984 he has lectured in the Department of Fine Art, Glasgow School of Art.

In McIntyre there exists a fine representative of the figurative graphic-led artist, central to the Scottish tradition in art. His is also an artist who seeks to maintain strong and healthy links with the community from which it springs.

McIntyre's paintings and drawings exude a strong sense of place and of theatricality: the sheer force of draughtsmanship in his work provokes the attention of the spectator and engages the senses directly. Heightened colour in his paintings is usually a device used by the artist to emphasise the drawing and compositional strength rather than being an end in itself.

Throughout his career, McIntyre has maintained a fascination with the formality and deep power of ritual in its various forms, be it in dancing, acting or in religious worship. From 1983, when he moved to the small town of Moffat, Dumfriesshire, he became intrigued by traditional occupations and symbols which dominated the locality. He produced a powerful series of drawings based on a civic sculpture of 'The Moffat Ram', which became for McIntyre a symbol for ancient archetypes and also male sexual power.

Since then, his works have become more obviously theatrical. His part-factual, part-fictional painted narratives seem to dance across the canvas. Not surprisingly, McIntyre's most recent major commission was for the theatre — in 1990, he painted huge backdrops for the 'image theatre' event *Jock Tamson's Bairns*. Luridly coloured figures and animals loom out, such in *Devil Dogs Dancing*, strongly reminiscent of both German Expressionist painting and theatre. The artist conjures up a bizarre and fantastic world in a tradition of Expressionism which stretches from Bosch in the 15th century to Immendorf in the 20th century. McIntyre's striking compositions will continue to excite our imagination for a long time to come.

The artist has had many one-person exhibitions in the United Kingdom and is

Angels with Bare Arses, 1989,
Oil on board, 183 x 152.5 cm,
Courtesy RAAB Gallery, London

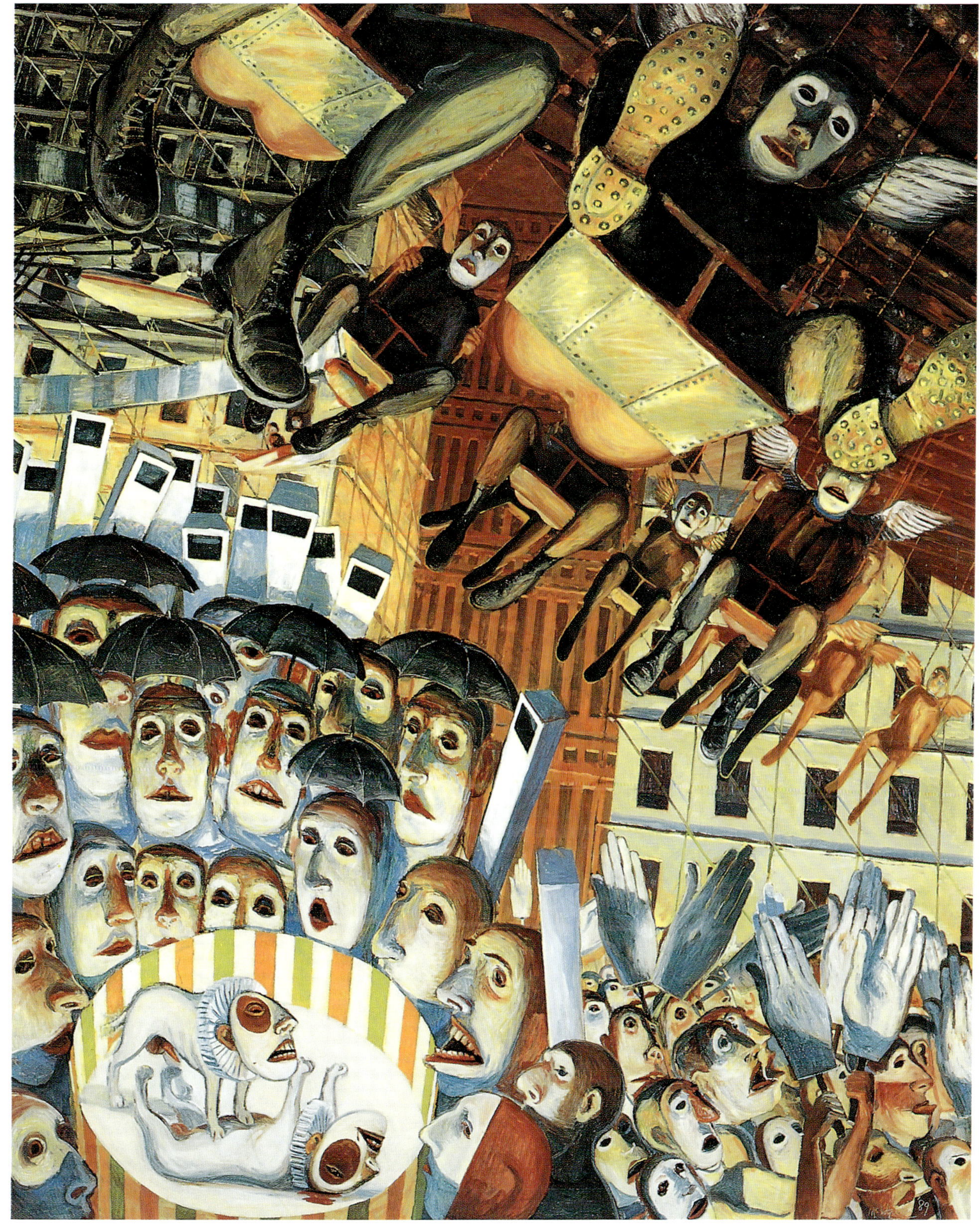

represented in public and private collections in the United Kingdom, including the
Scottish National Gallery of Modern Art.

Artist's Comment

*In a lot of Celtic culture, humour and sadness go hand in hand. I've experimented
with many different areas, but I keep coming back to ideas which are
unapologetically Scottish. It's a big nasty world, but within it are little human
elements. These are the anchor points for my paintings.*

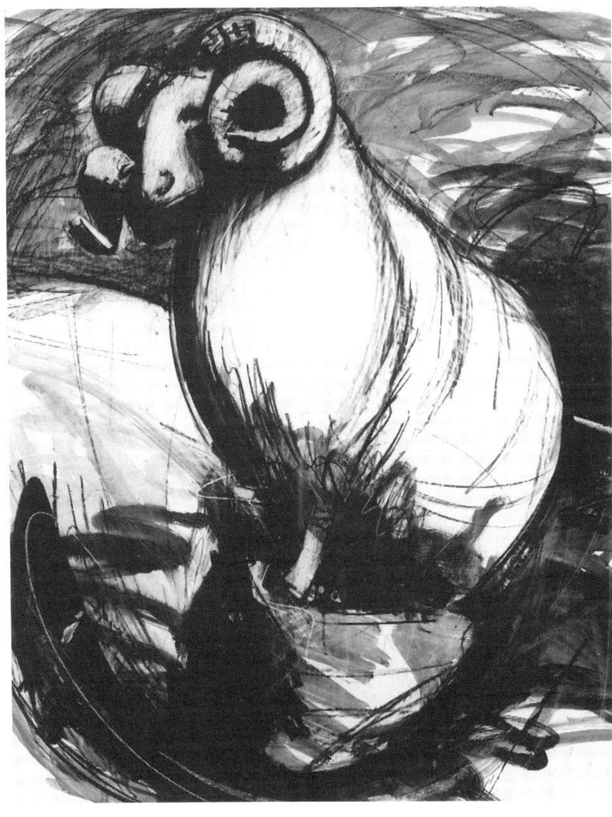

Moffat Ram, 1986,
Ink and charcoal on paper, 152 x 122 cm,
Collection of the Royal Bank of Scotland

Our Worldly Possessions, 1988,
Oil on canvas, 244 x 214 cm,
Courtesy RAAB Gallery, London

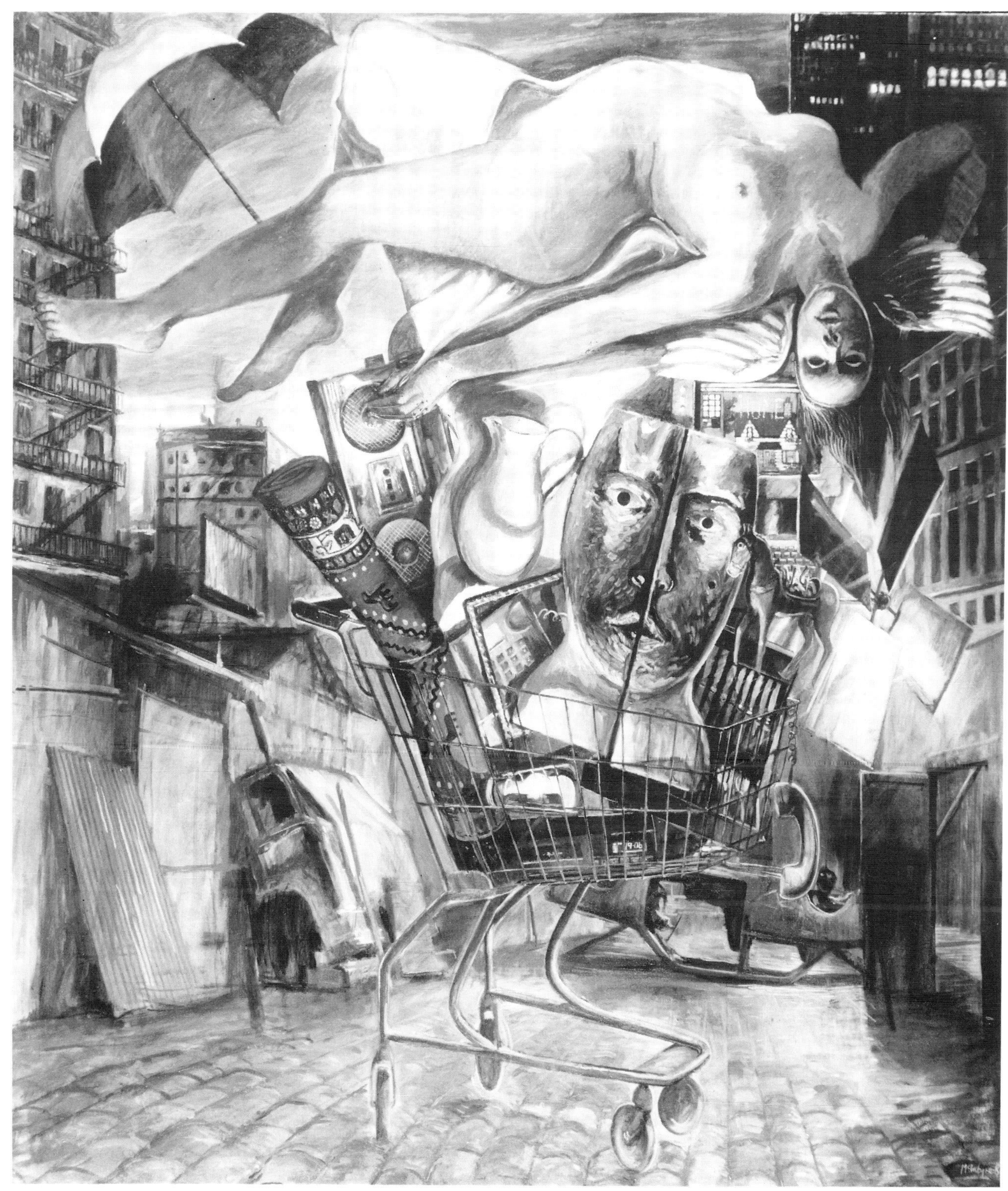

BRUCE McLEAN

Bruce McLean was born in Glasgow in 1944 and studied at Glasgow School of Art from 1961–63, thereafter attending the advanced sculpture course at St Martin's School of Art, London from 1963–66. He currently lives and works in London.

Bruce McLean's work has been among the most varied and provocative in Scottish art, utilising painting, performance, photography and ceramics. His style is marked by an unconventional and irreverent wit, aimed often at the pretentions of the art world and polite society — formal concerns such as colour, balance and space have been of minor importance and, if used, are usually present to satirise those artists of the establishment who take these considerations seriously. In the 1960s he produced a number of works in natural materials, returning landscape subjects back to Nature but using deliberately quirky techniques — *Seascape* involved laying photographic paper across the sea, registering changes in light. McLean moved on to reconsider the centrality of the body in art in a number of performances and posed photographs, most notably in his 1972 *Pose Work for Plinths* where, in a sequence of 12 images, the artist takes up absurd positions across three sculpture plinths.

McLean's technique is to criticise his subjects through mockery and at an ironical distance. As the artist says: 'The only way to see life is through humour. Humour is the nearest to truth that you can get.' Comparisons with the tactics of Duchamp and even Hogarth often appear in writings on his work.

McLean's painting style was once described as 'weaving its way from Matisse to Rolf Harris'. It is theatrical, colourful and graphic, deriving its impact from the immediacy of advertising and design, rather than from the tradition of painting.

McLean has had one-person exhibitions worldwide and has also taken part in a number of performances and exhibitions throughout Europe, the United States and Japan. Major group exhibitions include 'A New Spirit in Painting' (London, 1981), 'Zeitgeist' (Berlin, 1982), and 'British Art in the 20th Century' (London, 1987).

His work is held in major public and private collections in the United Kingdom and abroad, including the Tate Gallery, London, and the Scottish National Gallery of Modern Art.

Yucca Gloriosa, 1980,
Acrylic on wax crayon on photographic
paper, 170.2 x 137.2 cm

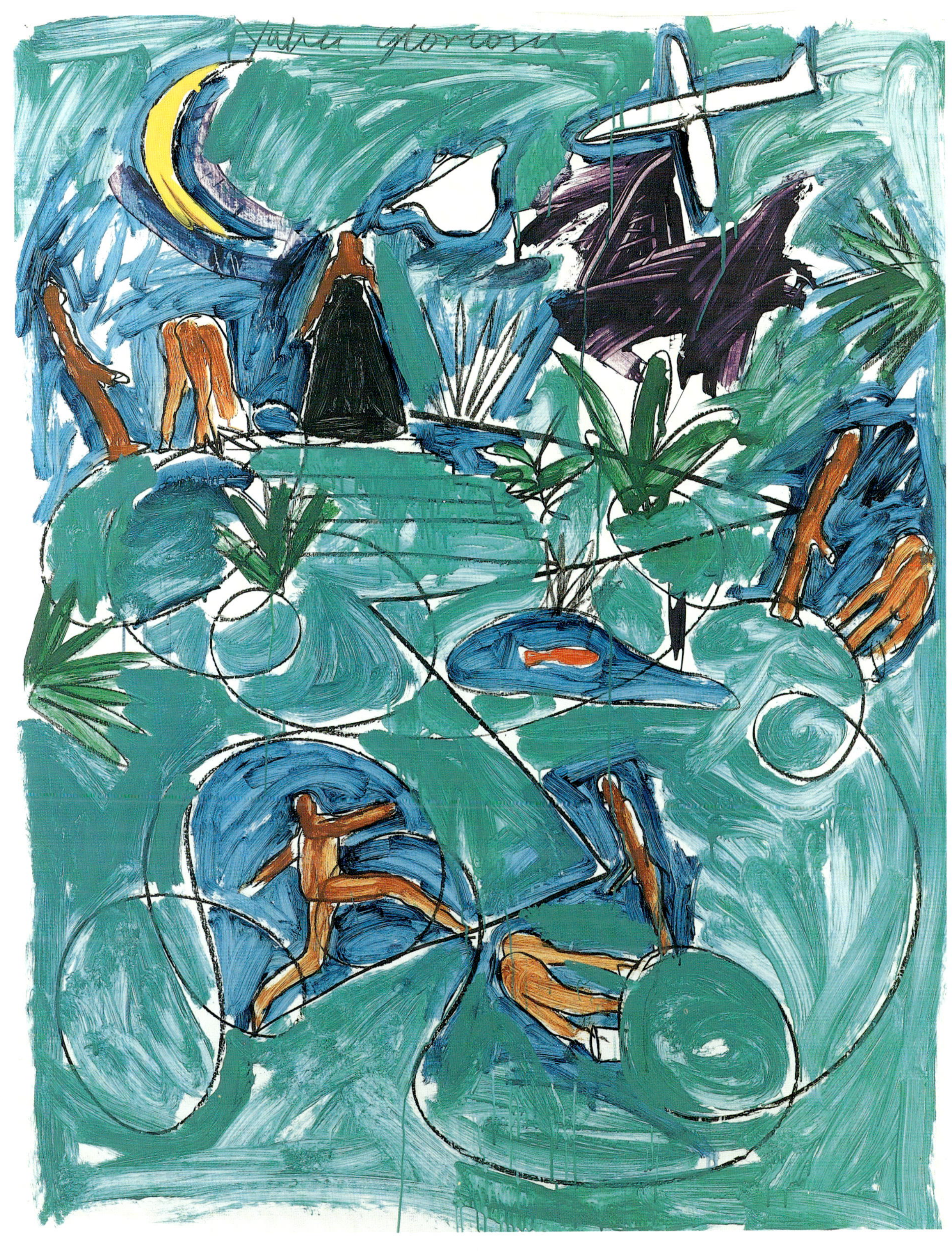

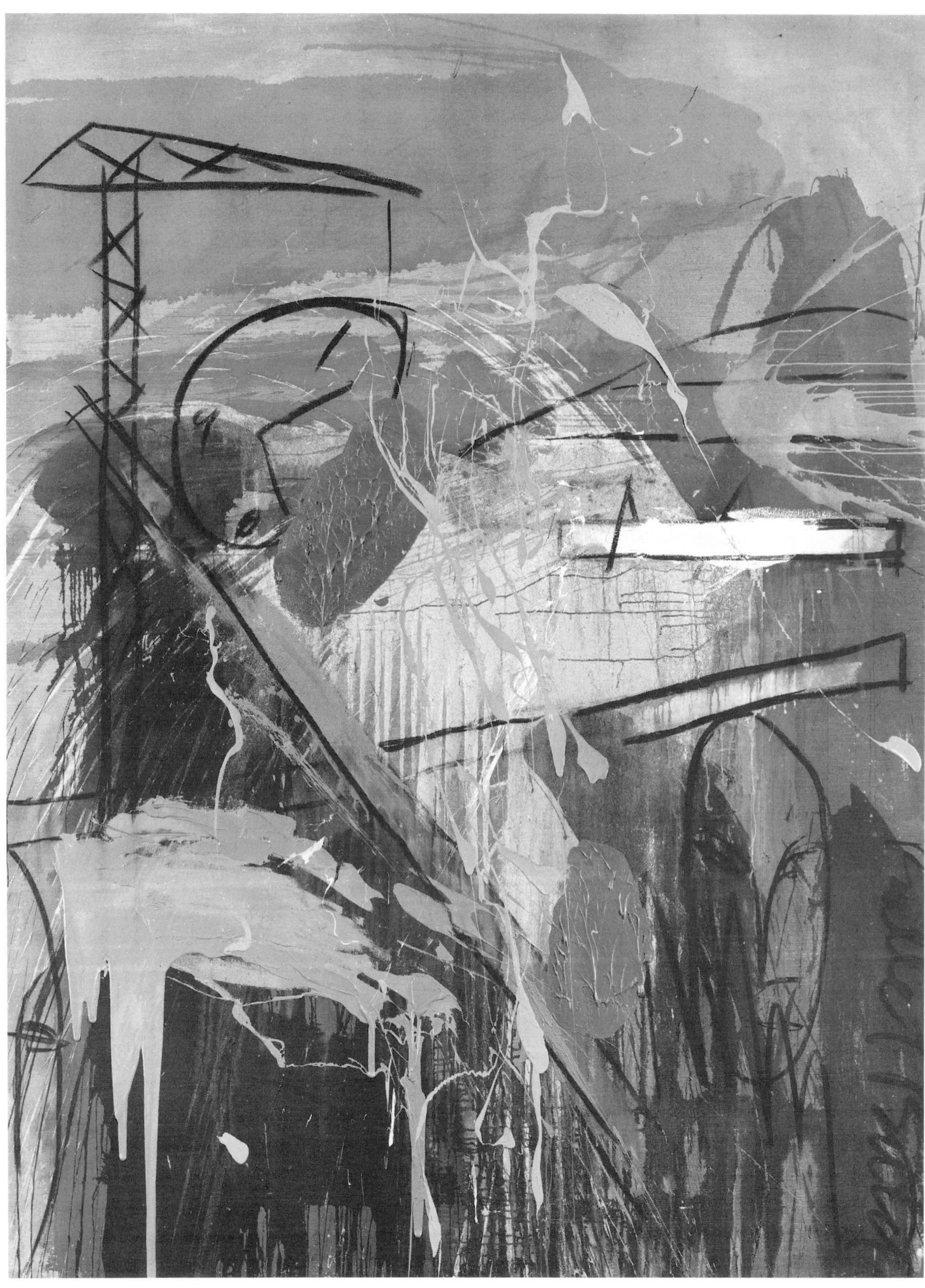

Ballet Butu, 1988,
Acrylic and charcoal on
canvas, 259 x 198 cm,
Courtesy Anthony d'Offay
Gallery, London

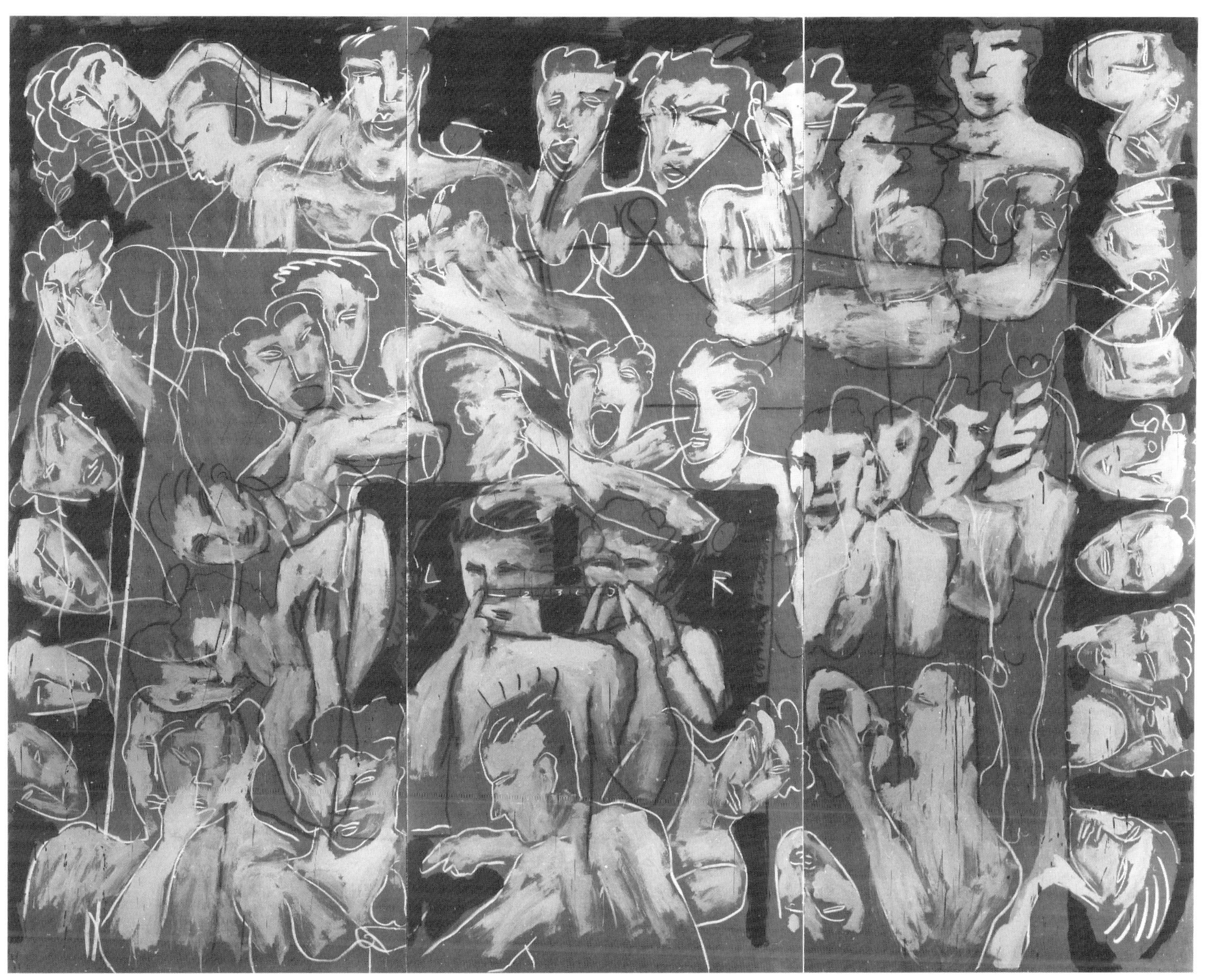

Big Night out on Frankfurterstrasse, 1982,
Acrylic, chalk and charcoal on cotton,
3 parts, each 300 x 150 cm, overall size 300 x 450 cm,
Courtesy Anthony d'Offay Gallery, London

JOHN McLEAN

John McLean was born in Liverpool in 1939 and grew up in Arbroath where his father Talbert McLean, a distinguished painter of the post-war generation, still lives and works. He studied at St Andrews University (1957–62) and then moved to London to study art history at the Courtauld Institute (1963–66). Although now a full-time painter, he has taught at various colleges in Britain and abroad in Canada and USA. Since 1974 he has won major awards from the Arts Council of Great Britain and the British Council. He was the first artist-in-residence at Edinburgh University in 1985–86.

How Scottish John McLean's paintings are would be hard to argue, let alone define, and the artist himself would be the first to protest at such ready labelling. He would point out that, although brought up in Scotland and encouraged by an artistic family background, the work he produced then was in a figurative mode which he has long since abandoned. It was when he went to London in 1963 and saw the work of American painters such as Louis and Noland that he fully realised the course of his development would be as an abstract painter. As he has said, 'For me the directness of their painting seemed to open up the future.' (Of course 'directness' is one of the characteristic features of the best of Scottish painting —Raeburn, McTaggart, Eardley, for instance.) However, it was to trans-Atlantic influences (Sam Gilliam, Jack Bush, for example) that McLean continued to look throughout the 1960s and early 1970s to help him get rid of the unnecessary intricacy in his work of that time. Also his regular studio contacts with Canadian painters such as Robert Christie, during his period in Saskatchewan, were important experiences for McLean.

Yet, despite his critical interest in the best of post-war abstraction, the formulating force on his own work is the pressure he puts on himself in the studio, as he responds to the 'suggestions the painting itself makes'. There the artist must exercise his 'independence of visual judgment'. Ultimately, for McLean, even external visual stimuli are subservient. It is the artist's eye which is the arbiter as he discerns the most subtle relationships between colour, form and space.

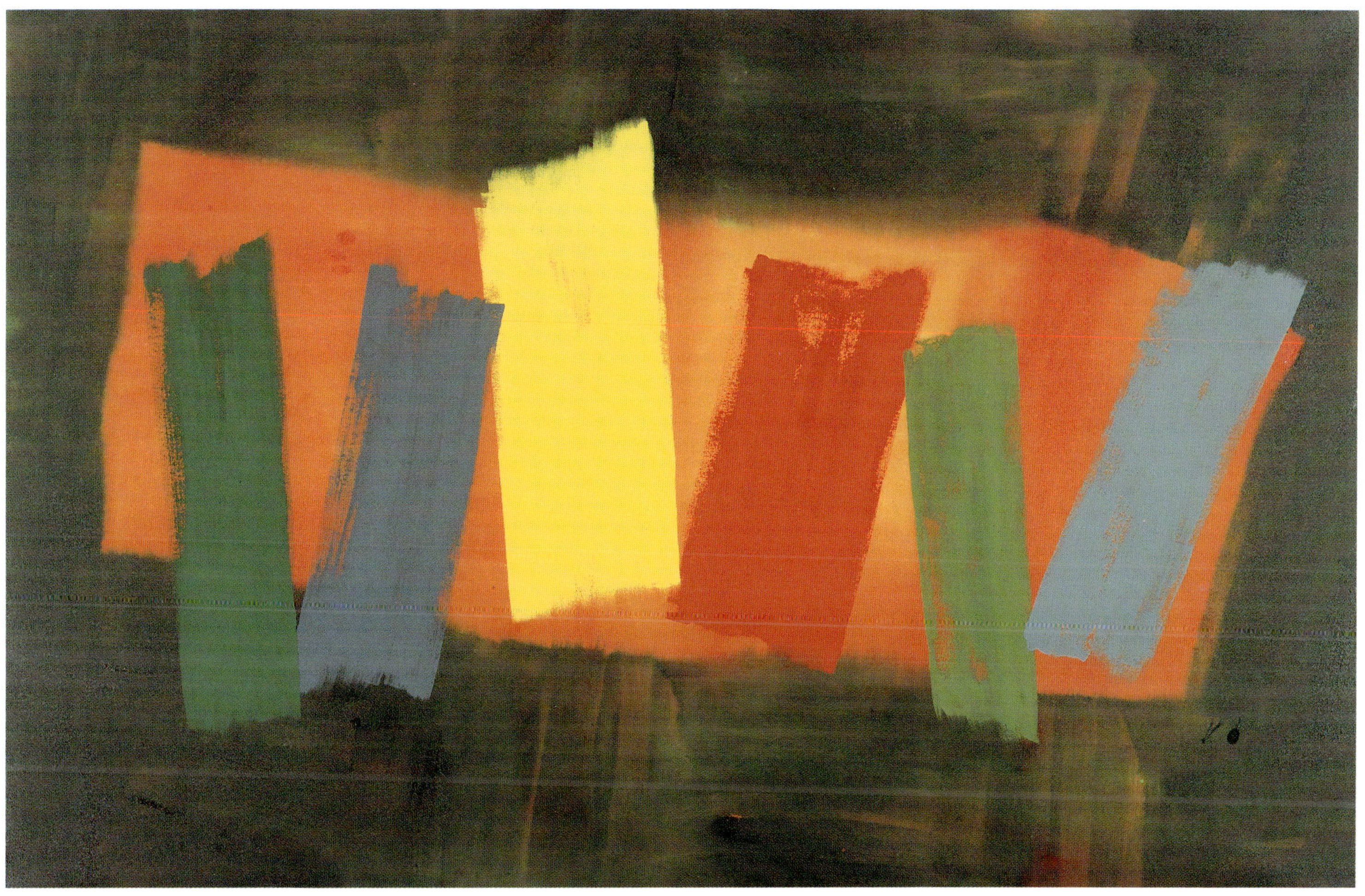

Firebox, 1989,
Acrylic on canvas, 138 x 218 cm,
Francis Graham-Dixon Gallery, London

However, for McLean, what gives each work its unique quality is the 'feeling' of the painting. This is where the question of technique comes in — the touch of the artist. As with many abstract artists, he has invented methods of painting which serve his own specific requirements. Always aware that his approach to each work is related to its scale, he has found that working on large unstretched canvases on the ground with a squeegee mop can give him an exciting play-off between the surety of his control and unforeseen accidents. Each painting is a prolonged process of exploration; however, the finished picture is marked by a decisiveness of execution along with a spontaneousness of expression. To some, McLean's paintings may appear disconcertingly simple and straightforward, but that is only because 'all the hard work isn't apparent'.

John McLean has had numerous one-man exhibitions since the 1960s, both in Britain and Canada and the USA (Louisville, 1984; New York, 1988). His work has appeared in most of the important abstract exhibitions in the last decade. He exhibits with Francis Graham-Dixon Gallery, London, and his work is represented in many private and public collections, both in Britain and abroad, including the Scottish National Gallery of Modern Art, the Arts Council of Great Britain and the Tate Gallery.

Artist's Comment

There is nothing I can say about my paintings that, if you look hard enough, you cannot see for yourself. They are not obscure. Their directness hides the hard work. The one thing at the root of it all is colour.

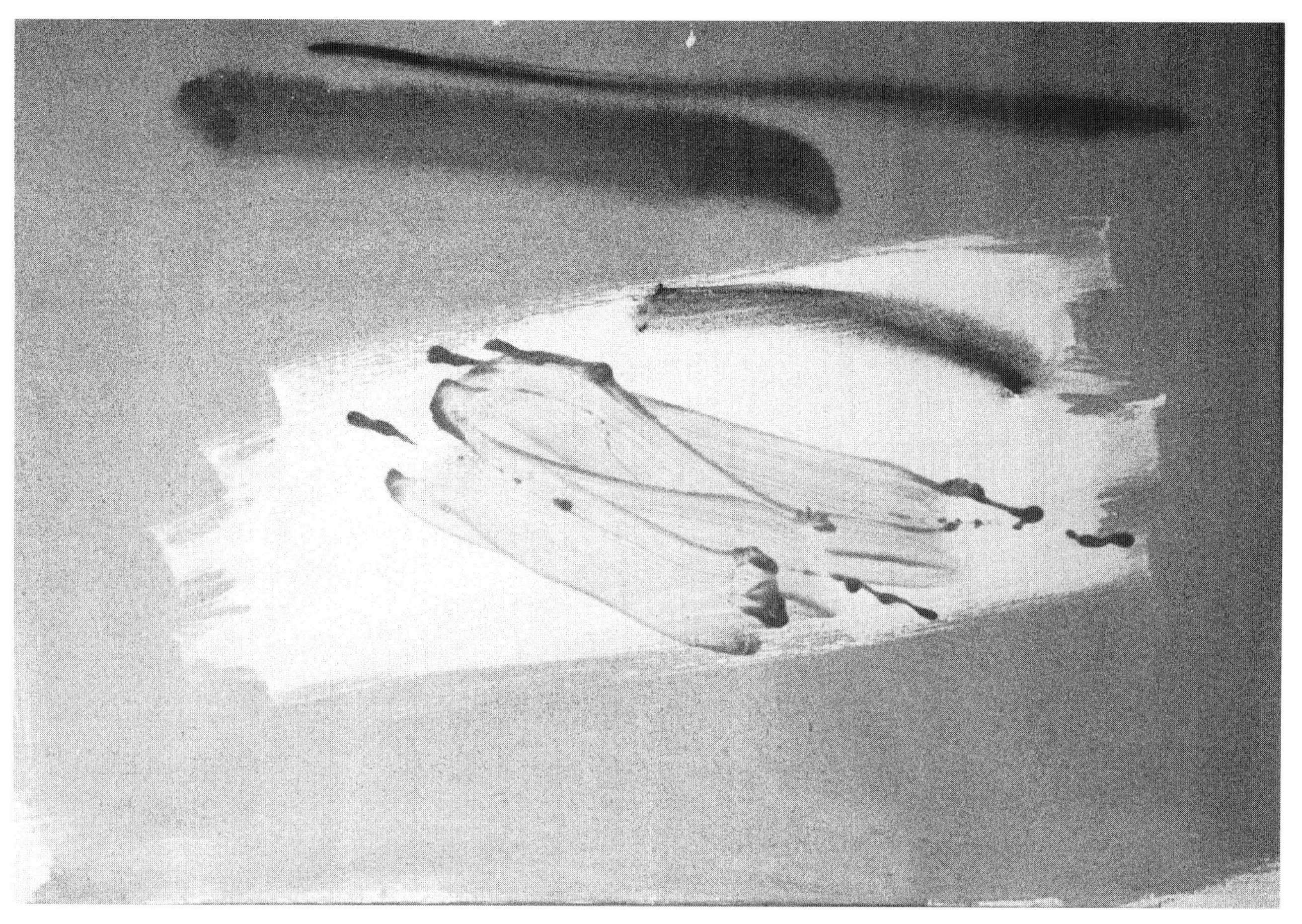

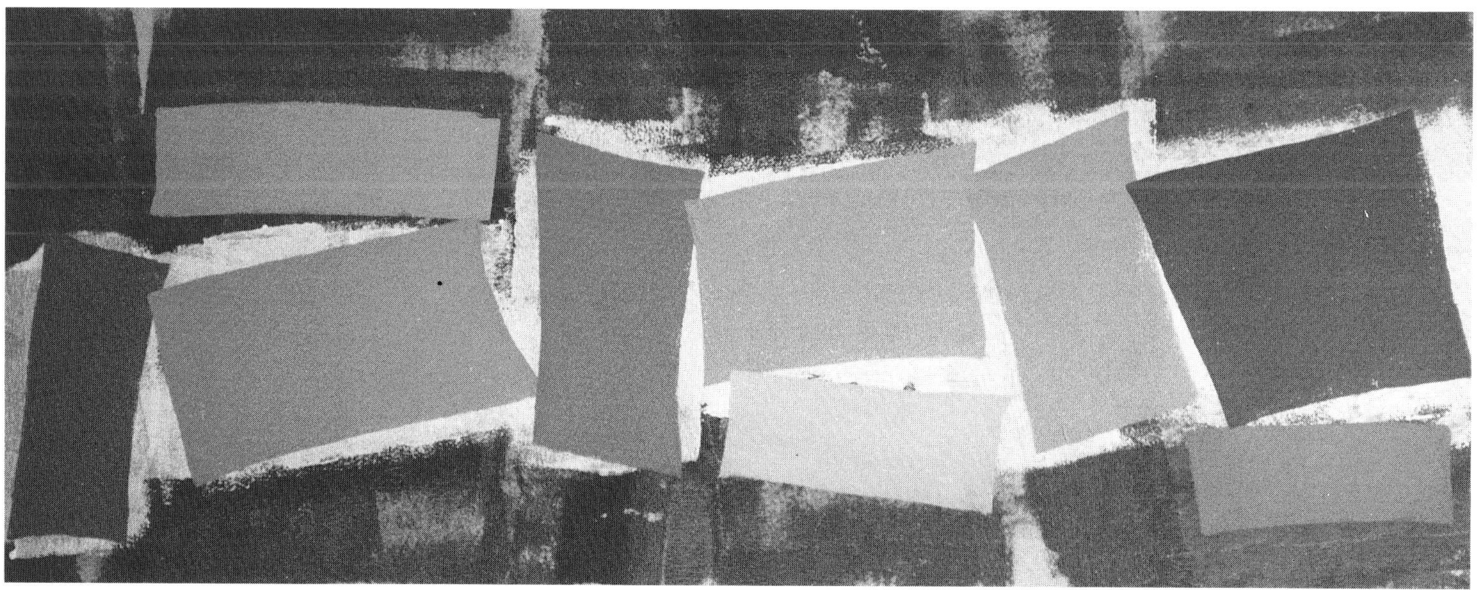

Alexander Moffat was born in Dunfermline, Fife in 1943. After training in painting at Edinburgh College of Art he held a variety of positions including Director of the New 57 Gallery, Edinburgh, visiting lectureships around Britain and, from 1979, teaching painting at Glasgow School of Art where he is currently Senior Lecturer.

Moffat has become widely respected both as a teacher and as a painter — it was under his tutelage that many of the significant figurative artists from Glasgow came to prominence. His firmly held belief in the power of figurative art has influenced many, and his own artistic influences — such as Léger, Munch and Beckmann — have also, in turn, inspired his students. Although the division between figurative and abstract art can be an arbitrary one, many artists (and indeed the public at large) feel that abstraction can too easily negate the essentials of life, resulting in a loss of contact with reality and popular appreciation. Moffat is just one example of how an artist has sought to reconcile the politics of the Left with the art of the avant-garde. As he asserts: 'Beckmann's statement "The elimination of the human component from artistic representation is the cause of the vacuum which makes us all suffer in varying degree …" has always been my credo.

Throughout his career, Moffat has concentrated on portraits where his distinctively linear style has won him many significant commissions, such as a series on Scottish poets including Sorley MacLean, Hugh MacDiarmid and Norman MacCraig. Of MacDiarmid, above all, he says: 'It was he who convinced me that art could be much more than a pretty picture.' MacDiarmid, like Moffat, saw himself as both part of the tradition of European Radicalism as well as an exponent of the living traditions of Scottish culture. Historically, it has sometimes been difficult for artists to believe in, or be accepted for holding, this principle.

More recently, Moffat has reverted to an earlier genre, that of landscape painting, to record the momentous changes occurring in Germany and also, in true history painter tradition, warning of the disasters which befell that country during the rise of Fascism. The artist's moral seriousness may be said to be echoed in his

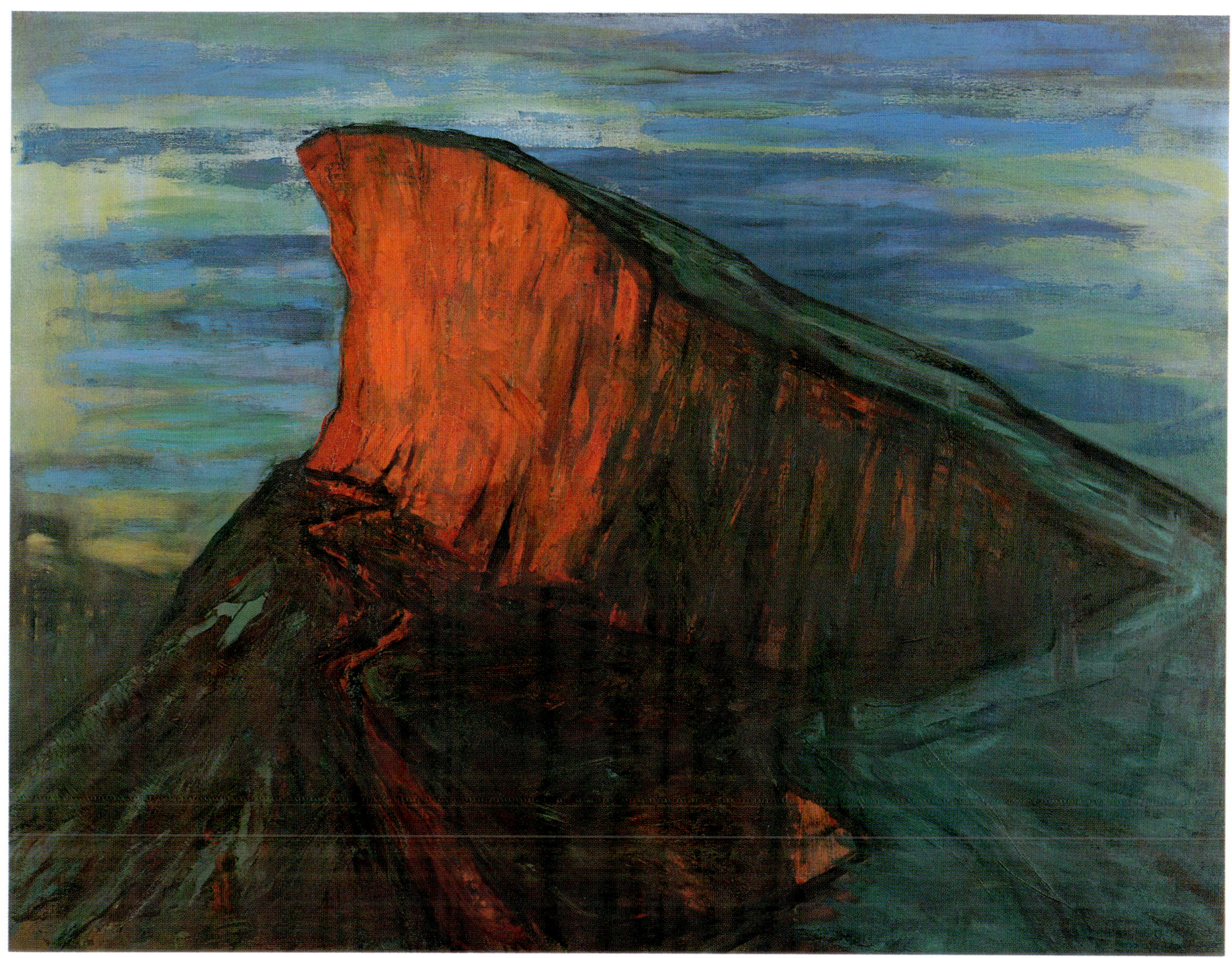

The Rock, 1989–90,
Oil on canvas, 137 x 183 cm,
Photograph: Antonia Reeve
Collection of the artist

technique, as his style allows little concentration on the physical, sensual qualities of paint, deliberately eschewing the *belle peinture* tradition of the College where he trained. Moffat permits us no relaxation.

The artist has had one-person exhibitions in Poland, Glasgow and Edinburgh and been involved in numerous group exhibitions. In 1984 he co-curated the British Art Show 2 and his work is represented in numerous private and public collections.

Artist's Comment

I've no wish to make any sensational show of temperament in my work: only to make people more aware of, and so perhaps enrich, the life around them. What interests me in Expressionist art is this absolute preoccupation with humanity, from the individual right through to the social.

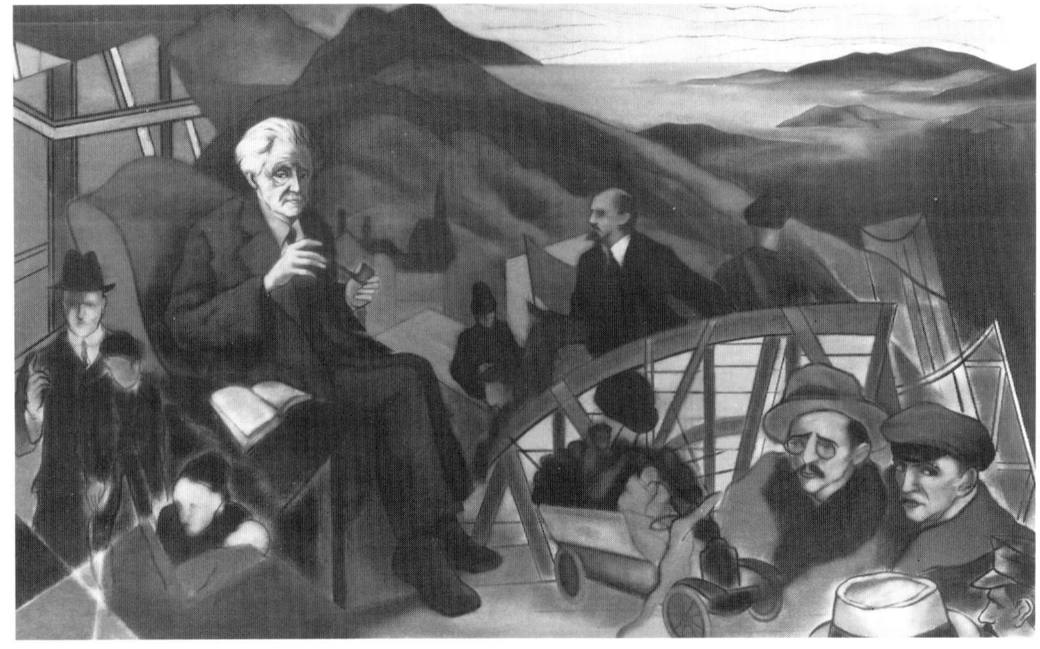

Hugh MacDiarmid (Hymn to Lenin),
1979,
Oil on canvas, 114 x 190 cm,
Photograph: Tom Scott,
Collection of The Scottish Arts Council

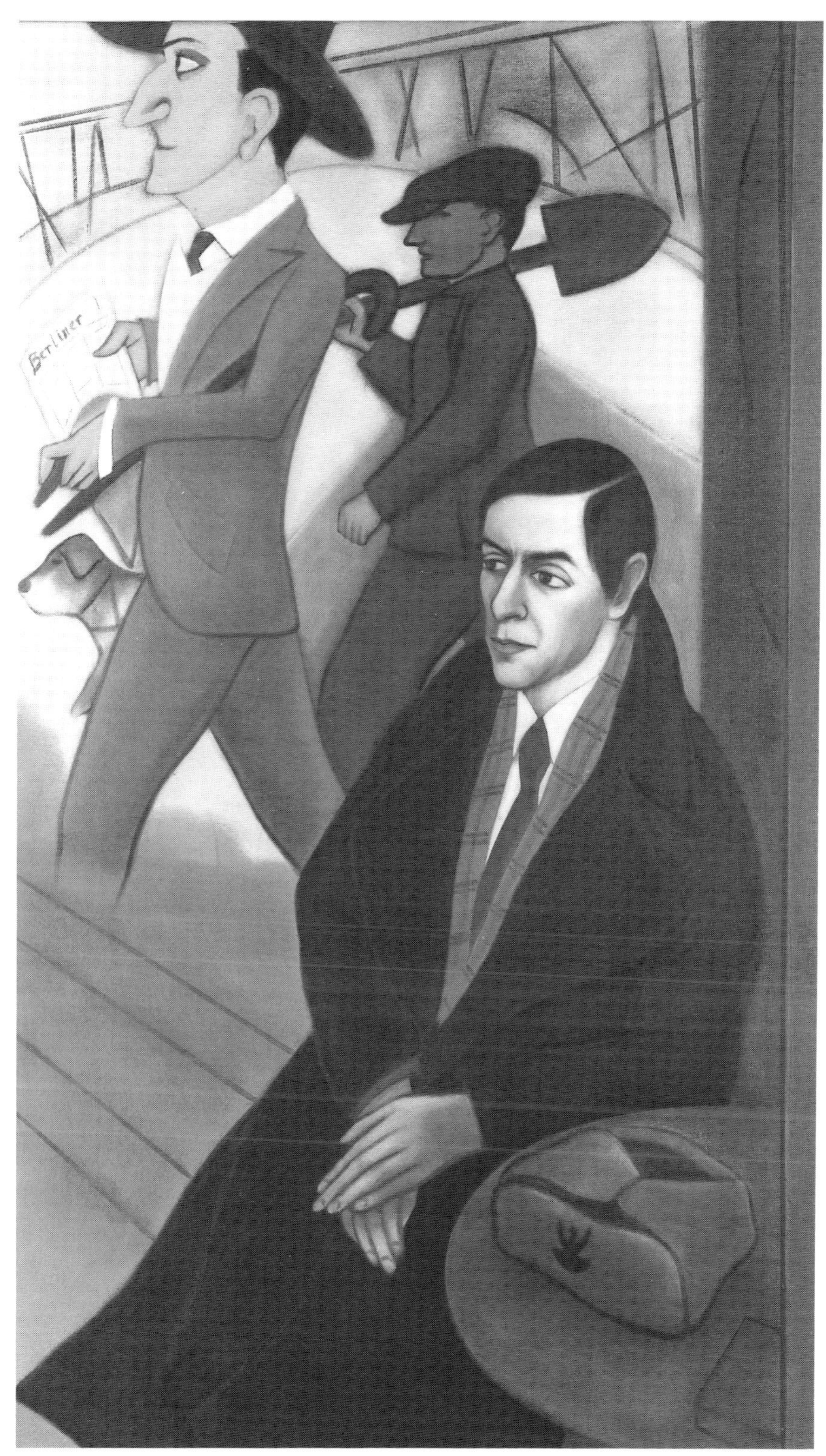

Portrait of Neal Ascherson, 1977,
Oil on canvas, 126 x 76 cm,
Photograph: Tom Scott,
Collection: Neal Ascherson

John Mooney was born in Edinburgh in 1948. He studied at Edinburgh College of Art (1966–70), then completed his postgraduate qualifications the following year. He is now a full-time lecturer in the Drawing and Painting Department at Edinburgh College of Art.

John Mooney is yet another artist who contradicts the 'painterly' tradition of Scottish art. There is no spontaneous expressionism in his work, except maybe in his smaller watercolours. His technique is tightly controlled, with painstaking attention to detail. His style, which owes something to Magritte's deadpan parody of academic painting, is one of highly wrought graphic illusionism. As such the visual impact of Mooney's work arises from the marked contrast between strictly disciplined technique and the anarchistic behaviour of the subjects in the paintings. Every object and figure seems to be in a continuous process of change from one state or identity to another. While the artist uses a hard-edged style and grid-like compositional presentation to pin down his subjects, they in themselves thumb their nose at such pigeon-holing as they jump from one stage of metamorphosis to another.

John Mooney's art can be seen as part of the continuing Scottish interest in the elusiveness of identity, which takes its most celebrated form in Robert Louis Stevenson's story of *Dr Jekyll and Mr Hyde*, where Stevenson deals with the dichotomy between public mask and private face in society. Mooney is fascinated with the shifting relationship between art and illusion. Furthermore, through the word-play in his titles he wittily challenges us to test the ability of language to pin-point the connection between words and images. Poetic metaphor, sensual symbolism, visual punning — all are deployed to keep this game of linguistic hide-and-seek constantly on the move.

Finally, as if to turn his pictorial world of contrast and contradiction through the full circle, Mooney also produces 'straight' still-lifes of cacti and house plants where the objects are painted with such illusionistic skill that ironically the paintings can look more real than the things that modelled for them.

Maybe because of the time involved in producing each painting, John Mooney is

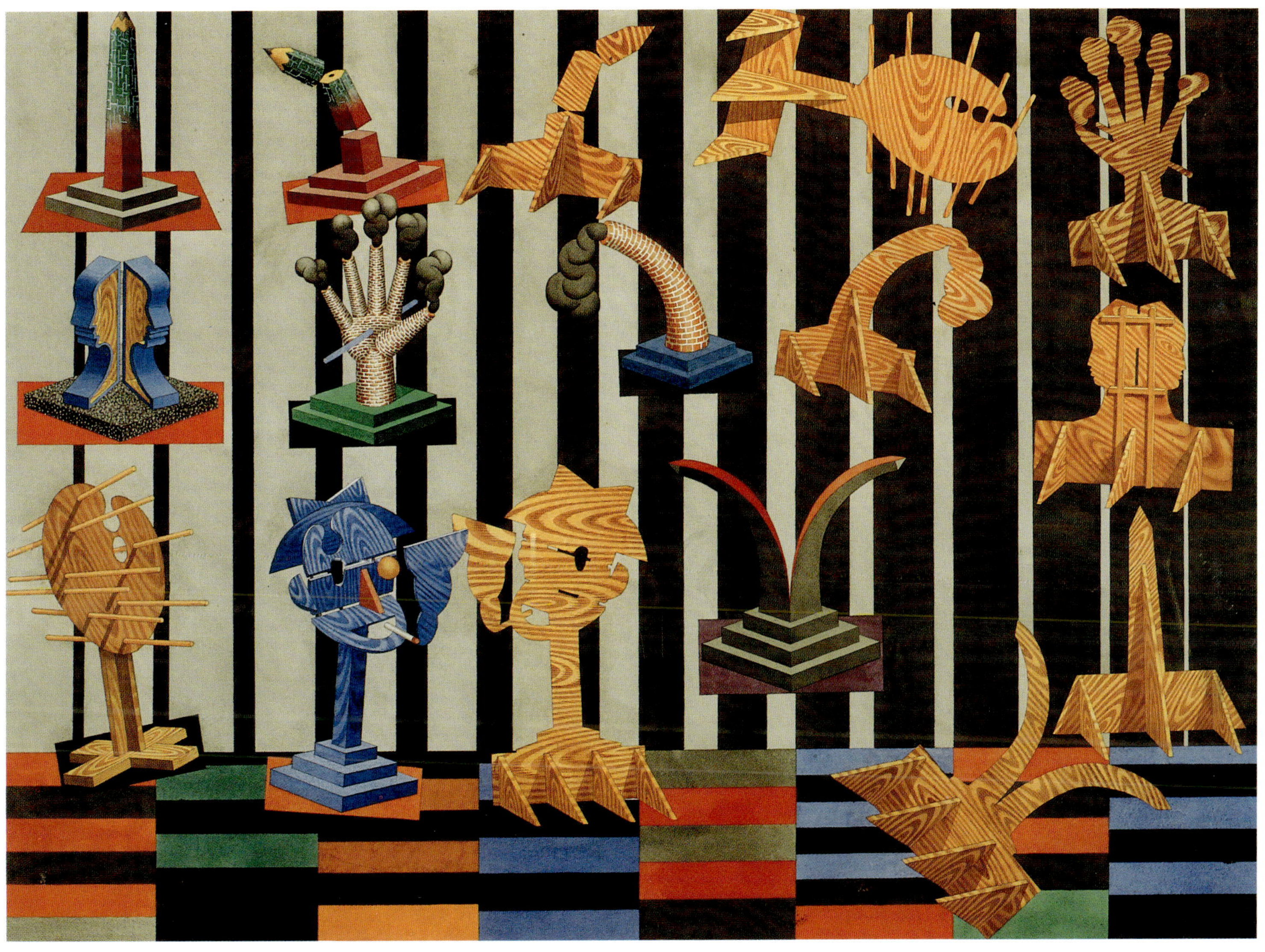

Operation Without an Aesthetic, 1990,
Acrylic on canvas, 58 x 80 cm

not a prolific exhibitor. Since the early 1970s he has had six or seven solo exhibitions, mainly with galleries in Edinburgh. His work is represented in a number of private and public collections, such as the Scottish National Gallery of Modern Art and the Contemporary Art Society, London.

Artist's Comment

The cactus, obelisk, chimney stack and lighthouse have a common, symbolic denominator that has always interested me. Double meanings plus the games that can be played between written and visual language are central to my work and, hopefully, invite the viewer to enjoy the pictures on a number of different levels.

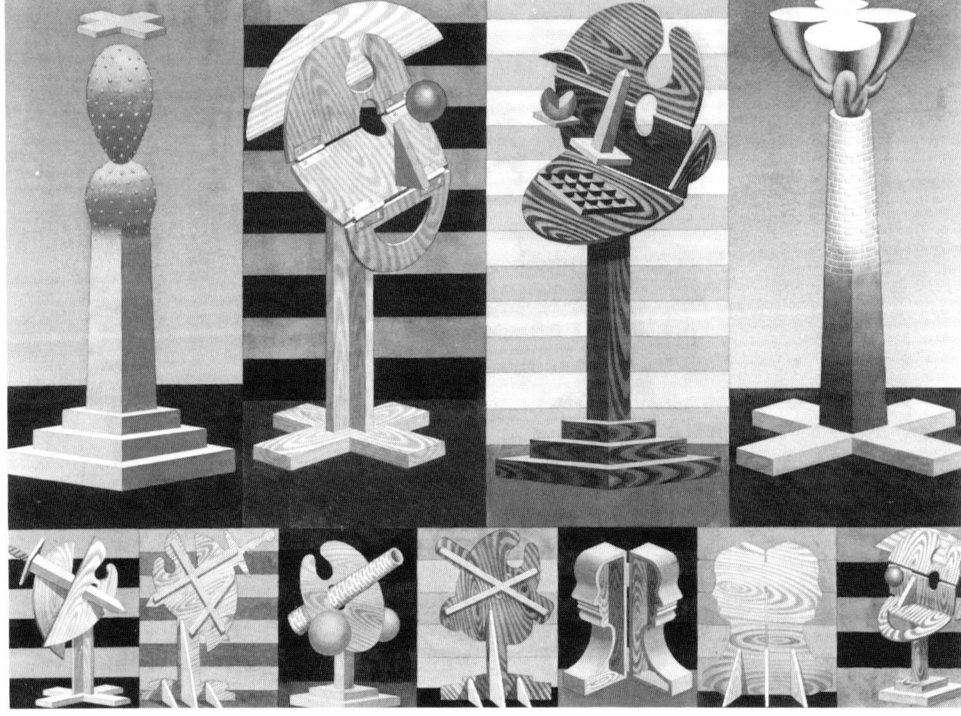

Coming to a Head, 1989,
Watercolour, 58 x 81 cm,
Photograph: Joe Rock

Still Life with Cactus, 1988,
Acrylic on canvas, 192 x 127 cm,
Photograph: Joe Rock

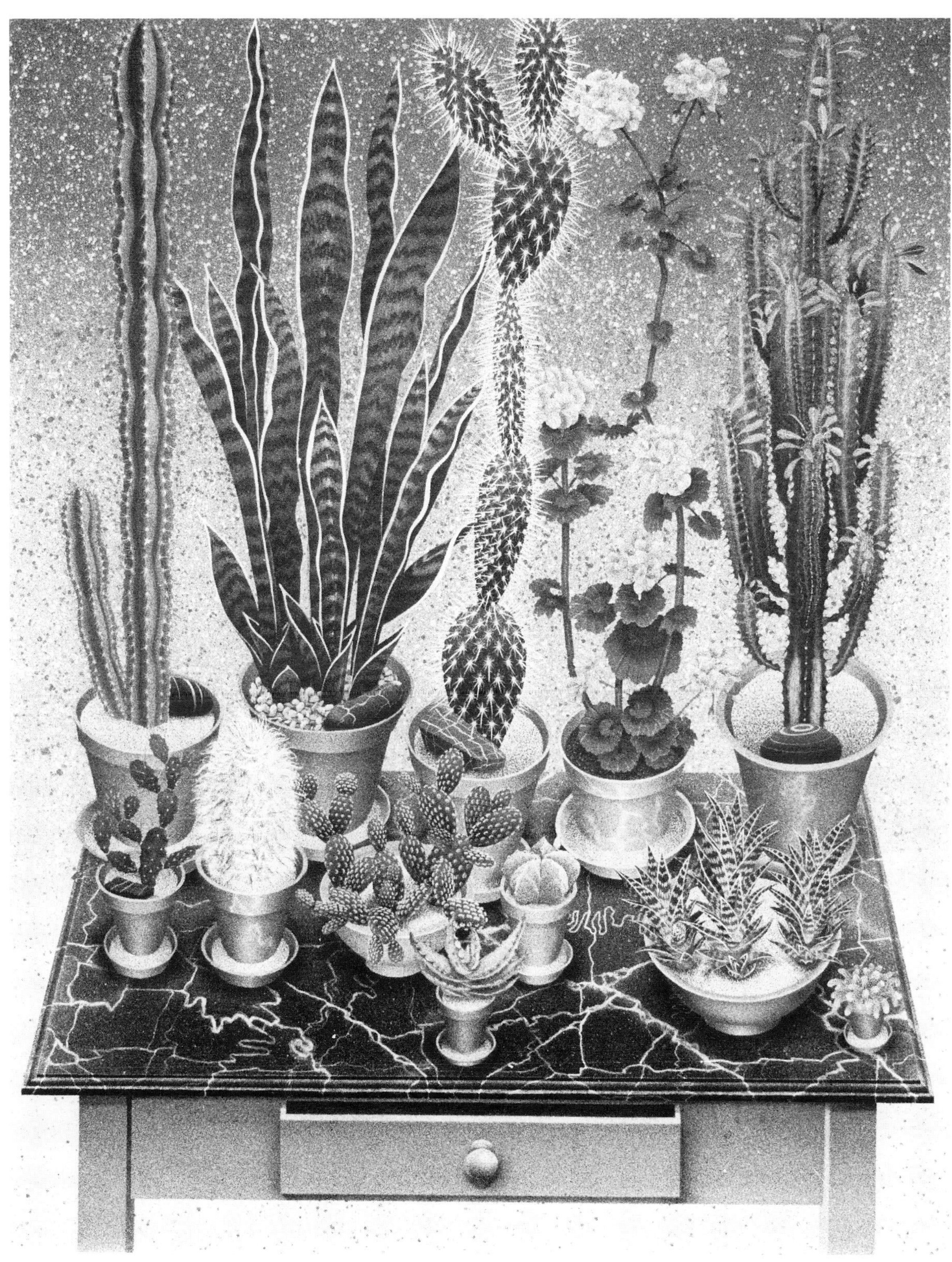

ELIZABETH OGILVIE

lizabeth Ogilvie was born in Aberdeen in 1946. She studied sculpture at Edinburgh College of Art, 1964–49 and gained her postgraduate qualifications there in 1970. She currently lives in Fife and teaches in the Fine Art Department of Edinburgh College of Art.

Although trained as a sculptor, for much of her career Ogilvie has concentrated on two-dimensional work, developing a fastidious and breathtaking facility in the art of large-scale drawing. Perhaps due to her training in sculpture, her work studiously avoids the temptations of colour, so characteristic of painting in Scotland. Her subject matter — the action of water, rock formations and beach and tide debris — has led her to a dramatic and highly romantic depiction of natural phenomena, but one pursued with an extraordinary singularity of purpose. Constant visits to the remote coastlines of Scotland have furnished Ogilvie's imagination with powerful imagery, often of plumes, foams and splashes of water as it cascades against rock.

The minute, obsessive delicacy of her technique means we are invited further into the core of natural experience — she creates meditative essays on the ebb and flow of life, as captured in drawing. In concentrating on depictions of the sea, the artist evokes a long established history of artistic endeavour, from Hokusai to Turner and Monet, which has found inspiration in contemplating water and its infinitely varied activity, yet paradoxically captured at an instant by the artist.

In order to expand the evident poetic associations of her work, Ogilvie has produced drawings and text in hand-made book form, some of which cite the oral poetry traditions of the island community which once inhabited St Kilda — where ancestors of the artist once lived. These texts are often placed, seemingly randomly, across the picture surface alongside other images, such as seaweed, pebbles and shells to imply the organic relationship these objects can have with each other, as if washed up on the beach and discovered by accident. Again, expanding into new areas and opening up new possibilities in her art, Ogilvie has collaborated on live, performance-based work with the Scottish Chamber Orchestra and the theatre group, The Kosh.

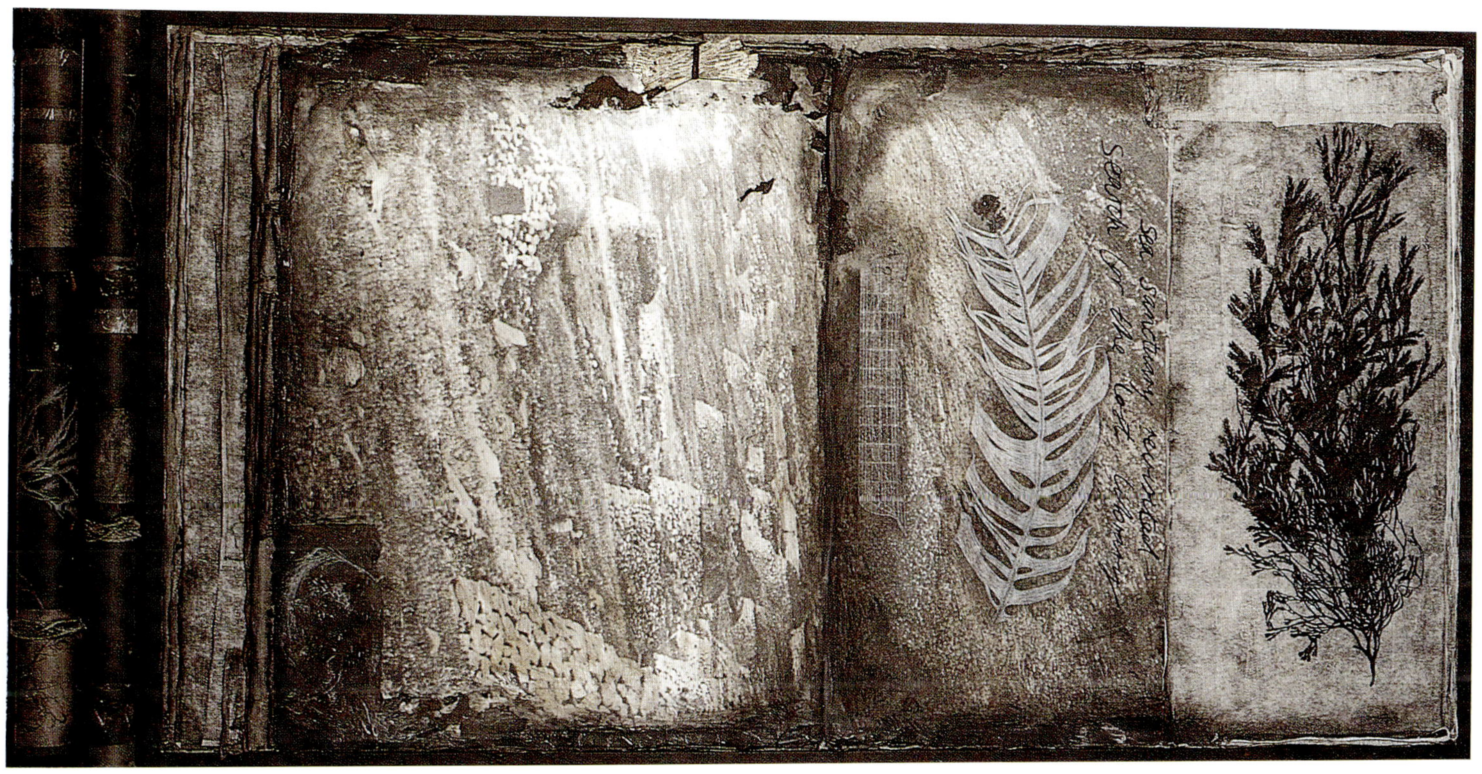

Sea Sanctuary Revisited — Search for the Lost Library, 1990,
Ink, photograph graphite, charcoal paint, crayon, handmade paper, 133 x 266 cm,
Collection of the artist

Ogilvie has exhibited extensively in United Kingdom and abroad. She is represented in major public and private collections including the Tate Gallery, London, and the Scottish Arts Council.

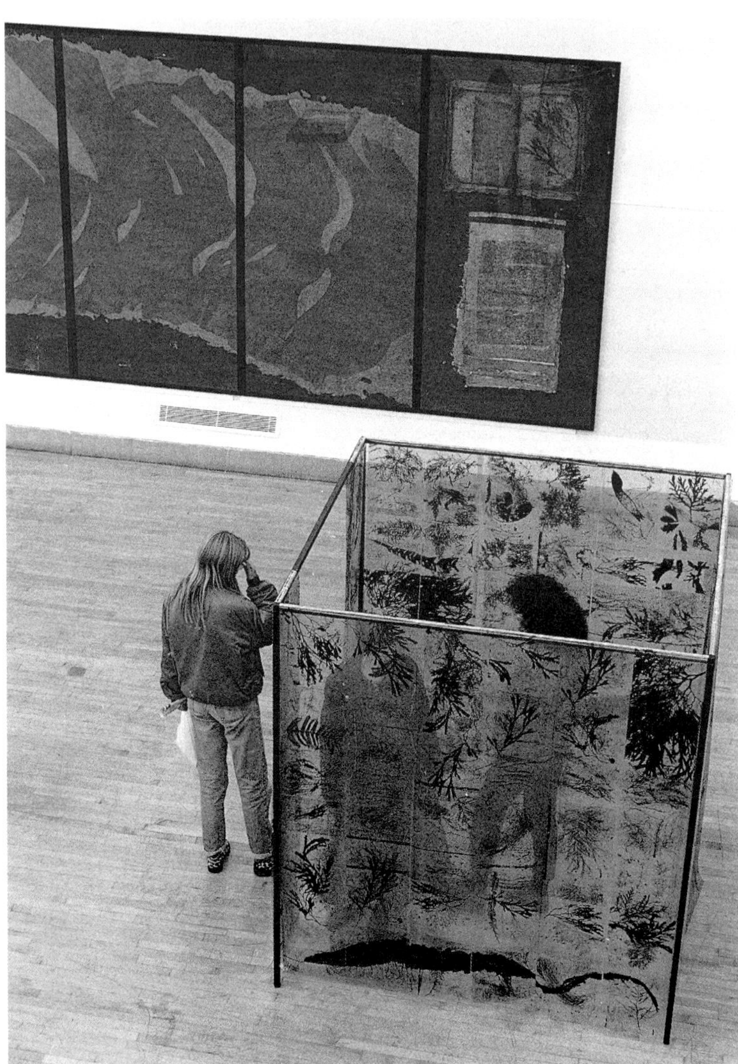

'Sea Sanctuary' Exhibition, 1988,
Talbot Rice Gallery,
Photograph: Joe Rock

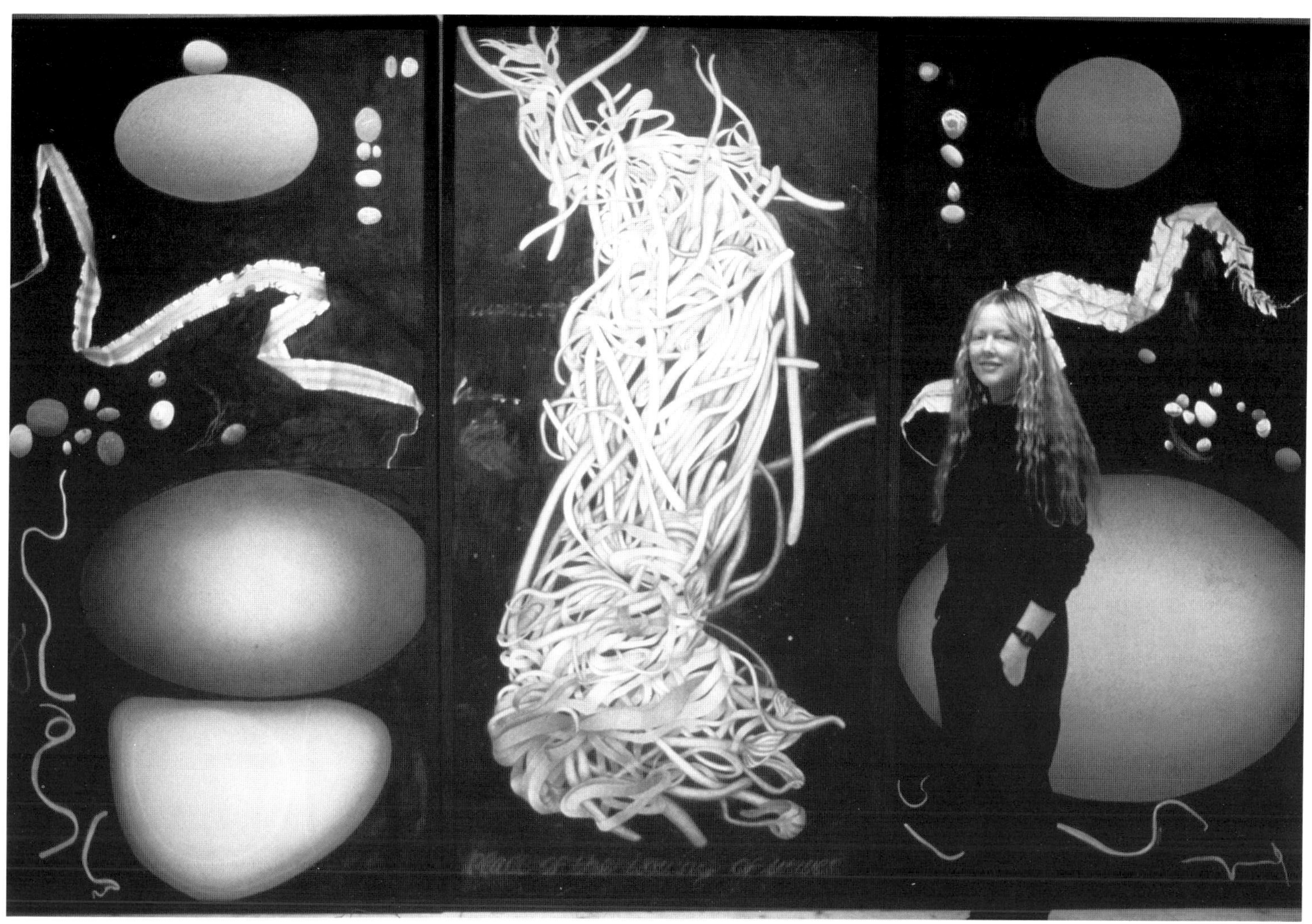

Place of the Issuing of Waves, 1988,
Ink, graphite, paint, crayon, 244 x 366 cm,
Photograph: Bob Callender,
Collection of the artist

Glen Onwin was born in Edinburgh in 1947. He studied painting at Edinburgh College of Art from 1966–71, where he now teaches in the Drawing and Painting Department.

Onwin deals with issues on a global scale in his art, mixing symbols of ancient alchemy and science, industrial progress and the natural landscape. In complex assemblages and paintings he adopts the vocabulary of chemical and organic change and transformation, often with an environmentally concerned message. Both in the titles and in the subjects of works such as *Acidification* (1985), *Toxic Waste* (1985) and *Land Disposal* (1986), we are given a powerful image of destruction imposed on the landscape — a traditional genre subject given a haunting and modern context.

Although this direct attention to humanity's crimes against Nature is strongest in Onwin's new work, it does have its roots in earlier projects, concerned as it is with natural substances. Particularly important is a major series of 1978 called *The Recovery of Dissolved Substances* — a photographic and constructed catalogue of salt in its many forms: under a microscope, across a beach and mass-produced in a factory. As an important constituent of our own bodies as well as the world outside, this 'salt of the earth' might be seen as one of the most fundamental subjects possible for art. It also opens up the question of the relationship between the structures underlying our planet and our understanding of ecology, a subject expanded upon in later work.

In national terms, Onwin may be said to be treating subjects of relevance to Scotland in a particularly Scottish way. Within this country of extraordinary natural beauty exists a small but potent industrial presence — in our modern world the two clash violently. The direct attack on these scientific, yet very human, realities make Onwin's art both cautionary and yet optimistic — pointing the way to a better future.

Onwin has exhibited widely in the United Kingdom and Europe. He is represented in private and public collections, including the Scottish Arts Council.

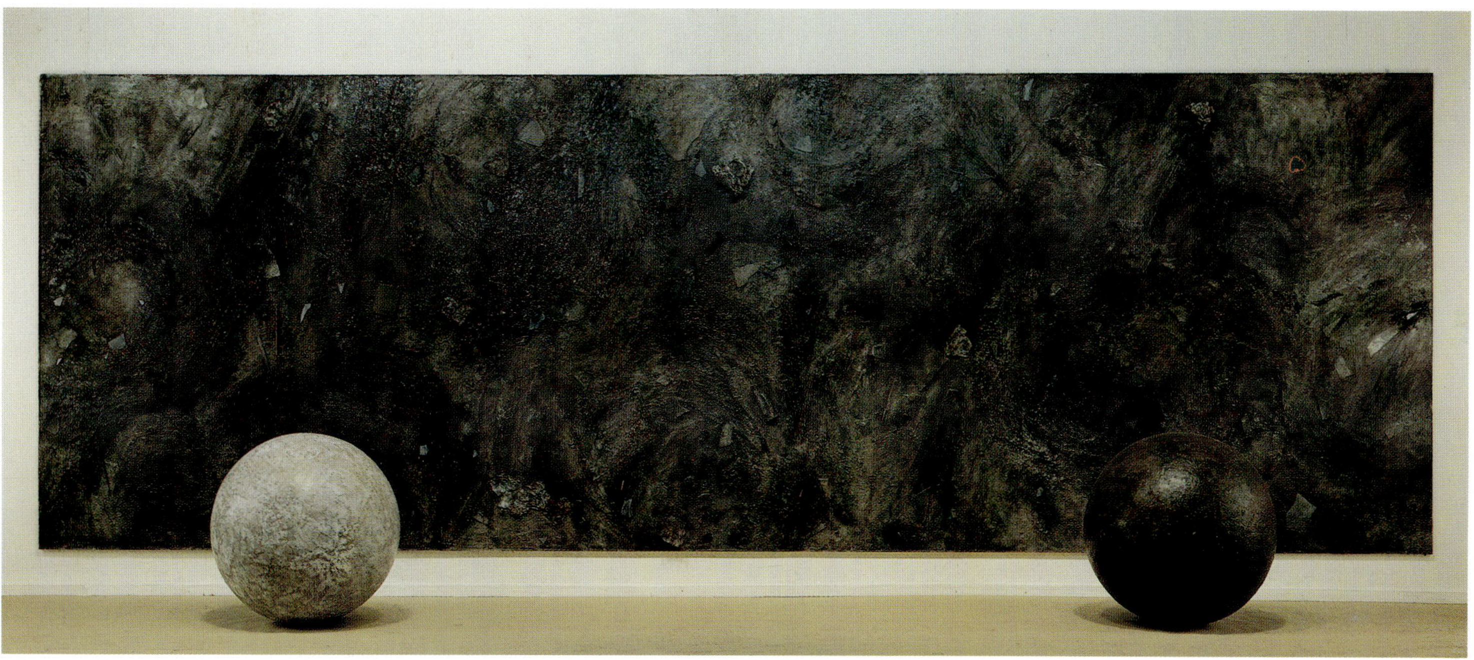

Unthinkable, 1985,
Mixed media, 244 x 732 cm,
Photograph: Duncan McQueen
Collection of the Art Gallery and Museum Kelvingrove, Glasgow

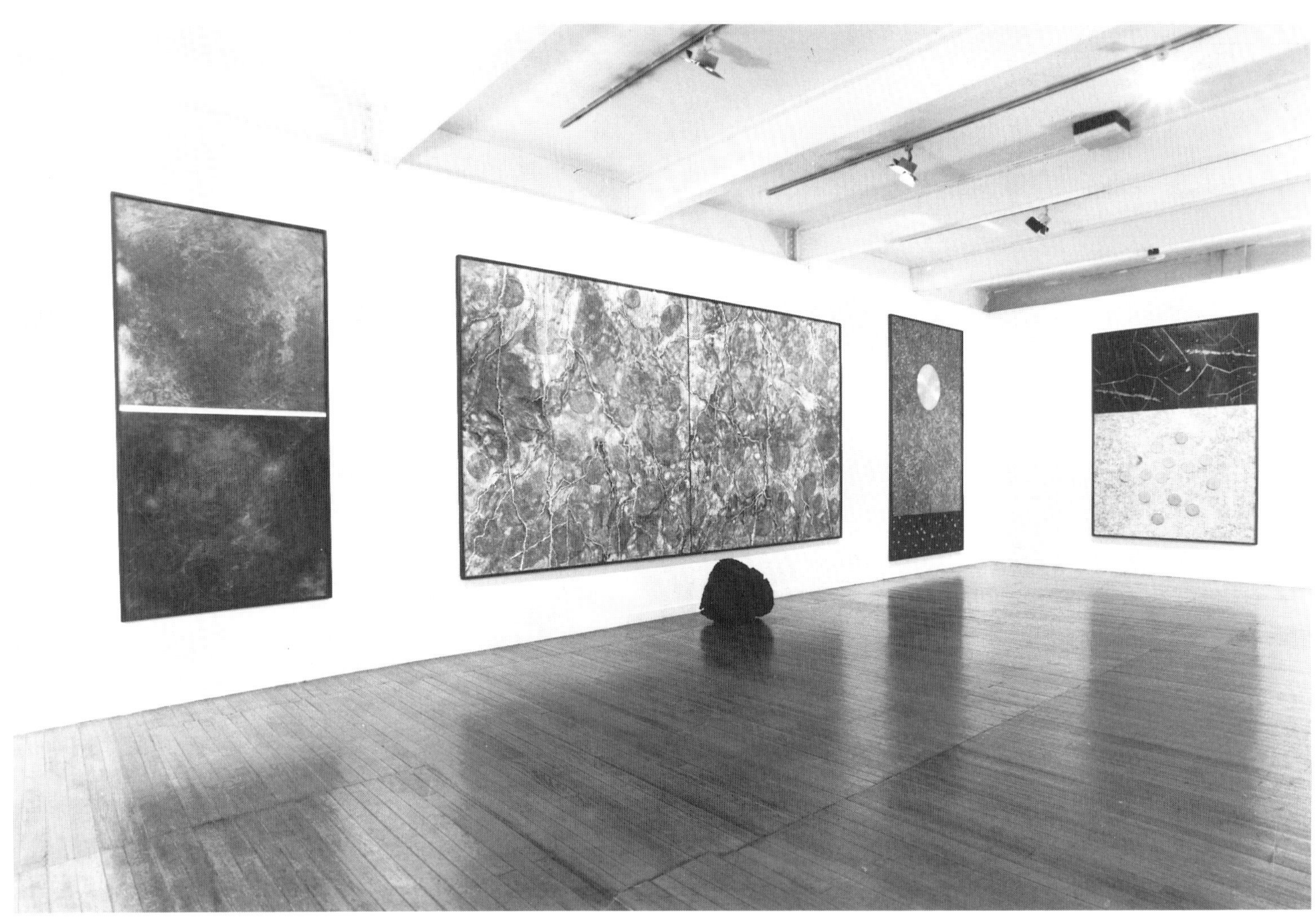

Revenges of Nature, detail of installation showing from left to right:
Carbon, Oxygen, Water, 1987,
247 x 122 cm,
First Life, 1986,
244 x 489 cm,
Photosynthesis, Open the Kingdom, 1987,
305 x 183 cm,
Land Disposal, 1986,
267 x 183.5 cm,
Photograph: Ian Logan,
Courtesy Fruitmarket Gallery, Edinburgh

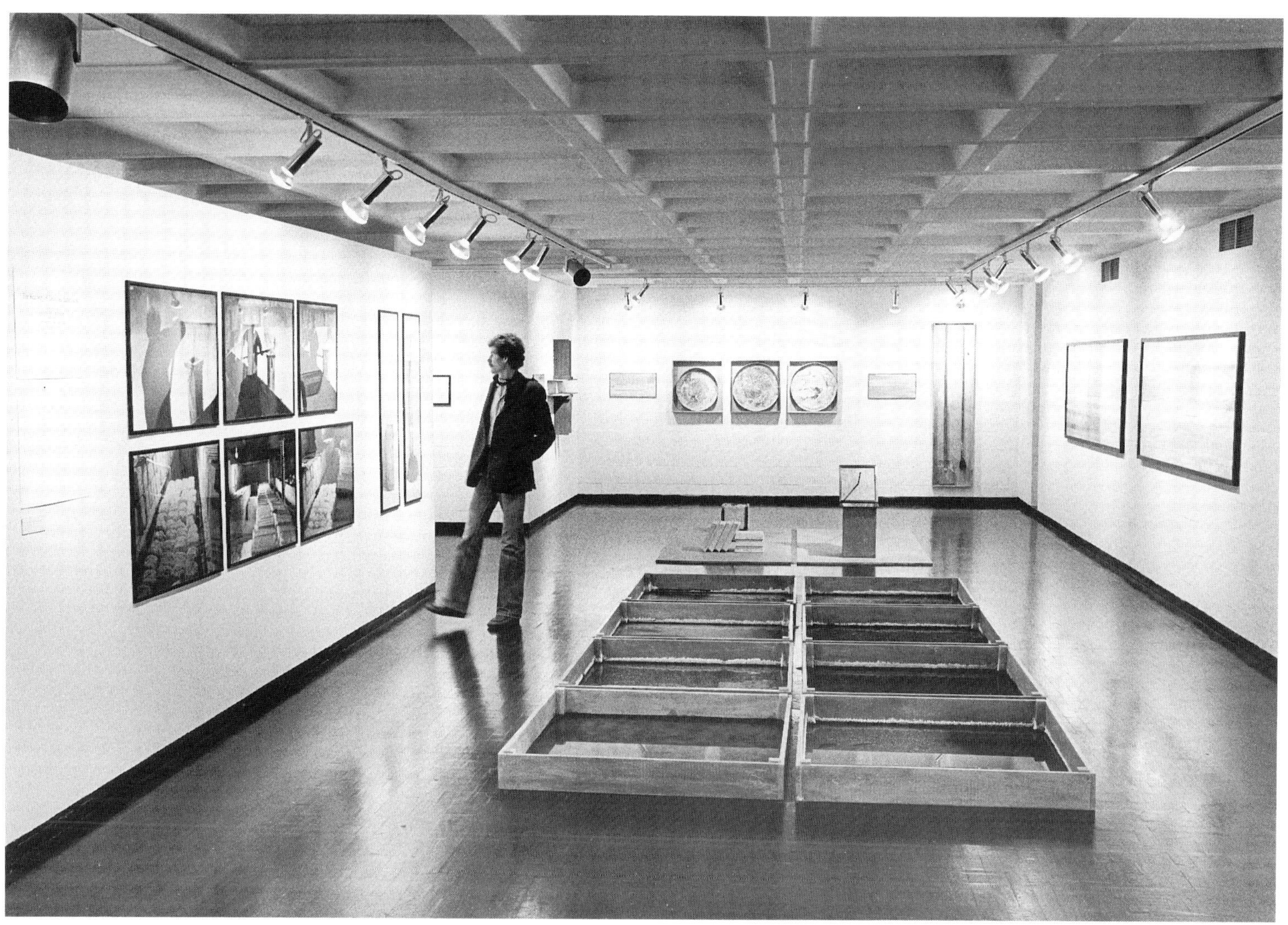

The Recovery of Dissolved Substances (detail of installation), 1979,
Courtesy of Arnolfini Gallery, Bristol

JAMES PATTISON

James Pattison was born in Dundee in 1955. Pattison studied Architecture at Duncan of Jordanstone College of Art, Dundee, for one year before transferring, in 1974, to the Drawing and Painting Department where he graduated with a post-diploma in 1979. From 1979–80 he took his Art Teaching qualification at Moray House College of Education, Edinburgh. He is the recipient of many awards, most notably the Scottish Arts Council Bursary, Amsterdam, 1988–89. He currently lives and works in Glasgow.

The appeal of highly-charged and brightly coloured painting has been an important element of modern Scottish painting since the time of The Colourists, who worked in the first few decades of this century. They and their followers have taken one thread of modern art, that of the liberating and positive associations of pure colour, and developed it with reference to the real world — concentrating especially on portraits, landscape and still-life subjects. However, it is perhaps the revolution in American painting after the Second World War which has been of even greater importance to this artist.

Whilst American painting has had its adherents in Scotland, the commitment to pure abstraction, free from any direct reference to the outside world, is less in evidence here, though it is a central concern of Pattison. Over the last ten years the artist has created an original synthesis of various methods of abstract painting and printmaking. On a single canvas, Pattison unites coolly air-brushed passages of paint with more directly expressive, active gestures. The contrasting clash of control and abandon are collaged together, evoking another innovation in modern art — that of Synthetic Cubism.

As no explicit subject is intended by the artist, each painting is created using formal laws of abstraction to create a vibrant, orchestrated picture surface. To raise the visual excitement to an overpowering pitch, Pattison uses particularly strong colours and applies the paint in different ways; sometimes watered down and translucent, at other times laid on thickly and aggressively.

The wide varieties of textures Pattison employs are occasionally culled from

Moonstone, 1989,
Acrylic on canvas, 152 x 152 cm,
Photograph: James Pattison
Collection of the artist

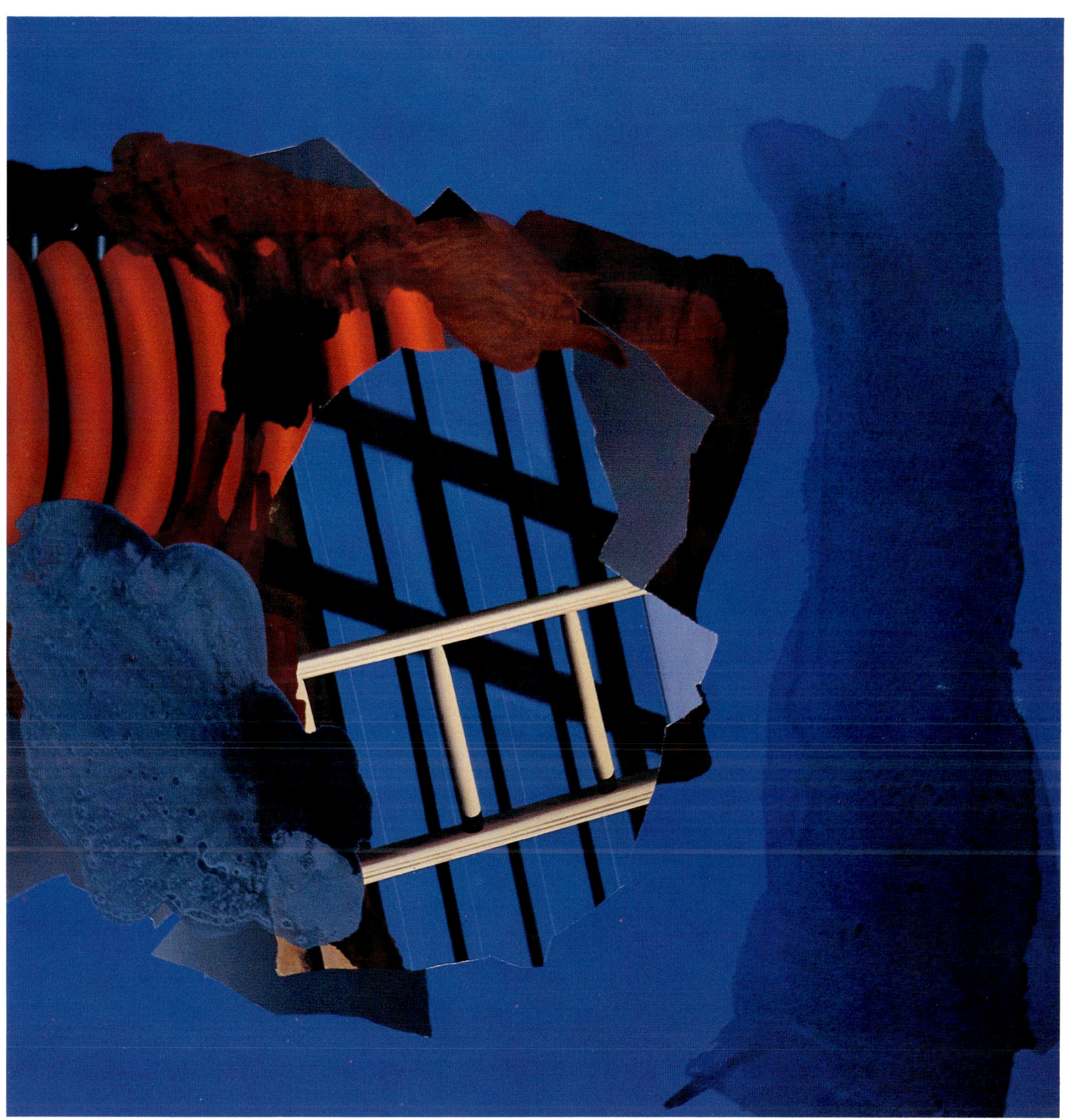

magazines, which gives a contemporary edge to what are otherwise non-specific subjects. In this he shows the explicit relevance of abstract painting in highlighting the ways we perceive the outside world today, so varied in appearance and form.

Pattison has held one-person exhibitions throughout Britain and has been represented in group exhibitions across Europe. He is represented in public and private collections across the United Kingdom, including the Scottish Arts Council.

Artist's Comment

I have recently been working with, and from, collage and am interested by the sudden abrupt changes in focus which collage can achieve. Various intuitive, softer marks are painted and printed in relation to the pictures as they progress. I am trying to eventually produce a satisfactory synthesis of these various and seemingly disparate elements and marks.

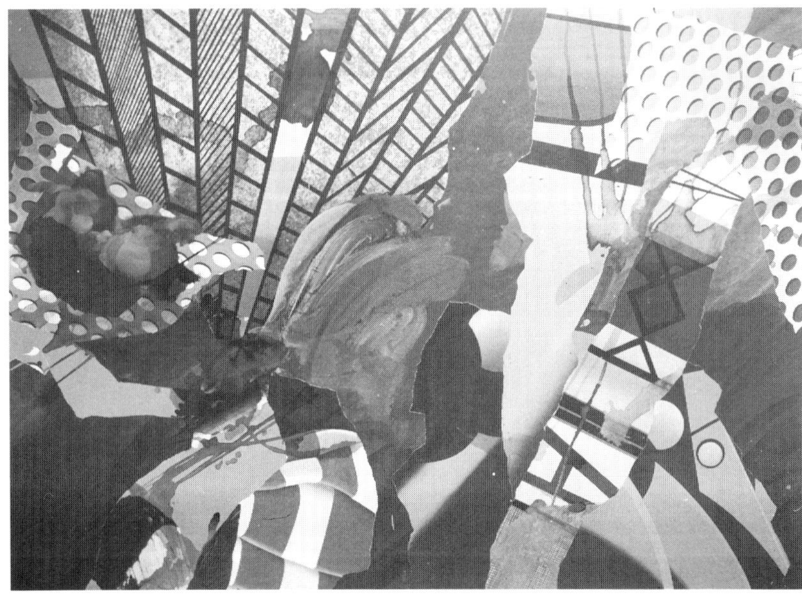

Painting (6) '87, 1987,
Acrylic on canvas, 152 x 213 cm,
Photograph: James Pattison,
Collection of the artist

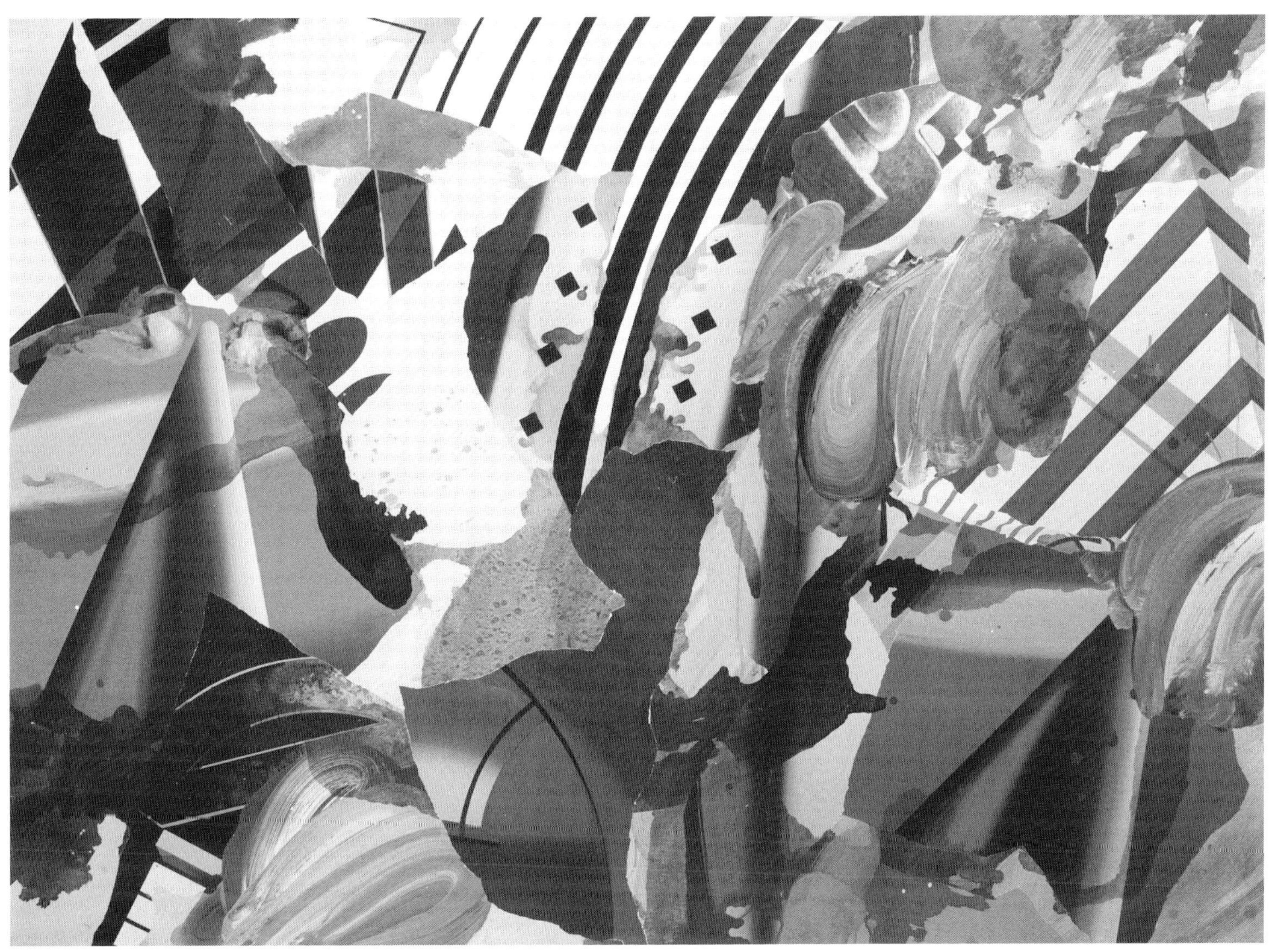

Painting (8) '86, 1986,
Acrylic on canvas, 152 x 213 cm,
Photograph: James Pattison,
Collection of the artist

FRED POLLOCK

Fred Pollock was born in Glasgow in 1937. He studied at Glasgow School of Art (1955–59) and since then has taught at various art colleges in England — at Brighton and Canterbury, for example — as well as being invited as guest artist at the Triangle Art Workshop, New York, in 1984. He has lived and worked in London for many years and is associated with the Stockwell Depot group of abstract painters.

If man's relationship with Nature was the dominant concern of art in the 19th century, then in this century modern art has shifted its attention elsewhere. Two things in particular have obsessed the art of our times — object and colour. Why this should be is too complex to pursue here, but both these central themes in modern art relate to Fred Pollock's work.

As colour is so obviously the integral issue of his paintings, maybe the 'object' aspect should be dealt with first. The type of painting that Pollock has evolved for himself is clearly linked to a form of abstraction that was developed in America and particularly New York in the 1940s and 1950s. On the whole, that is a tradition of modern painting that is taken up with purely pictorial concerns. Many artists working in this mode have tried to focus exclusively on the optical properties of painting; for example, by staining their pigments into the canvas and allowing the colour to speak for itself. Pollock, however, has shifted away from such an approach and thickened his paints so that the physical properties and the various methods of application of his materials are emphatically drawn to our attention. Furthermore, the 'objectification' of his paintings is continued by the actual shape they take, which, although decided in the final stages, tends always towards the panel-like; an extended rectilinear format either in the vertical or the horizontal. Thus, it is much more difficult for the viewer to treat these paintings in a conventional manner, as pictures into which one looks. Rather, we are forced to see them as flat shapes onto which paint has been applied. Looking at a Pollock work, one is reminded of Meyer Shapiro's observation that a painting is the last hand-made object produced by a skilled craftsman.

Irish Night, 1990,
Acrylic on canvas, 170 x 124.5 cm,
Private collection,
Courtesy Vanessa Devereux Gallery, London

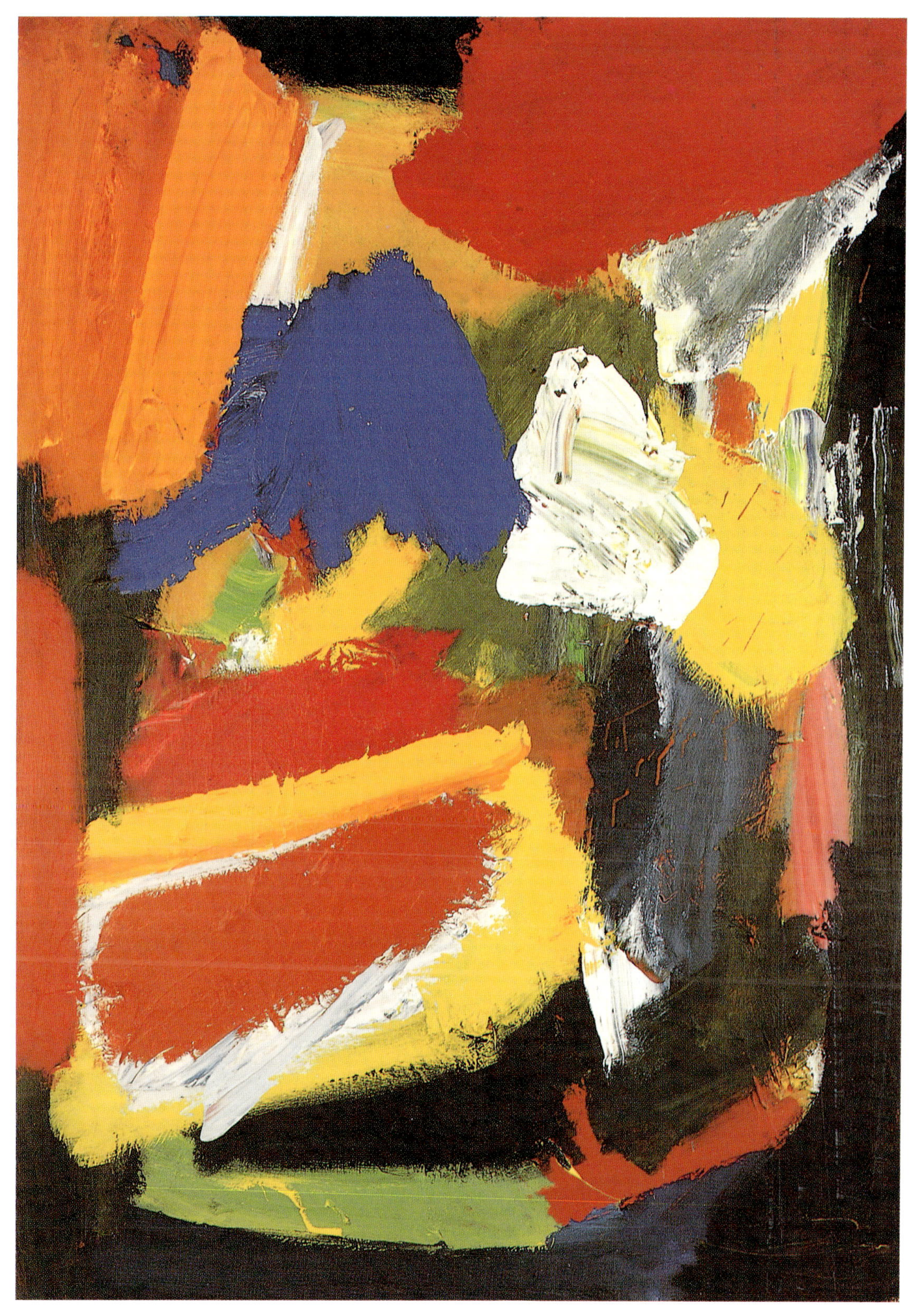

Colour, of course, is the major preoccupation of Pollock's painting. Yet, even here there is an emphasis of solidity which adds significantly to the sheer presence of the work. This strong sense of pictorial physicality is achieved through various strategies. Firstly, each individual application of colour, although sustained within the whole pictorial arrangement, has its own distinctive identity. Secondly, as the result of what has just been said, there is no illusionism; the whole process of how each painting is constructed is clearly presented as each slab of pigment butts or overlaps its neighbour. Thirdly, the colour relationships are bold, but self-supporting, thus creating a strong feeling of thrusting patterns of internal forces not unlike a piece of constructive sculpture. This sculptural vigour must have struck Anthony Caro, who commented on Pollock's work: 'These paintings don't only look good at first acquaintance; they stay good.'

Fred Pollock has shown widely in Britain, on the Continent and USA. He exhibits with the Vanessa Devereux Gallery, London, and his work is represented in many private and public collections, both in Britain and abroad.

Artist's Comment

My aim is to make the painting as visually exciting and aesthetically stimulating as possible through an intuitive use of colour and space.

Three Yellows on Golden Brown, 1988–89,
Acrylic on canvas, 213.5 x 173 cm,
Photograph: Peter White,
Courtesy Vanessa Devereux Gallery, London

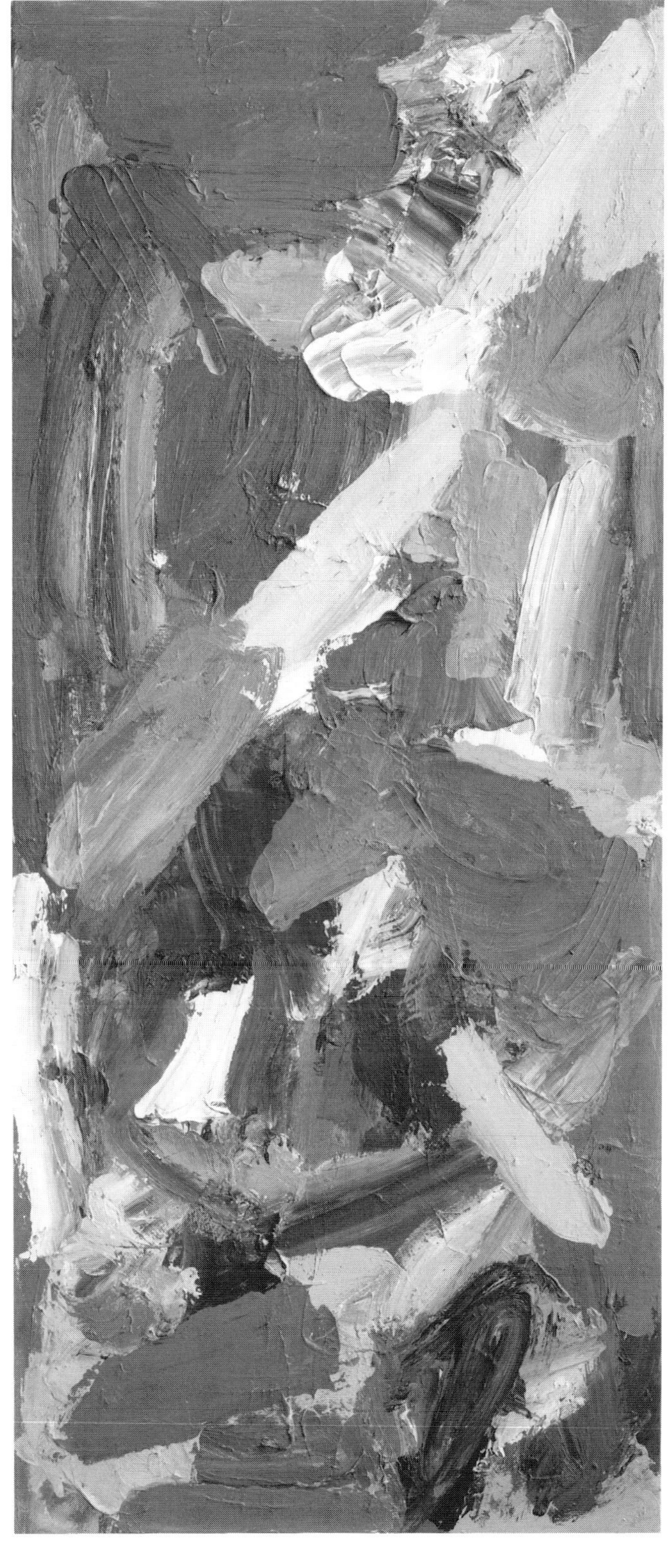

Dutch Spring II, 1991,
Acrylic on canvas, 221 x 97 cm,
Photograph: Peter White,
Courtesy Vanessa Devereux Gallery, London

BARBARA RAE

Barbara Rae was born in 1943 and grew up in Crieff, Perthshire. She studied at Edinburgh College of Art (1961–65) and then went into secondary school art education (1968–72). Since 1975 she has taught in the Drawing and Painting Department at Glasgow School of Art. She has won many awards for her painting and was elected President of the Society of Scottish Artists in 1983.

On first acquaintance one might be forgiven for regarding Barbara Rae's paintings as purely abstract compositions. However, on closer inspection, as in a cubist picture, their outside source of inspiration begins to emerge. Elements from the language of landscape painting, a distinct high horizon, a foreground tree shape for example, being to catch the eye. Furthermore, the titles, whether of a remote west of Scotland beach or a quarry in Tuscany, give each painting a claim to a specific experience involving the artist and her subject, which locates it both in time and place.

It could be argued that the history of landscape painting is the pictorial record of the changing relationship between the artist and the natural world. Towards the end of the last century a crisis arose when the Impressionists, scientifically inspired ideal of a totally objective record of observed reality began to appear as an unrealisable dream. Not only did it start to strike them that appearances were too fugitive to be pinned down with any certainty, but also the object/subject relationship between the painter and his/her motive was much more complex and interrelated than was originally conceded. Artists were forced to seek various solutions and out of this crisis modern art was born.

One course which was taken, and to which Rae's work is heir, was that initiated by Gauguin and the Synthesists. Here the artist will still seek out inspirational aspects of natural scenery or the man-made environment and sketch on the spot the dominant characteristics of the subject observed. However, the creative process may not really get under way until much later in the studio. Only then, after the artist has mentally and emotionally distilled these initial objective impressions, can they be transformed into a decorative arrangement that not only has to work within the

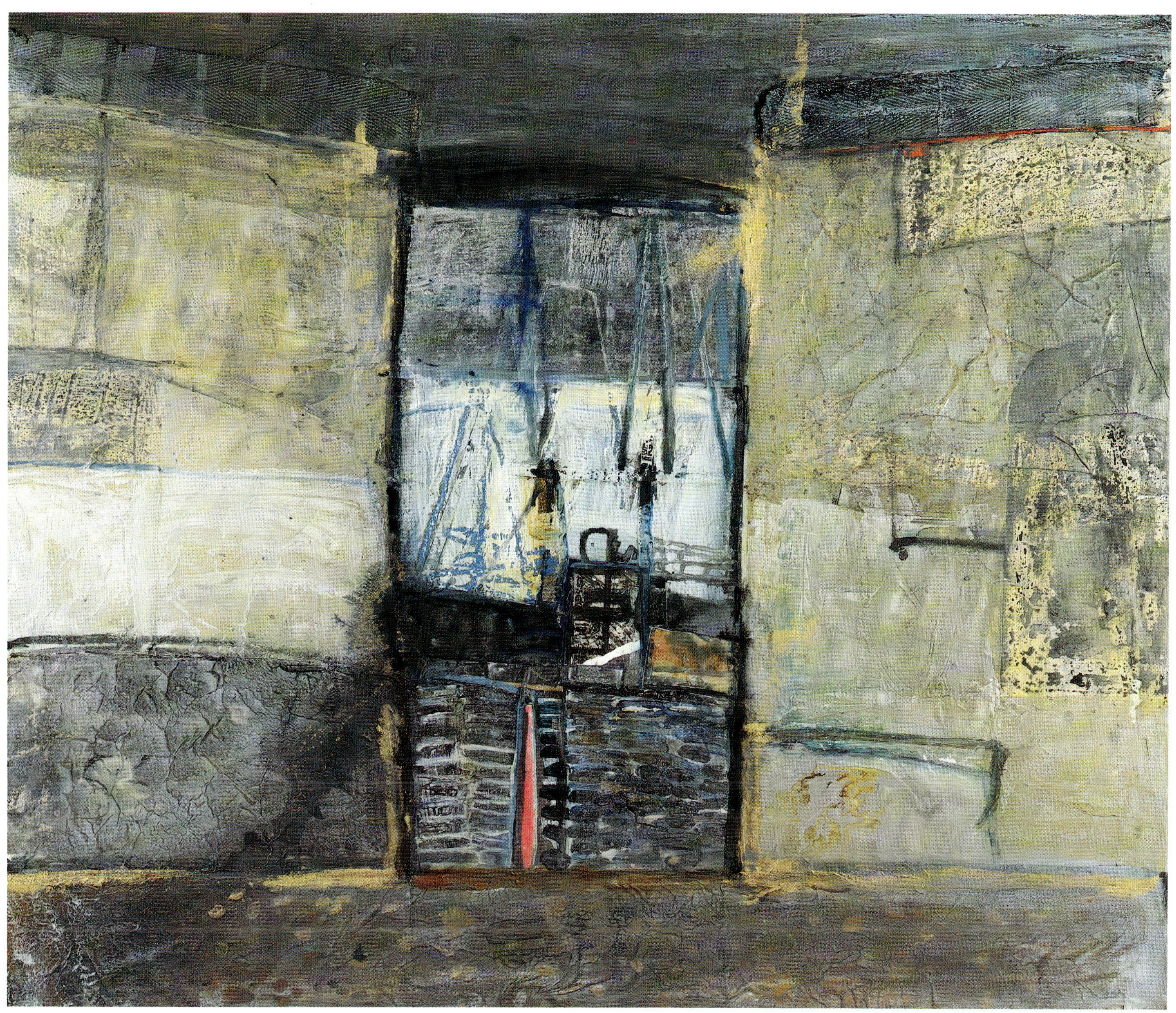

Leith Morning, 1989,
Oil on canvas, 152 x 183 cm,
Photograph: Antonia Reeve

chosen pictorial format, but also expresses the subjective feelings that the artist has developed towards the subject — and the painting of the subject. For the actual painting, if successful, has to stand as an object — a *talisman* — to work wonders in its own right. Within this particular tradition of modern art, Barbara Rae's paintings are extremely successful. Through the varied use of bold compositions, strong contrasting colours and richly textured painted and collaged surfaces, her landscapes not only delight the eye with their assured sense of decorative order but also stimulate emotional associations by their evocative mood and atmosphere.

Barbara Rae has a very impressive exhibition record, having shown her work in prestigious galleries and art fairs throughout Britain and abroad. She has strong links with the Scottish Gallery and showed in their new London Gallery in 1990. Her work is represented in many private and public collections, both in Britain and abroad, including the Scottish National Gallery of Modern Art and the British Museum.

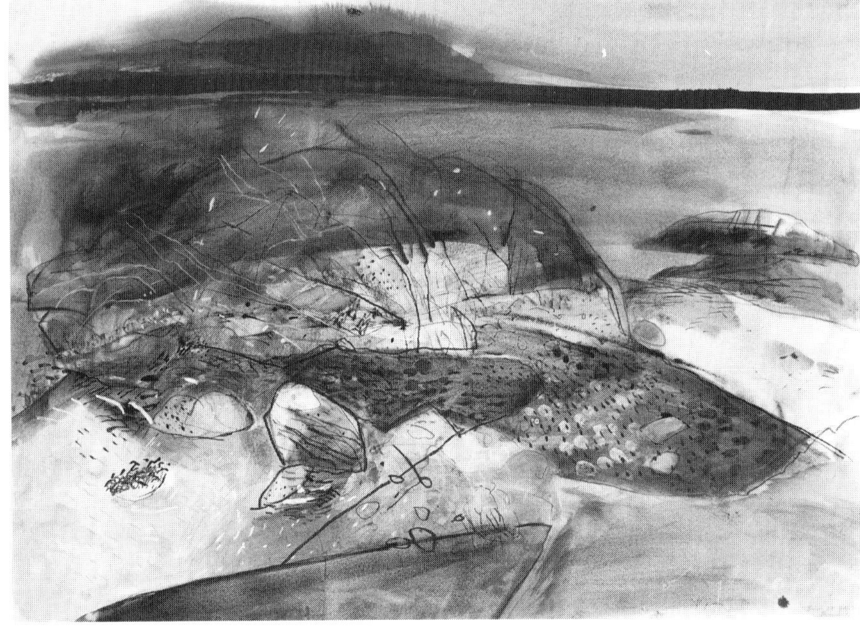

Beach at Ardtoe, 1984,
Ink and chalk on paper, 76 x 102 cm

January Quarry Ballachulish, 1985,
Oil and collage on canvas, 183 x 183 cm

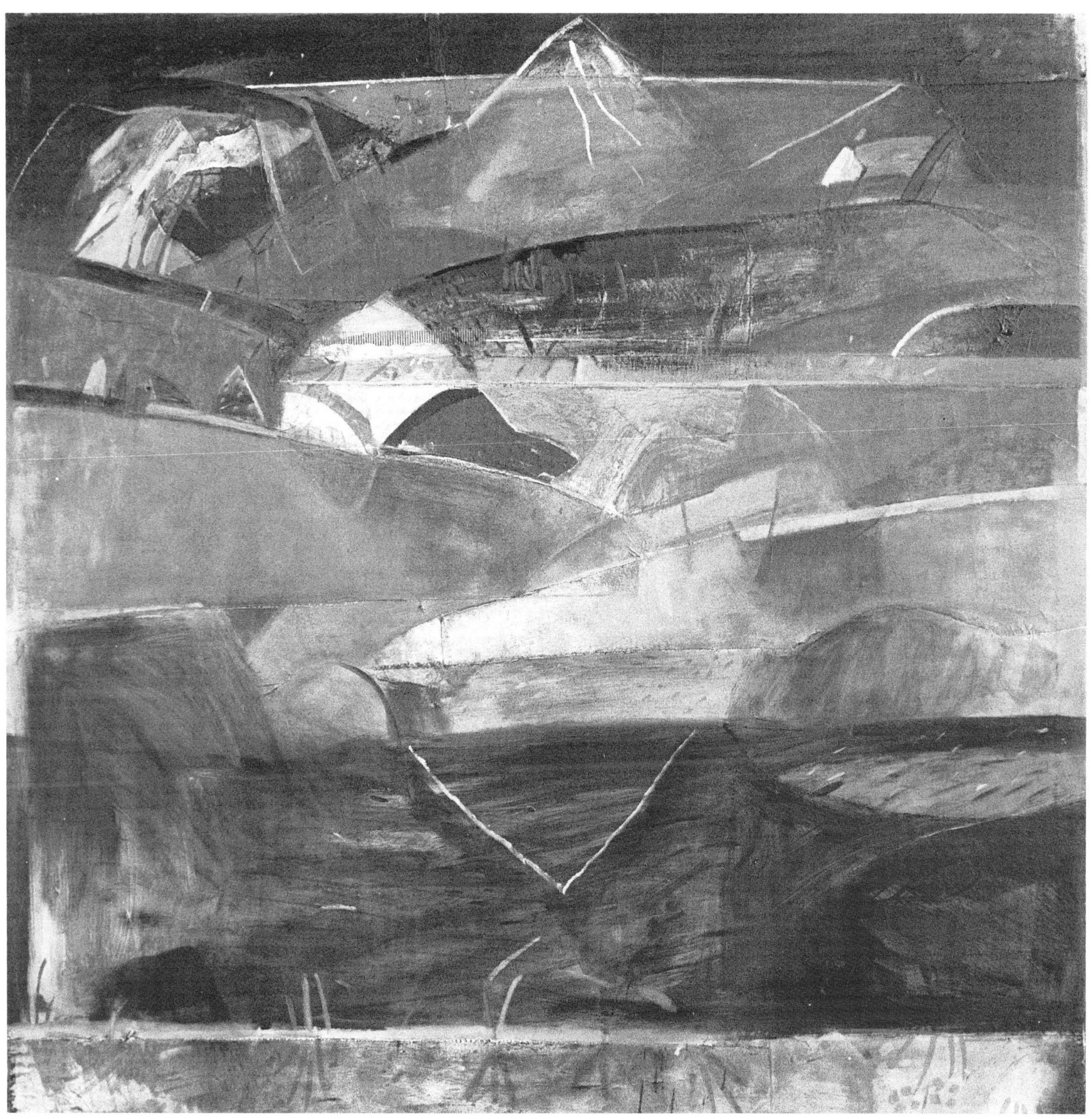

JUNE REDFERN

June Redfern was born in St Andrews, Fife, in 1951 and trained at Edinburgh College of Art (1968–72). After college she taught at a secondary school in Leith, Edinburgh, then at Preston Polytechnic (1982–83), followed by a junior artist-in-residency at the National Gallery, London. Since 1986 she has been a visiting tutor to various art colleges in Scotland and England. She lives and works in London.

Surely it is only a coincidence, but it is interesting that June Redfern was born in St Andrews, a major centre in Scottish Church history, for she is that rare phenomenon in the late 20th century — a religious painter. Her paintings are not religious in any conventional sense. They are poetic not iconic. Fond of allusion, she strenuously avoids presenting any specific meaning in her pictures. However, her work does touch on issues of profound concern — whether of a private personal nature or of wider universal significance — such as the divine and angelic forces in human affairs and Man's perverse resistance to their guidance. Furthermore, it is not only the chosen themes in her work that place her as an heir to the great history of religious art, but also the manner in which she finds expression for these human and spiritual matters. If her paintings can be linked thematically to the ideas of religious art, then stylistically they are within the Baroque tradition of that type of painting. Through the artist's intuitive free handling of paint, which can become expressive in its own right, she infuses into her work the same soaring movement, the operatic grandeur, the virtuoso dexterity and rich sensual colouration that can be found in a 17th century master such as Rubens. As with the great Baroque artists, Redfern's paintings, at their best, can be highly dramatic and, at the same time, deeply moving. Having rejected in her early work a realistic approach to painting, she, like her inspiring Scottish predecessor, Joan Eardley, has developed her concentration on the power of colour, texture and gesture, rather than descriptive forms, to convey the emotional impact of her pictures. As in all great art, but particularly religious painting, the ultimate meaning of her work cannot be rationally explained. The significance of the poetic imagery in the paintings, the crouching pensive figures, the wooded river bank, the twilit landscape, can only become apparent through the

Boy with Blossoms, 1989–90,
Oil on canvas, 137 x 107 cm,
Photograph: J. Morris-Ebbs

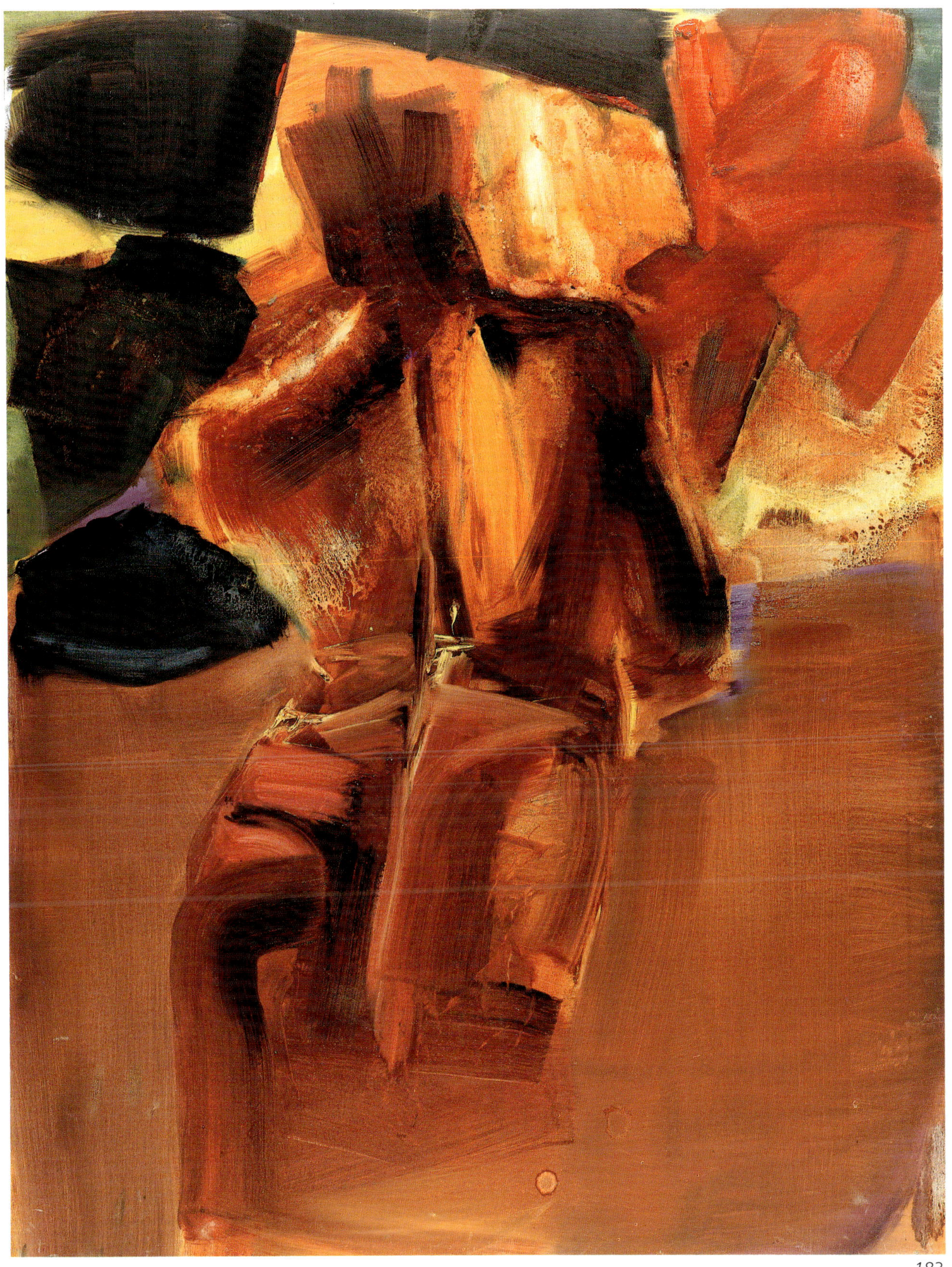

unfolding of the viewer's emotional reaction to the complex range of feelings which the artist expresses in each painting.

June Redfern's paintings are not finished statements, but open-ended impulses of a deeply subjective nature. She paints from memory and in her recent work the thematic aspects of her pictures have become more autobiographical. Using the power of painting to evoke memories of her own life history, the latest work investigates how the artist can use the gift of memory to activate the subconscious to produce free associative feelings and images in the search for self-discovery. A much more introspective mood pervades these new paintings and maybe June Redfern is now moving away from Rubens and coming closer to Rembrandt in her own distinctive manner of Baroque painting.

Since 1976 June Redfern has had nearly 20 solo exhibitions in Scotland, England and USA. Her work is represented in a number of private and public collections, including the National Gallery, London, and the Scottish National Gallery of Modern Art, Edinburgh.

Artist's Comment

I want to make my work more and more daring, but more intense and personal.
I wish I could paint like people make music — paint an aria!

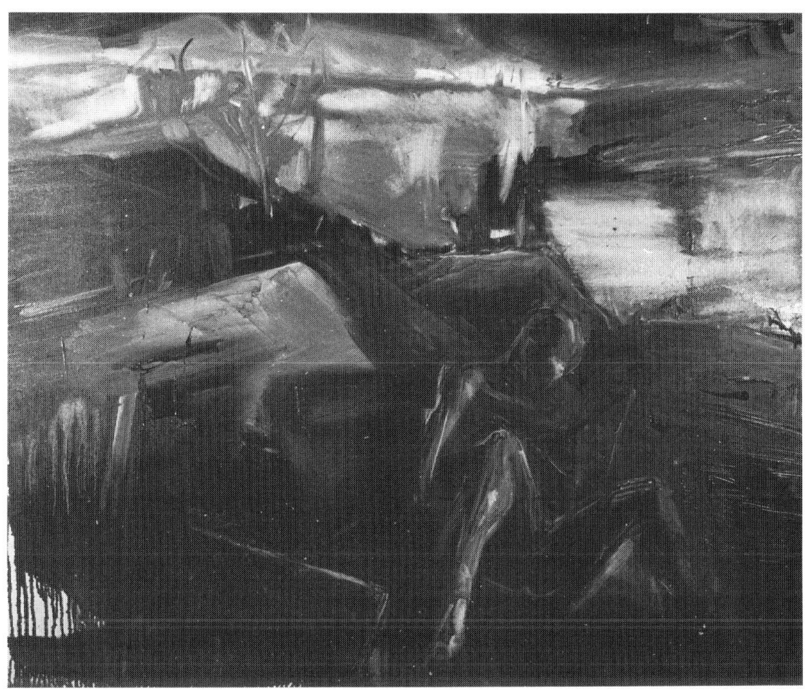

Fisherman, 1988,
Oil on canvas, 97 x 117 cm,
Private collection

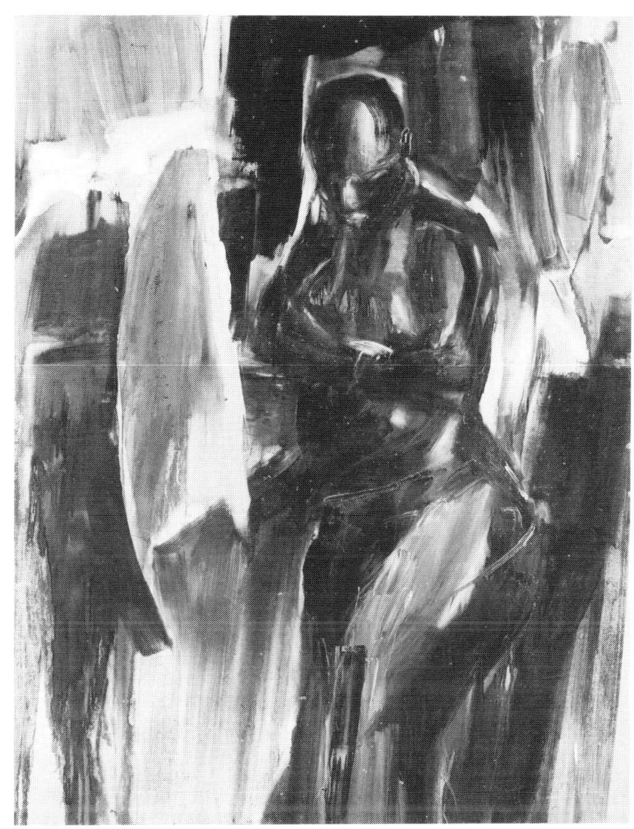

Big Blue Nude, 1990,
Oil on canvas, 168 x 152 cm,
Private collection

Iain Robertson was born in Nicosia, Cyprus. Educated in Edinburgh, he did not go to art school until he was in his early 20s. He trained in England — at Cumbria College of Art, Carlisle (1978–79) and Exeter College of Art (1979–82) — and remained in Exeter, working at the SPACEX studios (1982–86). He has won the prodigious Pollock-Krasner Foundation award (1988) and a Scottish Arts Council award (1990). In 1988 he returned to Edinburgh where he now lives and works as a full-time painter.

As with the best of contemporary abstract painting, the 'eye' is the motivating, controlling factor and for Robertson it is the visual delight that colour and texture can directly express in themselves which is the main theme of his work. In order to convey and intensify the visual excitement in his work, he has gradually, over the past ten years, developed his technical facility in handling paint, along with a heightening of his critical senses, leading to a greater control over the step-by-step process of picture making. Whereas his earlier paintings were tentative exercises in muted colours — composed with clear positive and negative areas of activity — he now has the experience to develop his practice so that all aspects of his paintings are equally a part of the overall interconnection of sensual colour, gestural shape and textured surface. Also, when the works are seen as a group, this feeling of interrelationship increases, linking the paintings themselves with each other and so creating an overall sense of organic process. Robertson tends to paint his canvases in square or strong vertical forms which adds to their material presence. The raw, intuitive manner of application also gives an immediacy to his paintings which stresses the actuality of their physical being.

As Robertson builds up his paintings through the expressive application of oil paint, the whole process through which each picture evolves to its independent existence can be witnessed by the viewer's discerning eye. Therefore, the meaning of each painting is itself the sum of what the artist puts into it and what the viewer gets out. The sheer celebration of sensual pleasure in textures and colours makes Robertson's paintings Gardens of Earthly Delights for those who allow their eye and

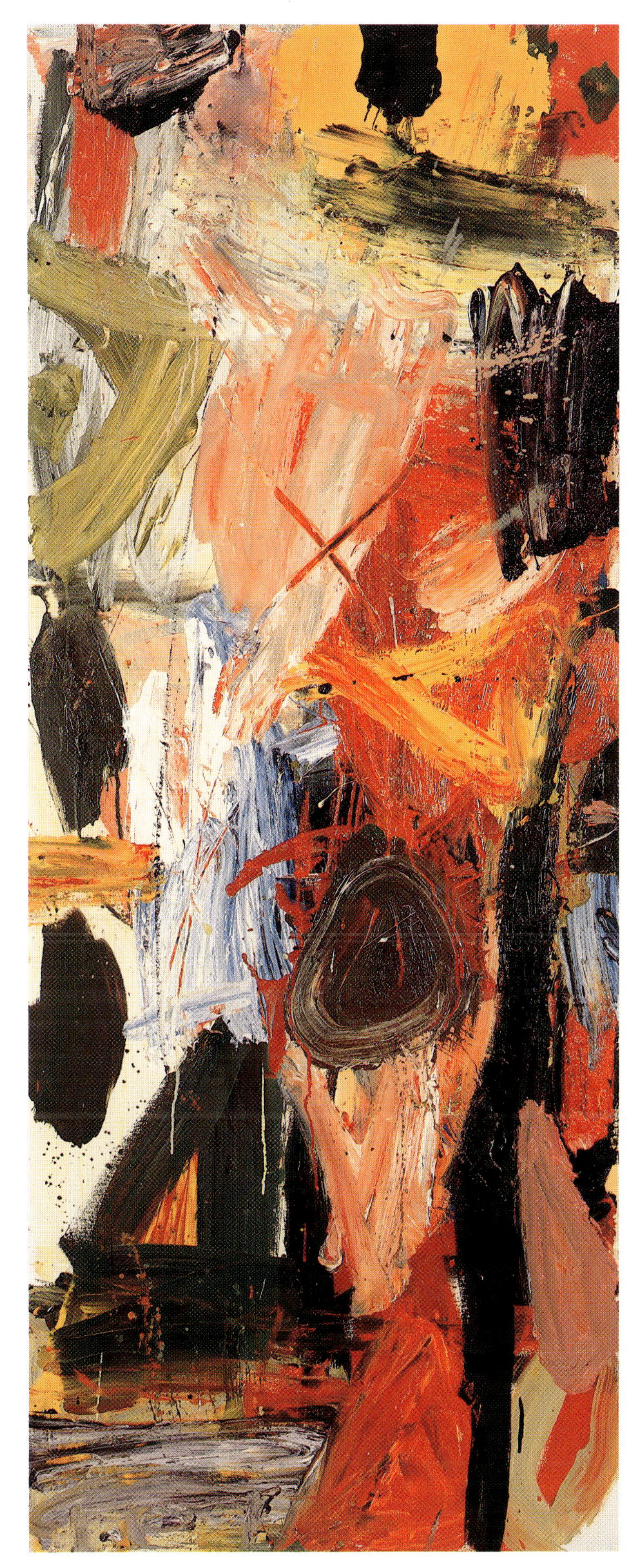

Honeydripper, 1991,
Oil on canvas, 180 x 73 cm,
Photograph: Catriona Grant
Collection of the artist

their senses to act as one.

Iain Robertson has exhibited not only in Great Britain, but also in France and the USA.

Artist's Comment

My paintings are abstract. Through the physical act of painting I spontaneously put down colour and shape, working intuitively and directly onto the canvas from all four sides. A period of improvisation persists until my participation is no longer necessary, and the work takes on a life of its own.

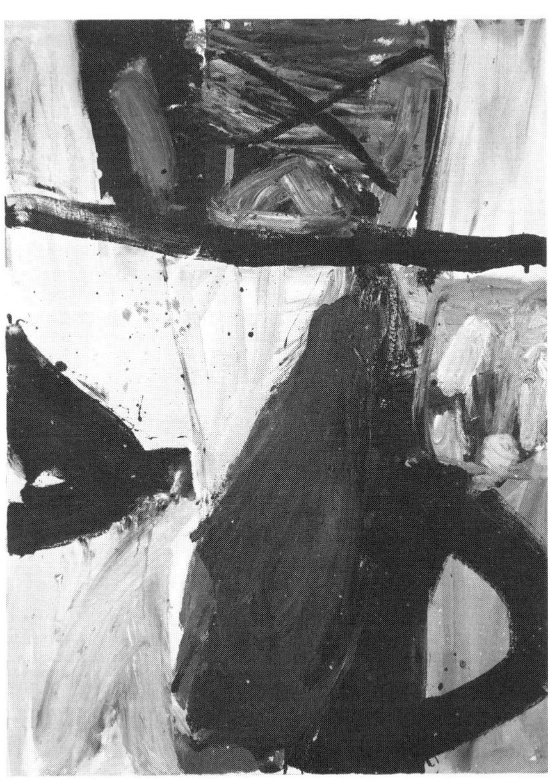

CW, 1991,
Oil on canvas, 122 x 91 cm,
Photograph: Catriona Grant,
Collection of the artist

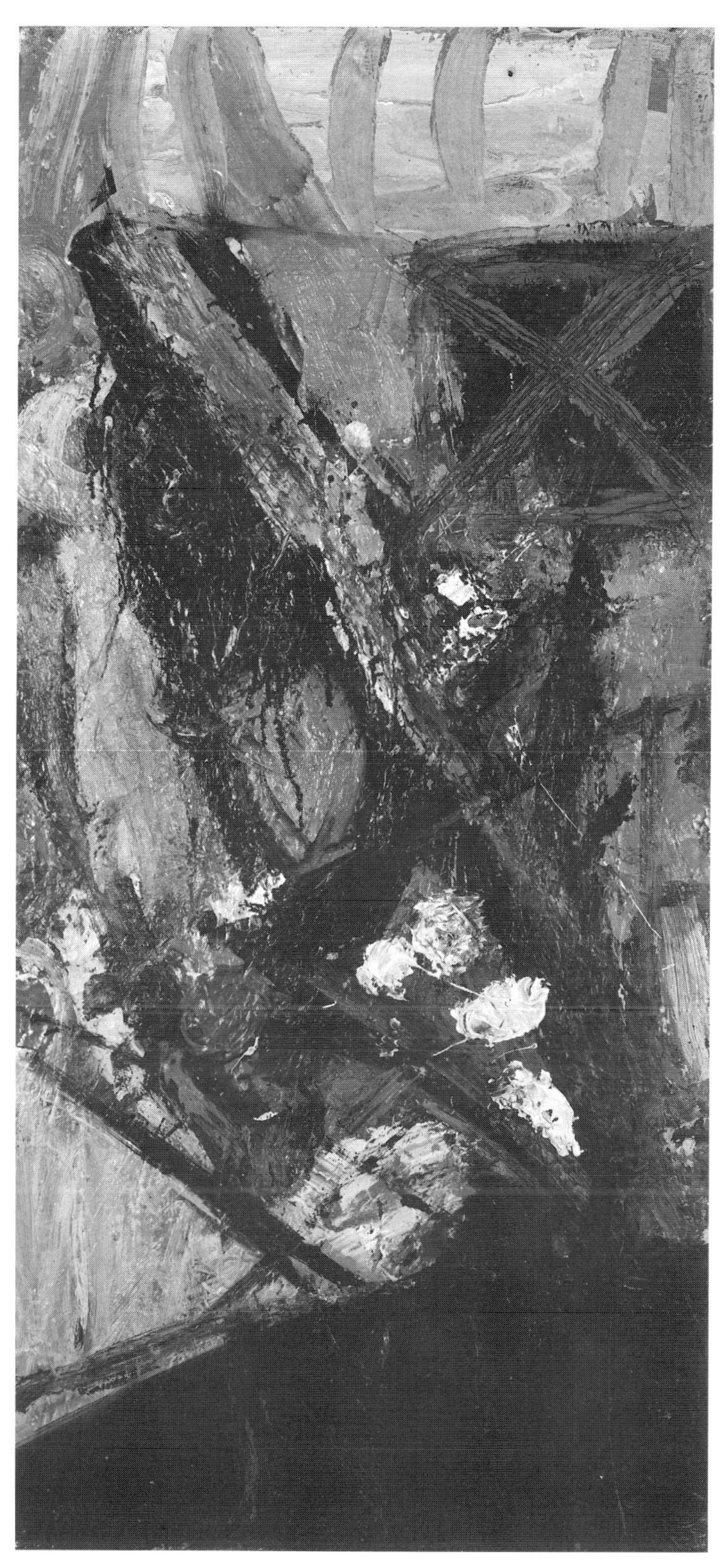

Untitled, 1985,
Oil on canvas, 107 x 51 cm,
Photograph: Catriona Grant,
Collection of the artist

DUNCAN SHANKS

Duncan Shanks was born in Airdrie in 1937. He studied at Glasgow School of Art and went to Italy on a post-diploma scholarship. He taught as a part-time lecturer at Glasgow School of Art until 1979. Over the years he has won a number of awards for his paintings from the Scottish Arts Council, the Royal Scottish Academy and Royal Glasgow Institute. He now lives and works as a full-time painter in the Clyde valley in Lanarkshire.

If, as many would like to believe, the Scottish landscape was the birthplace of European romanticism, then the Clyde valley was the cradle of that great movement. For over 20 years Duncan Shanks has lived and worked from this area of the Scottish countryside, which has been a source of inspiration to poets and artists since the 18th century. The sweeping grandeur and the ancient historical associations of Cora Linn and the Falls of the Clyde made such a strong impression on the Scottish romantic imagination that a series of paintings of that subject, by Jacob More, was hailed as the first 'national' landscapes. Of course, romanticism and nationalism were always deeply interconnected but in Scotland's case the relationship was crucial. Scotland lost its independent sovereignty with the Union in 1707 and as such its quest for national identity had to have a cultural rather than a political basis. Thus, this rise of the importance of landscape north of the border. For it was there, in the landscape, that Scottish artists and their fellow countrymen sought to find through the untamed natural scenery the fundamental qualities of the Scottish character. If the German landscape painters sought to communicate with the divine spirit and the English yearned for a return to a rural arcadia, then the Scots searched for their lost identity when they confronted the natural world.

Through the lineage of McTaggart and Eardley, Duncan Shanks' landscapes continue the romantic tradition in Scottish art. His paintings are not immediate objective records of what he witnesses, but prolonged subjective reactions to what he sees and feels. They are not topographical but poetical. They are not descriptive, but discursive. As with all true romantic art, his paintings suggest questions, rather than state answers. The investigative nature of his work, however, is not as in the

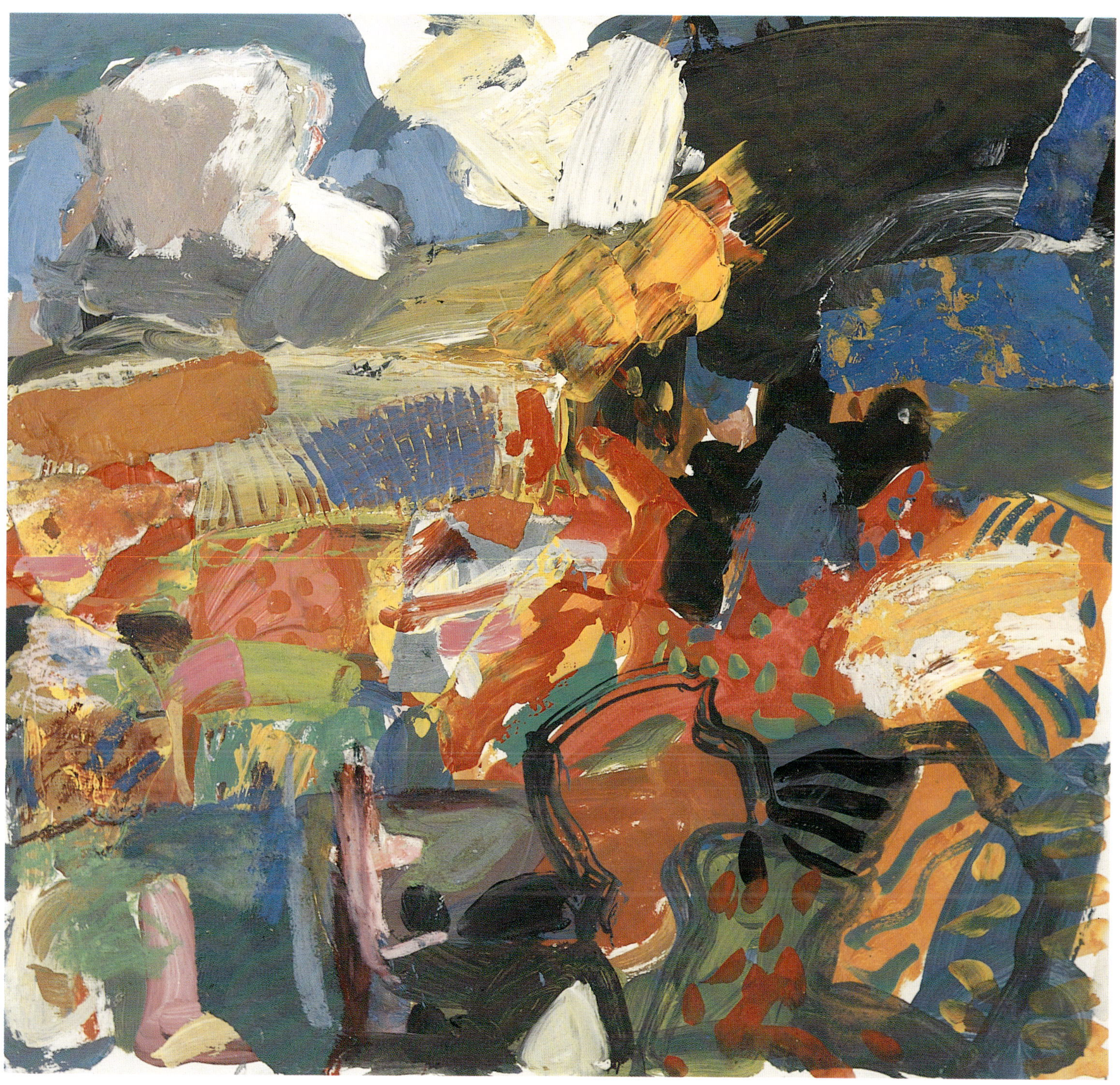

Fruit Fields, 1990,
Acrylic on paper with collage, 41 x 44 cm,
Photograph: Marilyn Muirhead
Collection of the artist

18th century manner a quest for identity within the processes of history, but rather within the dialectics of modern art; a continual exploration within the natural world of the relationship between image and experience, representation and reality. His best paintings are an ongoing struggle. They are full of all kinds of inner tension; between pictorial space and surface manipulation, between spontaneous gesture and representational significance, between independent colour and associative description and ultimately between the act of painting and the final image.

Duncan Shanks is rapidly becoming one of the most successful painters in Scotland. He mainly shows in Edinburgh and Glasgow. His work is represented in many private and public collections, such as the Scottish Arts Council, the Arts Council of Great Britain and three of the Scottish universities.

Artist's Comment

I never feel I finish a painting. One solution is left and the search continues on another canvas.

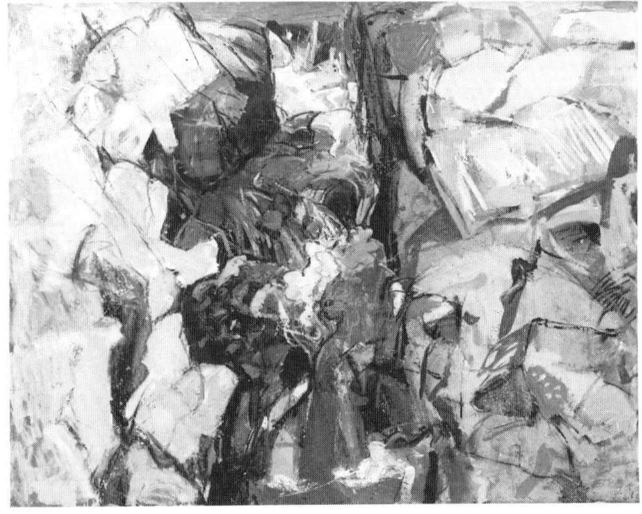

Dipper's Gully, 1990,
Oil on canvas, 152 x 198 cm,
Photograph: R. Marilynn Muirhead,
Collection of the artist

Straight Dykes, 1989,
Oil on canvas, 152 x 152 cm,
Photograph: R. Marilynn Muirhead,
Collection of the artist

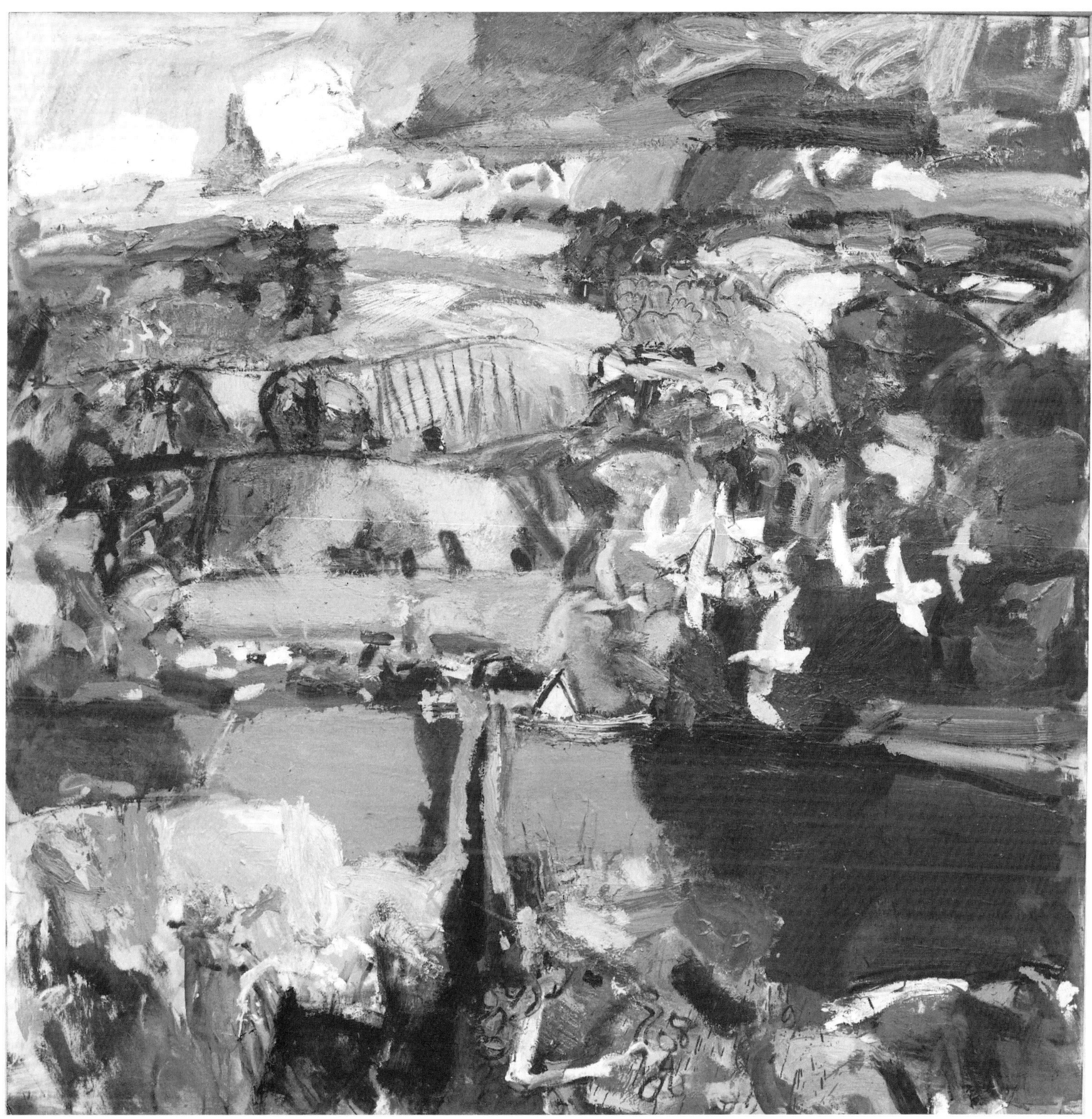

Peter Thomson was born in Glasgow in 1962 and studied at Glasgow School of Art (1980–84). He has remained in Glasgow where he works as a full-time artist and is a member of the Artists' Collective Gallery, Transmission. He was awarded a Scottish Arts Council assistance grant in 1990.

Despite its promotional success in creating a new image for itself, especially as a centre for cultural innovation, beneath the surface Glasgow remains a deeply divided city. It requires an artist with a concerned knowledge of its history and the history of painting to deal with such a complex subject. Although still in the early stages of his career Peter Thomson is such an artist. His major achievement to date has been to present, within the great tradition of European humanist art, his own reactions as a 'lapsed Catholic, working class male' to the environmental, social and psychological experience of living in the former second city of the Empire as it tries to shed its industrial past for a new consumer-oriented identity. To place his paintings within the lineage of Breughel, Rembrandt, Hogarth, Goya, Courbet, Grosz, Beckmann and Dix is not to commend him for his art-historical awareness, but to recognise the profoundly challenging nature of his work. As with those radical artists of the past he is committed to the belief that the primary duty of the artist, as social critic, is to strip away conventional appearances and prejudices and confront his public with the dark distorting forces in the human psyche and society which really condition the true nature of contemporary experience.

As is the case within the radical tradition of European painting, Thomson takes a pessimistic view of the world he paints. His perplexed pictures of nightmare landscapes and urban wastelands, inhabited by physically and socially deformed figures, are bleak to the point of despair. There is an all-pervasive atmosphere of alienation between social groups divided by cultural, religious, economic and sexual differences, while everywhere the bond between the human and the natural world is deeply fractured. However, what saves his pictures from being terminally despondent is that they are painted with such an intensity of commitment to the individual character of each aspect of the subject that the paintings take on — tragic or

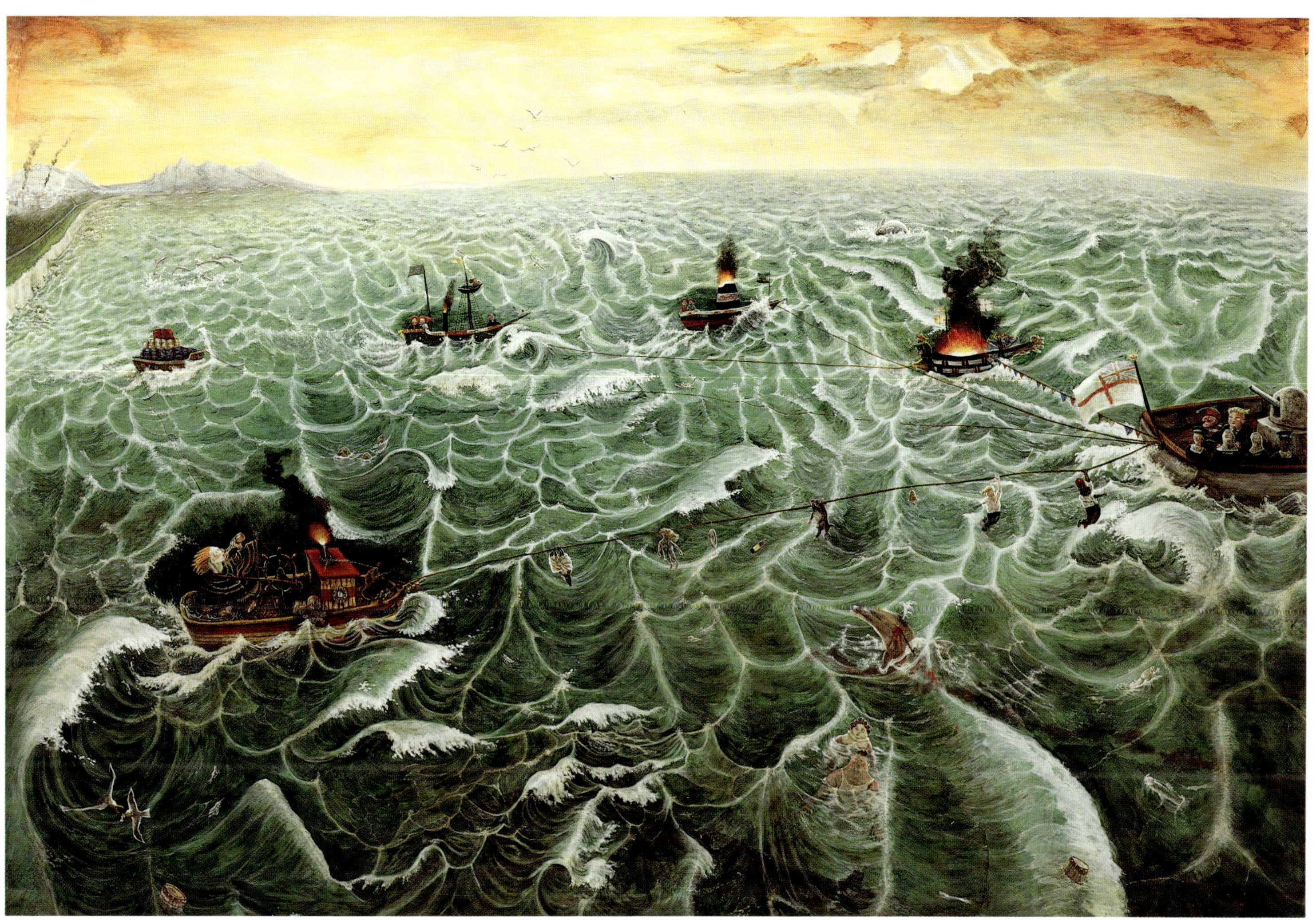

British Seascape, 1990,
Acrylic on paper, 102 x 147 cm,
Collection of the artist

comic dimensions which can still celebrate the human spirit. Remarkably, at such an early stage in his development, Thomson has acquired a means of presentation which can encompass both the personal and private as well as the public and historical. By using the expressive language of modern figurative art along with the stylistic authority of history painting, his work rises above mere illusionistic social realism and through the power of visual metaphor and allegory is able to address the moral complexities of modern life within a specific Scottish context.

Peter Thomson has shown in various group shows in Scotland and London and had his first major exhibition at Transmission Gallery in 1990. His work is represented in the Scottish Arts Council's collection.

Artist's Comment

Class, religion, the legacy of British imperialism, feelings of political impotence — part of the modern Scottish cultural and political make up — are the most important themes recurring in my painting.

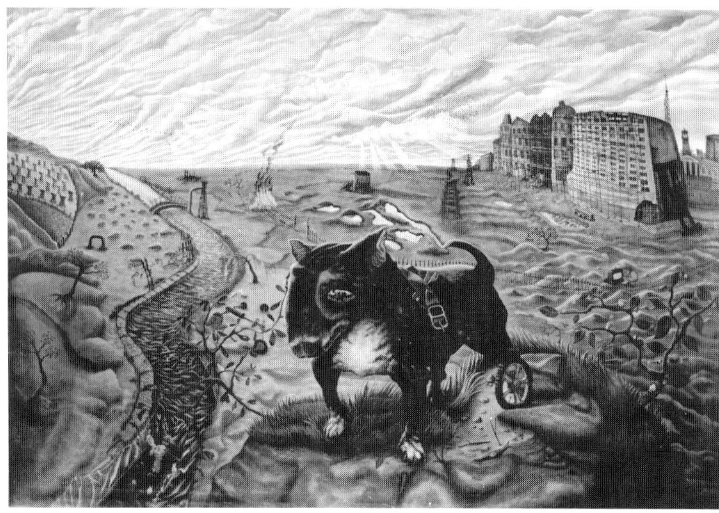

Garden City, 1989,
Acrylic on paper, 117 x 163 cm,
Collection of the artist

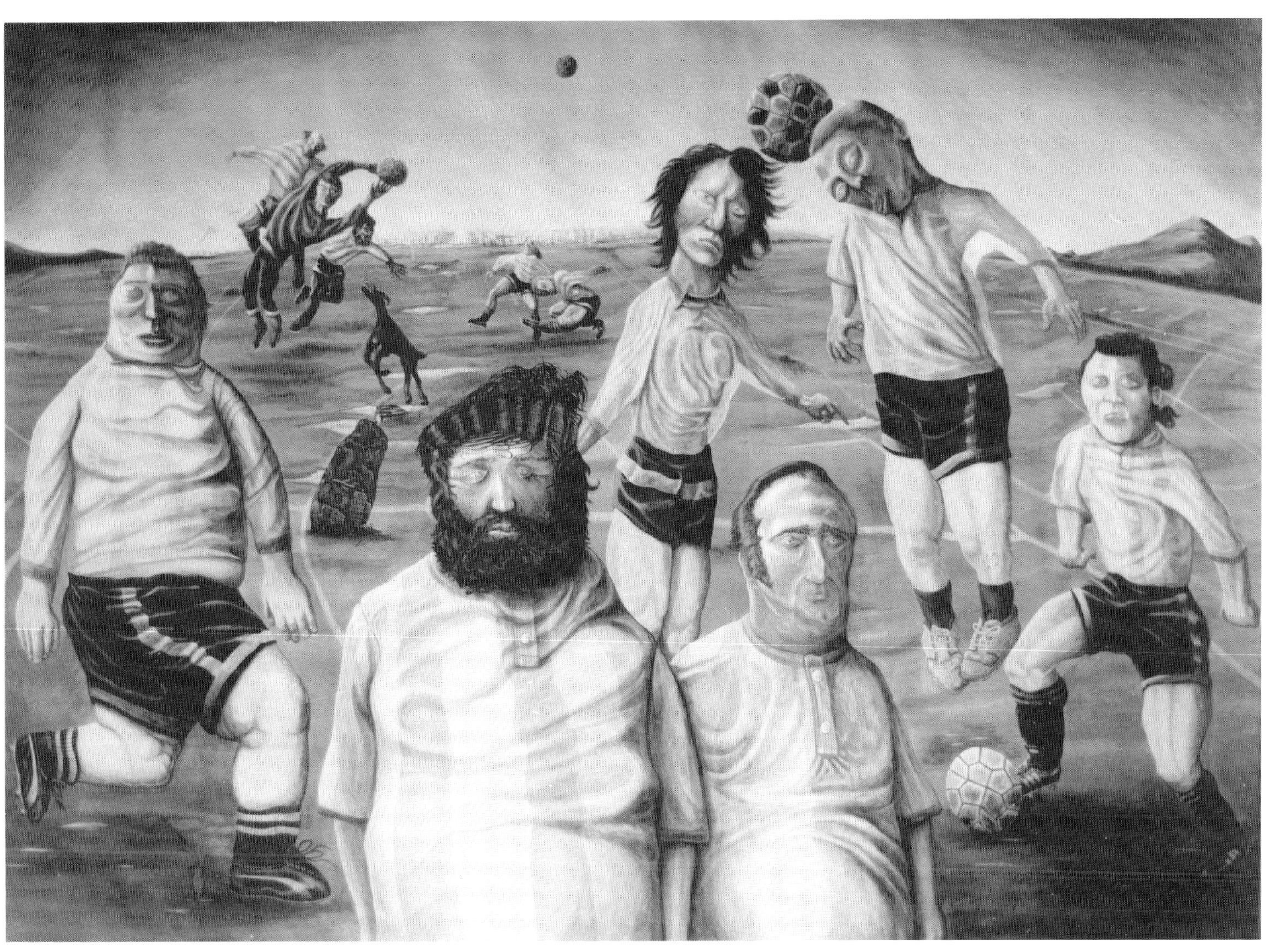

Pub Team, 1990,
Acrylic on paper, 102 x 152 cm,
Private collection

FRANCES WALKER

Frances Walker was born in Kirkcaldy, Fife, in 1930. She trained at Edinburgh College of Art (1947–53) and took her teaching diploma at Moray House College in 1956. After a spell as Visiting Teacher for Art in the islands of Harris and North Uist, Western Isles (1956–58), she became a long-serving teacher of drawing and painting at Gray's School of Art (1958–85) in Aberdeen. Retired from teaching, she can now more fully pursue her career as a landscape painter living and working alternatively in Aberdeen and on the isle of Tiree, where she has one of the few remaining thatched-roof houses as her home.

Frances Walker's landscapes are not what is usually associated with Scottish Art. They are distinctive both in subject and treatment. She avoids the obvious scenic beauties of Scotland and seeks out remote scenes of bare rocky coast-line. Furthermore, her treatment of such subjects is not typical of the Scottish landscape tradition. A superb draughtswoman, she never inclines to the Scottish *belle peinture* manner, but prefers a restrained objective approach, with the emphasis on line and structural form rather than gesture and decorative colour.

Apart from her deep attention to pictorial construction, Frances Walker has two main concerns as a committed landscape artist. Firstly, she absorbs herself in an intense analysis of geological forms to delve beneath the immediate surface of shifting appearances and, in her own words, 'reveal the structure, anatomy and dramatic origins of the landscape'. Secondly, she is always concerned to make aware the ever changing relationship between the natural environment and the human presence. Even if many of her landscapes appear uninhabited the man-made is subtly alluded to by a few distant standing stones, a ruined cottage, pieces of washed-up fishing tackle or a rusting beer can in a rock pool. Frances Walker's pictures transcend the merely topographical or the picturesque by her intense powers of observation, her sensitivity to atmosphere and her evocative associations of individual details to the landscape as a whole. She will also treat the same scene in various different media, conveying a profound sense of change and continuity not unlike the late series of paintings by Monet.

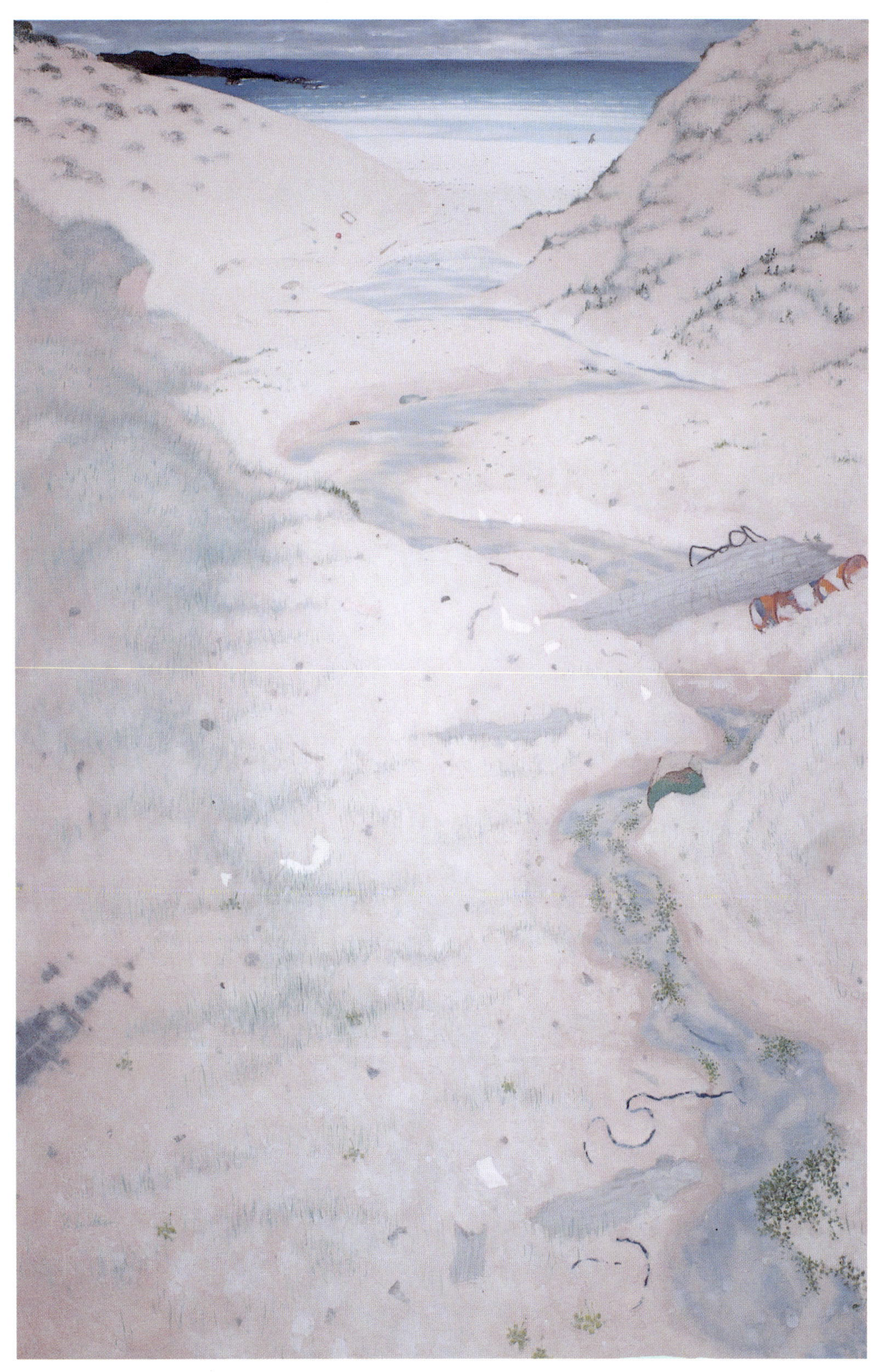

Tiree Shore, 1988,
Oil on canvas, 122 x 76 cm,
Photograph: Alistair Pebbles,
Collection of Mrs F. MacDonald

Frances Walker has had several one-person shows throughout Scotland since her
first in Edinburgh in 1957. Her work is represented in many private and public
collections, including the Scottish Arts Council.

Artist's Comment

*You paint because you are lonely. You paint because you are unhappy. I believe that
is often so, but it sounds negative —for although painting is a solitary and, by its
nature, isolating occupation, you are also, of course, by painting at all, making a very
positive assertion that you do not want to die — yet.*

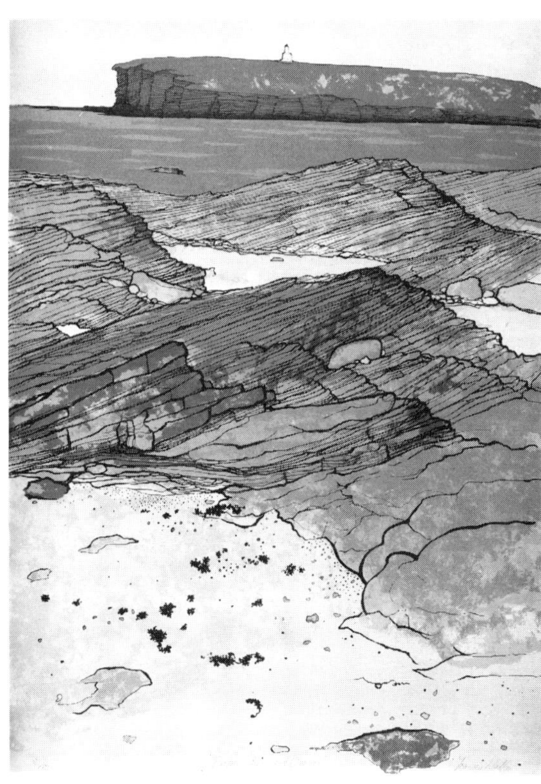

Birsay Shore and Brough, 1983,
Silkscreen, 79 x 58 cm,
Photograph: Joe Rock

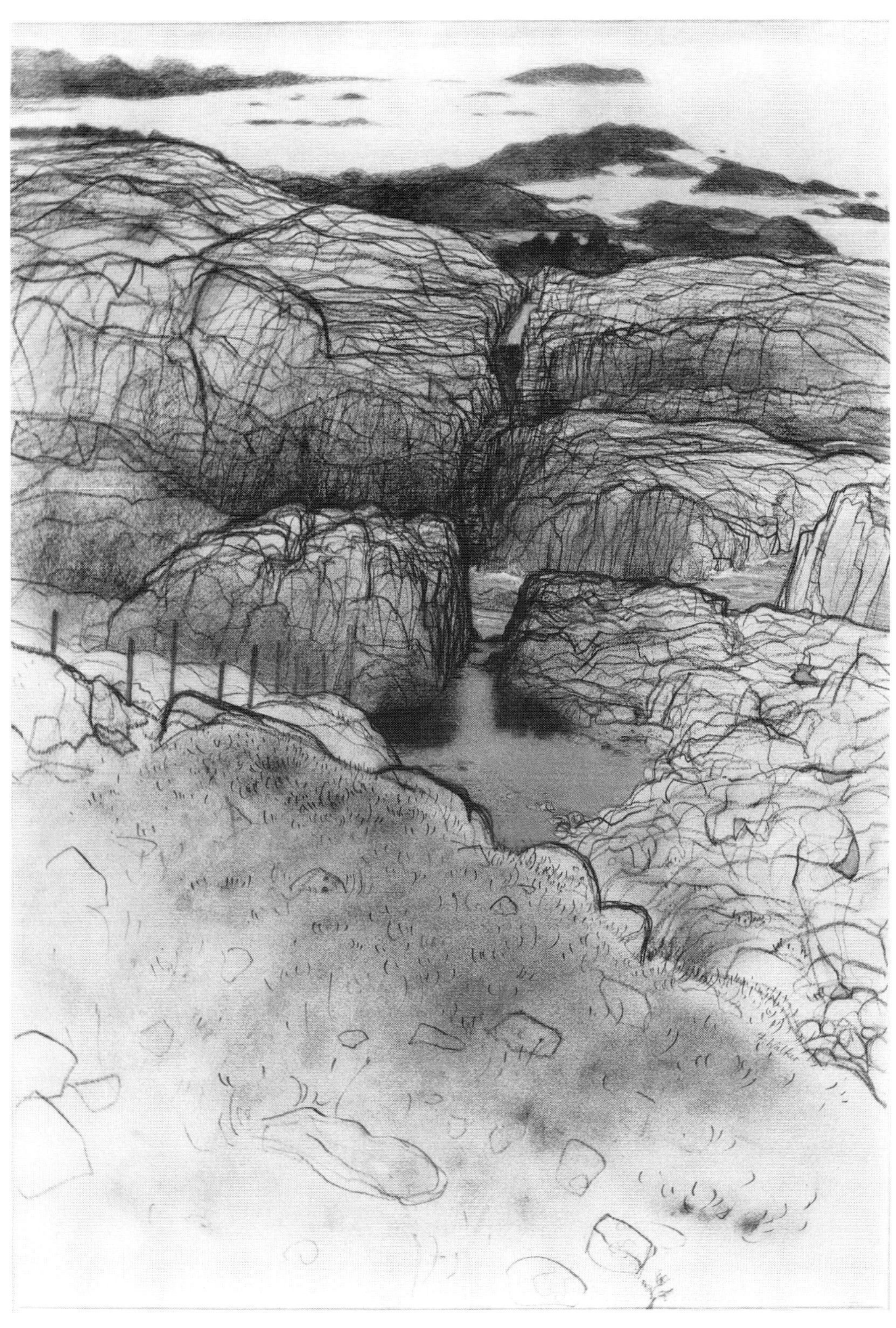

Rocks and Sea, Tiree, 1989,
Charcoal and chalk on paper,
76 x 53 cm,
Photograph: Alistair Pebbles

Alison Watt was born in Greenock, Scotland in 1965. She studied painting at Glasgow School of Art from 1983–87, receiving her Degree in Postgraduate Studies in 1988, and currently lives and works in Glasgow.

Since her graduation, Watt's immediate market success in Britain must be seen in the context of the slightly older generation of painters from Glasgow, in that much attention has been focused on figuration emanating from the School of Art. However, her art is in a distinctly quieter vein than the Expressionist-dominated work of painters such as Campbell and Wiszniewski. Watt's painting is solidly figurative, with a strong academic and restrained orientation. This was recognised by her winning of the John Player Portrait Award in 1987, when still a student at Glasgow, followed by her controversial portrait commission of the Queen Mother by the National Portrait Gallery in 1989. The debate centred around the artist's quiet relegation of strict anatomical concerns as well as a plain intimacy unusual for Royal representations.

In contrast to this very public picture, the majority of Watt's output is more domestic and elusive in orientation, comprising androgynous figures caught before us in symbolic postures. Many of the subjects look like Watt herself, and it is clear that a private meaning often lurks behind each painting. Always many-layered, Watt's pictures are slyly comic and mock-serious, gently satirising the Classical earnestness of Masters such as Fra Angelico, Poussin and Ingres.

Favourite motifs for Watt's paintings are kitchen objects — teacups, bowls, jugs, scissors — as well as water containers such as baths and tin tubs. The actual fabric of these objects — ceramics, stone, pewter, metal, varnished wood — all seem to echo the resistance to interpretation which Watt's main subjects evoke. Beneath the inorganic still-life that Watt sets out seems to lie a subtle and sometimes menacing presence which is highly charged. All expression, however, is tightly controlled by the artist's severe style. This is often echoed too in the way that the artist brings to the picture details of tamed Nature such as severed roses (severed from the outside world) or water, never rushing naturally but always contained in vessels. Here might

Marat and the Fishes, 1990,
Oil on canvas, 152 x 137 cm

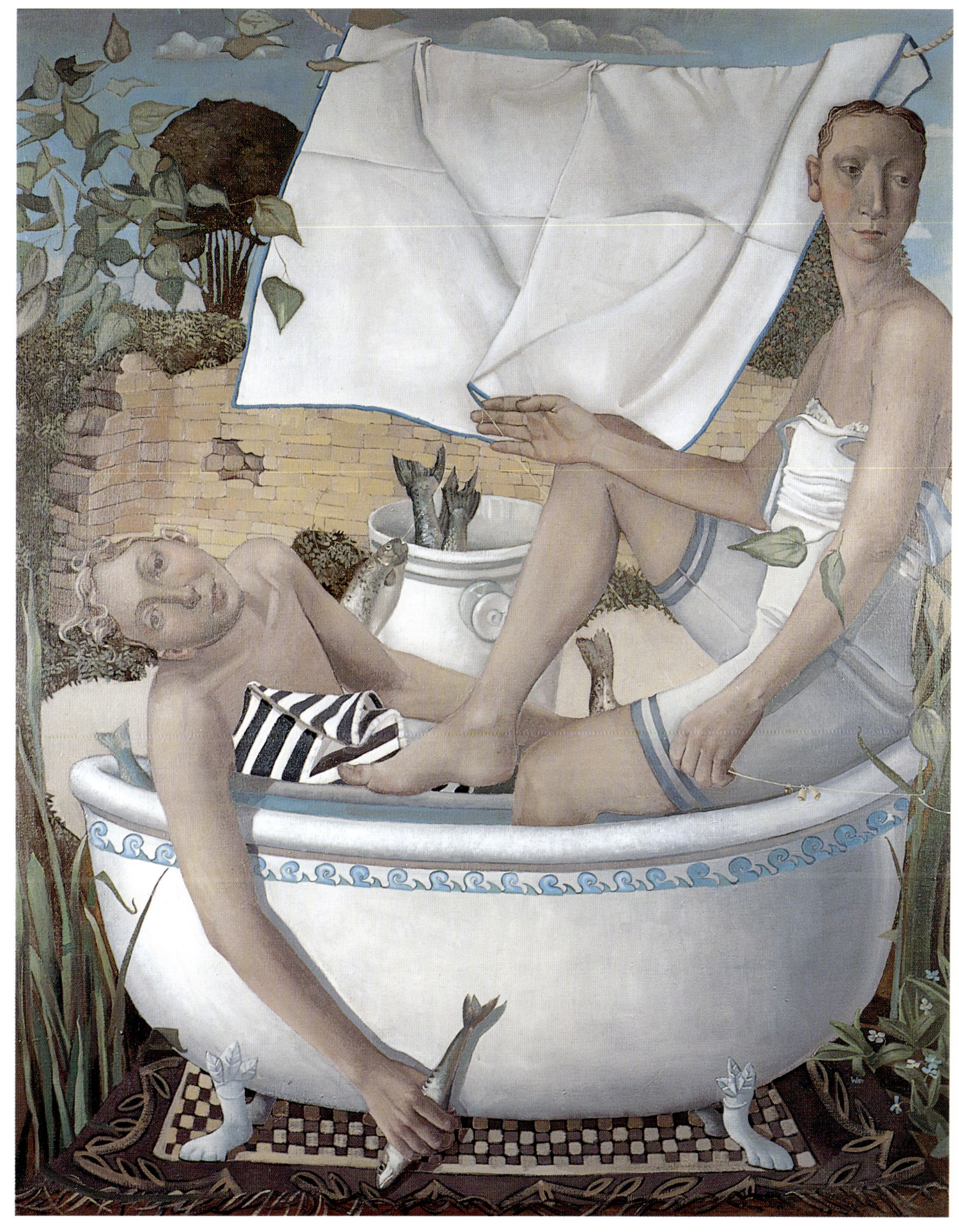

be typically Scottish references to restrained emotion and closely regulated experience.

Watt's first one-person exhibition was in London, in 1990. She has shown in a number of group exhibitions and is the recipient of numerous prizes and commissions in the United Kingdom. She is represented in various private and public collections.

Artist's Comment

I construct a title before I construct a painting. I tend to paint the same things again and again because I always think I could do it better. Next time.

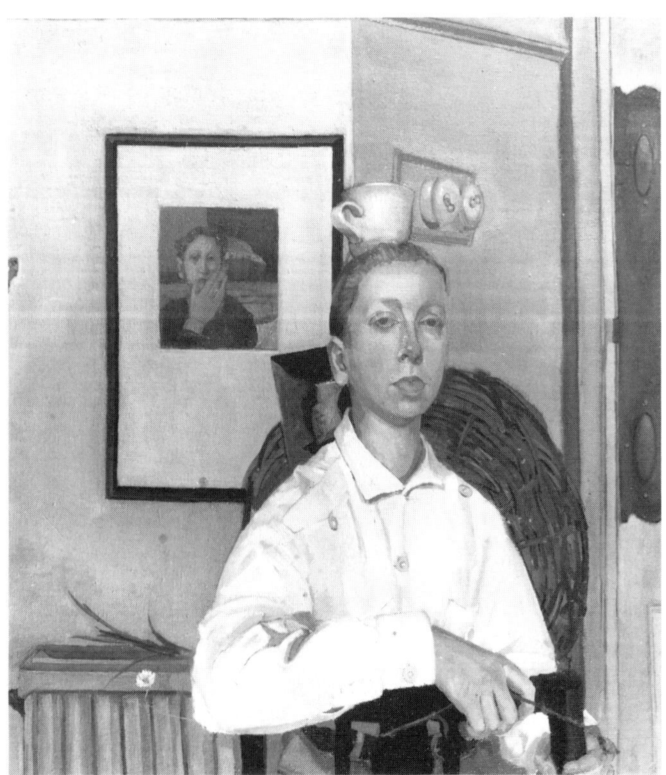

Self Portrait with Teacup, 1987,
Oil on canvas, 112 x 102 cm

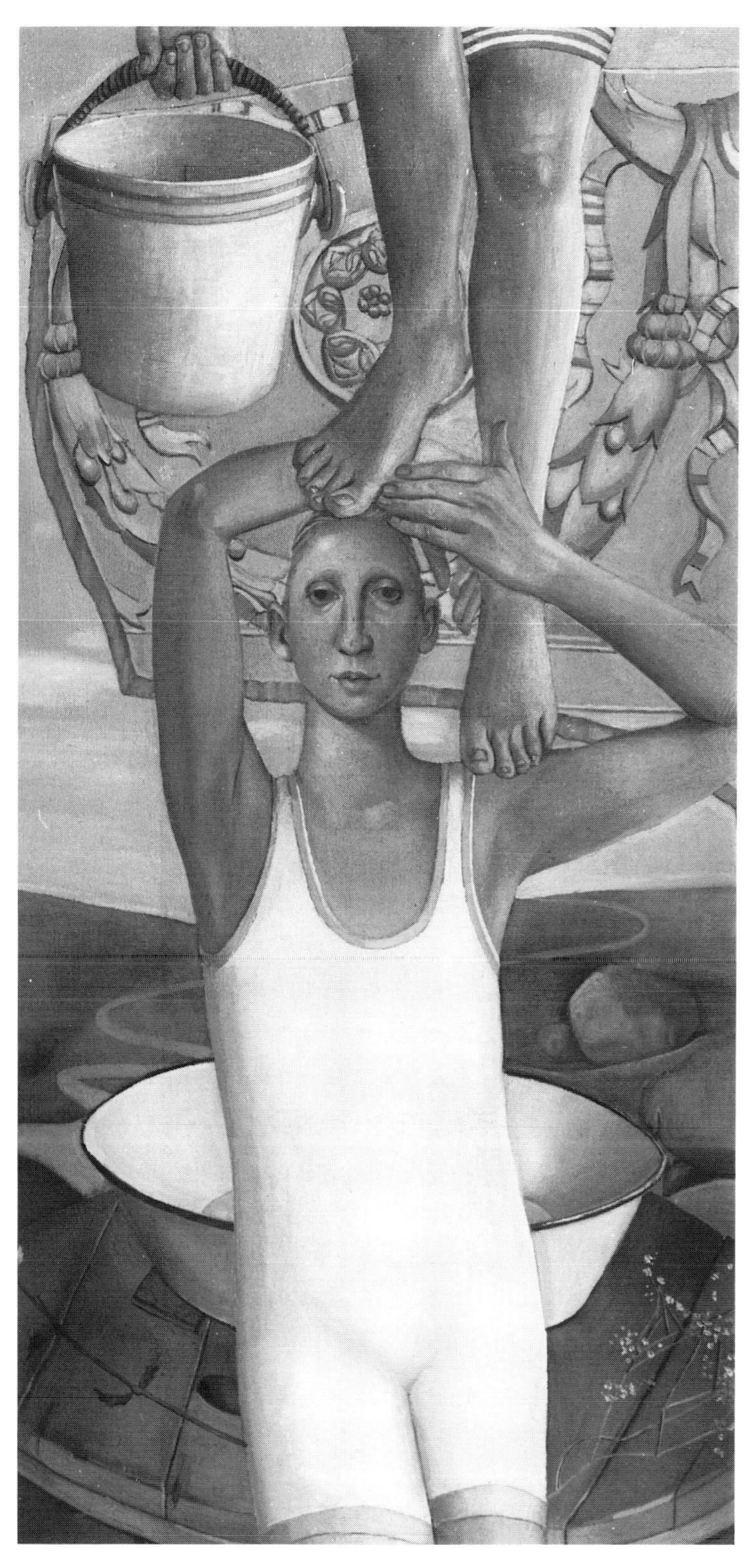

Water Carrier, 1989,
Oil on canvas, 152 x 77 cm

Kate Whiteford was born in Glasgow in 1952 and studied at Glasgow School of Art from 1969 to 1973. In 1977 Whiteford was awarded a British Council Scholarship to Rome. In 1987 she completed a major commission on Calton Hill, Edinburgh, as part of the TSWA Project, whilst in 1990 she participated in the Venice Biennale as part of the first ever Scottish Pavilion. She currently lives and works in London.

Whiteford is one of a select group of Scottish artists who have tried to express modern ideas in a contemporary form whilst rooting their approach in traditional references based on early civilisations. Abstraction and even Expressionism inform her handling of paint, yet the symbols she employs go back often to Pictish and Roman societies.

Most influential in her early career were European avant-garde artists such as Clemente, Kiefer and Penck, all of whose imagery and ideas were based on a feeling of national regeneration and reaffirmation. For Whiteford, being a Scots artist, this helped guide her to the powerful symbolic presence of early standing stones scattered throughout the Scottish landscape. However, according to the artist, her interests are largely formal, based on her fascination with the way in which unintelligible symbols from an ancient culture still exercise a hold over us even today.

In her application of paint, usually a strong red base with vibrant green marks drawn on top, Whiteford echoes the shallow relief of ancient carving. She is concerned with the power of drawing rather than the power of meaning. Yet, distinct meanings do seem to come to the surface: the power of memory, the passing of time and the emergence of ideas from the mind — all are symbolised in the shimmering lines in a Whiteford painting. Personal and ancient history are joined in this way. In using as a source the archaeology of early civilisations, the artist reminds us of our more immediate, personal 'archaeology'.

The importance of the overall effect of seeing her paintings together is illustrated in the meticulous way that Whiteford places her canvases in relation to each other when she exhibits. This helps to emphasise that her art is all-encompassing, deeply

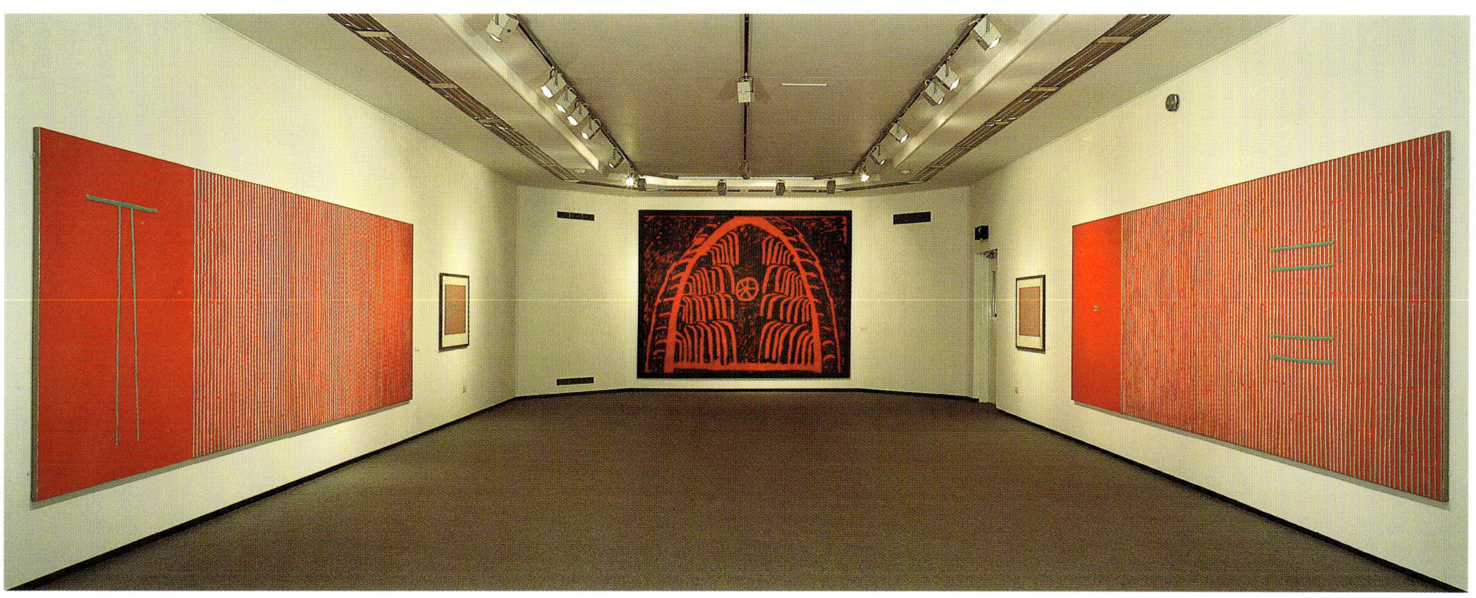

View of installation at Crawford Arts Centre, St Andrews for St Andrews Festival 1 24 February 1992,
Photograph: Colin Ruscoe
Courtesy the artist

meditative and rewards quiet study on behalf of the viewer.

Whiteford is represented in many private and public collections in the United Kingdom and abroad, including the Scottish National Gallery of Modern Art, the British Council, the Scottish Arts Council, the Tate Gallery, the Contemporary Art Society, London, and the Nomura Collection, Japan.

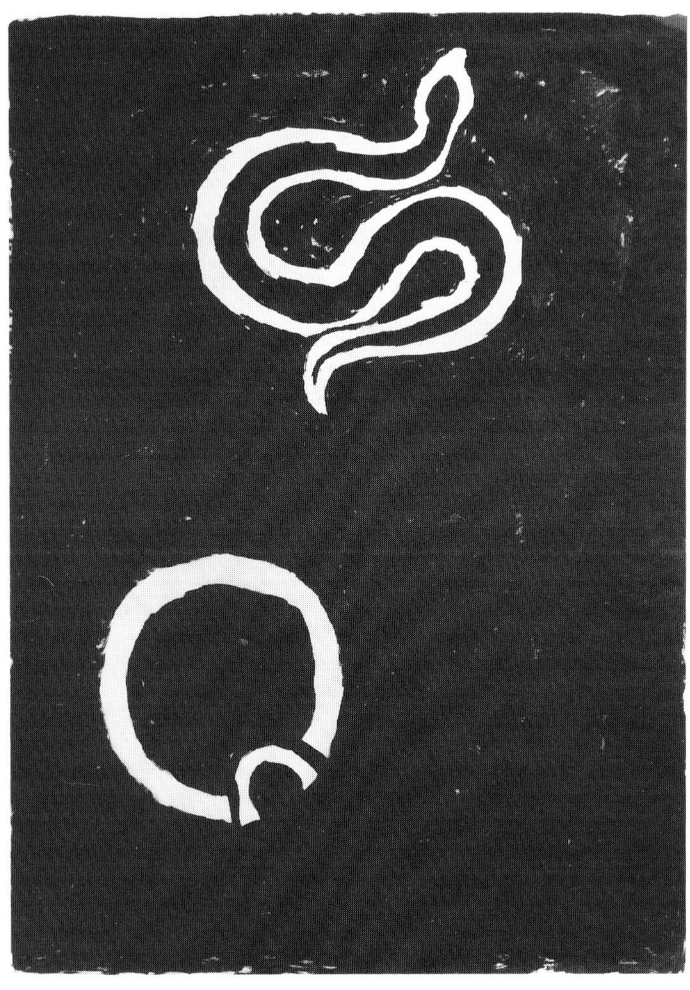

From the series 'Symbol Stones', 1983,
Paint on paper, 152 x 114 cm

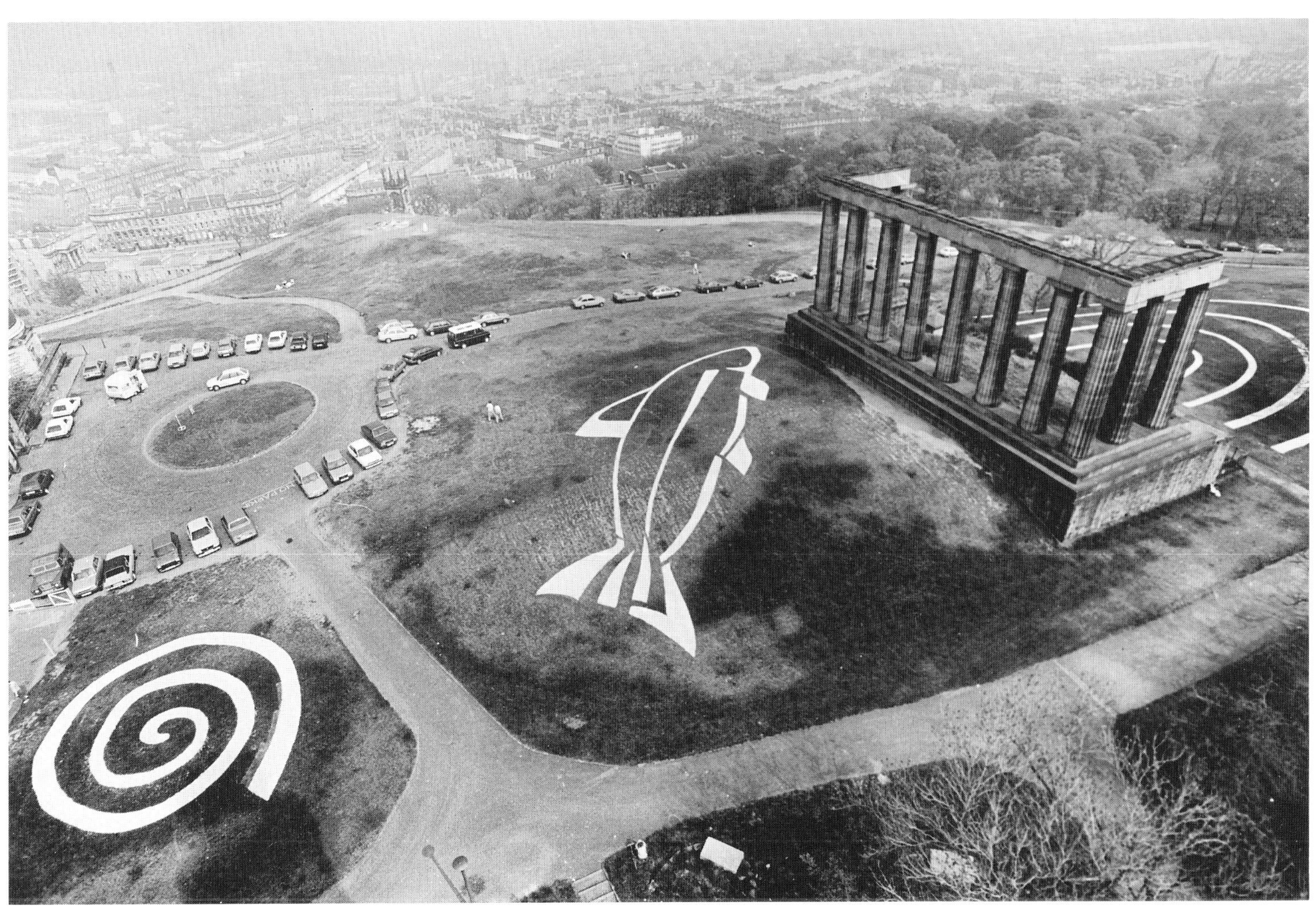

Sculpture for Calton Hill, 1987,
Photograph: Sean Hudson

I always make my figures in such a way that you can't tell the difference between somebody who's left wing or right wing, good or bad. You can't judge political convictions or morals from people's faces.

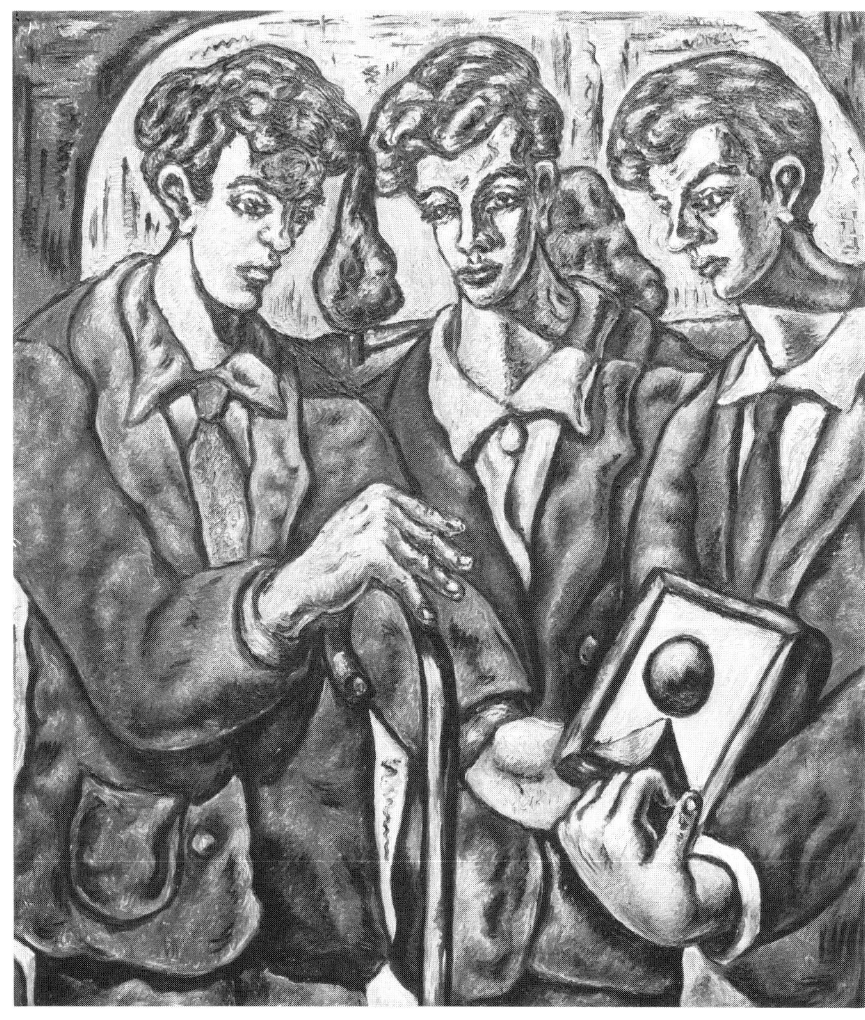

Modern Art, 1989,
Oil on canvas, 173.5 x 152.5 cm,
Courtesy Nigel Greenwood Gallery, London

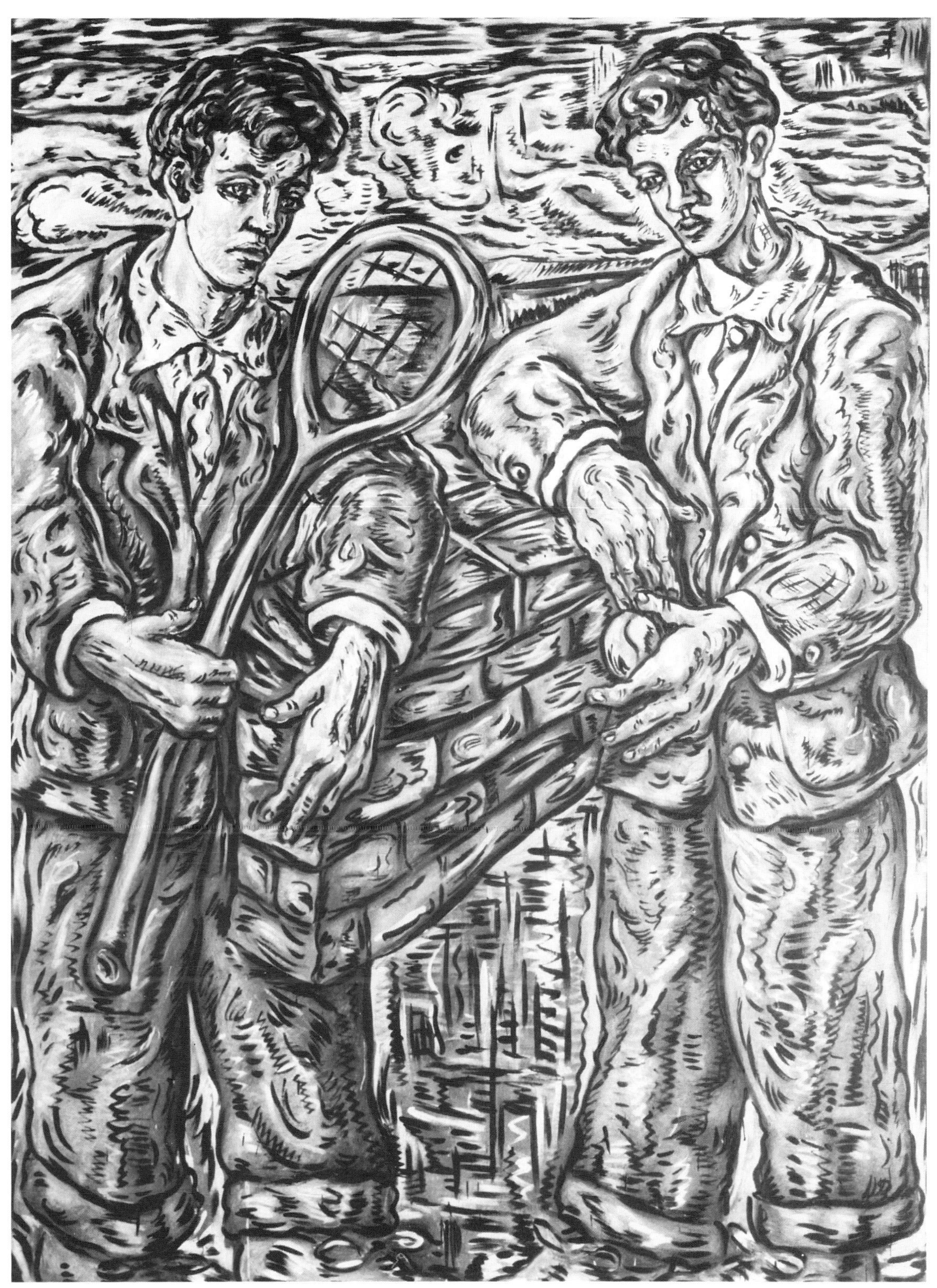

Tennis Players at the Wall,
1989,
Oil on canvas, 232 x 173 cm,
Courtesy Nigel Greenwood
Gallery, London

ONE-PERSON EXHIBITIONS

REINHARD BEHRENS

1982	'Further Exhibitions to Naboland', Edinburgh College of Art
1984	'An Expedition of Discovery into the Interior of Naboland', Glasgow School of Art
1984	'The Rediscovery of the Naboland journals', Touring Exhibition
1985	Printmakers Workshop, Edinburgh
1985	Smith Art Gallery and Museum, Stirling
1986	An Lanntair Gallery, Stornoway, Isle of Lewis
1986	Artspace Gallery, Aberdeen
1986	'Naboland — The Origin of Golf', Crawford Centre for the Arts
1987	Mclaurin Art Gallery, Ayr
1987	Open Eye Gallery, Edinburgh
1988	'Marooned on the Ice-Floe', Seagate Gallery, Dundee
1991	'The Last Yeti', Art and Nature Gallery, Bannack Street Museum, Dundee

JOHN BELLANY

1965	Dromidaris Gallery, Holland
1968	Edinburgh College of Art
1969	Winchester School of Art
1970	Drian Gallery, London
1970	Hendrix Gallery, Dublin
1971	New 57 Gallery, Edinburgh
1971	Printmakers Workshop, Edinburgh
1971	Drian Gallery, London
1972	RCA Galleries, London
1973	Triad Arts Centre, Bishop's Stortford, Herts.
1973	Edinburgh City Arts Centre
1973	Drian Gallery, London
1974	Drian Gallery, London
1975	Aberdeen City Art Gallery
1977	Acme Gallery, London
1978	Glasgow Print Studio Gallery
1978	Scottish Arts Council Gallery, Edinburgh
1978	Printmakers Workshop Gallery, Edinburgh
1978	Crawford Arts Centre Gallery, St Andrews
1979	Glasgow Print Studio Gallery
1979	Third Eye Centre, Glasgow
1979	Southampton City Art Gallery
1979	Newcastle Polytechnic Art Gallery
1979	Glasgow Print Studio Gallery
1980	Acme Gallery, London
1980	Moira Kelly Fine Art, London
1981	Goldsmith's College Gallery, London
1982	Rosa Esman Gallery, New York
1983	Paintings 1971–82, touring exhibition to: Ikon Gallery, Birmingham; Graves Art Gallery, Sheffield; Third Eye Centre, Glasgow; Rochdale Art Gallery; Hatton Gallery, Newcastle-upon-Tyne; Walker Art Gallery, Liverpool; MacLaurin Art Gallery, Ayr; Rosa Esman Gallery, New York; Christine Abrahams Gallery, Melbourne, Australia
1984	Dusseldorf Gallery, Perth, Australia
1984	Roslyn Oxley9 Gallery, Sydney
1984	Pier Arts Centre, Stromness Orkney
1984	Mercury Gallery, Edinburgh
1984	Rosa Esman Gallery, New York
1986	National Portrait Gallery, London
1986	Fischer Fine Art, London
1986	Galerie Krikhaar, Amsterdam
1986	Scottish National Gallery of Modern Art, Edinburgh and Serpentine Gallery, London (retrospective)
1986	Inaugural Exhibition for opening of Henry Moore Gallery, Royal College of Art, London
1987	The Peacock Gallery, Aberdeen
1987	Nigel Greenwood Gallery, London
1987	'"The Old Man and the Sea": Paintings and Prints', Compass Gallery, Glasgow
1987	Greenhill Galleries, Perth, Australia
1987	Roslyn Oxley9 Gallery, Sydney
1987	Butler Gallery, Kilkenny Castle, Ireland
1987	Hendrix Gallery, Dublin
1987	MacLaurin Gallery, Ayr, Scotland
1987	Third Eye Centre, Glasgow, Retrospective of prints
1987	'Recent Acquisitions', National Portrait Gallery, London
1988	Ruth Siegel Gallery, New York
1988	'Bellany as Printmaker 1965–85', Third Eye Centre, Glasgow, touring to: Printmakers Workshop Gallery, Edinburgh; Aberdeen Art Gallery; Beaux Arts Gallery, Bath
1988-89	Hamburger Kunsthalle and Museum am Ostwall, Dortmund (retrospective)
1989	'The Renaissance of John Bellany: Watercolours painted in Addenbrooke's Hospital, Cambridge', Scottish National Gallery of Modern Art, Edinburgh
1989	Fischer Fine Art, London
1989	'John Bellany — "A Renaissance"', Scottish National Gallery of Modern Art, Edinburgh
1989	Aberdeen Art Gallery
1989	Beaux Art Gallery, Bath
1990	RAAB Galerie, Berlin, West Germany
1990	Ruth Siegel Gallery, New York
1990	Compass Gallery, Glasgow
1991	Fitzwilliam Museum Cambridge
1991	Fischer Fine Art, London

ELIZABETH BLACKADDER

1959	57 Gallery, Edinburgh
1961	Scottish Gallery, Edinburgh
1965	Mercury Gallery, London
1966	Scottish Gallery, London
1966	Thames Gallery, Eton
1967	Mercury Gallery, London
1968	Reading Art Gallery and Museum
1968	Lane Art Gallery, Bradford
1969	Mercury Gallery, London
1970	Vaccarino Gallery, Florence
1971	Mercury Gallery, London
1971	Loomshop Gallery, Lower Largo, Fife
1972	Scottish Gallery, Edinburgh

1973 Mercury Gallery, London
1974 Scottish Gallery, Edinburgh, Festival exhibition
1974 Loomshop Gallery, Lower Largo, Fife
1976 Mercury Gallery, London
1976 Loomshop Gallery, Lower Largo, Fife
1977 Middlesborough Art Gallery and Museum
1977 Hambledom Gallery, Blandford, Dorset
1977 Stirling Gallery, Stirling
1978 Mercury Gallery, London
1978 Yehudi Menuhin School, Soke D'Abernon
1980 Mercury Gallery, London
1980 Oban Art Society
1981 Loomshop Gallery, Lower Largo, Fife
1981 Bohun Gallery, Henley-on-Thames
1981–82 Scottish Arts Council Retrospective Exhibition, Edinburgh, Sheffield, Aberdeen, Liverpool, Cardiff, London
1982 Mercury Gallery, London
1982 Mercury Gallery, Edinburgh, Festival Exhibition
1982 Theo Waddington Gallery, Toronto, Canada
1983 Lillian Heidenberg Gallery, New York
1984 Mercury Gallery, London
1985 Mercury Gallery, Edinburgh, Edinburgh Festival
1986 Lillian Heidenberg Gallery, New York
1987 Henley-on-Thames Festival of Music and the Arts
1987 Salisbury Festival Exhibition
1987 Glasgow Print Studio
1988 Mercury Gallery, London
1989 Aberystwyth Arts Centre Retrospective Touring Exhibition, Aberystwyth, Brighton, Bangor, Cardiff, Bath, Lancaster
1990 Abbot Hall, Kendal

DENNIS BUCHAN
1965 Douglas and Foulis Gallery, Edinburgh
1974 Saltire Society, Edinburgh

1975 Compass Gallery, Glasgow

JOYCE CAIRNS
1980 Compass Gallery, Glasgow
1981 English Speaking Union, Edinburgh
1981 Peacock Printmakers, Aberdeen
1982 Senior Common Room, Aberdeen University
1984 Artspace Galleries, Aberdeen
1986 Perth Museum and Art Gallery
1986 369 Gallery, Edinburgh
1986 Third Eye Centre, Glasgow
1991 Talbot Rice Gallery, Edinburgh
1991 Peacock Printmakers, Aberdeen
1991 Odette Gilbert Gallery, London

STEVEN CAMPBELL
1983 Barbara Toll Fine Art, New York
1983 John Weber Gallery, New York
1984 Dart Gallery, Chicago
1984 Rhona Hoffman Gallery, Chicago
1984 Galerie Six Friedrich, Munich
1984 Riverside Studios, London
1985 The Fruitmarket Gallery, Edinburgh
1985 Barbara Toll Fine Art, Edinburgh
1985 Walker Art Center, Minneapolis
1985 Middendorf Gallery, Washington DC
1986 Galerie Pierre Huber, Geneva
1986 John Berggruen Gallery, San Francisco
1987 Marlborough Gallery Inc., New York
1989 Riva Yares Gallery, Scottsdale, Arizona
1990 'Steven Campbell: On Form and Fiction', Third Eye Centre, Glasgow and tour to Oriel Mostyn, Llandudno; Marlborough Fine Art, London; Aberdeen Art Gallery; Whitworth Art Gallery, Manchester; Southampton Art Gallery

RUSSELL COLOMBO
1978 Royal Edinburgh Hospital
1985 Talbot Rice Gallery
1986 Wyeside Arts Centre, Builth Wells
1986 Y Bout Gallery, Pontypridd

1988 The Scott Gallery, Hawick Museum
1990 Talbot Rice Gallery

CALUM COLVIN
1983 Compass Gallery, Glasgow
1983 Richard Demarco Gallery, Edinburgh
1985 Chapter Arts Centre, Cardiff
1985 Bezalel Academy of Arts and Design, Jerusalem
1985 'Ten out of Ten', Hamilton Gallery, London
1985 'The 85 Degree Show', Serpentine Gallery, London
1986 'Recontres Internationales de la Photographie', Arles
1987 Seagate Gallery, Dundee
1987 'Towards a Bigger Picture', Victoria and Albert Museum, London
1987 Kathleen Ewing Gallery, Washington DC
1987 Sander Gallery, New York
1987 'True Stories and Photofictions', Ffotogallery, Cardiff
1987 Riverside Studios, London
1987 'The Vigorous Imagination', Scottish National Gallery of Modern Art, Edinburgh
1988 Friedman-Guinness Gallery, Heidelberg
1988 Haggerty Museum, Wisconsin
1988 'Juxtapositions', Salama-Caro Gallery, London
1988 Foco '88, Circulo de Bellas Artes, Madrid
1988 'The Male Nude', Salama-Caro Gallery, London
1988 'Recontres Internationales de la Photographie', Arles
1988 The Ludwig Museum, Cologne
1988 Galeria 57, Madrid
1989 California State University, Long Beach, California
1989 'Towards a Bigger Picture, Part II', Victoria and Albert Museum
1989 'Towards a Bigger Picture, Contemporary British Photography',

Tate Gallery, Liverpool
1989 Portfolio Gallery, Edinburgh
1989 Salama-Caro Gallery, London
1989 Photographic Art in Britain, Barbican
Art Gallery
1989 Friedman-Guinness Gallery, Frankfurt
1989 Kunstverrin, Munich
1989 Kunsthalle, Nurnberg
1989 Kunstverein, Karlsruhe
1989 Forum, Bremen
1989 Harris Museum and Art Gallery,
Preston
1989 Piers Art Centre, Orkney
1990 Haggerty Museum, Wisconsin
1990 Glenn/Dash Gallery, Los Angeles
1990 Torch, Amsterdam
1990 Fruitmarket Gallery, Edinburgh
1990 Aberdeen City Art Gallery
1991 ICA Chicago

STEPHEN CONROY
1989 Marlborough Fine Art, London, and
tour of part of the exhibition to
Glasgow Art Gallery and the
Whitworth Art Gallery, Manchester

FRED CRAYK
1977 Duncan of Jordanstone College of
Art, Dundee
1978 Torrance Gallery, Edinburgh
1979 369 Gallery, Edinburgh
1982 369 Gallery, Edinburgh
1984 Greenock Theatre Arts Centre,
Greenock
1987 Compass Gallery, Glasgow
1991 Talbot Rice Gallery, Edinburgh

KEN CURRIE
1982 'Art and Social Commitment',
Glasgow Arts Centre
1986 'New Work from Glasgow', Arnolfini,
Bristol
1987 People's Palace Museum, Glasgow
(permanent installation)
1988 Third Eye Centre, Glasgow
1988 RAAB Galerie, Berlin

1990 'Story from Glasgow', Kelvingrove
Art Gallery and Museum, Glasgow
1991 RAAB Gallery at Millbank and
Riverside Studios, London
1991 Talbot Rice Gallery, Edinburgh

ALAN DAVIE
1946 Grant's Bookshop, Edinburgh
1948 Galleria Michelangelo, Florence
1948 Galleria Sandri, Venice
1950 Gimpel Fils, London
1951 Gimpel Fils, London
1952 Gimpel Fils, London
1953 Gimpel Fils, London
1954 Gimpel Fils, London
1955 Gimpel Fils, London
1956 Gimpel Fils, London
1956 Catherine Viviano Gallery, New York
1957 Catherine Viviano Gallery, New York
1958 Retrospective: Walker Art Gallery,
Liverpool
Whitechapel Art Gallery, London
Nottingham University
Wakefield Art Gallery
1960 Gimpel Fils, London
1960 Esther Robles Gallery, Los Angeles
1960 Galleria del Naviglio, Milan
1960 Martha Jackson Gallery, New York
1960 Galerie Rive Droite, Paris
1960 Carnegie Institute, Pittsburgh
Museum of Art
1962 Retrospective: Stedelijk Museum,
Amsterdam
1962 Retrospective: RBA Galleries, London
1963 Retrospective: Kunsthalle, Baden-
Baden
1963 Retrospective: Kunsthalle, Bern
1963 Gimpel Fils, London
1963 Retrospective: Kunstnernes Hus, Oslo
1963 Retrospective: Kunstgewerbeverein,
Pforzheim
1963 Galleria La Medusa, Rome
1963 VII Bienal de Bellas Artes, Sao Paulo
1963 Museo de Bellas Artes, Caracas
1963 Museu de Arte Moderna, Riode
Janeiro

1963 Gimpel and Hanover Galerie, Zurich
1965 Galerie d'Aujourd'hui, Brussels
1965 Galerie Rudolf Zwirner, Cologne
1965 Court Gallery, Copenhagen
1965 Gimpel Fils, London
1965 Martha Jackson Gallery, New York
1965 Graves Art Gallery, Sheffield
1965 Galerie Bleue, Stockholm
1966 Commonwealth Institute Gallery,
Edinburgh
1966 Queen's Gallery, Leeds
1966 Usher Gallery, Lincoln
1966 Gimpel Fils, London
1966 Castle Museum, Norwich
1966 Haaken Gallery, Oslo
1966 Rotterdamsche Kunstring, Rotterdam
1967 Art Club of Chicago, Chicago
1967 Kestner-Gesellschaft, Hannover
1967 Gimpel Fils, London
1967 Galerie de France, Paris
1967 Gimpel and Hanover Galerie, Zurich
1968 Hudson Gallery, Detroit
1968 Kunstverein fur die Rheinlande,
Dusseldorf
1968 Westfalen
1968 Richard Demarco Gallery, Edinburgh
1969 Kunstmuseum, Basel
1969 Gimpel Fils, London
1969 Gimpel and Weitzenhoffer Gallery,
New York
1970 Gimpel Fils, London
1970 Galerie Stangl, Munich
1970 Gallerie La Medusa, Rome
1970–77 Retrospective: Austin, Texas;
Montreal, Canada; Oakland,
California
1971 Galerie Lambert Monet, Geneva
1971 Gimpel Fils, London
1971 CCAC GAllery, California College of
Arts and Crafts, Oakland
1971 Gimpel and Hanover Galerie, Zurich
1972 Gimpel and Weitzenhoffer Gallery,
New York
1972 Gimpel and Hanover Galerie, Zurich
1975 Art '75, Basel
1975 Gimpel Fils, London

1975 Comsky Gallery, Los Angeles
1975 Gimpel and Weitzenhoffer Gallery, New York
1975 Galerie de France, Paris
1975 Kilcawley Center, Youngstown University, Youngstown
1975 Gimpel and Hanover Galerie, Zurich
1976 Hokin Gallery, Chicago
1976 Galleria La Medusa, Rome
1976 Rubiner Gallery, Royal Oak
1977 City of Aberdeen Art Gallery and Museum, Aberdeen
1977 Zoumboulakis Gallery, Athens
1977 Carone Gallery, Fort Lauderdale
1977 Gimpel and Weitzenhoffer Gallery, New York
1977 La Demeure, Paris
1978 Galerie Brinkman, Amsterdam
1978 Galeria am Palmengarten, Frankfurt
1978 Gimpel Fils, London
1978 Galerie Maercklin, Stuttgart
1978 Gimpel and Hannover Galerie, Zurich
1979 Galeria Ado, Bonheiden
1979 Ray Hughes Gallery, Brisbane
1979 Carone Gallery, Fort Lauderdale
1979 Gimpel Fils, London
1979 Lister Gallery, Perth, Australia
1979 Art of Man Gallery, Sydney
1980 Gimpel and Weitzenhoffer Gallery, New York
1980 Gimpel and Hanover, Zurich
1980 Lister Gallery, Perth, Australia
1981 Gimpel Fils, London
1981 Galerie Van Loe, Frankfurt
1982 Rosenberg Fine Arts Ltd, Toronto
1982 The Scottish Gallery, Edinburgh
1982 The Arcade Gallery, Harrogate
1982 Hong Kong Arts Centre, Hong Kong
1982 Galerie de Raam, Breda, Netherlands
1982 FIAC, Paris
1983 Galerie d'Eendt, Amsterdam
1983 Gimpel Fils, London
1984 Festival Gallery, Bath
1984 Community Arts Centre, Windsor
1984 Galerie Van Loe, Frankfurt
1984 Bede Gallery, Jarrow

1984 Loft Gallery, Ware
1985 Galerie Apicella, Bonn
1985 Galerie Peccolo, Livorno
1985 Gimpel Fils, London
1985 Arizona Yares Gallery, Scotsdale
1986 Gimpel and Weitzenhoffer Gallery, New York
1987 'Major Works of the Fifties', Gimpel Fils, London
1987 Moray House Gallery, Edinburgh
1987 Galerie Louis Carre, Paris
1987 FIAC, Paris
1988 'Magic Fountains', Gimpel Fils, London
1988 'Alan Davie: Paintings from 1956–1988', South West Galleries Association, touring eight cities in Scotland
1989 'Works on paper 1960–1985', Gimpel Fils, London
1989 Galleri G, Helsingborg, Sweden
1989 'Drawings', Kunsthandel, Vienna
1989 'Works on paper', Galerie Louis Carre, Paris
1989 'Major Works of the Sixties', Gimpel Fils, London
1990 'Alan Davie in the '70s', Galleri G, Helsingborg, Sweden
1991 Triennale Grafiki, Krakow, Poland
1991 'Recent Paintings', Wolf At The Door, Penzance, Cornwall
1991 'Recent Work', Gimpel Fils, London
1991 Galerie Bock, Copenhagen
1992 'The Alan Davie Retrospective - 1937 to the present', McLellan Galleries, Glasgow

DAVID DONALDSON
1961 Henry Hellier's studio, Glasgow
1973 Festival exhibition, The Scottish Gallery, Edinburgh
1974 The French Institute, Glasgow
1794 The Fermoy Gallery, King's Lynn, Norfolk
1980 The Mall Galleries, London
1982 Festival exhibition, The Scottish

Gallery, Edinburgh
1983 The Macaulay Gallery, Stenton, East Lothian
1983–84 Restrospective Exhibition, Glasgow, Dundee, Edinburgh, London
1983 'Recent Works', Fine Arts Society, Glasgow
1986–87 'Donaldson at 70', Fine Arts Society, Glasgow, Edinburgh
1987 Fresno Metropolitan Museum, California
1988 Everard Read Gallery, Johannesburg, South Africa
1990 'Some Time in France, Recent Paintings', Fine Arts Society, Glasgow, London

KATE DOWNIE
1982 'Drawings and Paintings', Senior Common Room, Aberdeen University
1983 'Brewery on Canvas', Burton-on-Trent Community Centre Gallery
1984 'Social Events', Galleri Schottenburgh, Amsterdam
1984 'Installatie Drukwerk', Galleri Rechtboomsloot, Amsterdam
1985 'Coastlines', Drawings and Prints, Backroom Gallery, Edinburgh
1987 'Paintings and Drawings', Galleri Grijsdalen, Vejle, Denmark
1990–91 'Urban Circus' Exhibition, Work on paper, canvas and film installation, Collins Gallery, Glasgow; Tour: Cleveland Gallery, Middlesborough; MacManus Gallery, Dundee; Peacock/Artspace Gallery, Aberdeen

DAVID EVANS
1966 New 57 Gallery, Edinburgh
1968 Llantarnam Grange, Cwmbran Gwent
1969 University of York
1970 Majorie Parr Galleries, London
1972 Majorie Parr Galleries, London
1974 Majorie Parr Galleries, London
1977 Gilbert Parr Galleries, London

1980	Gilbert Parr Galleries, London
1982	Retrospective Exhibition, Fruit Market Gallery, Edinburgh
1985	Mercury Gallery, London
1991	Open Eye Gallery, Edinburgh

ALEXANDER FRASER

1964	57 Gallery, Edinburgh
1965	Drawings, Former Art College, Aberdeen
1970	The Arts' Tower, Sheffield University
1972	Richard Demarco Gallery, Edinburgh
1974	Compass Gallery, Glasgow
1974	Stirling Gallery, Stirling (with Jack Knox and Bill Scott)
1975	Sheffield University
1977	Park Square Gallery, Leeds
1978	Stirling Gallery, Stirling (with Fred Bushe)
1979	Imperial College, London
1979	Peacock Printmakers, Aberdeen
1982	Peacock Printmakers, Aberdeen
1984	New 57 Gallery, Edinburgh
1984	Aberdeen Art Gallery, Aberdeen
1987	Talbot Rice Gallery, Edinburgh
1988	Art Space, Aberdeen

LYS HANSEN

1960	Commonwealth Institute, London
1969	Strathclyde University, Glasgow
1974	Crowsteps Gallery, Blairlogie, Stirling
1976	University of Stirling
1977	MacRobert Arts Centre, Stirling University
1978	Strathclyde University, Glasgow
1978–80	Stirling Gallery, Stirling
1980	Greenock Arts Centre
1980	Henderson Gallery, Edinburgh
1983	Open Eye Gallery, Edinburgh
1984	The Third Eye Centre, Glasgow
1985	Octagon Gallery, Belfast/University of Ulster at Belfast (Northern Ireland Arts Council)
1985	Project Arts Centre, Dublin (Irish Arts Council)
1986	Camden Arts Centre, London

1986	Artspace, Aberdeen
1986	369 Gallery, Edinburgh
1986	Alying Porteous Gallery, Chester
1988	City Art Centre, Edinburgh
1990	McLaurin Gallery, Rozelle, Ayr

GWEN HARDIE

1984	Studio Gallery, Glasgow
1986	Paton Gallery, London
1987	Fruitmarket Gallery, Edinburgh, travelling to: Seagate Gallery, Dundee; Artspace, Aberdeen; John Hansard Gallery, Southampton; Artsite, Bath; McLaren Gallery, Ayr; Pier Art Centre, Stromness, Orkney
1988	Kettle's Yard, Cambridge
1988	Paton Gallery, London
1990	Scottish National Gallery of Modern Art, Edinburgh
1990	Fischer Fine Art, London

JOHN HOUSTON

1958	57 Gallery, Edinburgh
1960	The Scottish Gallery, Edinburgh
1962	Festival exhibition, The Scottish Gallery, Edinburgh
1965	The Scottish Gallery, Edinburgh
1966	Mercury Gallery, London
1967	Festival exhibition, The Scottish Gallery, Edinburgh
1968	Mercury Gallery, London
1969	Lane Gallery, Bradford
1969	Wustum Museum of Fine Arts, Racine, Wisconsin
1969	Johnson Foundation, Racine, Wisconsin
1970	Mercury Gallery, London
1970	Cerberus Gallery, New York
1970	The Loomshop Gallery, Lower Largo, Fife
1971	Festival Exhibition, The Scottish Gallery, Edinburgh
1972	Mercury Gallery, London
1972	The Loomshop Gallery, Lower Largo, Fife
1974	The Loomshop Gallery, Lower Largo,

	Fife
1974	Oban Art Society
1975	Festival exhibition, The Scottish Gallery, Edinburgh
1975	Mercury Gallery, London
1976	The Loomshop Gallery, Lower Largo, Fife
1977	Mercury Gallery, London
1978	Lamp of the Lothians Collegiate Centre, Haddington
1979	Mercury Gallery, London
1979	The Loomshop Gallery, Lower Largo, Fife
1979	Middlesborough Art Gallery
1980	Festival exhibition, The Scottish Gallery, Edinburgh
1981	Mercury Gallery, London
1983	Festival Exhibition, Mercury Gallery, Edinburgh
1984	Mercury Gallery, London
1985	Mercury Gallery, Edinburgh
1985–86	Portraits of Sir Alexander Gibson for the Scottish National Portrait Gallery
1986	The Loomshop Gallery, Lower Largo, Fife
1987	Works on Paper 1962–1987, Talbot Rice Gallery, The University of Edinburgh, Aberdeen Art Gallery and Maclaurin Art Gallery, Ayr
1989	Mercury Gallery, London

IAN HOWARD

1973	'Different Realists', Talbot Rice Art Centre, Edinburgh
1976	Edinburgh International Film Festival
1979	Recent Acquisitions, Scottish Arts Council Gallery, Edinburgh
1979	Cleveland Drawing Biennale, Middlesborough, London and tour
1980	'Fine Artists', 369 Gallery, Edinburgh
1981	Recent Purchases, Scottish Arts Council, Fruitmarket Gallery, Edinburgh
1982	'Grease and Water', Scottish Arts Council touring exhibition
1982	'Four North-East Artists', Fruitmarket

Gallery, Edinburgh
1982   Aberdeen Art Gallery, Aberdeen
1984   'Dunbar and Howard', Glasgow Arts
        Centre
1984   Scottish Print Open 3, touring
        exhibition
1984   Contemporary Scottish Printmakers,
        Mercury Gallery, London
1984   Contemporary Drawing, Fine Art
        Society, Edinburgh and Glasgow
1984   Peacock 10, Aberdeen Art Gallery
1984–85 'Sculptors' Drawings', Arts Council
        touring show
1985   Tolly-Cobbold Eastern Arts 5th
        National Exhibition, Cambridge and
        tour
1985   'Ian Howard — New Drawings',
        Compass Gallery, Glasgow
1985   Scottish Prints, Warwick Arts Trust,
        London
1985   Contemporary Arts Society Art
        Market, London
1986   Anne Berthoud Gallery, London (with
        Nick Freeman)
1986   'The Human Touch', Fischer Fine Art,
        London
1986   British/Malaysian Exhibition, Kuala
        Lumpur, British Council Exhibition
1987   Recent British Painting and Printing,
        British Council Touring Exhibition;
        Bangkok, Singapore, Hong Kong
1987   'Northern Lights — Contemporary
        Scottish Painting', Assembly Rooms,
        Norwich
1987   'Ian Howard — Paintings, Prints and
        Related Works', Touring: Third Eye
        Centre, Glasgow; Artspace Galleries,
        Aberdeen; Seagate Gallery, Dundee;
        Talbot Rice Art Centre, Edinburgh
        University
1987   Scottish Contemporary Art, Clare
        Hall, Cambridge
1987   Contemporary Arts Society Art
        Market, London
1987   Royal Overseas League, Overseas
        House, London

1987   'Eight Artists', Kingfisher Gallery,
        Edinburgh
1988   'The Scottish Show', Welsh Arts
        Council Touring Show
1988   'Scottish Art in Yugoslavia', Richard
        Demarco Gallery Touring Show in
        Yugoslavia
1988   'Metropolis', RAAB Gallery, London
1989   Contemporary Art Society, Smiths
        Gallery, London
1989   London Art Fair
1990   'In the Directors Chair', Open Eye
        Gallery, Edinburgh
1990   Recent Scottish Painting, Fine Art
        Society, Edinburgh and Glasgow
1990   Guthrie Award Winners, Fine Art
        Society, Edinburgh and Glasgow
1990   Jordanstone Folio, A collaboration
        with Writer-in-Residence included in
        'Kindred Spirits' exhibition, Ancrum
        Gallery and Duncan of Jordanstone
1990   The Compass Contribution,
        Tramway, Glasgow
1990   Leicestershire Art for Schools
        Exhibition,Loughborough
1990   Stevenson Collection, Warwick Arts
        Trust, London
1990   Royal Scottish Academy, Summer
        Exhibition
1990   Duncan of Jordanstone School of
        Fine Art Staff Exhibition at the
        McManus Galleries
1990   Contemporary Scottish Painting,
        Compass Gallery, Glasgow

PETER HOWSON
1983   Wall Murals, Feltham Community
        Association, London
1985   New Paintings and Drawings,
        Mayfest, Glasgow
1985   Print Studio Gallery
1985   Peter Howson — New Paintings,
        Crawford Centre for the Arts,
        University of St Andrews
1987   Washington Gallery, Glasgow
1987   Angela Flowers Gallery, London

1988   New Works on Paper, The Scottish
        Gallery
1988   Small Works on Paper, The Scottish
        Gallery
1988   Small Paintings and Works on Paper,
        Angela Flowers Gallery, London
1988   The Twilight Zone, Cleveland Gallery,
        Middlesborough and Quay Arts
        Centre, Isle of Wight
1989   Saracen Heads, Flowers Graphics,
        London
1989   Paintings and Drawings, Flowers
        East, London
1989   New Prints, Flowers Graphics,
        London
1989   Drawings, Tegnerforbundet, The
        Drawing Art Association of Norway
1990   Drawings and Small Paintings,
        Agarte, Rome
1990   New Work, Glasgow Print Studio
        Mayfest Exhibition, Glasgow
1990   Los Angeles International Art
        Exposition
1991   New Prints, Flowers Graphics,
        London
1991   New Paintings, Lannon/Cole Gallery,
        Chicago, USA
1991   Paintings and Drawings, Flowers
        East, London

MARGARET HUNTER
1986   Galerie IX Atelier, Berlin
1986   Rozelle House Gallery, Ayr
1988   'Berlin-Scotland-Transfer', Galerie IX
        Atelier, Berlin
1988   369 Gallery, Edinburgh
1988   Vanessa Devereux Gallery, London
1988   Galerie Werkstatt, Berlin
1989   Kunstraum Klapperhof, Cologne
1990   Petrus-Kirche, Berlin
1990   Maclaurin Gallery, Ayr
1990   369 Gallery, Edinburgh
1990   Vanessa Devereux Gallery, London

MATTHEW INGLIS
1985   The Collective Gallery, Edinburgh

| 1988 | Territory, The Crawford Arts Centre, St Andrews, Edinburgh College of Art |
| 1991 | Sylvia, 369 Gallery, Edinburgh |

CALLUM INNES
1986	Artspace Gallery, Aberdeen
1988	369 Gallery, Edinburgh
1990	Frith Street Gallery, London
1990	Jan Turner Gallery, Los Angeles
1991	Frith Street Gallery, London

ALAN JOHNSTON
1973	Konrad Fischer, Dusseldorf
1974	Von der Heydt Museum, Wuppertal
1974	Nigel Greenwood, London
1975	Nigel Greenwood, London
1976	Nigel Greenwood, London
1977	Graeme Murray Gallery, Edinburgh
1978	Museum of Modern Art, Oxford
1979	Graeme Murray Gallery, Edinburgh
1980	John Hansard Gallery, Southampton
1983	Graeme Murray Gallery, Edinburgh
1983	Jack Tilton Gallery, New York
1984	Shimada Gallery, Yamaguchi, Japan
1985	De Zaak, Groningen, Netherlands
1986	Galerie Cora Holzl, Dusseldorf, West Germany
1986	Paul Steen Gallery, Edinburgh
1986	Jack Tilton Gallery, New York
1987	Shimada Gallery, Yamaguchi, Japan
1987	Corridor Gallery, Reykjavik, Iceland
1987	Pier Art Gallery, Stromness
1987	The Fruit Market Gallery, Edinburgh
1988	The Orchard Gallery, Derry
1988	The Arnolfini, Bristol
1988	The Living Art Museum, Reykjavik, Iceland
1988	Jack Tilton Gallery, New York
1989	Cora Holzl Gallery, Dusseldorf, West Germany
1989	Shimada Gallery, Yamaguchi, Japan
1989	Bernard Jordan Gallery, Paris
1990	Jack Tilton Gallery, New York
1990	Forum, Dusseldorf, West Germany
1991	Transmission Gallery, Glasgow

JOHN KIRKWOOD
1972	New 57 Gallery, Edinburgh
1974	Printmakers' Workshop Gallery, Edinburgh
1976	New 57 Gallery, Edinburgh
1981	Talbot Rice Art Centre, Edinburgh
1983	War Prints and photomontages, Printmakers' Workshop, Edinburgh

JACK KNOX
1961	57 Gallery, Edinburgh
1966	The Scottish Gallery, Edinburgh
1969	Richard Demarco Gallery, Edinburgh
1971	Serpentine Gallery, London
1972	Buckingham Gallery, London
1972	Civic Arts Centre, Aberdeen
1983	Retrospective, Edinburgh, Fruitmarket, Glasgow, Third Eye and touring
1989	The Scottish Gallery, Edinburgh
1990	Kelvingrove Art Gallery and Museum, Glasgow

HENRY KONDRACKI
1979	Traverse Theatre Club, Edinburgh
1984	The Artist's Collective Gallery, Edinburgh
1987	Vanessa Devereux Gallery, London
1988	Michael Wardell Gallery, Melbourne, Australia
1989	Vanessa Devereux Gallery, London
1991	William Jackson Gallery, London

EILEEN LAWRENCE
1969	57 Gallery, Edinburgh
1975	Richard Demarco Gallery, Edinburgh
1976	New 57 Gallery, Edinburgh
1978	Arnolfini Gallery, Bristol, Chapter, Cardiff
1978	Institute of Contemporary Art, London
1980	Fischer Fine Art, London
1985	Fischer Fine Art, London
1986	Artsite, Bath
1987	The Barn, Lincolnshire
1988	Beaux Arts, Bath

THOMAS LAWSON
1977	'In Camera', Artists Space, New York
1980	Mercer Union Gallery, Toronto
1981	Metro Pictures, New York
1982	Metro Pictures, New York
1983	Metro Pictures, New York
1983	Richard Kuhlenschmidt Gallery, Los Angeles
1984	OR Gallery, Vancouver
1984	Christminster Gallery, New York
1985	Metro Pictures, New York
1986	Civic Virtues, City University Graduate Center Mall, New York
1987	'The Party's Over', Metro Pictures, New York
1987	Anthony Reynolds Gallery, London
1987	La Jolla Museum of Contemporary Art, La Jolla, California
1988	Kuhlenschmidt/Simon, Los Angeles
1989	Metro Pictures, New York
1989	TOO Gallery, Vancouver
1990	Third Eye Centre, Glasgow
1990	Anthony Reynolds Gallery, London
1990	Battersea Arts Centre, London

KEITH McINTYRE
1982	Shore Gallery, Leith
1984	369 Gallery, Edinburgh
1985	Compass Gallery, Glasgow
1985	Pittenweem Arts Festival, Fife
1986	369 Gallery, Edinburgh
1987	RAAB Galerie, Berlin
1988	RAAB Gallery, London
1990	'The Paintings for Jock Tamson's Bairns', Tramway Theatre, Glasgow/RAAB Gallery, London
1991	'Paintings for the Falling Angel', Kelvingrove Museum and Art Galleries, Glasgow

BRUCE McLEAN
1969	Konrad Fischer, Dusseldorf
1970	'King for a Day', Nova Scotia College of Art Gallery, Halifax
1971	'Objects no Concepts', Situation, London

1971	Galerie Yvon Lambert, Paris
1972	'King for a Day', Tate Gallery, London
1972	Galeria Francoise Lambert, Milan
1975	'Early Works 1967–1975', Museum of Modern Art, Oxford
1975	Robert Self Gallery, Newcastle
1975	'Nice Style: The End of an Era 1971–1975', PMJ Self, London
1977	'New Political Drawings', Robert Self Gallery, London and Newcastle
1978	'The Object of Exercise?', The Kitchen (performance sculpture and drawing installation with Rosi McLean), New York
1979	University Gallery, Southampton
1979	Barry Barker, London
1979	InK, Zurich
1980	'New Works and Performance/Actions Positions', Third Eye Centre (travelled to Fruit Market Gallery, Edinburgh and Arnolfini, Bristol), Glasgow
1981	Chantal Crousel, Paris
1981	Musée d'Art et d'Industrie, St Etienne
1981	Art and Project, Amsterdam
1981	Kunsthalle, Basel
1981	Anthony d'Offay Gallery, London
1982	Greta Insam, Vienna
1982	Kanransha Gallery, Tokyo
1982	Mary Boone Gallery, New York
1982	Modern Art Galerie, Vienna
1982	Chantal Crousel, Paris
1982–83	Van Abbemuseum, Eindhoven
1983	Kanransha Gallery, Tokyo
1983	Kiki Maier-Hahn, Dusseldorf
1983	DAAD Gallery, Berlin
1983	Dany Keller, Munich
1983	Whitechapel Art Gallery, London
1983	Institute of Contemporary Arts, London
1984	Galerie Fahnemann, Berlin
1984	Badischer Kunstverein, Karlsruhe
1984	Dany Keller, Munich
1984	Art Palace, New York

1984	Kanransha Gallery, Tokyo
1984	Bernard Jacobson Gallery, New York
1985	Anthony d'Offay Gallery, London
1985	Bernard Jacobson Gallery, London
1985	Galerie Gmyrek, Dusseldorf
1985	Tate Gallery, London
1986	Bernard Jacobson Gallery, London
1986	Anthony d'Offay Gallery, London
1986	The Scottish Gallery, Edinburgh
1987	Anthony d'Offay Gallery, London
1987	Galerie Fahnemann, Berlin
1987	Hillman Holland, Atlanta
1988	Museum von Hedendaagse, Netherlands
1988	Galerie Gmyrek, Dusseldorf
1988	Kanransha Gallery, Tokyo
1989	Galerie Fahnemann, Berlin
1989	Scottish Gallery, London
1990	Arnolfini Gallery, Bristol
1990	Kanransha, Tokyo
1990	Glasgow Print Studio, Glasgow
1990	Dean Clough, Halifax

JOHN McLEAN

1975	Talbot Rice Art Centre, Edinburgh University
1978	House Gallery, London
1980	Nicola Jacobs Gallery, London
1981	Art Placement, Saskatoon
1982	Artspace Galleries, Aberdeen and touring Scotland
1982	Byck Gallery, Louisville, Kentucky
1983	Nicola Jacobs Gallery, London
1984	Martin Gerrard Gallery, Edmonton, Alta.
1985	Talbot Rice Art Centre, Edinburgh University
1986	Department of Architecture, Edinburgh University
1987	Kapil Jariwala, London
1988	Jariwala/Smith, New York
1988	Francis Graham Dixon Gallery, London
1989	Francis Graham Dixon Gallery, London
1989	Edinburgh College of Art, Edinburgh

ALEXANDER MOFFAT

1973	'A View of the Portrait', Scottish National Portrait Gallery, Edinburgh
1975	Gallery of the Press Club, Warsaw, Poland
1981–83	'Seven Poets', Third Eye Centre, Glasgow; Aberdeen Art Gallery and Museum, Aberdeen; Pier Arts Centre, Orkney (St Magnus Festival); Scottish National Portrait Gallery (Edinburgh Festival); Crawford Arts Centre, St Andrews; Ulster Museum, Belfast; Gardiner Arts Centre, Brighton; Winchester School of Art Gallery; Norwich School of Art Gallery
1984	Portraits Drawings, North East of Scotland Library and Museums Service (Booktable project)
1988	Portraits of Painters, Scottish National Gallery of Modern Art
1990	Glasgow Art Gallery and Museum, Glasgow

JOHN MOONEY

1973	New 57 Gallery, Edinburgh
1980	Talbot Rice Art Centre, Edinburgh
1984	Edinburgh College of Art
1985	Scottish Gallery
1989	Perth Art Gallery
1989	Academy of Fine Art, Belgrade

ELIZABETH OGILVIE

1974	New 57 Gallery, Edinburgh
1976	'Where the Sea Floats Up the Sky', New 57 Gallery, Edinburgh
1980	'Watermarks', The Fruitmarket Gallery, Edinburgh
1980	Third Eye Centre, Glasgow
1980	Aberdeen Art Gallery
1981	New Art Centre, Stoke Ceolfrith Art Gallery, Sunderland
1981	Serpentine Gallery, London
1984	Talbot Rice Art Centre, Edinburgh
1984	DLI Art Centre, Durham
1985	S.A.C. Travelling Gallery

| 1986 | Crawford Centre for the Arts, University of St Andrews |
| 1988 | Sea Sanctuary, Talbot Rice Art Centre, Edinburgh |

GLEN ONWIN

1971	Callender Park College of Education
1975	'Saltmarsh', Scottish Arts Council Gallery, Edinburgh
1975	'Saltmarsh', Serpentine Gallery, London
1976	'Salt Works, Seven Related Pieces', Eden Court, Inverness
1976	'Salt Works, The Recovery of Dissolved Substances', Folker Skulima Gallery, Berlin
1978	'The Recovery of Dissolved Substances', Arnolfini Gallery, Bristol
1978	I.C.A. Gallery, London
1979	'The Recovery of Dissolved Substances', Third Eye Centre, Glasgow
1979	Fruit Market Gallery, Edinburgh
1979	'False Geology', Peterloo Gallery, Manchester
1981	'Solve at Coagula', James IV LIbrary, St Andrews Festival
1981	'NaCl Related Works', The Salt Museum, Northwich
1982	'A Mineral Response to Nature', AIR Gallery, London
1988	'Earth Icons, The Chymical Garden', Artiste Gallery, Bath
1988	Glynn Vivian Art Gallery, Swansea
1988	'Revenges of Nature', The Fruitmarket Gallery, Edinburgh
1989	'Earth Icons, The Chymical Garden', Crawford Arts Centre, St Andrews
1989	Space-ex, Exeter
1989	'Revenges of Nature', Third Eye Centre, Glasgow
1990	'Mysterium Coniunctionis', Pier Arts Centre, Stromness
1991	'As above to Below', Square Chapel, Halifax

JIM PATTISON

1981	369 Gallery, Edinburgh
1982	Forebank Studios, Dundee
1984	Duncan of Jordanstone College of Art, Crawford Gallery
1987	Seagate Gallery, Dundee
1987	Glasgow Print Studio, Glasgow
1989	Black Bull Gallery, London
1990	Shelter Gallery, Glasgow

FRED POLLOCK

1963	New Charing Cross Gallery, Glasgow
1974	Garage, London
1986	Vanessa Devereux Gallery, London
1988	Vanessa Devereux Gallery, London
1990	Vanessa Devereux Gallery, London
1991	Galerie Josine Bokhoven, Amsterdam

BARBARA RAE

1967	New 57 Gallery, Edinburgh
1969	University of York
1971	New 57 Gallery, Edinburgh
1974	University of Aberdeen
1974	Aberdeen Art Gallery
1975	Peterloo Gallery, Manchester
1976	Stirling Gallery, Stirling
1976	Greenock Arts Guild
1977	Gilbert Parr Gallery, London
1978	University of Edinburgh
1979	University of Edinburgh
1979	The Scottish Gallery, Edinburgh
1983	The Scottish Gallery, Edinburgh
1985	Wright Gallery, Dallas, Texas
1986	Leinster Fine Art, London
1987	Glasgow Print Studio
1987	The Scottish Gallery, Edinburgh
1988	The Scottish Gallery, Edinburgh
1989	The Scottish Gallery, Edinburgh
1990	The Scottish Gallery, Edinburgh

JUNE REDFERN

1976	Scottish Arts Council, Edinburgh
1977	Third Eye Centre, Glasgow
1977	Leeds Education Authority Gallery
1978	Women's Art Alliance, London
1978	Henderson Gallery, Edinburgh

1980	The Smith Art Gallery and Museum, Stirling
1980	Drawings, Henderson Gallery, Edinburgh
1981	Pastels, 369 Gallery, Edinburgh
1984	Air Gallery, London
1985	Third Eye Centre, Glasgow
1985	Marianne Denson Gallery, Chicago
1986	National Gallery, London
1987	Mercury Gallery, Edinburgh Festival
1987	Bradford Art Galleries and Museums
1988	Aberdeen Art Galleries and Museums
1988	Towner Art Gallery, Eastbourne
1988	Mercury Gallery, London
1990	Trinity Gallery, London
1991	Compass Gallery, Glasgow

IAIN ROBERTSON

| 1984 | Recent Painting, Spacex Gallery, Exeter |
| 1992 | Talbot Rice Gallery, Edinburgh |

DUNCAN SHANKS

1974	Stirling University
1981	Scottish Gallery, Edinburgh
1984	Fine Art Society, Glasgow, Edinburgh
1988	Talbot Rice Gallery
1991	Fine Art Society, Glasgow, Edinburgh

PETER THOMSON

| 1990 | Transmission Gallery, Glasgow |

FRANCES WALKER

1957	57 Gallery, Edinburgh
1970	Richard Demarco Gallery, Edinburgh
1973	Durham University, Van Mildert College
1977	Richard Demarco Gallery, Edinburgh
1977	Stirling Gallery, Stirling
1978	Loomshop Gallery, Lower Largo, Fife
1979	Aberdeen University, Senior Common Room
1980	'Finnish Suite' (watercolours, drawings and prints), Peacock Printmakers Gallery, Aberdeen and further venues in Scotland 1981–82

| 1983 | 'Orkney Works', Pier Arts Centre, Stromness, Orkney and Artspace, Aberdeen and further venues in Scotland, 1984 |
| 1990 | 'Tiree Works', Talbot Rice Gallery, Edinburgh and Artspace, Aberdeen and further venues in Scotland 1990–91 |

ALISON WATT

| 1990 | The Scottish Gallery, London |
| 1990 | Glasgow Art Gallery and Museum, Kelvingrove |

KATE WHITEFORD

1983	University of St Andrews
1983	Institute of Contemporary Art, London
1984	Third Eye Centre, Glasgow
1984	Midland Group, Nottingham
1985	Ikon Gallery, Birmingham
1986	Riverside Studios, London
1988	Whitechapel Art Gallery, London
1990	Glasgow Museum and Art Gallery

ADRIAN WISZNIEWSKI

1984	Compass Gallery, Glasgow
1984	Air Gallery, London
1985	Nicola Jacobs Gallery, London
1986	Walker Art Gallery, Liverpool
1987	Walker Art Gallery, Liverpool
1988	Nigel Greenwood Gallery, London
1988	Glasgow Print Studios
1989	Rex Irwin Gallery, Sydney
1989	Galerie F17, Ghent
1990	Nigel Greenwood Gallery, London
1990	Gallery Aries, Tokyo
1990	Fruitmarket Gallery, Edinburgh
1991	Galerie F17, Ghent

BIBLIOGRAPHY

Art in Scotland 1978–1988, 369 Gallery, Edinburgh, 1988
Edward Gage, *The Eye in the Wind — Contemporary Scottish Painting since 1945*, Collins, London, 1977
Douglas Hall, *Twentieth Century Painting*, Edward Arnold, 1981
William Hardie, *Scottish Painting 1837 to the Present*, Studio Vista, 1990
Bill Hare, *20th Century Scottish Art*, The Artists' Publishing Co, 1989
Keith Hartley et al, *The Vigorous Imagination — New Scottish Art*, National Galleries of Scotland, 1987
Keith Hartley, *Scottish Art Since 1900*, National Galleries of Scotland/Lund Humphries, 1989
Wendy Kaplan (ed), *Scotland Creates, 5000 Years of Art and Design*, Weidenfeld and Nicolson, 1990
Duncan MacMillan et al, *Scottish Art Now*, Scottish Arts Council, 1982
Duncan MacMillian, *The Scottish Art Show*, Oriel 31, 1988
Duncan MacMillan, *Scottish Art 1460–1990*, Mainstream Publishing, 1990
Duncan MacMillan, *Scottish Art in the 20th Century*, The Royal West of England Academy/Redcliffe Press, 1991
Alexander Moffat, *New Image Glasgow*, Third Eye Centre, Glasgow, 1985
Cordelia Oliver, *Painters in Parallel*, Edinburgh College of Art, 1978
Scotland's Pictures, National Galleries of Scotland, 1991
The Visual Arts in Glasgow — Tradition and Transformation, Third Eye Centre, Glasgow, 1985

For individual articles on contemporary Scottish painting consult such publications as *Alba* magazine, *Cencrastus* and *The Green Book*, and the exhibition catalogues which are listed in the individual bibliographies.

REINHARD BEHRENS
Stavanger Aftenblad, 19 October 1981
'Print Annual II' catalogue, 1981–82
'On Tour in Europe' catalogue, Printmakers Workshop, Edinburgh, 1982
The Scotsman, 22 February 1982
The Scotsman, 1 March 1982
Glasgow Herald, 7 June 1982
Glasgow Herald, 13 August 1982
Edinburgh Evening News, 14 August 1982
'New Scottish Prints' catalogue, 1983
'Scottish Art, 2 Generations' catalogue, 1983
'Scottish Print Open 3' catalogue, 1983
'Scottish Prints Now' catalogue, Edinburgh Printmakers Workshops, 1983
'Sixth International Drawing Biennale' catalogue, 1983
Glasgow Herald, 16 April 1983
Arts Review, April 1984
Glasgow Herald, 5 June 1984
Glasgow Herald, 31 December 1984
Guardian, 12 June 1984
Guardian, 12 October 1984
Glasgow Herald, 2 November 1984
Guardian, 2 November 1984
'Stonework' catalogue, SAC, 1985
The Scotsman, 11 February 1985
The Scotsman, 18 February 1985
Glasgow Herald, 20 February 1985
Arts Review, March 1985
'As An Fheararm' catalogue, from the land, Mainstream, Third Eye Centre, an Lanntair, 1986
'ALBA' catalogue, Autumn 1986
'Ninth British International Print Biennale' catalogue, Bradford, 1986
'On A Raised Beach' catalogue, illustrations to Hugh MacDiarmid, published by Valda Grieve, 1986
Stornoway Gazette, 29 March 1986
Evening Express (Aberdeen), 20 June 1986
Guardian, 4 October 1986
The Courier and Advertiser, 11 September 1986
St Andrews Citizen, 19 September 1986
Glasgow Herald, 24 September 1986
The Scotsman, 1 November 1986
'Scottish Print Open 4' catalogue, 1987
Arts Review, June 1987
Glasgow Herald, 5 June 1987
East Fife Mail, 22 July 1987
'Audio visueel Experimenteel Festival' catalogue, Arnheim, 1988
'Fifth Biennal of European Graphic Art' catalogue, Heidelberg, 1988
'Fruitmarket Open' catalogue, 1988
'Into the Highlands' catalogue, Dundee Art Gallery, 1989
Scottish World/Canada, May 1989
The Scotsman, 22 May 1989
'The Whale and the Artist' catalogue, Dundee Art Gallery, 1990
Glasgow Herald, 1 March 1990
Life and Work, April 1990
'Ash Gallery First Anniversary' catalogue, 1991
'The Last Yeh' catalogue, National History Museum, Dundee, 1991
'The Travelling Gallery' catalogue, Arts in Fife Touring Bus, 1991
'The First 100 Years' catalogue, History of the SSA, 1991
Scotland on Sunday, 2 June 1991
'Seven from Scotland' catalogue, Malaspina Printmakers Society, Vancouver BC, 1991

JOHN BELLANY
Edward Gage, 'Positive evidence of new Edinburgh School', *The Scotsman*, 4 September 1969
Oswell Blakeston, *Arts Review*, Vol 22, No 9, p 290, 1970
William Packer, *Art and Artists*, Vol 5, May, p 30, 1970
Alan Bold, catalogue, Drian Gallery, London, 1970
Alan Bold, 'Scottish Realism' catalogue, Scottish Arts Council Touring Exhibition, 1970
Interview in 'Scottish Realism' catalogue, 1971
Cordelia Oliver, *The Guardian*, 14 May 1971
Catalogue, group exhibition with William Crozier, Rodick Carmichael and Peter Stitt, Arcardia Fine Art, Edinburgh, 1971
Eddie Wolfram, *Arts Review*, Vol 23, No 17, p 515, 1971
Oswell Blakeston, *Arts Review*, Vol 23, No 15, p 464, 1971
Alan Bold, catalogue, Triad Regional Arts Centre, Bishop's Stortford, 1973

William Crozier and Eddie Wolfram, catalogue, Drian Gallery, London, 1973
Eddie Wolfram, *Arts Review*, No 4, p 108, 24 February 1973
Eddie Wolfram, *Art and Artists*, Vol 8, p 48, September 1973
Barbara Wright, *Arts Review*, No 20, p 672, 8 October 1973
Alan Bold, catalogue essay of group exhibition with John Bellany, Neil Dallas Brown, Bill Gillon, Alexander Moffat at Fruitmarket Gallery, Edinburgh, 1975
Alan Bold, catalogue, Acme Gallery, London, 1977
Martin Green, 'John Bellany: Paintings', *Art Monthly*, No 14, p 16, February 1978
Felix McCullough, *Arts Review*, No 5, p 141, March 1978
Simon Vaughan Winter, *Artscribe*, No 10, p 44, January 1978
Marina Vaizey, *The Times*, p 36, 8 January 1978
Felix McCullough, 'Edinburgh Festival 1979', *Arts Review*, No 17, p 455, 31 August 1979
William Packer, catalogue, Acme Gallery, London, 1980
Lucy Ellman, *Arts Review*, No 12, p 250, 20 June 1980
John Roberts, *Artscribe*, No 24, p 58, August 1980
Stuart Morgan, *Art Forum*, p 87, April 1980
Marina Vaizey, *The Times*, p 41, 22 June 1980
Heather Waddell, 'The Painter's Inheritance', *Glasgow Herald*, 14 June 1980
Mary Rose Beaumont, *Arts Review*, p 233, 5 June 1981
Mick Vonjoll, *Artline*, 1981
Edward Lucie-Smith, *Artscribe*, No 27, p 30, February 1981
Mary Rose Beaumont, 'The language of allegory', *Art and Artists*, No 181, pp 20–23, October 1981
Mary Rose Beaumont, *Art and Artists*, No 183, p 20, December 1981
Monica Petzal, 'British Artists — an exhibition about painting?', British Council Touring Exhibition in Aachen, 1982

Edward Lucie-Smith, *Art International*, Vol 25/3–4, pp 81–82, March–April 1982
'John Bellany, Paintings 1973–1982', catalogue, Ikon Gallery, Birmingham, 1983
Robert Ayers, *Studio International*, Vol 196, No 1001, p 43, 1983
Peter Fuller, *Art Monthly*, No 65, p 14, April 1983
Irene McManus, 'Vision from the outer edge', *The Guardian*, 8 March 1983
John Fowler, 'Bellany goes to extremes to reflect the hard life', *Glasgow Herald*, 7 June 1983
Rasaad Jamie, 'John Bellany at the Ikon', *Artscribe*, No 40, pp 46–47, April 1983
William Packer, interview, *Artline*, No 6, pp 8–9, 1983
Marina Vaizey, *The Times*, p 43, 20 March 1983
Glasgow Herald, 9 June 1983
Mary Rose Beaumont, *Arts Review*, p 207, October 1983
James Burr, *Apollo*, No 117, p 410, May 1983
Alexander Moffat, catalogue, Pier Arts Centre, Stromness, Orkney, 1984
Art Monthly, No 79, p 22
Felix McCullough, *Arts Review*, p 428, August 1984
'John Bellany in Australia: a conversation with Jeff Makin', *Studio International*, Vol 197, No 1005, pp 32–34, 1984
Julian Andrews, catalogue 'The British Council Collection 1934–1984', 1984
Max Wykes-Joyce, *Art and Artists*, Vol 215, p 31, August 1984
The Times, p 7, 21 August 1984
Max Wykes-Joyce, *Arts Review*, p 508, 11 October 1985
Clare Henry, *Glasgow Herald*, p 4, 26 March 1985
Hugh Clayton, 'Athena takes a leaf out of Booker's books', *The Times*, p 14, 4 September 1985
Art in America, No 73, p 160, March 1985
William Packer, Robin Gibson, catalogue 'John Bellany: New Portraits', National Portrait Gallery, London

Richard Cork, catalogue 'Bellany's Voyage', Fischer Fine Art Limited, London, 1986
Alistair Hicks, *The Times*, 25 March 1986
Clare Henry, 'Personal view of Botham the folk hero', *Glasgow Herald*, 28 January 1986
Giles Auty, 'Fish Philosopher', *The Spectator*, 8 March 1986
Richard Cork, *The Listener*, 13 March 1986
Frances Spalding, *British Art Since 1900*, London, 1986
Catalogue for Christies Auction, London and New York, 1986
Newart New World, 22 April 1986
Catalogue of Acquisitions 1982–84, Tate Gallery, 1986
Dennis Bowern and Derrick Culley, catalogue, Madrid Toumy Exhibition, June 1986
Christopher Johnstone, *Fifty Twentieth Century Artists*, Scottish National Gallery, 1986
One City A Patron, British Art of the 20th Century from the Collection of Southampton Art Gallery, March 1985
Ninth British International Print Bienniale, March 1986
Catalogue 'John Bellany', Scottish National Gallery of Modern Art, Edinburgh and The Serpentine Gallery, London, Trustee of the Scottish National Gallery of Modern Art, 1986
Clare Henry, *The Glasgow Herald*, 12 August 1986
John Fowler, *The Glasgow Herald*, 14 August 1986
John Russell Taylor, 'Bellany Wins A Titanic Struggle', *The Times Review*, 12 August 1986
Mary Rose Beaumont, *The Financial Times*, 12 August 1986
The Sunday Telegraph, 10 August 1986
Edward Gage, 'A Voyage to Hell and Back', *The Scotsman*, 12 August 1986
Waldemar Januszczak, 'Edge of Darkness and Beyond', *The Guardian*, 14 August 1986
Marina Vaizey, *The Sunday Times*, 17 August 1986
Giles Auty, *The Spectator*, 16 August 1986
Terence Mullaly, *The Daily Telegraph*, 25 August 1986

William Feaver, *The Observer*, 24 August 1986
Edward Gage, 'Face to Face with Bellany', *The Scotsman*, 8 September 1986
Allan Wright, 'Bellany's Glowing Summer', *The Scotsman*, 28 October 1986
Alastair Hicks, 'New Scottish Colourists', *Vogue*, 1986
William Feaver, *The Observer*, 14 December 1986
John McEwan, *Studio International*, Winter Issue, 1986
Catalogue 'Trienniale Europea Dell' Incisione', Grado, Italy, 1987
William Feaver, *The Observer*, 7 June 1987
Waldemar Januszczak, *The Guardian*, 8 June 1987
Brian Fallon, *The Irish Times*, 31 August 1987
Dorothy Walker, 'Bellany at Kilkenny Castle', *The Irish Independent*, 29 August 1987
John Hutchinson, 'Flower of Scotland', *Sunday Press*, 6 September 1987
Aidan Dunne, *Sunday Tribune*, 30 August 1987
Catalogue, Biennale of Graphic Art Ljubljana, Yugoslavia, 1987
The Whitechapel Auction, Whitechapel Art Gallery, London, *Sotheby's Catalogue*, 1 July 1987
Sarah Howell, 'Artists Face to Face', *Observer Colour Supplement*, 13 September 1987
Sean Kelly and Edward Lucie-Smith, *The Self Portrait — A Modern View*, Sarema Press, London, 1987
William Hardie, *Scottish Painting, 1837 to the Present*, 1990
Duncan MacMillan, *Scottish Art 1460–1990*, 1990

Film
BBCTV Film, *John Bellany*, directed by W Gordon Smith, 30 minutes, 1973/4
BBCTV Film, *John Bellany*, directed by Keith Alexander, 30 minutes, 1986
BBCTV Film, *John Bellany — The Making of a Portrait*, with Joan Bakewell, 15 minutes, 1986
BBCTV Film, Heart of the Matter, *Is Life Worth Living? It Depends on the Liver*, 1989

ELIZABETH BLACKADDER
Emilio Coia, 'Elizabeth Blackadder A.R.A.', *Scottish Field*, November 1966, pp 60–61
T Elder Dickson, 'Scottish Painting: the Modern Spirit', *Studio International*, December 1963, pp 236–43
'Elizabeth Blackadder, Still Life: Objects and Flowers', in *Henley Festival of Music and the Arts*, souvenir programme, 1987, pp 9–12
Douglas Hall, 'Elizabeth Blackadder', The *Scottish Art Review*, Vol IX, No 4, 1964, pp 9–12, 31
William Packer, *Elizabeth Blackadder*, Mercury Gallery, London and Edinburgh, 1985
Philip Vann, 'R.A. Travel: Eastern Eden. Elizabeth Blackadder R.A. tells Philip Vann of her Japanese inspirations', *R.A. Magazine*, 15, 1987, pp 46–48
Judith Bumpus, *Elizabeth Blackadder*, Phaidon Press, London, 1988

Catalogues
William Packer (foreword by Carel Weight), *Elizabeth Blackadder*, Scottish Arts Council exhibition, Edinburgh, 1981
William Packer, *Elizabeth Blackadder and John Houston*, Glasgow Print Studio Gallery, 1987

Writings by the artist
With Dr Brinsley Burbidge, introduction to the catalogue of *The Plant: Images of plants, from the scientifically accurate to the purely imaginative, selected from artists working since the war and closely connected with Scotland*, Scottish Arts Council, Edinburgh, 1987
Statement in Charlotte Parry-Crooke (ed), *Contemporary British Artists with Photographs by Walia*, London, 1979

Broadcast material
Conversations with Artists: Elizabeth Blackadder, Interview with Edward Lucie-Smith, BBC Radio 3, 18 October 1982, Produced by Judith Bumpus
A Feeling for Paint: Four Artists and their Materials (Elizabeth Blackadder, David Tindle, Robin Philipson and Bert Irvin), BBC 2, 4 April 1983, Produced and directed by Anne James
Interview with Roger Billcliffe in *Tuesday Review*, BBC Radio Scotland, 5 May 1987, Produced by Caroline Adam

DENNIS BUCHAN
'Scottish Painting', *The Studio*, 1962
Edward Gage, *The Eye in the Wind — Contemporary Scottish Painting since 1945*, Collins, London, 1977
Painters in Parallel, S.A.C. Festival Exhibition, Selected by Cordelia Oliver, 1978

JOYCE CAIRNS
Catalogue 'Five Artists from Aberdeen' (Cairns, Dunbar, Howard, Watson, Young), 369 Gallery, 1980
Stuart Macdonald, catalogue 'The Art of Thinking', Peacock Printmakers Touring Show
Euan McArthur, interview, *Alba*, 1986
David Alston, catalogue 'Under the Cover of Darkness: Night Prints', 1986
Catalogue 'The Scottish Show Oriel 31', 1988
'Art in the Age of Pluralism', *Art and Design*, 1988
'Reproduction and Small Piece', *Interior*, 1988
Clare Henry, *Arts Review*, November 1989
Bill Findlay, interview 'Wounding the Surface', *Cencrastus*, Spring, 1989
Cyril Gerber, catalogue 'Compass Contribution at Tramway', 1990

STEVEN CAMPBELL
Peter Hill, 'Scottish Art Now', *Artscribe*, October 1982
John Russell, 'Reviews-Art: Summertime Discoveries at the Galleries', *New York Times*, 24 June 1983
John Russell, 'Reviews: Steven Campbell', *New York Times*, 9 December 1983
Kim Levin, 'Reviews: Steven Campbell', *Village Voice*, 20 December 1983
Guy Trevay, 'Voice Centerfold-Art: Steven Campbell', *Village Voice*, 27 December 1983
Barry Yourgrau, 'Review: Steven Campbell', *Arts Magazine*, January 1984
Jacqueline Brody, 'New Editions: Steven Campbell', *The Print Collector's Newsletter*,

Vol XIV, No 6, January–February 1984
Theodore Wolff, 'Art as a Warning', *The Christian Science Monitor*, 26 January 1984
Nicholas Moufarrege, 'The Mutant International; VII: Time and Timing, Shelter and Storm', *Arts Magazine*, March 1984
Peter Hill, 'Review: Steven Campbell', *Artscribe*, February–April 1984
Lisa Liebmann, 'Review: Steven Campbell', *Artforum*, April 1984
Brooks Adams, 'Review: Steven Campbell' *Art in America*, May 1984
Harold Haydon, 'Galleries: Campbell Makes Tales Come Alive on Canvas', *Chicago Sun-Times*, 27 April 1984
Alan Artner, 'Galleries: Curious Mix of Odd Style, Grotesquerie', *Chicago Tribune*, 27 April 1984
Michael Brenson, 'Art: Swimming and Other Pools', *New York Times*, 29 June 1984
Marian Pallister, 'Painting the Big Apple Red', *Glasgow Evening Times*, 5 July 1984
Stuart Morgan, 'Soup's on: An Audience with Steven Campbell', *Artscribe*, September–October 1984
Stuart Morgan, catalogue 'Steven Campbell: Between Oxford and Salisbury', Riverside Studios, London and The Fruitmarket Gallery, Edinburgh, November 1984
Ronny Cohen, 'Jumbo Prints', *Artnews*, October 1984
William Packer, 'The Great British Show Hits the Road', *Financial Times*, 6 November 1984
Richard Cork, 'Second City First', *The Listener*, 8 November 1984
Marina Vaizey, 'Painting Takes to the Stage', *Sunday Times*, 2 December 1984
Waldemar Januszczak, 'Galleries Briefing: Steven Campbell', *The Guardian*, 4 December 1984
William Packer, 'A Scot Comes to Artistic Judgement', *Financial Times*, 4 December 1984
Stuart Morgan, 'The Case of the Waggling Leg', *Artforum*, December 1984
Sandra Miller, 'Putting Flesh on to Oil Painting: Steven Campbell New Paintings', *The Times*,

4 December 1984
Waldemar Januszczak, 'When Christ Came to Cookham', *The Guardian*, 12 December 1984
Nigel Pollitt, 'New Reviews' Steven Campbell', *City Limits*, 14–20 December 1984
William Feaver, 'Quirky Charades', *The Observer*, 16 December 1984
Sarah Kent, 'Steven Campbell', *Time Out*, 20 December 1984–2 January 1985
William Feaver, 'Reviews', *Vogue*, January 1985
Waldemar Januszczak, 'The Church of the New Art', *Flash Art*, January 1985
Patrick Bishop, 'Young, Scots and Expressionist', *Literary Review*, January 1985
Clare Henry, 'An International Hot Property with his Feet on the Ground', *Glasgow Herald*, January 1985
Allen Wright, 'Artistic Filling of Gap Site', *The Scotsman*, January 1985
Robert Merritt, 'Drawings Represent Several Approaches', *Richmond Times*, 27 January 1985
James Collins, 'A Travelogue: Love and Loathing in Europe', *Flash Art*, March 1985
Caroline Collier, 'Review: Steven Campbell', *Flash Art*, March 1985
John Russell, 'Reviews: Steven Campbell', *New York Times*, 12 April 1985
Lucinda Bredin, 'Campbell Finds His Kingdom', *Scottish Field*, February 1985
Michael Spens, 'On the Plight of any Artist', *Studio International*, March 1985
Eduardo de Benito, 'Steven Campbell, La Pintura como Genero Literario', *Lapiz*, May 1985
Joan Hugo, 'Pick of the Week', *Los Angeles Weekly*, August 1985
Waldemar Januszczak, 'The Glow that Came from Glasgow', *The Guardian*, 13 August 1985
Clare Henry, 'Glasgow Stealing the Show for Art', *Glasgow Herald*, 14 August 1985
William Feaver, 'Welcome to Prehistory', *The Observer*, 25 August 1985
Alexander Moffatt, catalogue 'New Image Glasgow', Third Eye Centre, Glasgow, August 1985
Marge Goldwater, catalogue 'Of Hikers and

Humeians', Walker Art Centre, Minneapolis, September 1985
Peter Fuller, 'Review: The Hayward Annual', *Artscribe*, September 1985
Andrew Graham-Dixon, 'Is it Miles Better in Glasgow?', *Sunday Times*, October 1985
Leslie Geddes-Brown, 'On the City Full of Northern Promise', *Sunday Times*, 6 October 1985
Waldemar Januszczak, 'New Image Glasgow', *The Guardian*, 17 October 1985
Marina Vaizey, 'Paintings Hot off the Easel', *Sunday Times*, 19 October 1985
Mary Rose Beaumont, 'New Image Glasgow', *Arts Review*, 25 October 1985
John Russell Taylor, 'Galleries: New Image Glasgow', *The Times*, 29 October 1985
Clare Henry, 'Five Scottish Artists', *Glasgow Herald*, 27 Nvember 1985
Mel Gooding, 'New Image Glasgow', *Art Monthly*, November 1985
Helen Kohen, 'Focus New York — Hails Latest in Art', *The Miami Herald*, 10 January 1986
Richard Francis, catalogue 'Steven Campbell: *Bonjour Monsieur Foucault*', Tate Gallery, Liverpool, Summer 1986
Tony Godfrey, *The New Image: Painting in the 1980s*, Phaidon Press, Oxford, 1986
James Collins, 'Interview with Steven Campbell', *Flash Art*, February–March 1987
Tony Godfrey, catalogue 'The Recent Paintings of Steven Campbell', Marlborough Fine Art, London, April 1987
Tony Godfrey, 'Steven Campbell: *The Dangerous Early and Late Life of Lytton Strachey*', *Burlington Magazine*, April 1987
Clare Henry, 'Scottish Whimsy', *Studio International*, August 1987
Andrew Wilson, catalogue 'The Frozen Gesture: Recent Paintings by Steven Campbell', Marlborough Gallery Inc, New York, September 1988
Hugh Cumming, 'New Figurative Art: A Survey', *Art and Design*, Vol 4, No 9/10, October 1988
Judith Higgins, 'Steven Campbell', *Artnews*, November 1988

Robin Nicholson, 'Scottish Neo-Romantics', *The Antique Collector*, August 1989
Martin Gayford, 'Art Now Belongs to Glasgow', *The Daily Telegraph*, 6 January 1990
Virginia Fraser, 'City Lights', *Vogue*, Feburary 1990
Catalogue, Euan McArthur, 'Steven Campbell's Uncertainty Principle', and Stuart Morgan, 'Leaves from a Campbell Notebook', Third Eye Centre, Glasgow, March 1990
Clare Henry, 'Campbell Third Eye-Catching', *Glasgow Herald*, 10 March 1990
Clare Flowers, 'Campbell on Form', *Scotland on Sunday*, 11 March 1990
Meg Milne, 'Painter's Transformation Scene', *Sunday Express*, 11 March 1990
Emilio Coia, 'A First for Golden Old Boy', *The Scotsman*, 12 March 1990
Cordelia Oliver, 'Steven Campbell', *The Guardian*, 17 March 1990
W Gordon-Smith, 'Tongue in Chic from the Prodigal', Observer Scotland, 18 March 1990
Todd McEwan, 'Steven Campbell: Through the Ceiling, Through the Floor, and Through the Streets of Glasgow', *Modern Painters*, Vol 3, No 1, Spring 1990
Andrew Gibbon-Williams, 'Glasgow's Painter in Residence', *The Times*, 6 April 1990
Andrew Nairne, catalogue 'Steven Campbell', Tate Gallery, Liverpool, May 1990
Film Interview
Alistair Scott, 'Steven Campbell/Adrian Wiszniewski', *Arena*, BBC Television, February 1986
Interview with Professor Martin Kemp, *The Third Ear Programme*, BBC Radio 3, 23 March 1990

RUSSELL COLOMBO
Bill Hare, *Alba* 2, 1986

CALUM COLVIN
D Brittain, 'Calum Colvin: keeping the beast chained tight', *Artline*, Vol 4, April/May 1989
P Core, 'Unnatural perspectives', *The Independent*, March 1988

C Glenn, *Calum Colvin*, California State University, Long Beach
Professor J Hedgecoe, *The Compelling Eye*, Royal College of Art
D Mellor, *Calum Colvin, Works, 1986/88*, Salama-Caro Gallery
D Mellor, 'Romances of Decay, Elegies for the Future', *Aperture*, 1988
J Laroche, *Zoom*, No 41

STEPHEN CONROY
Catalogue 'The Vigorous Imagination — New Scottish Art', Scottish National Gallery of Modern Art, Edinburgh
Alice Bain, 'Young Scots Fly the Banner', *Glasgow Herald*, 10 August 1987
Douglas Hall, 'Scottish Art Alive and Kicking', *The Scotsman*, 10 August 1987
Emilio Coia, 'Explosive Impact of the Young Scots', *The Scotsman*, 10 August 1987
Keith Hartley, 'The Vigorous Imagination', *The Green Book*, Vol 2, No 7
William Feaver, 'Queen Bee's Buzz', *The Observer*, 16 August 1987
Marina Vaizey, 'Window on the World', *The Sunday Times*, 16 August 1987
Andrew Graham-Dixon, 'The Scottish at Play', *The Independent*, 21 August 1987
Mathew Gwyther, 'Saatchi and Scottish art in Edinburgh', *Design Week*, 28 August 1987
Laurence Marks, 'Festival Diary — Stephen Conroy', *The Observer*, 30 August 1987
Andrew Graham-Dixon, 'A Painter's Progress', *The Independent*, 30 October 1987
Andrew Graham-Dixon, 'Unquiet Mood', *Vogue*, February 1988
Peter Fuller, 'Portrait of the Artist as a Naive Young Genius', *Sunday Telegraph*, 18 June 1989
Richard Dorment, 'A Young Painter's Nightmare', *Sunday Telegraph*, 18 June 1989
Emilio Coia, 'From Attic to Top Gallery', *The Scotsman*, 22 June 1989
Giles Auty, 'Conroy was here', *The Spectator*, 24 June 1989
William Feaver, 'Have his KKK and eat it', *The*

Observer, 25 June 1989
Andrew Graham-Dixon, 'Booked Up and Sold Out', *The Independent*, 27 June 1989
Peter Fuller, 'From Glasgow Boys to Glasgow Pups', *Sunday Telegraph*, 2 July 1989
Patrick Reyntiens, 'Galleries', *The Tablet*, 8 July 1989
William Packer, 'The Hedonist Smiles over his Geometry', *Financial Times*, 11 July 1989
Larry Berryman, 'Stephen Conroy, Marlborough Fine Art', *Arts Review*
Richard Dorment, 'Glasgow's Young Master', *Telegraph Weekend Magazine*, 15 July 1989
John Russell Taylor, 'Out of School, Galleries', *The Times*, 18 July 1989
Clare Flowers, 'Conroy's Quiet World Beyond Celebrity Hype', *Scotland on Sunday*, 13 August 1989
W Gordon Smith, 'Glasgow, Art', *Observer Scotland*, 27 August 1989
'Conroy, What the Critics Said', *Modern Painters*, Vol 2, No 3, Autumn 1989
Andrew Renton, 'Stephen Conroy: Part of a Discourse that is tantalisingly incomplete', *Flash Art*, November/December 1989
Brooks Adams, 'Hot Scot', *Interview Magazine*, January 1990
Sylvia Stevenson, 'Stephen Conroy: Fastidious Detachment', *Apollo*, August 1990
Allen Wright, *The Scotsman*, 14 December 1990
Alice Bain, 'Sir Steven's New Image', *Glasgow Herald*, 14 December 1990
Richard Jacques, 'Fine Tribute from Youth to Old Age', *The Scotsman*, 3 January 1991
Film
Keith Alexander, 'New Scottish Art — Stephen Conroy', BBC film, 25 May 1988

FRED CRAYK
Clare Henry, *The Glasgow Herald*, 1987
Tony McManus, *Cencrastus*, 1988
Jill and Cyril Gerber, catalogue 'Compass at the Tramway', 1990

KEN CURRIE
Mark Safford, 'Kenneth Currie', *Penumbra*,

Autumn, 1981
Ian Brotherhood, 'Ken Currie: a discussin on art and politics', *Artline*, No 5, March 1983
Alexander Moffat, catalogue 'Telling Stories', Third Eye Centre, Glasgow, 1985
Jeff Sawtell, 'Capitalism's crisis ends modernism', *Morning Star*, 19 October 1985
Marjorie Althorpe-Guyton, 'New Image Glasgow', *Artscribe*, October 1985
Mary Rose Beaumont, 'New Image Glasgow', *Arts Review*, No 37, October 1985
Mel Gooding, 'New Image Glasgow', *Art Monthly*, November 1985
Graham Ogilvie, 'Painting the town red', *Seven Days*, January 1986
Frances Morris, 'Making History', *Arnolfini Review*, May 1986
Malcolm Dickson, 'Polemics: Glasgow Painting Now', *Edinburgh Review*, No 73, 1986
Neal Ascherson, 'Enterprise and the Cult of Failure', *The Observer*, 17 August 1986
Jeff Sawtell, 'Problems of Marxism today', *Morning Star*, 14 January 1987
Justine Picardie and Dorothy Wade, 'The Shock of the Noo', *The Face*, No 87, July 1987
Andrew Graham-Dixon, 'The Scottish at Play', *The Independent*, 21 August 1987
Brandon Taylor, catalogue 'Critical Realism', Nottingham Castle Museum, 1987
Michael Wilson, 'Revival or Myth?', *Scotsman Magazine*, Vol 8, No 5, August 1987
John Griffiths, 'Heroes and Dreamers: Scottish Figurative Art in the 1980s', *Art and Design*, Vol 3, No 7/8, 1987
Clare Henry, 'Seeing ourselves as others didn't', *Glasgow Herald*, 28 August 1987
Allan Harkness, 'The Social Imagination: Ken Currie's Glasgow Murals', *Cencrastus*, Autumn, 1987
Timothy Hyman, 'The Vigorous Imagination', *Burlington Magazine*, November 1987
Catalogue 'The Vigorous Imagination: New Scottish Art', Scottish National Gallery of Modern Art, Edinburgh, 1987
Waldemar Januszczak, 'Backs to the Wall', *The Guardian*, 17 September 1987

Sally Kinnes, 'Angry Arts: Ken Currie', *Blueprint*, No 42, November 1987
Bernard Levin, 'Passion and Platitude', *The Times*, 16 November 1987
Richard Cork, catalogue 'Art History: artists look at contemporary Britain', Hayward Gallery, London, 1987–88
Justine Picardie, 'Heightening Glasgow's sense of history', *The Sunday Times*, 17 April 1988
Clare Henry, 'Using a paintbrush for a lance', *The Glasgow Herald*, 15 July 1988
Alice Bain, 'Thistle in the gutter', *The List*, July 1988
Jack McLean, 'Profile of Ken Currie', *The Glasgow Herald*, 23 August 1988
Bill Hare, 'Divided City', *Radical Scotland*, August/September 1988
Tom Lubbock, 'Red Clyde by torchlight', *The Independent*, 8 August 1988
John Griffiths, 'British artists of the '80s', *Art and Design*, Vol 4, No 9/10, 1988
Lewis Biggs, catalogue 'Cries and Whispers', British Council Collection, 1988
Mark Van Royen, 'And now, Scotland', *Artweek*, Vol 19, No 33, 1988, San Francisco
Carolyn Cohen and Judith Higgins, catalogue 'The New Painting', Cincinnati Contemporary Arts Centre, 1988
Paul Wood, 'On Ken Currie: The Dotage of Authenticity', *Edinburgh Review*, No 80–81, 1988
James D Young, 'Culture and Socialism', *Worker's City*, Clydeside Press, 1988
Alexander Moffat, 'Life Grows Harder', *Alba*, Winter, 1988
Anne McDonald, 'Interview with Ken Currie', *Shift*, Vol 3, No 1, San Francisco
John Griffiths, 'Current Trends', *Art and Design*, Vol 5, No 3/4, 1989
Carolyn Cohen, 'The New British Painting', *Art and Design*, Vol 5, No 3/4, 1989
Timothy Hyman, 'Scottish Art since 1900', *Times Literary Supplement*, 28 July–3 August 1989
Alan Bold, 'Scottish Art', *Modern Painters*, Vol 2, No 3, 1989

Stewart Hennessy, 'Artist at war with complacency', *Observer Scotland*, 2 July 1989
Norbert Lynton, catalogue 'Picturing People: British Figurative Art since 1945', British Council, 1989
Ian Spring, 'Born in the shadow of the Fairfield crane', *The Phantom Village: The Myth of the New Glasgow*, Polygon, 1990
Alan Bold, 'Bellany and Scottish Painting', *An Open Book*, MacDonald Publishers, Edinburgh, 1990
Keith Hartley, catalogue 'Scottish Art since 1900', Scottish National Gallery of Modern Art, Edinburgh, 1989
Edward Lucie-Smith, 'New Scottish Painting', *Art in the Eighties*, Phaidon Press, 1990
William Hardie, 'Contemporaries: Abstraction and New Figuration', *Scottish Painting 1831 to the Present*, Studio Vista, 1990

Selected Films and Interviews
BBC 2, 'Art and Upheaval: Art and Society', 13 October 1987
BBC Radio 4, *Kaleidoscope*, 'Diego Rivera and Art History', 2 November 1987
BBC Radio 3, *Third Ear*, Interview with Julian Spalding, 1 February 1988
BBC 2, 'New Scottish Art: Ken Currie', 24 May 1988
Channel 4, 'Glasgow By the Way: Part four — May Day', 30 August 1988
BBC Radio Scotland, Tuesday Review, Interview with George Byatt, 10 January 1989
ZDF West Germany, 'Warum Glasgow? Uber die Kulturhauptttstadt Europas 1990', 8 January 1990

ALAN DAVIE
Herbert Read, *Contemporary British Art*, Penguin Books, London, 1951
Patrick Heron, *The Changing Forms of Art*, Routledge and Kegan Paul, London, 1955
Patrick Heron, *Arts Digest*, New York, 1955
Herbert Read, 'A Blot on the Scutcheon', *Encounter*, London, 1955
Patrick Heron, *Arts*, New York, 1956
Anton Ehrenzweig, 'The Modern Artist and the

Creative Accident', *The Listener*, London, 1956
David Lewis, 'Alan Davie', *Accent* 1, Leeds,
1958
Bryan Robertson, 'Alan Davie', *Books and Art*,
London, 1958
David Lewis, catalogue, Wakefield
Retrospective, 1958
Bryan Robertson, catalogue, Whitechapel
Retrospective, 1958
Sam Hunter, *Art in America*, No 3, 1959
Alan Bowness, 'Alan Davie', *Aujourd' hui* 26,
Paris, 1960
Alan Bowness, catalogues, Gimpel Fils, London,
Galerie Charles Lienhard, Galleria Del Naviglio,
1960
Robert Melville, 'Contemporary British Painters'
(1), *Motif* 7, 1961
W Sandberg and HLC Jaffe, *Pioneers of Modern
Art*, McGraw-Hill, London, 1961
W Sandberg, catalogue, FBA/Amsterdam
Retrospective, 1962
David Sylvester, 'Alan Davie and the Cult of
Painting Big', *The Sunday Times*, London, 1962
Robert Harvey, 'The True Meaning of the
Wheel', interview, *Granta*, Cambridge, 1962
Michael Horovitz, *Alan Davie*, Methuen,
London, 1963
Michael Horovitz, 'Notes on Alan Davie',
Cimaise 10, No 1, Paris, 1963
Dietrich Mahlow, catalogue, Baden Baden
Retrospective, 1963
Alan Bowness, catalogue, Sao Paulo Bienal
Exhibition, 1963
Robert Melville, 'The Unintensionalism of Alan
Davie', *Quadrum* 14, Brussels
Bryan Robertson, John Russell, Lord Snowden,
Private View, Nelson, 1965
Werner Haffmann, *Painting in the Twentieth
Century Vol 2*, Lund Humphries, London, 1965
*7 Decades 1895–1965, Crosscurrents in Modern
Art*, Public Education Association, New York,
1965
Alan Davie, Alan Bowness, *Studio International*,
September 1966
Will Groham, *Art of Our Time*, Verlag M
Dumont Schankery, Cologne, 1966

Alan Bowness, 'British Art Today', *Art of Our
Time*, Thames and Hudson, 1966
Alan Bowness, *Alan Davie*, Lund Humphries,
1967
Alan Bowness, 'Alan Davie un Veggente', *ARTI*,
T17, No 6, 1967
Pierre Cabanne, 'Alan Davie', *Arts Loisirs*,
No 75, Paris, 1967
'Alan Davie Unvoyant', *Revue Mensuelle*, No 41,
La Galerie des Arts, Paris, 1967
Barrie Sturt-Penrose, 'Alan Davie', *The Sunday
Observer Colour Supplement*, 21 May 1967
J Burr, 'Magic and Ritual', Apollo, Vol 110,
No 211, 1979
JR Taylor, 'Out on His Own', *Art and Artists*,
No 181, October 1981
Roger Berthoud, 'Encounter with Alan Davie',
Illustrated London News, September 1985
Jacques Roche-Villiers, catalogue, Galerie Louis
Carre, Paris, 1987
Douglas Hall, catalogue, South West Arts
Association, Travelling Exhibitions in Scotland,
1988–89
Keith Patrick, 'An Interview with Alan Davie',
The Green Book, Vol III, 1989
Charles Booth-Clibborn, 'Monotypes', Print
Quarterly VI (3), p 318, 1989
Keith Patrick, '70th Birthday Tribute', *Art Line*,
October 1990
William Crozier, 'A Beacon in the Gloaming',
Art Line, October 1990
Anna Markowska, catalogue, Gallery 'M',
Krakow, 1991
Michael Tucker, 'Music Man's Dream', *Alan
Davie*, Lund Humphries, London, 1991
Douglas Hall, 'Introducing Alan Davie', *Alan
Davie*, Lund Humphries, London, 1991

DAVID DONALDSON

RH Westwater, 'David Donaldson', *Scottish Art
Review*, Vol 8, No 4, 1962, pp 5–8
Pierre Lavalle, 'David Donaldson', *Scottish Field*,
August 1963
Alison Downie, 'A compulsion to paint people',
The Glasgow Herald, 13 December 1975
Edward Gage, *The Eye in the Wind —*

Contemporary Scottish Painting since 1945,
Collins, London, 1977, p 37
Jack Firth, *Scottish Watercolour Painting*,
Edinburgh, 1979, p 35
David Donaldson, 'The enjoyment of painting',
The Scottish Review, No 13, February 1979
The Art Magazine, Summer, 1981

KATE DOWNIE

Artists in Industry, West Midlands,
Wolverhampton Art Gallery, 1984

DAVID EVANS

Edward Gage, *The Eye in the Wind —
Contemporary Scottish Painting since 1945*,
Collins, London, 1977
Jack Firth, *Scottish Watercolour Painting*,
Ramsay Head Press, 1979
Paul Stirton, *David Evans*, New 57 Gallery, 1982

LYS HANSEN

Alba, 1986
The Self-Portrait, A Modern View, Sarema Press,
1987
Clamjamfrie, Broad Sheet, Issue No 1
Clamjamfrie, Broad Sheet, Issue No 3
Liz Lochhead, *Dreaming Frankenstein*
Interviews
BBC Television, *Profile*, 'The Lunch Party', 1984
BBC Radio 4, *Tuesday Review*, 1986
BBC Radio 4, 'For a' That' Burns Exhibition,
1990
BBC Radio 4, Exhibition and book review

GWEN HARDIE

Murdo Macdonald, *Weightlessness and Gravity*,
Festival Times, August 1984
Sandy Moffat, 'Artists in Exile', *Edinburgh
Review*, Feburary 1986
Sean Kelly, Edward Lucie-Smith, *The Self-
Portrait, A Modern View*, Sarema Press, 1987
Wendy Beckett, *Contemporary Women Artists*,
p 49
Keith Hartley, *Scottish Art since 1900*, , National
Galleries of Scotland/Lund Humphries, 1989,
pp 136, 109

Edward Lucie-Smith, Carolyn Cohen, Judith Higgins, *The New British Painting*, pp 65, 104
Marjorie Allthorpe-Guyton, *Gwen Hardie: Paintings and Drawings*
Keith Hartley, *Gwen Hardie*, Fischer Fine Art, London
Films
Sean Kelly, *The Self-Portrait, A Modern View*, HTV
Keith Alexander, *New Scottish Art — Gwen Hardie*, 20 minutes, BBC2

JOHN HOUSTON
Cordelia Oliver, *Manchester Guardian*, May 1960
T Elder Dickson, 'Scottish Painting, The Modern Spirit', *Studio International*, December 1963
Emilio Coia, *Scottish Field*, August 1968
James G Mowat, catalogue 'John Houston Retrospective Exhibition', Dunfermline, 1974
Edward Gage, *Edinburgh Ten 30*, Scottish Arts Council, Welsh Arts Council, 1975
Richard Calvocoressi, *John Houston*, Scottish Arts Council, Gaelic College, Skye, 1976
Edward Gage, *The Eye in the Wind — Contemporary Scottish Painting since 1945*, Collins, London, 1977
Jack Firth, *Scottish Watercolour Painting*, 1979
William Packer, *Mercury Magazine*, Summer Issue, 1983
Alastair Hicks, 'The New Scottish Colourist: Bruce McLean, John Bellany, John Houston', *Vogue*, October 1986
Duncan MacMillan, *John Houston, Works on Paper 1962–1987*, 1987
Alice Bain, 'Mayfest Review', *Glasgow Herald*, 13 May 1987
William Packer, catalogue 'Elizabeth Blackadder and John Houston', Glasgow Print Studio, 1987
Clare Henry, *Glasgow Herald*, 13 March 1987
Duncan MacMillan, catalogue 'The Scottish Show', Oriel, Wales, 1988
Clare Henry, *Galleries*, October 1989
Keith Hartley, *Scottish Art since 1900*, , National Galleries of Scotland/Lund Humphries, 1989
Judith Bumpus, *Arts Review*, 22 September 1989

IAN HOWARD
Isobel Johnstone, *Four N.E. Artists*, Peacock Printmakers, Aberdeen, 1983
Professor Norbert Lynton, Tolly-Cobbold Eastern Arts Fifth National Exhibition', Eastern Arts, 1985
James Bustard, *Sculptors Drawings*, Scottish Arts Council, 1985
Mary Rose Beaumont, *The Human Touch*, Fischer Fine Art Ltd, London, 1986
Mary Rose Beaumont, *Side by Side*, British Council, 1986
Ian Robertson, 'Ian Howard interviewed', *Alba*, Summer, 1986
Peter Hill, *Ian Howard: Paintings, Prints and Related Works*, Third Eye Centre, Glasgow, Peacock Printmakers, Aberdeen, 1987
John Griffiths, 'Heroes and Dreamers: Scottish Figurative Art in the '80s', *Art and Design*, Vol 3, No 7/8, 1987
Duncan MacMillan, 'The Scottish Story', *Oriel* 31, Wales, 1988
John Griffiths, 'Deconstructionist Tendencies in Art', *Art and Design*, Vol 4, No 3/4, 1988
John Griffiths, 'Movements in Contemporary Art', *Art and Design*, Vol 4, No 7/8, 1988
John Griffiths, 'Scottish Art Now', *Art and Design*, Vol 4, No 7/8, 1988
The Compass Contribution 1969–1990, Compass Gallery, Glasgow, 1990
Duncan MacMillan, *Scottish Art 1460–1990*, Mainstream, Edinburgh, 1990

PETER HOWSON
D Howell, catalogue 'Wall murals', Feltham Community Association, London, 1982
Alexander Moffat, catalogue 'Pictures of Ourselves', Scottish Arts Council, Edinburgh, 1982
William Buchanan, catalogue 'Grease and Water: The Art and Technique of Lithography', Printmakers Workshop, Edinburgh, 1983
Alexander Moffat, catalogue 'New Image Glasgow', Third Eye Centre, Glasgow, 1985
Marjorie Allthorpe-Guyton, *Artscribe*, October 1985
Waldemar Januszczak, *The Guardian*, 17 October 1985

Mary Rose Beaumont, *Arts Review*, 25 October 1985
John Russell Taylor, *The Times*, 29 October 1985
Mel Gooding, *Art Monthly*, November 1985
Peter Hepburn, catalogue 'Unique and Original', Glasgow Print Studio, 1985
Robert Livingstone and Peter Howson, catalogue 'Peter Howson: New Paintings', Crawford Centre for the Arts, University of St Andrews, 1986
Ray McKenzie, catalogue 'The Eye of the Storm', The Smith Art Gallery and Museum, Stirling, 1986
Philip Wright, catalogue 'New Art from Scotland', Warwick Arts Trust, London, 1986
Clare Henry and Keith Hartley, catalogue 'Scottish Art Today: Artists at work', Edinburgh International Festival, Edinburgh College of Art, 1986
Andrew Graham-Dixon, 'The Glasgow Connection: Peter Howson and Stephen Barclay', *Harpers and Queen*, May 1986
Clare Henry, 'Explosion of Scottish Talent — Scottish Art Today', *Glasgow Herald*, 6 August 1986
Tessa Jackson, 'Peter Howson', *The Green Book*, Vol 12, No 6, 1986
Clare Henry, 'Ex-bodybuilder shapes up', *Glasgow Herald*, 6 February 1987
Paula Vazelay, *London Arts Review*, 8 May 1987
John Russell Taylor, *The Times*, 15 April 1987
Michael Wilson, 'Revival or Myth', *The Scotsman Magazine*, August 1987
Waldemar Januszczak, catalogue 'Saracen Heads', Angela Flowers Gallery, London, 1987
Giles Auty, *The Spectator*, 17 October 1987
Mary Rose Beaumont, *Arts Review*, 23 October 1987
Guy Burn, *Arts Review*, 6 November 1987
Clare Flowers, 'Peter Howson: Heroes and Villains', *Cencrastus*, Spring, 1988
Donald Kuspit, catalogue 'Fables and Fantasies', Paintings from the collection of Susan Kasen and Robert D Summer, Duke University Museum of Art, USA, April 1988
Lucinda Bredin, 'Painters from the Glasgow School of Art', *Elle*, May 1988
Sarah Kent, *Time Out*, 27 July 1988

Robert Heller, catalogue 'The Twilight Zone',
Cleveland Art Gallery, September 1988
Edward Lucie-Smith, catalogue 'The New British
Painting', The Contemporary Arts Center,
Cincinnati, USA, 1988
Hugh Cumming, 'New Figurative Art: A Survey',
Art and Design, Vol 4, No 9/10, 1988
Edward Lucie-Smith, catalogue 'The Self-Portrait:
A Modern View', Fischer Fine Art, London, 1988
Arts Review, 24 February 1989
Amanda Sebestyen, 'Keep the Beer Mat Flying',
New Statesman and Society, 4 August 1989
Marina Vaizey, catalogue 'Peter Howson: Paintings
and Prints', Glasgow Print Studio, 1990
Robert Heller, catalogue, LA Art Fair Solo
exhibition
Alan Jackson, *20 20 Magazine*, 1991

MARGARET HUNTER
Lesley Geddes-Brown, 'Trying to Stop the Talent
Drain', *The Sunday Times*, July 1985
Dr Olav Münzberg, *Zitty Magazine*, Berlin, June
1986
Art News, Kyle and Carrick District Council, Ayr,
July 1986
Peter Kravitz, *Edinburgh Arts Review*, January
1986
Alice Bain, *The Glasgow Herald*, May 1987
Catalogue 'Art in Exile', May 1987
Dorothy Wade and Justine Picardie, 'Here Come
the Glasgow Girls', *The Independent*, June 1987
Anthony Jones, catalogue 'The Vigorous
Imagination', August 1987
Catalogue 'The Smith Biennial 1987', September
1987
Clare Henry, *The Glasgow Herald*, January 1988
Konrad Jule Hammer, catalogue '1. Mai Salon
1988', May 1988
Clare Henry, 'Glasgow Truly in the Picture', *The
Glasgow Herald*, June 1988
'Tre artiste europee a confronto', *La Nazione*,
Firenze, October 1988
Murdo Macdonald, *The Scotsman*, October 1988
Geraldine Prinze, 'Two distant cultures …', *The
Independent*, October 1988
Giles Auty, 'Women Dealers', *London Galleries

Guide*, November 1988
Clare Henry, *Arts Review*, November 1988
Christian Ebel, *Zitty Magazine*, Berlin, February
1989
Alexandra Glanz, 'Bis in die Hutkrempe', *Der
Tagesspiegel*, Berlin, February 1989
Alexander Moffat, catalogue 'New Directions',
February 1989
'Suche nach der Inspiration', *Frankenpost*,
Germany, May 1989
Sabine Gebhardt, *Selber Tageblatt*, Germany,
1 June 1989
Ralf Sziegoliet, *Frankenpost*, Germany, 1 June
1989
W Gordon Smith, 'Nine Decades of Scots
Painters', *Observer, Scotland on Sunday*, 18 June
1989
'Malaktion beschliesst Ausstellung', *Selber
Tageblatt*, 23 June 1989
Clare Henry, *The Glasgow Herald*, 30 June 1989
Keith Hartley, catalogue 'Scottish Art Since 1900',
June 1989
The Scotsman, 18 September 1989
W Gordon Smith, *Observer, Scotland on Sunday*,
1 October 1989
Dr Penny Dunford, *Dictionary of Women Artists in
Europe and America since 1850*, Harvest and
Wheatsheaf, October 1989
Marlis Pfiffer, Goethe Institute catalogue 'Three
European Artists', Glasgow, June 1990
Clare Henry, *The Glasgow Herald*, 22 June 1990
The List, June 1990
Tom Levine, 'Nun Heilen wirdie Mauer', *Hessische
Algemeine*, Germany, 16 September 1990
Murdo Macdonald, *The Scotsman*, 8 October
1909
Hilary Robinson, *The List*, 12–25 October 1990
Clare Flowers, *Spectrum*, 7 October 1990
Penny Taylor, 'Self Expressionism', *The
Independent*, 6 November 1990
Sandy Moffat, catalogue, Vanessa Devereux
Gallery, November 1990
Francis Spalding, '20th Century Painters and
Sculptors', *Dictionary of British Art*, Vol VI,
Antique Collectors Club, 1990
Elizabeth Anson, 'The Vibrancy of June Redfern',

Women's Art Journal, March/April 1991
Zakiah Omar, 'Art that engenders world view of
women', *New Straits Times*, Malaysia, 9 May 1991
Catalogue 'East', National Open Art Exhibition,
Norwich Gallery, July 1991
Tim Hilton, 'Full of Eastern Promise', *The
Guardian*, 17 July 1991
Television and radio interviews
'Three European Artists', exhibition interview,
Scottish Television, 14 June 1990
East Side Gallery Wall Project, interview, 'Heute
Journal', German Television, 31 August 1990
East Side Gallery Wall Project, interview, 'Today',
BBC World Service, 1 September 1990

MATTHEW INGLIS
Murdo Macdonald, 'The Serious and Funny Side of
Life', *The Scotsman*, August 1988
Bill Hare, 'Territory and Terrorism', interview, *Alba*,
No 10, Winter, 1988

CALLUM INNES
Philip Wright, catalogue 'New Art From Scotland',
Warwick Arts Trust, 1985
Murdo Macdonald, *The Scotsman*, October 1988
Kevin Henderson, 'Callum Innes, Recent Work,
369 Gallery', *Alba*, Spring, 1989, p 77
Murdo Macdonald, 'Fruitmarket Open', *The
Scotsman*, June 1989
Andrew Nairne and artists, catalogue 'Scatter',
Third Eye Centre, Glasgow, 1989
Peter Hill, *Alba*, Summer, 1989
Murdo Macdonald, *The Scotsman*, 24 July 1989
Cordelia Oliver, *The Guardian*, 31 July 1989
Murdo Macdonald, catalogue 'The Smith Biennal,
1989', 1989
Murdo Macdonald, *The Scotsman*, 23 October
1989
W Gordon Smith, *The Observer, Scotland on
Sunday*, 15 October 1989
Clare Flowers, *The Observer, Scotland on Sunday*,
14 October 1989
Caroline Collier, David Ward, Andrew Nairne,
catalogue 'The British Art Show 1990', 1990
Kate Bush, *Artscribe*, May 1990
Mary Rose Beaumont, *Arts Review*, March/April

1990
Sue Hubbard, *Time Out*, 18–25 April 1990
Teme Celeste, Spring, 1990
Yvonne Sporre, 'White on White', *Mirabella*, American issue, December 1990

ALAN JOHNSTON
Grey Marks in the Village, Von der Heydt Museum, Wuppertal, 1974
From the Mountain to the Plain, Museum of Modern Art, Oxford, 1978
Irrawaddy, Düsseldorf, 1981
Irrawaddy, Museum Journal, Amsterdam, 1983
Torn Bough, Edinburgh, 1983
Drukwerk de Zaak, de Zaak, Groningen, 1985

JOHN KIRKWOOD
Douglas Gray, 'The Assault of Technology', *Penumbra II*, 1981
Bill Hare, 'Pie in the Sky', *Alba* I, 1986

JACK KNOX
Sandy Fraser, *Scottish Art Now*, Scottish Arts Council Publication, 1982
Cordelia Oliver, *Jack Knox 1960–1983*, Scottish Arts Council, 1983
Keith Hartley, *Scottish Art Since 1900*, National Galleries of Scotland/Lund Humphries, 1989
William Hardie, *Scottish Painting 1837 to the Present*, Studio Vista, 1990
Duncan MacMillan, *Scottish Art 1460 –1990*, Mainstream Publishing, 1990
Edward Gage, *The Eye in the Wind — Contemporary Scottish Painting since 1945*, Collins, London, 1977
Judith Bumpus, 'A Most Vigorous Force', *The Collector*, August 1990

HENRY KONDRACKI
The Observer, 29 December 1985
William Feaver, *Arts Review*, 14 February 1986
Marina Vaizey, *The Sunday Times*, 16 February 1986
Oona Strathern, *Arts Review*, 3 July 1987
William Feaver, *The Observer*, 26 July 1987
Oona Strathern, *Arts Review*, 21 December

1987
Charles Hall, *Arts Review*, 17 November 1989
William Feaver, *The Observer*, 26 November 1989
SCAM, August 1990
Giles Auty, *The Spectator*, 30 April 1991

EILEEN LAWRENCE
Christopher Johnstone, *Arnolfini Review*, Bristol, 1977
Catalogue 'Biennale de Paris', Paris, 1977
'Art Actual', *Skira Annual*, 1978
Keith Hartley, catalogue 'Eileen Lawrence Recent Work', Fischer Fine Art, London, 1980
Catalogue 1978/80, Tate Gallery, London, 1980
Sheena Wagstaff, catalogue 'Eileen Lawrence Artsite', Bath, 1986
Catalogue 'Looking into Paintings', A.G.B., 1986
The Green Book, 1987
Brian Redhead, *The Inspiration of Landscape*, Phaidon Press, 1989
Keith Hartley, *Scottish Art Since 1900*, National Galleries of Scotland/Lund Humphries, 1989
Catalogue 'Images of Paradise', Christies/Survival International, 1989
Fiona McLeod, catalogue 'New North', Tate Gallery, Liverpool, 1990
The Journey, Usher Gallery in association with Radcliffe Press, 1990

THOMAS LAWSON
John Ashbery, 'Yule Log', *New York Magazine*, 31 December 1978
Flavio Caroli, 'Giovani, Americani, Malati di privato', *Corriere della Sera*, 22 April 1979
Achille Bonito Oliva, 'The Bewildered Image', *Flash Art*, March 1980
Flaminio Gualdoni, 'Paesaggio di Paesaggi', *Salone degli Specchi del Teatro Comunale*, S Maria, Lombardy, 1980
Flavio Caroli, *New Image; A Generation and Half of Young International Artists*, XVI Triennale, Regione Lombardia, Milan, 1980
Carter Ratcliff, catalogue 'Illustration and Allegory', Brooke Gallery, New York, 1980

Kay Larson, *Village Voice*, 21 May 1980
Hilton Kamer, *New York Times*, 23 May 1980
Carrie Rickey, 'Advance to the Rear Guard', *Village Voice*, 21 May 1980
Carrie Rickey, 'Naive Nouveau and Its Malcontents', *Flash Art*, Summer, 1980
Valentin Tatransky, *Arts Magazine*, September 1980
Deborah Phillips, *Arts Magazine*, September 1980
Joan Simon, 'Double Takes', *Art in America*, October 1980
William Zimmer, *Soho News*, 26 November 1980
Valentin Tatransky, *Flash Art*, January/February 1981
Martin Sumner, catalogue 'Art', Manhattan, April 1981
Valentin Tatransky, *Figuring*, Hallwalls, Buffalo, New York, 1981
Joan Casedemont, 'Thomas Lawson, Metro Pictures', *Artforum*, September 1981
Matthew Collings, 'Nothing Deep', *Artscribe*, August 1981
Paul Kopecek, 'Previews: 8 Artists from New York', *Art Monthly*, September 1981
Michael Newman, 'Closed Circuits', *Art Monthly*, November 1981
John Roberts, 'Real Life Magazine Presents … at Nigel Greenwood', *Artscribe*, December 1981
Martha Beck and Marie Keller, *New Drawing in America*, The Drawing Center, New York, 1982
Kay Larson, 'Eight Critics in Search of an Exhibition', *New York Magazine*, 15 February 1982
Peter Schjeldahl, 'Mind Over Matter', *Village Voice*, 9 March 1982
Donald Kuspit, 'Critical Perspectives PSI and New Drawing in America at the Drawing Center', *Artforum*, April 1982
Roberta Smith, 'Surface Values', *Village Voice*, 13 April 1982
Flavio Caroli, 'Magico Primario', *Gruppo Editoriale Fabbri*, Milan, 1982
Donald Kuspit, 'Thomas Lawson, Metro Pictures', *Artforum*, May 1982
Valerie Smith, 'Painting, Metro Pictures', *Flash Art*, May 1982

Nora Halpern, *Frames of Reference*, The Whitney Museum, Downtown Branch, New York, 1982
Carter Ratcliff, 'Art and Resentment', *Art in America*, Summer, 1982
Hal Foster, 'Between Modernism and the Media', *Art in America*, Summer, 1982
Hans Muller, 'Bilder wie Unfalle', *Bassler Zeitung Magazine*, No 24, 19 June 1982
Geralyn Donahue and Joan Wallace, 'The Difference Between Absence and Not Being Missed', Journal, *LAICA*, Summer, 1982
Howard Singerman, 'Paragraphs Toward an Essay Entitled Restoration Comedies', Journal, *LAICA*, Summer, 1982
Nicolas Moufarrege, 'The Erotic Impulse', *Arts Magazine*, November 1982
Janet Kardon, *Image Scavengers: Painting*, ICA University of Pennsylvania, Philadelphia, 1982
Paul Krainak, *New Art Examiner*, December 1982
Russell Bowman and Peter Schjeldahl, *New Figuration in America*, Milwaukee Art Museum, 1982
Christopher English, 'New Figuration in Old Milwaukee', *New Art Examiner*, January 1983
Roberta Smith, 'Appropriation uber Alles', *Village Voice*, 11 January 1983
Michael Starenko, 'What's an Artist to do? A Short History of Postmodernism and Photography', *Afterimage*, January 1983
Grace Glueck, 'Artists who Scavenge from the Media', *New York Times*, 9 January 1983
John A Walker, *Art in the Age of Mass Media*, Pluto Press, London, 1983
Robert Rooney, 'Interview with Thomas Lawson', *Art and Text*, No 8, 1983
Richard Rhodes, *Real Lives*, Vanguard, Feburary 1983
Peter Schjeldahl, 'Falling in Style: The New Art and our Discontents', *Vanity Fair*, March 1983
Judith Russi Kirschner, 'Compassionate Images', *Artforum*, May 1983
Flavio Caroli, *La Forma e l'Informe*, Galeria d'Arte Moderna, Commune di Bologna
Donald Kuspit, 'New Figuration in America at the Milwaukee Art Museum', *Art in America*, September 1983

DA Robbins, 'An Interview with Thomas Lawson', *Arts Magazine*, September 1983
Hunter Drohojowska, 'Closed Captions', *Los Angeles Herald Examiner*, 11 November 1983
Emily Hicks, 'Stories About Painting', *Artweek*, 12 December 1983
Richard Armstrong, 'Other Views', *Artforum*, December 1983
Michael Brenson, 'Thomas Lawson', *New York Times*, 10 January 1983
Kim Levin, 'Thomas Lawson', *Village Voice*, 10 January 1984
Laurel Wood Adams, *New Art Examiner*, January 1984
Walter Robinson, *East Village Eye*, February 1984
Lisa Liebmann, 'Thomas Lawson, Metro Pictures', *Artforum*, March 1984
Eleanor Heartney, 'Thomas Lawson, Metro Pictures', *Art News*, March 1984
Thomas Lawson and Ken Lum, 'A conversation between two artists', *Flash Art*, April–May 1984
Kate Horsefield, *Profile: Thomas Lawson*, Video Data Bank, Art Institute, Vol 4, No 2, March 1984 (Reprinted in *Artspeak 2: Discourses on the Early Eighties*, Jeanne Siegel, ed, UMI Research Press, Ann Arbor)
Linda Cathcart, *A Decade of New Art*, Artists Space, New York, 1984
Donald Kuspit, *Art in America*, June 1984
William Olander and Andy Grundberg, *Drawings: After Photography*, Independent Curators, New York, 1984
JW Mahoney, *Art in America*, September 1984
Linda Cathcart and Craig Owens, *The Heroic Figure*, Museum of Contemporary Art, Houston, 1984
Roberta Smith, 'Painting With Two Minds About It', *Village Voice*, 25 September 1984
Alice Thorson, *New Art Examiner*, November 1984
Richard Martin, *Arts Magazine*, November 1984
Susan Morgan, *Unrecognised Inheritances*, Contemporary Perspectives 1984, Center Gallery, Bucknell University
Catherine Fox, 'Suspects Focuses on Media's Influence', *Atlanta Journal/Constitution*, 31 March 1985

James Corcoran, '20/20', *Dialogue*, May/June 1985
Jeane Silverthorne, *Artforum*, Summer 1985
Ronald Jones, 'Seeing is Believing: New Paintings by Thomas Lawson', *Arts Magazine*, Summer 1985
Carter Ratcliff, 'Cassandra Critics', *Art in America*, Summer 1985
David Carrier, 'Suspicious Art, Unsuspecting Texts', *Arts Magazine*, November 1985
Alan Jones, *Correspondences*, Laforet Museum, Tokyo, 1986
Anne Berriman, 'A Critical Operation: The Sixth Biennale of Sydney', *Follow Me*, No 22, Sydney, April/May 1986
Terence Maloon, 'Parody Saves a Scrambled Biennale', *Sydney Morning Herald*, Sydney, 17 May 1986
Nick Waterlow *et al*, *Origins, Originality and Beyond*, The Biennale of Sydney, Sydney, 1986
Janet Malcolm, *The New Yorker*, 27 October 1986
Lucy Lippard, *Por Encima del Bloqueo*, Il bienal de la Habana, Centro Wilfredo Lam, Havana, 1986
Ronald Jones, 'Thomas Lawson: The Decay of Lying', *Artscribe*, March 1987
Daniela Salvioni, *Flash Art*, May 1987
Holland Cotter, *Art in America*, May 1987
Susan Morgan, *Thunder Mountain*, Athony Reynolds Gallery, London, 1987
Waldemar Januszczak, 'The Devil in a Dour Scot', *The Guardian*, 1 July 1987
Michael Brenson, 'Art: Brooklyn Painters', *New York Times*, 25 June 1987
Eleanor Heartney, 'Working in Brooklyn', *Art News*, September 1987
Michael Phillipson, *Artscribe*, November/December 1987
Michael Archer, *Artforum*, November 1987
Amelia Jones, 'Connections to the Real', *Artweek*, 26 March 1988
Marlena Donahue, *Los Angeles Times*, 11 March 1988
Michael Brenson, *New York Times*, 15 July 1988
Ronald Jones, 'Hover Culture', *Artscribe*, Summer 1988
Mark Hinson, 'Critical Art Ensemble brings tough

critic to town', *Tallahassee Democrat*, 9 September 1988

J Molina, 'Thomas Lawson se lleva el arte kitch de un bar sevillano', *El Correo de Andalucia*, 7 October 1988

Critical Art Ensemble, *Atlanta Art Papers*, January/February 1989

Mary Jane Jacobs, Anne Goldstein, Anne Rorimer, Howard Singerman, *A Forest of Signs*, MoCA, Los Angeles, 1989

Nancy Princenthal, *Art of Renewal*, Orchard Gallery, Derry, 1989

Susan Morgan, 'On the walls of Derry', *Arena Internacional del arte*, October 1989

Joan Tedeschi, 'City Statues Come to Municipal Building', *Battery News*, 6 November 1989

David Brett, *New Installations at the Orchard Gallery*, Circa November/December 1989

Sarah Kent, 'Art', *20/20*, May 1990

Cliff Blakey, 'Art Out in the Open', *imag*, May 1990

Declan McGonagle, Thomas McEvilley et al, 'A New Necessity', *First Tyne International*, Tyne and Wear Museum Services, 1990

Paul Usherwood, 'Viz(ual) Arts: *The First Tyne International*, Edge 90', *Art Monthly*, July 1990

BRUCE McLEAN

Charles Harrison, 'Some Recent Sculpture in Britain', *Studio International*, Vol 177, No 907, 1969

Willoughby Sharp, 'Body Works', *Avalanche*, No 1, 1970

John Hulton, catalogue 'Road Show', Sao Paolo Biennale, 1971

Charles Harrison, 'Virgin soils and Old Land', *Studio International*, Vol 181, No 933, 1971

Richard Cork, 'Humour as the Weapon to Demolish the Establishment', *Evening Standard*, 5 November 1971

Caroline Tisdall, 'King for a Day', *The Guardian*, 11 March 1972

Lucy Lippard, 'Dematerialisation of the Art Object', *Studio Vista*, New York, 1973

Michael Hartney, 'Nice Style at Garage', *Studio International*, Vol 188, No 971, 1984

Richard Cork, 'What a Send Up! — The Automated Lounge Lizards', *Evening Standard*, 17 October 1974

Paul Overy, 'Irony at Oxford', *The Times*, 13 May 1975

Caroline Tisdall, 'Centre Victory', *The Guardian*, 14 December 1986

John McEwen, 'Jibulee Joke', *Spectator*, 16 April 1977

RoseLee Goldberg, 'Performing Burden, and the Legendary Bruce McLean, Piece', *Art-Rite*, 1977

Marc Chaimowicz, 'Furlong/McLean: Academic Board', *Studio International*, Vol 193, No 986, 1977

Mona Sulzman, 'The Kitchen: Measuring Our Lives in Teaspoons', *Soho Weekly News*, New York, 23 November 1978

William Furlong, catalogue 'Performance: Art or is it?', Cultureel Animatiecentrum Beursschowburg Brussela, October 1978 and Performance Art programme, Arts Council of Northern Ireland Gallery, Belfast, November 1978

Sarah Kent, 'Masterworks of Mediocrity', *Time Out*, November 1979

Alex Hamilton, 'Enter Stage Left: Acrobats with Fork Lift Truck', *The Guardian*, 6 November 1979

RoseLee Goldberg, *Performance: Live Art 1909 to the Present*, Thames & Hudson, London, 1979

William Furlong, catalogue for Hayward Annual, Arts Council of Great Britain, London, 1979

Nena Dimitrijevic, 'Pose Performance of Bruce McLean', *Art Monthly*, No 24, 1979

Andrew Clements, 'The Masterwork', *Financial Times*, 7 November 1979

Nena Dimitrijevic, 'Bruce McLean', *Un Certain art anglais*, Musee d'Art Moderne de la Ville de Paris, 1979

Meirion Browne, 'Masterwork', *The Guardian*, 9 November 1979

Sarah Kent, 'The Biography Drawer' in catalogue 'Bruce McLean', Third Eye Centre, Glasgow, 1980

David Brown, 'Bruce McLean — Oh Really — The Appearance of Non-Prodigal Son or Can You Hear Me at the Front?' in catalogue 'Bruce McLean', Third Eye Centre, Glasgow, 1980

Nena Dimitrijevic, 'There's a Sculpture on My Shoulder' and 'Nice Style: The World's First Pose Band' and 'Performance, Installations, Paintings' in catalogue 'Bruce McLean', Kunsthalle Basel, Whitechapel Art Gallery, London and Stedelijk van Abbemuseum, Eindhoven, 1981

Catalogue 'Bruce McLean', Musee d'Art et d'Industrie, St Etienne, 1981

Catlaogue 'A New Spirit in Painting', Royal Academy of Arts, London 1981

Catalogue 'Documenta 7', Kassel, 1982

Catalogue 'Aspects of British Art Today', Metropolitan Museum of Art, Tokyo, 1982

Catalogue 'Vision in Disbelief', 4th Biennale of Sydney, 1982

Catalogue 'Zeitgeist', Berlin 1982

Catalogue 'Bruce McLean' Galerie Dany Keller, Munich, 1983

Catalogue 'Bruce McLean: Berlin/London', Whitechapel Art Gallery, London and DAAD Galerie, Berlin, 1983

Catalogue 'Bruce McLean: Paintings and Drawings', Munich, 1983

New Art, Tate Gallery, London, 1983

M Amaya, *Bruce McLean*, Art Palace, New York, 1984

Jean Christophe-Ammann, *Bruce McLean*, Galleria fina Bitterlin, Basel, Florence, 1984

Andreas Vominckel, *Bruce McLean*, Badischer Kunstverein, Karlsruhe, 1984

An International Survey of Recent Paintings and Sculpture, The Museum of Modern Art, New York, 1984

1965 to 1972, When Attitudes Become Form, Kettle's Yard Gallery, Cambridge, 1984

Norman Rosenthal, *Simple Manner of Physical Violence*, Galerie Gmyrek, Dusseldorf

Bruce McLean, Tate Gallery, London, 1985

Bilder Fur Frankfurt, Bestandskatalog des Museums fur Moderne Kunst, Frankfurt, 1985

Mary Rose Beaumont, *Bruce McLean*, Edinburgh Festival, Scottish Galleries, Edinburgh, 1985

Mel Gooding, *Bruce McLean*, Galerie Fahnemann, Berlin, 1987

Tom Baker, 'Striking a Pose', *Arena*, May/June 1987

Mary Rose Beaumont, 'Bruce McLean: The Floor,

The Fence, The Fireplace', *Arts Review*, 27 March 1987
Paul Ticknell, 'Easel Rider', *Elle*, April 1987
Tom Baker, 'On an off the fence', *The Face*, April 1987
Andrew Graham-Dixon, 'The name of the pose', *The Independent*, 11 March 1987
Deyan Sudjic, 'The Arnolfini Grows Up', *Blueprint*, February 1988
Alastair Best, 'Culture without Quiche', *Designers Journal*, February 1988
Judith Mackrell, 'Moving on the Edges', *The Independent*, October 1988
John Percival, 'Inspired Steps', *The Times*, 28 October 1988
Mel Gooding, *Bruce McLean*, Phaidon Press, 1988
Clare Henry, 'Bruce McLean', *Glasgow Herald*, 12 October 1990

JOHN McLEAN
Sydney Goodsir Smith, 'Annual Exhibition of R.S.W.', *The Scotsman*, 26 January 1963
Christopher Grier, 'Encounters Artistic', *The Scotsman*, 17 July 1965
Norbert Lynton, 'Around the Galleries', *The Guardian*, 23 July 1965
Guy Burn, 'Shiela Marshal, Geoffrey Smedley, Michael Macleod, John McLean', *Arts Review*, Vol XVII, No 14, July 1965
Norbert Lynton, 'London Galleries', *The Guardian*, 31 March 1966
Norbert Lynton, 'London Letter', *Art International*, May 1966
Norbert Lynton, 'Three Young Painters', *The Guardian*, 25 January 1967
Guy Brett, 'Axion for Young Painters', *The Times*, 28 January 1967
Nigel Gosling, 'All Tied Up', *The Observer*, 29 January 1967
Edward Lucie-Smith, *Studio International*, March 1967
Norbert Lynton, 'London Letter', *Art International*, March 1967
Caroline Tisdall, 'Action Man', *The Guardian*, 12 March 1971
Tim Hilton, *Studio International*, June 1971

Judy Marle, *The Guardian*, 10 August 1971
Michael McNay, *The Guardian*, 11 July 1972
Judy Marle, *The Guardian*, November 1975
John McEwan, *The Spectator*, December 1975
Fenella Crichton, *Art International*, January 1976
Ben Jones, 'Interview with Alan Gouk, Richard James, John McLean, Fred Pollock', *Artscribe*, No 5, February 1977
Duncan MacMillan, *Four Abstract Artists*, Scottish Arts Council, 1977
Clement Greenberg, *Four Scottish Painters*, Scottish Arts Council, 1977
Cordelia Oliver, 'Four Abstract Artists', *Artscribe*, No 10, January 1978
Tim Hilton, catalogue 'John McLean', House Gallery, 1978
John McEwan, 'Explorative', *The Spectator*, 16 September 1978
Maria Vaizey, *Arts Review*, Vol 30, No 14, 4 August 1978
Maria Vaizey, *Sunday Times*, August 1978
Maria Vaizey, *Sunday Times*, September 1978
Adrian Searle, *Artscribe*, No 14, October 1978
William Feaver, *The Observer*, August 1978
John McEwan, *The Spectator*, 16 June 1979
Tim Hilton, 'Mr Packer Picks His Team', *Times Literary Supplement*, 7 December 1979
Saranjeet Walia, *Contemporary British Artists*, Bergstrom and Boyle, London, 1979
Alan Gouk, 'Stockwell, a Viewpoint on the Paintings', *Artscribe*, No 20, November 1979
William Packer, *The British Art Show*, Arts Council of Great Britain, 1980
Tim Hilton, *A Force Against the Basilisk*, Art Council of Great Britain, 1980
William Feaver, 'In Search of Beauty', *The Observer*, 31 August 1980
Michael McNay, 'Abstract Art Comes out of Hiding', *The Guardian*, 2 September 1980
William Packer, 'The Fourth Annual', *Financial Times*, 2 September 1980
John McEwan, 'Pastiches', *The Spectator*, 13 September 1980
Kenworth Moffett, *The New Generation*, Rhineburgh Press, New York, 1980
Terry Fenton, The Edmonton Art Gallery Bulletin,

1980
Stuart Bradshaw, 'It All Depends', *Artscribe*, No 27, February 1981
Joan Murray, 'Jack Bush in Great Britain', *Art Magazine*, No 52, February/March 1981
Rene Micha, 'Lettre de Paris', *Art International*, March/April 1981
Karen Wilkin, 'Andre Emmerich, New York, The New Generation, A Curator's Choice', *Art Magazine*, No 53/54, 1981
Ken Kiff, 'A Dialogue Between Ken Kiff and Wynn Jones', *Artscribe*, No 31, October 1981
Tim Hilton, *The Observer*, February 1982
Terry Fenton, 'Jack Bush's Influence', *Update*, May/June 1983
Shelagh Nolan, 'The Continuing Heritage of Jack Bush', *Artswest*, June 1983
Rashid Jamie, 'John McLean's Paintings', *Artscribe*, October 1983
David Nicholson, 'Painters of Winchester', *Artscribe*, October 1984
Mary Rose Beaumont, *Recent British Paintings and Prints*, British Council, 1986
Bill Hare, 'Interview with John McLean', *Alba*, Winter, 1987
Ann Grant, 'John McLean', *Alba*, No 9, 1988
Peter Davies, 'John McLean', *Arts Review*, 13 June 1988
Tim Hilton, 'The Ecology of Colour', *The Guardian*, 8 June 1988
Kaleidoscope interview, BBC Radio 4, 1988
Michael Tooby, *He Presence of Painting*, Arts Council, 1988
Keith Hartley, *Scottish Art Since 1900*, Scottish National Gallery of Modern Art, 1989
William Cook, *The Scotsman*, 15 November 1989
Cordelia Oliver, 'Irvin/McLean', *The Guardian*, 1 December 1989
Margaret Garlake, 'Denis Bowen; Cornelia Parker; John McLean', *Art Monthly*, December 1989/ January 1990
Duncan MacMillan, *Scottish Painting*, Edinburgh, 1990
Pamela Johnson, 'Working in the Abstract', *Business Magazine*, November 1990

ALEXANDER MOFFAT
Alan Bold, catalogue 'Scottish Realism', Scottish
Arts Council Touring Exhibition, 1971
Edward Gage, 'Smouldering Emotion set in Realist
drabness', *The Scotsman*, 27 August 1973
Alan Bold, catalogue 'Bellany, Dallas, Brown,
Gillon, Moffat', Fruitmarket Gallery, Edinburgh,
1985
Emilio Coia, 'Alexander Moffat, *Scottish Field*,
October 1975
Edward Gage, *The Eye in the Wind —
Contemporary Scottish Painting since 1945*,
Collins, London, 1977
Cordelia Oliver, *Painters in Parallel*, Edinburgh
College of Art, 1978
Lynda Morris, catalogue 'Gould, Moffat, Williams',
Midland Group, Nottinham, 1978
Timothy Hyman, 'Narrative Painting: A Second
Generation', *Artscribe*, No 19, 1979
Timothy Hyman, catalogue 'Seven Poets', Third
Eye Centre, Glasgow, 1981
Hugh MacDiarmid, *Aesthetics in Scotland*,
Mainstream, 1984
Duncan Thomson, *Portrait Drawings*, Booktable
Project, Scottish Arts Council, 1984
Timothy Hyman, catalogue 'In Their
Circumstances', Usher Gallery, Lincoln, 1985
John Griffiths, 'Scottish Art Now', *Art and Design*,
Vol 4, No 7/8, 1988
Keith Hartley, *Scottish Art Since 1900*, National
Galleries of Scotland/Lund Humphries, 1989
Douglas Hall, catalogue 'Turning the Century',
Raab Gallery, London and Berling and Gian Ferrari
Milan, 1990
Norbert Lynton, catalogue 'Picturing People:
British Figurative art since 1945', British Council,
1990
Duncan MacMillan, *Scottish Art 1460–1990*,
Mainstream, 1990

ELIZABETH OGILVIE
Cordelia Oliver, *Painters in Parallel*, Edinburgh
College of Art, 1978
Duncan MacMillan, *Modernia Taidetta
Skotlannista*, Amos Anderson Gallery, Helsinki,
1978

Hugh Adams, *Watermarks*, Scottish Arts Council,
1980
Adrian Henri, Serpentine Gallery, London, Arts
Council of Great Britain, 1982
Art and the Sea, I.C.A., 1982
Robert Callender, *Sea Papers*, Talbot Rice Gallery,
Edinburgh, 1984
Elements of Nature, Arts Council of Great Britain,
1984
Diana Sykes, *Floating Images*, Scottish Arts
Council, 1985
Christopher Andrea, *The Christian Science
Monitor*, New York, 1986
Robert Livingston, *Sea Changes*, Crawford Centre
Gallery, St Andrews, 1986
Sea, Greenpeace, London, 1988
Sea Sanctuary, Talbot Rice Gallery, Edinburgh,
1988
Duncan MacMillan, 'Letters from the Edge of the
World', *The Scottish Picture Show*, STV, 1988
Geraldine Prince, 'Suffused by the Sea', *Scotland
on Sunday*, 1988
Duncan MacMillan, *Art into Botany*, Talbot Rice
Gallery, 1988
Clare Henry, *Arts Review*, 1989
Keith Hartley, catalogue 'Scottish Art since
1900', Scottish National Gallery of Modern Art,
Edinburgh, 1989
Waving at the Tide, Kosh STV, 1990
Deborah Krasner, *Celtic*, Thames & Hudson,
Great Britain and Viking Penguin, USA, 1990

GLEN ONWIN
Glen Onwin, *Saltmarsh*, Edinburgh, 1974
David Brown, catalogue 'Saltmarsh', Scottish
Arts Council, Edinburgh, 1975
Edward Gage, 'The Tangible Facts', *The
Scotsman*, 20 January 1975
Cordelia Oliver, 'Glen Onwin', *The Guardian*,
27 January 1975
William Packer, catalogue 'Scottish Sculpture
'75', Demarco Gallery, Edinburgh, 1975
William Packer, 'Summer Show III', *Arts Review*,
Vol XXVII, No 16, 8 August 1975
Marina Vaizey, 'Creative Patron', *The Sunday
Times*, 10 August 1975

Jasia Reichardt, 'Artists Exploring Landscape',
Architectural Design, Vol XLV, No 9, September
1975
Catalogue 'Aspects of Landscape', The British
Council, 1976
Jasia Reichardt, *Time, Words and the Camera*,
Neue Galerie am Landesmuseum, Joanneum,
Graz, 1976
Paul Overy, catalogue 'Inscape', Scottish Arts
Council, Edinburgh, 1976
Cordelia Oliver, 'Inscape', *The Guardian*,
11 November 1976
Marina Vaizey, 'The Fascination of Gold', *The
Sunday Times*, 14 November 1976

FRED POLLOCK
Frederick Gore, R.A. Catalogue 'British Painting
1952–1977', Royal Academy, 1977
Clement Greenberg, catalogue 'Four Scottish
Painters', Fruitmarket Gallery, Edinburgh, 1977
Ben Johns, 'Alan Gouk, Richard James, John
McLean, Fred Pollock in conversation with Ben
Johns', *Artscribe*, February 1977
Muriel Wilson, catalogue 'Certain Traditions:
Recent British and Canadian Art', British Council
touring exhibition, 1977–79
Tim Hilton, *The Poole Arts Centre Modern art
Exhibition*, Seldown Gallery, 1980
Tim Hilton, 'Out of the Underground', *The
Guardian*, 30 March 1988
John Hoyland, *Hans Hoffman: Late Paintings:
An interview with Anthony Caro, Sheila Girling,
Fred Pollock, Alan Gouk, Basil Beattie*, Tate
Gallery, 1988
David Lillington, *Time Out*, April 1990
William Packer, 'Good Jokes on thin ice',
Financial Times, 24 April 1990
Ian Vines, catalogue 'Colour in Modern
Painting', Stoke on Trent museum, 1991

JUNE REDFERN
Cordelia Oliver, *The Guardian*, 24 October 1979
Cordelia Oliver, *The Guardian*, 26 October 1980
Clare Henry, *The Glasgow Herald*, November
1981
Catalogue 'British Drawing', The Hayward

Annual Exhibition, 1982
Cordelia Oliver, 'Pictures of Ourselves', *The Guardian*, April 1982
Emilio Coia, *The Scotsman*, June 1983
Clare Henry, *The Glasgow Herald*, June 1983
Sarah Kent, *Time Out*, 1984
Lyn McRitchie, *City Limits*, 1984
James Holloway, catalogue 'Portraits on Paper', Scottish Arts Council, Edinburgh, 1984
Monica Petzl, *Time Out*, October 1984
Andrew Nairne, catalogue 'Hand Signals', Ikon Gallery, Birmingham, 1985
Richard Chapman and Lyn McRitchie, catalogue 'The River', Third Eye Centre, Glasgow, 1985
Cordelia Oliver, catalogue 'The River', Third Eye Centre, 1985
Caroline Collier, 'Five Painters and the Irrational', *Artscribe*, No 49, 1985
Catalogue, National Gallery, London, 1986
Monica Petzl, *Time Out*, 23 July 1986
Mary Rose Beaumont, *Arts Review*, 23 July 1986
Catalogue, Festival exhibition, Mercury Gallery, Edinburgh, 1987
Keith Hartley *et al*, *The Vigorous Imagination — New Scottish Art*, National Galleries of Scotland, 1987
Alice Bain, *List Magazine*, August 1987
Emilio Coia, *The Scotsman*, August 1987
Mary Rose Beaumont, *Financial Times*, 11 August 1987
Allen Robertson, *Time Out*, August 1987
William Ferguson, *Times Educational Supplement*, August 1987
Clare Henry, *The Glasgow Herald*, August 1987
Felix McCullough, *Arts Review*, August 1987
Giles Auty, *The Spectator*, August 1987
Murdo Macdonald, *The Scotsman*, August 1987
Richard Dorment, *Daily Telegraph*, August 1987
John Russell Taylor, The Times, 18 August 1987
Alistair Smith, catalogue, Bradford Art Gallery, 1987
Rose Paterson, *Daily Telegraph*, 31 December 1987
Robert Clark, *The Guardian*, 11 January 1988
John Hewitt, *Arts Review*, January 1988
Mary Rose Beaumont, *Arts Review*, 15 January 1988
Hugh Adams, *New Art Examiner*, May 1988
Mary Rose Beaumont, catalogue 'Naked II', Aberystwyth, 1988
Tony Godfrey, catalogue 'Figuring out the '80s', 1988
Penny Johnson, *The Independent*, September 1988
Larry Berryman, *Arts Review*, October 1988
The Times, June 1989
Womens Artists Slide Journal, No 27, 1989
Sarah Jane Checkland, 'The Art of Staying in the Picture', *The Times*, 14 July 1989
Keith Harvey, catalogue '100 Years of Scottish Painting', 1989
Sue Hubbard, 'June Redfern, Artist in Profile', *Green Book*, Vol III, November 1989
Marina Vaizey, catalogue, Cleveland International Drawing Biennale, 1989
Sue Hubbard, *Time Out*, March 1990
Pip Seymour, *Painters in Print*, April 1990
Marina Vaizey, 'Drawing out the Feminine', *Sunday Times*, November 1990
Mary Rose Beaumont, *Arts Review*, November 1990
William Hardie, *Scottish Painting 1837 to the Present*, Studio Vista, 1990
Libby Ansom, 'June Redfern', *C.V. Magazine*, December 1990–February 1991

IAIN ROBERTSON
Gordon Dean, interview, *The Scotsman*, 30 November 1988

DUNCAN SHANKS
Duncan MacMillan, catalogue 'Falling Water', Talbot Rice Gallery, 1988
Duncan MacMillan, catalogue 'The Scottish Show', Welsh Arts Council, 1989
Duncan MacMillan, *Scottish Art 1460–1990*, Mainstream, Edinburgh, 1990
William Hardie, *Scottish Painting 1837 to the Present*, Studio Vista, 1990

ALISON WATT
Andrew Graham-Dixon, 'Not Just A Pretty Face', *The Independent*, 27 May 1987
Clare Henry, 'Glasgow School of Art Degree Show', *The Glasgow Herald*, 17 June 1987
Muriel Gray, 'Portrait of Muriel Gray', *The Observer*, 10 July 1988
John Griffiths, 'Movements in Contemporary Art', *Art and Design*, October 1988
John Griffiths, 'Scottish Art Now', *Art and Design*, October 1988
Jean Rafferty, 'Sombre Visions Don't Reflect A Fiery Outlook', *The Sunday Times*, 13 November 1988
Clare Henry, 'Six Women Artists', *The Glasgow Herald*, 14 November 1988
Hugh Cummings, 'New Figurative Art: A Survey', *Art and Design*, November 1988
John Griffiths, 'British Artists of the '80s', *Art and Design*, November 1988
Hugh Cummings, 'Three Scottish Artists', *Modern Painters*, Spring 1989
The Times Leader, 'Tea With Royalty', *The Times*, 4 August 1989
Clare Henry, 'Tale of The Queen MOther and a Teacup', *The Glasgow Herald*, 4 August 1989
Clare Henry, 'Morrison Portrait Award,' *The Glasgow Herald*, 3 November 1989
Clare Henry, 'Scottish Exhibitions', *Arts Review*, November 1989
John Griffiths, 'Portrait of Alison Watt', *The Green Book*, Vol III, No 4, 1990
Clare Flowers, 'Self Portrait', *Scotland on Sunday*, 11 February 1990
Clare Henry, 'Arts Page', *The Glasgow Herald*, 6 March 1990
Giles Auty, 'Oddly Enough', *The Spectator*, 17 March 1990
William Packer, 'Artists With A Touch Of Class', *The Financial Times*, 17 March 1990
Rosalin Sadler, 'Exhibition Reviews — Alison Watt', *Modern Painters*, Spring 1990
The Compass Contribution 1969–1990, Compass Gallery, Glasgow, 1990
Sir Roy Strong, 'Mirrors of Majesty', *The Sunday Times*, 29 July 1990
Miranda Carter, 'The Tote Gallery', *Harpers & Queen*, August 1990

Film interviews
'Reporting Scotland', 1 June 1987
'Scotland Today', 2 June 1987
Stuart Cosgrove, 'Halfway to Paradise', 2 October 1988
Ed Hayward, 'Artwork — Appearances', BBC Schools Programmes, 23 February 1989
Ishbel McLean, 'The Portrait', BBC Schools Programmes, February 1990
Ishbel McLean, 'Excess', BBC Scotland, 9 April 1990
BBC 2, 'Rough Guide To Glasgow', June 1990
Ishbel McLean, 'Two Boys and a Girl from Glasgow', August 1990
James McLean, 'State of the Arts', Scottish Television, December 1990

KATE WHITEFORD
Martin Kemp, 'Kate Whiteford: A Personal Impression', *Votives and Libations in summons of the Oracle*, University of St Andrews, 1983
Iwona Blazwick, 'Kate Whiteford', *Offshore*, Galerie Wittenbrink, 1984
Michael Archer, *Rites of Passage*, Third Eye Centre, Glasgow, 1984
Mel Gooding, *British Art: Twelve British Artists*, Contemporary Art Society, London, 1986
Mel Gooding, *Puja: Ritual Offerings to the Gods*, Riverside Studios, London, 1986
Marjorie Allthorpe-Guyton, *The Golden Thread?*, Harris Museum and Art Gallery, Preston, 1987
Richard Cork, 'Beyond the Tyranny of the Predictable', *TSWA 3D Catalogue*, Television South West and South West Arts, 1987
David Reason, 'Drawing Lines', *Internationale Triennale der Zeichnung 4*, Nurnberg, 1988
Julien Robson, *Excavations*, John Hansard Gallery, University of Southampton, 1988
Keith Hartley *et al*, *The Vigorous Imagination — New Scottish Art*, National Galleries of Scotland, 1987
Alex Noble, *From Art to Archaeology*, South Bank Centre, 1991
Junichi Shioda (ed), catalogue, 'British Art Now: A Subjective View', Asah Shimbun and the British Council, Tokyo, 1990

Video
Two Videos about Six Artists, Whitechapel Art Gallery, 1984

ADRIAN WISZNIEWSKI
Peter Hill, 'The Land of the Mountain and the Flood', *Studio International*, Vol 196, 1983
Clare Henry, *The Glasgow Herald*, 31 October 1984
Marjorie Allthorpe-Guyton, Alexander Moffat, Jon Thompson, catalogue 'The British Art Show', Arts Council of Great Britain, London, 1984
William Feaver, *The Financial Times*, 6 November 1984
Richard Cork, *The Listener*, 8 November 1984
Patrick Bishop, *The Literary Review*, January 1985
Mary Rose Beaumont, Nancy Balfour, catalogue '10 Years at Air: A Retrospective', Air Gallery, London, 1985
Patrick Kinmouth, *Vogue*, Feburary 1985
Caroline Collier, 'Room at the Top', *Flash Art*, No 122, April/May 1985
Waldemar Januszczak, 'The Glow the Came from Glasgow', *The Guardian*, 13 August 1985
Clare Henry, 'Glasgow Stealing the Best Show for Art', *The Glasgow Herald*, 14 August 1985
Andrew Graham-Dixon, 'Is it Miles Better in Glasgow?', *The Sunday Times*, 6 October 1985
John Russell Taylor, 'And Why Should Painting Not Be Decorative', *The Times*, 8 October 1985
William Packer, 'Coming Down to Earth', *The Financial Times*, 17 October 1985
Waldemar Januszczak, 'Prospects of Mysterious Britain', *The Guardian*, 17 October 1985
Marina Vaizey, 'Paintings Hot off the Easel', *The Sunday Times*, 20 October 1985
Margaret Garlake, 'Adrian Wiszniewski', *Art Monthly*, November 1985
Alexander Moffat, catalogue 'New Image Glasgow', Third Eye Centre, Glasgow, 1985
Marjorie Allthorpe-Guyton, *Artscribe*, No 54, September/October 1985
Clive Turnbull, 'Signs of Dreaming', *The Green Book*, Vol 2, No 4, 1985
Peter Hepburn, catalogue 'Unique and Original', Glasgow Print Studio, 1985

Caroline Collier, *Artscribe*, No 55, December 1985/January 1986
Francis Spalding, British Art Since 1900, *Thames & Hudson*, 1986
Philip Wright, catalogue 'New Art From Scotland', Warwick Arts Trust, London, 1986
Tony Godfrey, *The New Image: Painting in the 1980s*, Phaidon Press, Oxford, 1986
John Griffiths, 'Modern Movements in British Art', *Art and Design*, Vol 3, Nos 1/2, 1987
John Griffiths, 'Heroes and Dreamers: Scottish Figurative Art in the '80s', *Art and Design*, Vol 3, Nos 7/8, 1987
Alex Kidson, catalogue, Walker Art Gallery, Liverpool, 1987
Edward Lucie-Smith and Sean Kelly, *The Self Portrait — A Modern View*, Sarema Press, London, 1987
Keith Hartley *et al*, *The Vigorous Imagination — New Scottish Art*, National Galleries of Scotland, 1987
Mary Rose Beaumont, *Arts Review*, 11 March 1988
Peter Hill, 'Behind Closed Doors', *Alba*, No 8, 1988
Tony Godfrey, *Art in America*, September 1988
Carolyn Cohen, Judith Higgens, Edward Lucie-Smith, *New British Painting*, Phaidon Press, Oxford, 1988
John McDonald, 'Searching for the Sublime Romantic', *Sydney Morning Herald*, 25 March 1989
Keith Hartley, *Scottish Art Since 1900*, National Galleries of Scotland/Lund Humphries, 1989
Tony Godfrey, *Drawing Today: Draughtsmen of the Eighties*, Phaidon Press, Oxford, 1990
William Hardy, *Scottish Painting: 1837 to the Present*, Cassell, London, 1990
Clare Flowers, *Scotland on Sunday*, 2 December 1990
John Griffiths, 'Talking to Adrian Wiszniewski', *The Green Book*, Vol 3, No 7, 1990
Duncan MacMillan, *Scottish Art 1460–1990*, Mainstream, Edinburgh, 1990